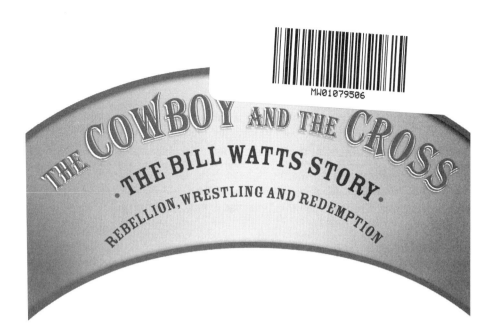

THE COWBOY AND THE CROSS

THE BILL WATTS STORY

REBELLION, WRESTLING AND REDEMPTION

"Cowboy" Bill Watts and Scott Williams

ECW Press

Published by ECW PRESS
2120 Queen Street East, Suite 200, Toronto, Ontario, Canada M4E IE2

LIBRARY AND ARCHIVES CANADA CATALOGUING IN PUBLICATION

Watts, Bill, 1939–
The cowboy and the cross : the Bill Watts story : rebellion, wrestling,
and redemption / "Cowboy" Bill Watts and Scott Williams.

ISBN 1-55022-708-4

1. Watts, Bill, 1939– 2. Wrestlers — United States — Biography. I. Williams, Scott (Scott
E.) II. Title.

GV1196.W38A3 2005   796.812'092   C2005-904302-4

Editor: Michael Holmes
Cover and Text Design: Tania Craan
Production: Mary Bowness
Cover Photo: From the Bill Watts Collection
Back cover photo: Kathy Sue Photography
Printing: Transcontinental

This book is set in AGaramond and Algerian

DISTRIBUTION
Canada: Jaguar Book Group, 100 Armstrong Ave., Georgetown, ON L7G 5S4
United States: Independent Publishers Group, 814 North Franklin Street,
Chicago, IL 60610

PRINTED AND BOUND IN CANADA

ECW PRESS
ecwpress.com

Dedication

I firmly believe that all things will pass and that only what is done for Christ will last!

As I journey longer into this life here on earth, my relationship with Him, which was "renewed" in 1984, after about 20 years "in the desert of rebellion," has led me to look at my life from a completely different perspective.

My goodness, don't you, too, believe there has to be more to life than the material, the surface and self? That there is more to our lives than to just exist here on earth and then die, and that ends it? Don't you, too, realize that this life on earth is but a journey, a "beginning," that we have eternal souls that will live forever, and that there is a battle for our souls between God and Satan — between heaven and hell?

Thankfully for us, all we have to do is make a decision as to the side we desire to be on. Then, if we have selected Jesus as Savior and Lord, it is done, and it is "out of our hands." We are saved eternally, though our daily lives "in relationship" allow us to make choices to follow in relationship with Him, or to rebel against His will for us — with the consequences of those choices — good or bad.

So this book is dedicated to my Lord and Savior, Jesus Christ, and for the hope that those who read it will also look deep into their own selves and their own lives in discovery. I hope they realize that they do have a "greater purpose for being" and a Creator who loves them and has provided for them a way for an eternal relationship with Him through His Son, Jesus Christ. He loves us and accepts us, "just as we are." And at that miraculous moment, our lives begin anew in Him, and our growth in relationship begins and continues until we are called home to Him.

I dedicate this book to Him, revealing so many of my choices and their consequences — whether you think they are good or bad — and trying to then put them into this eternal perspective.

ACKNOWLEDGEMENTS

This project is something I really did not want to face. I always felt that if I wrote a book, it would have to be "bigger in purpose" than just about me, and I did not know how to tie the two things together — the world of my life and my spiritual evolution. Without a lot of encouragement, it might never have happened, so I want to acknowledge all those who love and support me and have encouraged me in this. I might not have mentioned all of them in the book, because they might not have been involved in that part of my life — wrestling and athletics — but their contribution is just as important.

That starts with my wife, Suzanne, and she (along with others) can certainly testify to the fact that I am not easy to live with. In the same vein, my children, who I dearly love (even if I have revealed a lot of the pain I caused them with the resulting consequences, only revealed so that too may somehow help others).

Father Brian Mullady — though I am definitely not Catholic, we are dear friends, and he has encouraged me tremendously in so many things and ways. Brian Bumpas, a dear friend, who has loved me and encouraged me to truly get in touch with my inner self. Alvis Reeves and Jim Myers, who have become very close friends. Pete Maguire, another who has become a dear friend, who has encouraged me.

And certainly Scott Williams, my co-author, who has become a dear friend and who persisted in this project with ECW PRESS, along with editor Michael Holmes at ECW PRESS. Without Scott, this would never have happened.

— Bill Watts

Months ago, I started keeping a list of people who helped me out with a particular factoid of history, or who helped by reading over a chapter and offering corrections, keeping me honest.

Two computer crashes and a hurricane evacuation later, I realize that list is dust. As I try to recreate it now, please forgive me, if you helped me in some way, and I did not mention you here. I know I'll leave out someone; I just don't know who it will be. Whoever you are, I apologize.

Mitch Hartsey, Dan Chernau, Dave Meltzer and Max Levy have offered insights, dates, places and other nuggets of information from their respective wealths of knowledge about the history of the strange business that is professional wrestling.

Barry Rose (visit his wonderful Florida wrestling Web site, at www.cwfarchives.com) and Rich Tate (his Georgia wrestling site is also a treasure trove of history, at www.georgiawrestlinghistory.com) were very gracious with their time, in looking over the chapters dealing with their states.

Thanks also to Jims Cornette and Ross, two of the smartest gentlemen the wrestling business has ever known, for sharing some Mid-South memories with me, and for providing two wonderful introductions. Many thanks as well to Emil "Peppi" Bruneau, for his insightful introduction.

The *Galveston County Daily News* has kept me employed through all of my strange endeavors, and I appreciate everyone there.

The photographs in the book come courtesy of Mr. Watts' collection, but I owe a ton of gratitude to good friends Jim Sukman and Michael Steenbergen for their invaluable assistance in converting the original photographs into digital images, for publication here.

My other friends — among them, John Williams, Michael Mensik, Jason Hess, Amanda Belshaw, Xochitl Vandiver, everyone at Sonny's Place in Galveston and the always-hilarious Heath Grider — have been similarly invaluable, lending me ears and moral support.

Michael Holmes, like everyone else at ECW PRESS, has been fantastic to work with. I called Michael with the idea for this book, out of the clear blue, and he quickly became as excited about it as I was. The degree to which this story flows well and carries the desired impact is as much a credit to him as to anyone else involved.

And then, there's Bill Watts. Mr. Watts is one of the more controversial figures in wrestling history. One thing is for sure — very few people are ambivalent about him. I found him to be nothing but a pure joy to work with. His passionate commitment to his ideals made this book the strong story that it has become, and I greatly value the bond we've made, which will extend beyond this book, through our lives.

Of course, the good Lord has blessed me so often that I can never say thanks enough, but chief among my blessings are my wife Brenda, and our children, Brooke and Brody.

Finally, it was more than 20 years ago that my father, Charles E. Williams, took me to my first live wrestling event, one of Bill Watts' Mid-South Wrestling shows in Houston, promoted by Paul Boesch. Many times thereafter, he braved throngs of insane wrestling fans, when he would much rather have been home, watching baseball. I have been blessed with parents who have always supported me, but this time in particular, I need to say — Thanks, Dad.

— Scott E. Williams

CONTENTS

FOREWORDS

The "Big Cowboy" is one of a kind. His life has been as unpredictable and controversial as that of any figure I have known in the wrestling business. I met Bill Watts over thirty years ago, and at times I loved him like a brother, while at other times I hated the ground he walked on. Bill's people skills at one time were unique, to say the least. Bill could be bombastic, intimidating and totally overbearing at times. He could also teach the fundamental skills of the wrestling business as well as anyone I have ever met to anyone who could accept his teaching methods and listen to his message. Bill was a brilliant individual whose contributions to this wild and crazy business will live on for generations to come.

Bill was my mentor in the wrestling business. Consequently, I have been blessed to have had over a thirty-year career in this business, with a fair amount of success, some say, and I owe the vast majority of it to "Cowboy" Bill Watts.

From being a super high school athlete, to playing football at the

University of Oklahoma for the legendary coach Bud Wilkinson, to becoming a regaled street fighter, to playing pro football, main-eventing every major wrestling territory in the world and upsetting the "establishment" virtually everywhere he went along the way before becoming a "player/owner" and eventually becoming one of the most respected television producers of wrestling of all time, Watts, as the late "Dean of Wrestling Broadcasters" Gordon Solie used to say (in his gravelly voice), "is indeed a strange enigma."

Bill's life journey has not been a smooth, bump-free ride, but it certainly is the stuff of which legends are made. His story is amazing. How the Big Cowboy survived it is a miracle. You will have a hard time putting this book down once you start it. Enjoy.

JIM ROSS

In the mid-1960s, a young warrior named William F. "Cowboy Bill" Watts came charging out of the University of Oklahoma. A renowned college athlete, he played professional football for a short time. Along the way, he developed a fondness for professional wrestling, and he had a lot more to offer in this venue, which at that time provided him with more earning potential than pro football did. Bill embarked upon a great career in 1962. New Orleans had always been a good venue for wrestling, and the young warrior charged into Louisiana in 1970.

My father, the late Emile Bruneau, was the chairman of the Louisiana State Athletic Commission. He had served as president of the World Boxing Council and as president of the National Wrestling Association. He immediately noticed Bill, whom he described as a cordial and bright young man with good business sense. My dad shared his wisdom of the wrestling business with Bill. He introduced me to him, and we became fast friends.

Wrestling in the late 1960s was somewhat dull. "Cowboy" Bill Watts revolutionized the world of professional wrestling. He had a rare combination of physical ability, athletic prowess and showmanship that made wrestling exhibitions exciting once again. His favorite move was the Oklahoma Stampede. He would pick his opponent up, hold him across his shoulder in one corner, then charge across the ring full speed and dive, landing on top of his opponent with all his force, plus his 297 pounds of muscle mass. He'd usually trample his opponent, to the utter delight of the fans.

It wasn't long before Bill entered the management aspect of professional wrestling too. He was a super promoter, pioneering the use of progressive television concepts to create fan enthusiasm. His booking business, Mid-South Sports, expanded in this area to cover Louisiana, Oklahoma, Mississippi, and parts of Arkansas and Texas. Bill had a true genius in developing talent, marketing such favorites as Andre the Giant, The Junkyard Dog, Ernie "The Big Cat" Ladd, Ted DiBiase, Jim "Hacksaw" Duggan, Steve "Dr. Death" Williams and many other wrestling stars. He pioneered the concept of the supershow, holding major events in the Louisiana Superdome.

I have many fond memories of these times with Bill. I remember Andre the Giant holding one of my sons in one hand. Bill would often visit my dad at his home to discuss wrestling matters. To this day, I still chuckle at my late mother serving Bill a demitasse of tea while he and my father were discussing business. Picture that, and you can't help but smile. He gave my sons a sense of business by having them tape the TV shows and sending them to a national wrestling magazine for review.

After my dad passed away, I began to represent Bill as his attorney. Wrestling in America had always been a regional business, but trends seemed to counter this. Mid-South continued to grow and was poised to go national. Unfortunately, interests from New York decided that they were going to control wrestling nationally, and they persuaded the governor at the time (now in federal prison) to direct the Boxing and Wrestling Commission to allow them to commence promotions in Louisiana. They also proceeded with a wholesale raid of talent. Soon buffoonery became the mainstay of professional wrestling. The business had changed — and not for the better. Bill sold his interests and retired from the wrestling business. He applied his talents in other areas and remains a highly successful businessman.

Although we don't see each other very often anymore, we are still in communication and remain close friends. Bill was and continues to be a person of the highest integrity who applies the Christian ethic to every aspect of his life. Today the warrior, no longer young, has some gray around his temples. Yet he remains the embodiment of the saying "The code of the warrior does not know the word *surrender.*" He never has; he never will.

EMILE "PEPPI" BRUNEAU
January 16, 2005

When I was asked to write this foreword, I was faced with a problem I'd never encountered before — I didn't know what to say. Or, more precisely, how to say it. What direction should I take in writing a foreword to the story of a man who had such a tremendous influence on my career? I could put him over, but he'll do enough of that in the next few hundred pages. Then I realized that the story is my story.

If not for "Cowboy" Bill Watts, I wouldn't have been asked to write a foreword to this book — or anything else anyone would read. This is not to slight any of the other great promoters and bookers whom I have had the good fortune to work with and learn from — Jerry Jarrett, Jerry Lawler, Dusty Rhodes, Ric Flair, Kevin Sullivan, Dutch Mantel, Jim Ross and so many more — but Bill gave me the chance to be a "star."

As he often did for others. Look at the early 1980s headliners in Mid-South Sports: The Fabulous Freebirds, The Junkyard Dog, The Rock & Roll Express, "Dr. Death" Steve Williams, "Hacksaw" Jim Duggan, The Midnight Express with Jim Cornette, Terry Taylor, Magnum T.A., Ted DiBiase — all big names, and all got their first chances to headline the cards in a major territory from Bill Watts.

Working for Bill was like going to a military school for pro wrestling — brutal road trips, violent fans, strict discipline — but those who paid attention also got a college course in how to book and present pro wrestling in a logical, credible and exciting manner that sold lots of tickets at prices people in that part of the country weren't used to paying for wrestling.

When Bill first saw me, I was twenty-two years old, had been managing for all of fourteen months and had never sold a ticket in my career. He took a chance and made me his top manager. He teamed me up with two men who had been friends of mine in Memphis, Bobby Eaton and Dennis Condrey, and gave me the team I would become synonymous with: The Midnight Express. Bill was the first to promote The Midnight Express — The Rock & Roll Express rivalry that would define tag-team wrestling in the decade and that would make such an impression that independent promoters would still be booking the match twenty years later.

Working for Bill Watts also introduced me to Jim Ross, who twenty years later is still a highly respected friend and adviser. It allowed me to observe the structure of television shows and angles, building to big events, playing to talents' strong points and other aspects of booking I would sorely need in later years when booking my own territories.

And working with Bill gave me career highlights — his "Last Stampede" coming-out-of-retirement tour in 1984, when he teamed with

JYD versus the Express, with yours truly. We set a record $1.2 million at the gate in fourteen dates, and we provoked some of the most rabid fan reactions I have ever witnessed. After a year in Mid-South, I could get booked with any promotion I chose.

Summing it up, Bill Watts gave me the knowledge and opportunity to make a very nice living in the wrestling business for the past twenty years. He knew how to get talent over, so I think it's only fitting that I write this foreword on behalf of all the young talent he was able to mentor. I only wish he hadn't fined me for delivering the copy late.

JIM CORNETTE

PREFACE

Time can fade memories — but it often enhances them. And, generally, it's the storyteller who becomes tougher, smarter, faster, better looking and sexier. Keep that in mind as I tell it "the way I remember it." Also keep in mind that the stories that follow are snapshots of my life from a certain moment.

It's like I tell my friends when we have a get-together: if you are not on hand to defend yourself, we will be merciless as we castigate you! So this is my story, and I'm telling it my way.

Much of my life was spent in rough surroundings, with language, actions and terminology that reflect those times and situations. We seldom edify or improve our surroundings. Sometimes we become more barbaric, more explosive or more hardened because of them — and thus notorious or even famous. Sometimes we even become "legendary" (in our own times and definitely in our own minds).

But I also have a spiritual side and a personal relationship with my

Lord, who faithfully pierced the "darkness" of my rebellion. Through most of my life, He surrounded me with godly people — not a majority, by any means, but they had a profound effect on me. I often ignored them initially, but they've never been forgotten. I remember Bud Carpenter of Young Life and his friend Will. I remember Brother Joseph. I remember hearing OU football players Bill Krisher, Clendon Thomas and Chuck Bowman giving their testimonies at a Baptist church I attended — and later they influenced my life by how they lived theirs. I remember the wife of that church's pastor, a wonderful, loving person.

My accountant, Jim Elliott, competed in high school and college football against me, although we were teammates in the first high school all-state game in Tulsa. We have had a relationship since the 1950s, and his gentle Christian demeanor was something I could never shake. And through Jim, I met Gene Griffen, whom the Lord used as an instrument when He called me back to Himself in 1984. There was Keith Henson, a young pastor I met by the Lord's lead, and Ernie Ladd, who became a Christian while working for me in wrestling.

I also want to remember the quiet and faithful servants of the Lord who have prayed for me over the years. My brother Bob's biblical understanding helped me through some challenging times. I'm so thankful for my sister Barbara Sue's prayers and for my mother and father praying for me faithfully and lovingly for so many years. Doug Miller, for a time, was so helpful, and Ted Anderson has been a faithful brother in the Lord. Port Robertson (OU's legendary wrestling coach) exhibited strong morals and a strong faith. And now I see many in pro wrestling, like Ted DiBiase, Terry Taylor, Hector Guerrero, Chavo Guerrero, Buddy Landel and Sting, take a public stand for the Lord. And I can't forget Virgie, a lady who worked in our home for a while, whom the Lord used to prevent me from taking a life.

People come into our lives for a time or a season, and we do not always know the reason. But looking back, I can see the "providence of God" in so many.

When I speak of tough guys in wrestling versus those I label "not so tough," please remember that these are my impressions. In general, they all were exceptional, or they wouldn't have survived within that community. I was blessed to know some of the most unique people of our times in a very unique industry.

There is an old saying about getting into a fight: "He who gets there first, with the most, wins." Even people I consider extremely tough could be caught in the right, or wrong, situation and get whipped. But when one of our peers overcame what seemed to be devastating odds, the story would be told and retold, and his reputation would grow comparatively among our band of brothers. Realize, too, that in the repetitious telling of these "legends" events could become embellished. I have heard people telling stories about me who were adamant about their testimonies, as if they had been eyewitnesses. But their stories would be so embellished that sometimes I could not even remember the event — at least not as described.

In my life, I've learned that you consider the consequences of taking action against someone you consider really tough, trying to estimate the cost. There have been those I felt I could "whip," but I also felt the price was too high. That certainly is a deterrent. Jeff Cooper, the famous founder of Gunsite, Arizona, who taught self-defense (primarily with the 1911 Colt .45-caliber gun), said, "An armed society is a polite society." His point was that, if you believe everyone is "carrying a gun," you would probably treat everyone with respect.

"Mad Dog" Maurice Vachon was just plain tough — not big, not overpoweringly strong, but *tough*. He was vicious in a street fight, where there were no rules, only survival. I had a huge amount of respect for him. I saw him in Winnipeg in a great street fight, which really showed me his heart. A guy had sucker-punched him and had him in bad shape. He ran Vachon's head into a steel door frame — the wound required several stitches and left Vachon without some vision in one eye — but this guy eventually "ran out of gas." There was no "quit" in the Dog, and he came back and really kicked the guy's ass.

Over the years, I've known guys with the kind of attitude that says, "If you kick my butt, I'll get you back — I'll get even." But this just doesn't happen when someone really gets beat. When you whip someone so bad that every morning when he shaves he sees a big scar that reminds him of you he "doesn't want no more."

I have never met anyone I believed could outdo Danny Hodge physically, whether it was running or wrestling. Was he vicious? No. But who would want to ever push him over the edge? There are good stories about him in this book.

Larry Hennig once got into it with a person with a huge reputation. And the guy probably was really tough — but he'd had too much to drink. It wasn't the right time for him to try a 320-pound strongman like "The Axe."

This kind of thing happened again and again in our business, and I am still often asked, "Is so-and-so really tough?" But as to who is the toughest guy I ever met, I really don't have an answer. It depends on the situation — there were a lot of tough guys.

But if you're asking me "Do you think you were tough?" well, my answer is *"No!"* I didn't like to fight (though as you read about my life that might seem like a lie). Because I was scared, I learned to trigger my temper to protect me. I was big, quick, agile and very strong, and I had good basic wrestling skills. I was also unscrupulous about the tactics I'd use to win — I was a dirty fighter who'd do anything not to lose, because I was afraid of getting hurt, afraid of the pain and humiliation of getting whipped. My temper became an anesthetic against pain — a way to lose myself in the viciousness of survival.

Of course, I didn't broadcast that I was afraid. And if someone thought I was tough, I allowed him to perpetuate that idea. I did feel I could take care of myself, and over time there were few who could whip me. Yet I felt that, if they did, I'd inflict a tremendous price. I never ran or backed down from anyone. If you were going to beat me, it wouldn't be a gift.

Now, in 2005, at sixty-six, it seems foolish to be talking of such childish things. When you are so self-centered, as we often are in wrestling, much of what you're wrapped up in has no moral or any real value.

Until I began removing myself from wrestling, I didn't have a clue about relationships. In my world, everything was totally self-centered. What a waste. After sharing my story with you, I hope you'll see through all this to the only thing of value — which is Jesus Christ, my Lord and Savior. What He did for you and me at Calvary *was* courage. *That* was love. He paid for our sins so we could be eternally saved. By that standard, my life is nothing.

For years, I couldn't figure out why He would love me, why He loves me now and forever, just as He loves you. Finally, I figured it out. God *is* love! That is His inherent nature: He must act according to His nature. He also desires a relationship with His creation, a personal relationship with each of us. It isn't based on any merit in me — there is nothing in me of merit to Him or that would help me achieve His righteousness. He does not "owe it to me." It is His free gift for each of us. He declares us righteous in His Son, and we are washed by the blood of that Lamb. He is in total control, and by His sovereignty He must provide for us, which He has through His only begotten Son.

So now I'm not afraid to die — just ashamed, seeing that so much of my life was in rebellion to His love and goodness. But, thank God, it isn't how we start this race but how we end it. I am saved by grace through faith in Jesus Christ, just as you can be. His salvation is available to everyone who accepts Him as Savior and Lord! Yes, salvation is conditional. It requires that you *accept it.*

Much of what you will read here will be the profanity of my life, but I hope you'll see there is nothing that the grace of God cannot overcome. And as you read, please sift through the stories to the real truth — that God loves you. If He can love me, He can and does love you. And to find the authority, along with absolute truth, just refer to the Bible, and read His revelation of Himself to us and His interaction with the saints He left so we could know Him.

I also need to mention the profanity of my language at times — unfortunately, it's something that's been with me throughout my life. I've heard it said that a person who uses profanity does not know how to communicate. I don't accept that. But I do feel that profanity seriously limits communication and heightens controversial or adversarial situations. If I curse you out, I am certainly in an adversarial position. Couple this with a testosterone-dominated business of extreme egos and you have a volatile mixture. I have even gotten into fights because my profanity was taken as a personal attack — when I was just using it as a "figure of speech."

Certainly, this relates back to my anger. And I have a lot of harbored anger, though I have released a lot too. But as soon as I am back in the business and talking about or participating in wrestling, my speech degrades, and my profanity increases. Sometimes it seems I'm unable to talk about my life in pro wrestling without swearing. Do I blame it on the business? No, I am responsible for my own actions. But after years of introspection, I know there are certain things I am better off keeping my distance from.

I loved wrestling. I loved the unique individuals I was able to interact with, and I am proud of what I accomplished. But my life has gone in a different direction. I know I needed to leave wrestling to have peace of mind, to have a progressive relationship with Jesus Christ. Writing this book again reveals that weakness in me.

For that, I'm sorry. I would love for you to see through it all, to the thoughts I feel have real value, but my lack of personal discipline might filter that message dramatically too. It's my hope there is a message here not occluded by the messenger.

I'd like to spend just a bit more of your time to really bring into focus how I view life and thus the purpose of telling this story. I believe in a sovereign God, our Creator and the Creator of the universe. He is one God, but triune in the Godhead, and we have relationships with Him as He has revealed Himself as the Father, the Son Jesus Christ and the Holy Spirit. He has revealed Himself to His creation by the divinely inspired work called the Bible and "in person" in the form of Jesus Christ. I consider His Word to be accurate and authoritative — the only source of absolute truth on Earth. I also realize that it challenges us, that we can misinterpret it and often do. But that does not take away from its infallibility.

I sprinkle biblical references throughout this book, and I encourage you to read them because what Bill Watts says is certainly biased and might even be exaggerated — or just not true. But what God says, in His Word, is the truth. I urge you to look up each reference and meditate upon it. I hope it will stimulate your heart and your mind in Him.

He has revealed to us that here on Earth we are involved in a struggle (Ephesians 6:12) between good and evil, which is sometimes characterized as "light and darkness." There is no *neutral ground.* You make a choice whether or not you're conscious of doing so, and making "no choice" is also a choice (and that is to choose against God). And there are consequences, good or bad. God has established His precepts for holiness and righteousness, and Romans 3:23 definitely reveals our "position" without Christ, and Romans 6:23 indicates the consequences! God, being sovereign, had to make a provision for us so that He could have an eternal relationship with us. He gave us the way to be redeemed and reconciled to Him forever. It was the finished work of Jesus Christ at Calvary, where He took our place on that Roman cross and died to pay our price for our sins. Start with the verse that reveals the greatest act of love this world has ever seen: "For God so loved the world that He gave His only begotten Son, that whosoever believeth in Him should not perish, but have everlasting life" (John 3:16).

There is a condition required of us. We must be reborn (John 3:3), which is the miraculous event that happens in an instant when we accept Jesus Christ as Savior and Lord and that begins our "spiritual life in Him." His Word also states that Jesus Christ is the only way to be reconciled to God (John 14:6; 1 Timothy 2:5).

To really begin to understand our salvation in Christ, in my understanding, there are three vital factors. First is the miraculous act whereby we realize our lost position and accept that we need a Savior and ask Jesus Christ into our hearts as our Savior and Lord. That is being "reborn" spiritually in Him and is eternal. Nothing, absolutely *nothing,* can change that! At that moment, we become forever positioned in Him!

Second is the process of our spiritual growth as we learn more of Him and strive to live as He would have us live. That process, just like any relationship, can have tremendous ups and downs. There is obedience and discipline, but we are never rejected, disqualified or thrown out of the family of God. Our relationship with Him is often termed "our communion with Him" or "our walk with Him." When we disobey Him and sin against Him, that communion, or relationship, is broken. But it can be restored by confessing our sins to Him and repenting for them.

And third is when He calls us home to Himself, when we will be "glorified" and given our "eternal bodies." What an awesome time to look forward to, being with Him forever!

Don't ever let anyone tell you that you can lose your salvation. You may question whether or not you have received it, but that is between you and God. Salvation is not performance based. Our works as followers of Christ are "our fruit." They count for rewards in Heaven, and we should want to do them out of our love for Christ. But they are not performed as a way to be saved or a method to become righteous. Our righteousness is only in His blood, in which we are "washed" when we accept Him as Savior and Lord.

My life reveals my struggle, the battle between darkness and light, between good and evil. Reading this, you should be appalled, angered or even horrified at the choices I've made.

My story is a warning. But it is also a story of hope as the light penetrates the darkness. Sometimes there's just a little, just a glimpse. Sometimes I seem to slam the door shut or take two steps forward and fall back three. But always a little light penetrates the deepest darkness, through God's Holy Spirit. God the Father, the source of all light, is faithful. And once we are His, this process of illumination begins for the rest of our lives!

Praise Him, I am saved. My hope and prayer are that anyone reading this story will seek out God's truth for his or her life and have a deep personal relationship with Him. In truth, that hope is my only reason for writing this book.

SUBTLE AS A TRAIN WRECK

To make a long story short, we ran into a speeding train.

It was 1960, and I was playing football at the University of Oklahoma in my sophomore year. With the size today of college players, especially linemen, can you believe that at 229 pounds I was the heaviest guy on the team? Normally, I weighed about 245 to 250 pounds, and at that weight I was still lean, well-proportioned and growing. OU coaches believed the players should be small, which to them correlated to being quicker, so they kept trying to pull us down in weight and never encouraged us to lift weights. Lifting weights is almost mandatory today because with that comes more size or mass. They didn't understand then the benefits of weight training and were too closed-minded to investigate. Their approach was horrible for a guy who was maturing, growing into his strength as an adult. In my case, it meant I was continually on a diet, or on their "fat man's team" for extra running, which also became, to me, one of their labels that created low self-esteem and insecurity.

I was with my first wife, Pat, but our marriage wasn't working out, and I was leaving her. My mother had come to Norman because I didn't own a car. Our only car had been Pat's father's, so my mother picked me up at ou in her 1954 Buick Century. She was upset about the entire situation.

We were back in Oklahoma City, on Meridian, heading north between Reno and 10th. As I recall, the railroad signal lights weren't working. We were told later that there had been seven previous deaths at that crossing from train wrecks. We hit the westbound train's second engine, which, we learned later, was traveling over the speed limit. Hitting one of the engines along the big "drive arm" of the train's wheels, our point of impact was, I now believe, providential. If we had hit the train's body, we probably would have gone underneath it and been crushed to death, because it took the train seven-tenths of a mile to stop.

The impact swung the driver's side away from the train and my side into it. The car was crushed, and I was thrown out of it. I landed about twenty yards away. I've often said, "I wish I had a videotape of that. It's probably the best bump I ever took." (Lenny Montana, a very funny wrestler who later played one of the mobsters in *The Godfather,* told me my beals were "not even as high as rice grows," so I was never noted for spectacular bumps taken, more for bumps given.)

I believe that everything is providential and that the days of our lives are in the hands of God. This accident happened in the middle of football season, so I was in good physical shape. My mother hit the steering wheel and was bruised some but wasn't badly hurt. By the time she got to me, I was instinctively trying to get up, although I couldn't. My pelvis was sprung, and I had crushed ribs, a concussion and a bunch of things internally they didn't even know about at the time. I'd be in and out of consciousness for the next few weeks.

My mother had major problems with depression. I believe now that she was manic-depressive or "bipolar." She also had terrible headaches and had prescriptions for them. She had some tranquilizers and painkillers and bravely crawled back into her car to get her purse, because she thought it would help to get a painkiller into me.

Initially, they left me in my clothes, possibly because they didn't think I was going to live and because they didn't know the extent of my injuries, so they didn't want to cut me out of my clothes until they could examine me. Fortunately, I had jeans on and an Oklahoma high school all-star football jacket they give you when you make all-state. I've still got that jacket, with blood on the sleeves and the cuff of the sleeve frayed from my landing. I bounced several times, I imagine, because I had cinders, dirt and filth embedded in my skin.

I was convulsing so badly that I was strangling on my own stomach lining vomiting, and they were trying just to stabilize me enough to put me on an x-ray table to see what was wrong with me. During this critical period, some well-meaning hospital worker came into my room and decided she'd clean me up, without the doctor's permission. She tried to roll me over, right onto my crushed ribs. The pain was so bad I came back to some form of consciousness, long enough to curse her out violently. About then, the doctor came in, and he went ballistic. I could hear him screaming at her in the hall as I lapsed back into unconsciousness. I was fortunate one of my broken ribs didn't puncture my lungs.

I weighed less than 200 pounds when released from the hospital, and it took six months before I could do even the most basic of football agility drills, like a rolling somersault and back to my feet in a hitting position. I started lifting weights to rehabilitate my injuries, and that dramatically changed my life.

If you are in a car, and have a run-in with a train, you are going to come in dead last. To live through something like that is a miracle! It took me nearly thirty years to realize that it wasn't luck. God is in control — and it just wasn't my time to go.

Even as a young boy, God was always in my life. However, as I became a young man, I began rebelling against my parents and all authority figures. I didn't really understand my rebellion or see it in the spiritual perspective until 1984. That was when I learned that God is faithful and that, once you are His, you are His forever.

See, all men want to know if they measure up, are accepted and can "make the team." Can they be a warrior, a winner? Understanding and grabbing hold of His assurance in relation to our salvation through His Son, Jesus Christ, is so important. At that miraculous moment, we become eternal children of God, fully redeemed from our sins, reconciled and accepted forever by Him. We become members of His family, forever.

I didn't understand that for years, until the 1980s, after He penetrated the calluses on my heart and began drawing me closer to Himself. The consequences of not understanding that "once saved, always saved," can be enormous!

We all want to be accepted and part of something — a family, a team. Well, our Creator loves us enough to provide eternal security in Him and to adopt us into His family, the body of Christ. Once saved, we are forever "positioned" in Him, in that unique family of God — *never, ever, to be rejected, kicked out, disqualified or "erased" from His Book of Life.* To know that is awesome and empowering, and it can make the most dramatic change in each of us. It can also create a self-esteem that is so healthy because of our position or status — our relationship with our God, our Creator and our Lord!

But a lot can happen in the process of living our lives here on Earth. As a young boy transitioning into manhood, I started failing in my efforts to live the Christian life. I spent years thinking I couldn't live this life, so why would Jesus Christ love me? My heart goes out to people who think they've failed and lost their salvation or feel they can't live the Christian life as represented by churches, which have all the best intentions but end up being legalistic and performance based.

Many churches become part of the problem by espousing rules for our lives, which I call "erroneous doctrine." It adds the burden of performance that can also result in feeling that we have failed God. Often this situation becomes repetitive: people fail, then repent, confess and try again. That vicious cycle of "failing God" is allowed to overshadow His love, His mercy and His grace, causing many to give up on their faith.

But God does not give up on us! Once you become a child of God and are reborn into the body of Christ spiritually, you are positioned forever. The struggle then becomes the "practical application" of that in our daily lives; we become a "work in process" until the day we are called home — our physical death here on Earth.

And we can have tremendous struggles in our walk with Him here on Earth, but they don't cause us to be kicked off His team or kicked out of the family of God! We are His forever! Knowing that frees you from any fear of feeling insecure. If your Creator has adopted you into His own family, that action should be the anchor for your self-esteem.

This does not contradict the model of how we should strive to live our lives by His example, nor does it encourage us to sin against God. In no way does His divine election of us as members of His family dull human responsibility. On the contrary, as Colossians 3:12–14 shows, it is precisely because the Christian has been elected to eternal salvation that he or she must put forth every effort to live the Godly life. For the Apostle Paul, divine sovereignty and human responsibility go hand in hand.

I was saved as a young boy by the grace of Jesus Christ through faith — not by my own merit, nor by my works or performance. I was saved by the work and performance of Jesus Christ at Calvary, and even through my years of rebellion I was still saved, even though I thought I'd lost my salvation.

But our growth is a process of experience and relationship with Christ, which allows us to experience more and more of His love for us, which becomes our motivation to become more like Him. Our motivation to live for Him comes from the love He expressed by going to the cross at Calvary and "taking our place" in judgment for our sins. He suffered and paid for our sins Himself, redeeming and reconciling us to the Father in Heaven forever. That act of unconditional love is the sustaining reason we struggle to live for Him. We are His!

I hope that, of all I write here, the *one thing* that really breaks through is that anyone — and I emphasize, as God promises us in John 3:16, *anyone* — can be saved eternally by accepting Jesus Christ as Savior and Lord, and once saved, always saved. There are no *if*s, *and*s or *but*s. So many seeming conditions for salvation are introduced by our religious doctrines. They are well intended but often seek to override God's simple truth as revealed in His Holy Word, the Bible. John 3:16 declares our eternal security through Christ. It doesn't say we "will have" salvation or place any other requirement on it. You have it right then — right when you accept Jesus Christ as Savior and Lord!

Once we repent and accept Jesus Christ, we begin a "process of relationship" with Him. That relationship can have challenges and problems, but our salvation through Jesus Christ is never in peril. Nothing can break it or change it. He knows that we will experience tremendous challenges in our lives, but, if we know we are His forever and can never lose our position with Him, we're free from the slavery of sin and condemnation. If we cling to that truth, then, when Satan tempts and tests us, we can be assured that our eternal life in Christ is secure! Being accepted by God, because of His Son's love and sacrifice, being made a permanent member of His team (the body of Christ) forever — isn't that awesome?

That is *huge* — to know He loves us, has accepted us into fellowship with Him and has paid the price for all our sins, past, present and future! We can "measure up" through Him; we are accepted by Him, forever, and we can be on His team forever. We can be warriors for Him, and we are winners in and through Him!

GROWING UP

I was born William F. Watts Jr., on May 5, 1939, in Oklahoma City, Wesley Hospital. I wasn't a big baby — just seven pounds, three ounces.

We spent my entire childhood in Oklahoma, except for two years, when I was four and five years old, when we lived in Wichita, Kansas. My father had been diagnosed with polio and failed the physical for the draft in World War II. He worked at Cessna Aircraft during the war, making his contribution to the war effort. We eventually settled in Warr Acres, a sub-urb of Oklahoma City, where I attended Putnam City schools until I graduated in 1957. I was the oldest, and my mother, Emma Lou, doted on me to the point that it created cross feelings between her and my father. Dad, I think, resented that this child had become the most important thing in her life. Her open promotion of me as her first-born and the child she loved the most also emotionally affected my brother and sister, though I didn't realize it then.

My mother loved me to an excessive degree, and this caused problems later when she became manic-depressive. Her expectations of me were so high that her reactions to me became extreme. She went from total love one day, or even one hour or moment, to brutality the next as I failed to live up to her expectations or didn't accomplish some assignment she had given me. By today's standards, some of the things she did to me would probably have caused her to face legal action. She was a strong disciplinarian, but her administration of discipline was so inconsistent and extreme that when I got older I really rebelled against her.

Some of the beatings I got were just phenomenal, for things like not getting the lawn mowed or for my attitude not being right. On certain occasions, when they determined I really needed a lesson, my parents would make me take a bath and go, naked, into my room. They would come in and beat me all over with a big belt until they were both exhausted. Those times were seared into my memory! As a less extreme punishment, I would have to grab her chest of drawers with my shirt off, and she'd beat me across the back with a belt. I still hate yardwork because I got beaten so many times over it.

Once, when I was in grade school, my mother wanted to cut my hair with hand clippers. She kept making mistakes and ended up shaving my head totally bald! I was standing there crying when my dad came home. All he said to her was, "Well, don't do that again." There was no empathy for me, and much less did he stand up to her for me.

Years later, when I confronted my mom and dad about these incidents, they both denied them, but my brother and sister remembered them.

As I mentioned, my mother had problems with depression, which the doctors seemingly didn't understand. Back then they didn't really know what was wrong or how to treat it. They hooked her on heavier and heavier tranquilizers and painkillers, many of which were mood altering. Like most prescription drugs, when your body builds up a resistance to them, doctors must up the dosage or try another drug.

When I was in college, her sickness had progressed to the point where I'd come home and she'd spend weekends in bed on strong medication, just crying. She had that slack-jawed, slobbering look, except when she was in a rage. She never had a drinking problem or anything like that. I believe fully that she had a disease, that she was bipolar. She would work all week at her job. Then she'd go home, take the stuff and just lay there, crying, with her mouth slack. My dad would clean the house and do everything. Of course, he had us kids also pitch in, and we had to be quiet so we didn't disturb her. I can look back now and realize her problem. Back then all I knew was that she was the person I loved the most, and while I knew she loved me I never knew where I stood from day to day.

I started working summer jobs when I was eleven, and my parents started charging me room and board in the summer. They were having a hard time because they couldn't manage money, so they had to come up with a plan to take the money I earned instead of disciplining themselves to live within their means.

When we get our self-esteem from others, the "keep up with the Joneses" syndrome dominates. One of the biggest tragedies in America is the desire to have it all materially. When that desire also requires the mother to work, the sacrifice is the children at home being deprived of their mother and her love. Parental interaction and discipline on a daily basis become surrogated to daycare centers, babysitters and their peers, TV and other influences that may not have kids' best interests at heart.

My mother wanted us to have a better lifestyle than what she felt we could have on my father's income, so she took on projects such as a preschool in our home. Then she found she could earn even more by working as an executive secretary. She went to work full time as a secretary for the vice president of all the Standard Humpty-Dumpty stores, but the more she earned the more she spent. I feel that the pressures of trying to earn more and more, in order to have more and more, also contributed to her mental condition. This is in no way derogatory to the single parent who has to do what is necessary to provide for a family. But the two-parent family really needs to weigh the supposed advantages against the possible consequences.

My dad got into car sales in Oklahoma City and later in sales in the steel industry. He was an ethical, hard-working guy. But Mom always spent beyond their means, and Dad was too dominated by her to intercede, so they would charge me rent based on what I made from my summer jobs. I resented it, but not that badly. If the family needed it, all they had to do was ask. I've never been one who doesn't give. But then Mom would come up with some trumped-up deal at the end of the summer if I had $400 or $500 (a lot of money in the early 1950s) saved up from working. She'd figure out a way to get mad at me and take all my money as punishment. She'd say, "You've been so bad, I'm just taking this," when the truth was she just needed it to pay bills. If she had just asked me, I'd have given it to her, but for her to take it like that, with some trumped-up excuse, crushed me. It ultimately triggered deep emotions of anger and eventually even hatred toward her.

I had to wash the dishes every day before school. If, for any reason, I was in a bad mood, she'd run me around the block. That might not sound bad, but around our block was about a mile. If I came back still in a bad mood, I had to run it again.

Some days Mom would take me to school on her way to work, but mostly I walked or rode my bicycle through my grade school and even junior high days. In high school, riding a bicycle to school wasn't cool, so I walked. This was another example of the insecurity that exists when we gain our self-esteem from our peers instead of from our Lord.

Sometimes my mother took me to school when I was in high school. We would pull up to the front entrance, where all "the boys" — the top athletes and school leaders — would congregate. When I would get out of the car and start walking toward them, she would honk at me, call me back and say, "Billy, come back here and kiss your mother good-bye."

I'd say, "Mom, not now. Everyone is looking."

She'd get mad and say, "Billy, you better kiss your mother good-bye right now!"

So I'd walk back to the car, with all the guys really hollering and giving it to me. I'd kiss her good-bye, and all the boys would chorus, "Billy, you'd better kiss your mother good-bye right now!"

It was so humiliating, so controlling, and it created so much anger in me. My pride was beginning to exert more and more control, and my rebellion was starting to seethe by my sophomore year.

I'm not saying that a lot of the discipline I received wasn't justified, but the way it was done was wrong. It was so controlling, and, if I was involved in a church I liked and she got mad at the pastor, she'd pull the family right out. We changed churches a lot, which created a lack of stability and relationship in that important area too.

I was raised in a church, and my mother was very serious about it. She read us Bible stories every day. She taught Bible class and could quote whole books of the Bible. We even went to church camps. I believe Mom was a devout Christian. She and I went every Monday night to Bible study with a converted Jew who had gone blind studying the Bible. His own family had his funeral when he converted. His name was Brother Joseph, and his Bible study was so in-depth I was mesmerized. This man loved the Lord! His love was so beautiful, and his spiritual knowledge was so awesome. I saved my money one summer and bought him the New Testament on records. I was given a great understanding for someone so young. So many unique people have been involved in my life, but only a few of them have been followers of Christ. Yet their impact has been dramatic and lasting, and the Lord has used them to be part of the process of my life, though I haven't always realized it at the time.

In many ways, my brother and sister were crapped on because of me, because there was no doubt I was number one with my mother. Bobby was crushed the most. She actually told him, "You're secondary." Even worse, the standard for him was set by my athletic ability and my school grades. He was not allowed to be himself.

A huge factor in our emotional well-being is self-esteem, how we feel about ourselves. Insecurity is powerful and can really maim or even destroy us emotionally. The environment in which we grow up is so important, along with positive feedback and encouragement. We all need reassurance and hope; we don't need to be torn down or criticized. If our parents are always comparing us to siblings and praising one more than the other, that is negative. God creates each of us as unique individuals, and the Lord doesn't make any mistakes! Each child should be loved and encouraged as a unique, special person and not made to feel he or she must live up to or "live down" to another member of the family or anyone else.

My dear brother was expected to live up to my athletic ability and my exceptional grades in school and all the other things gifted to me. In high school sports, Bobby seemed to become injury prone, and Dr. Freede gave a great understanding one time. He said, "His injuries are almost psychological. He's out there because he feels he has to be. There's a psychology in that, which is going to cause him to get injured."

Today Bobby and I are estranged, which I believe could be because of those expectations, and when I became "famous" and on TV all the time as "Cowboy" Bill Watts he couldn't duplicate that, nor did he really want to, but he was under expectations to excel similarly. And even though I love him tremendously and always told him "Bob, I can't change who I am, or what I am," subconsciously he may have thought he just couldn't live up to the expectations placed upon him by our mother. What a horrible burden to place on a child.

I believe my mother also really messed up my sister, Barbara Sue. She fought her weight and now has adult onset diabetes because my mother had her on every diet plan, every diet drug, in the world, which probably destroyed her metabolism. My sister is the only one of us who graduated from college. She taught school for years, and I love her tremendously.

Barbara Sue moved back in with my parents to take care of them when they were too ill to care for themselves in their final years. Even though my mother and I had tremendous confrontations, I was the only one who could penetrate her shell. When she had an episode and shut down the household, my sister would get word to me. I would go over there, and my job was to get my mother focused on me, which was easiest to do if she became mad at me. I'd confront her, tell her how horrible she was being, treating my sister and dad this way, and she would get so angry at me she'd rebond with my dad and Barbara Sue and be OK for a while. I used to tell my sister, when she was at her wit's end, "That's not Mom you're talking to — that's the prescription drugs and her disease." But realizing it doesn't make living it tenable.

My mother was a good person. As a young boy, I loved her with all my heart. When two friends and I played baseball in grade school, the closest organized league for kids our age was in downtown Oklahoma City. Mom took us every day.

One day, when we were on our way to a game, some kids were blocking the street. We didn't even know them, but my mother stopped, got out of the car and spanked them. She stood up for me in a lot of ways, but you never knew where you stood with her, and that was tough.

Football was big too. I think every kid, on some level, wants to be an athlete. Each high school game was The Event. The football stars were the studs of our school; other kids really looked up to them, and it seemed the prettiest girls dated players. Certainly, once I became aware of girls, I saw that I needed a letter jacket so a girl could wear it. That was the sign you were going steady. This custom meant totally different things. To a male, it was almost like ownership. My girlfriend was *my* girlfriend, an almost "proprietary" relationship, which I know now is totally wrong.

There was no football until eighth grade. By then, I was already 205 to 210 pounds, a big kid. I couldn't even do ten push-ups, though, because there was no physical training to that point. In eighth grade, you had to go to PE or try out for a sport.

As I went into eighth grade for my first structured physical exercise program, the organized football program, even though I was healthy and strong, I didn't know how to do push-ups or other basic calisthenics. Learning how to use our muscles and do simple exercises — teaching muscle control by experience — is also empowering and builds confidence.

Joe Garrison was the junior high football coach, and I was scared to death trying out. The ninth graders, the players already with a year's experience, just beat the crap out of me — in the tackling drills, the one-on-one blocking drills and the "bull-in-the-ring drill." I got creamed, and the ridicule by my peers and the coaches made the pain even worse, if that was possible. Plus, they were running me laps for screwing up, so I was blown up from that, crying, blubbering like a baby.

I quit after that first day. I told my parents how it went, and my dad said I should stick it out at least until the end of the year. Before I'd even got home, Garrison had called my parents and asked them to convince me to come back out, because he realized he had made a mistake. He never told me until years later, when he said, "Didn't you ever wonder why your parents already knew you had quit that day?"

I was scared most of that year, but I learned it was better to be the one delivering the blow with as much velocity as possible than the one receiving it. If you are bigger, stronger, have better technique and deliver the blow, you win. As I learned, I became a dominant player. Playing in high school, at a higher level, gave me status throughout the state too. I became "noticed" and started getting the most euphoric ego stroking back then, with articles in newspapers. Seeing your name in print is really ego building — self-pride is so intoxicating.

High school was where I first met Jack Brisco. He was a state champion wrestler and a football player from Blackwell. We hit it off right away. Later he ran around a bit with my brother, Bob.

From grade school through the ninth grade, one of my best friends was a kid named Clem McWhorter, along with Jerry Fredericks and Bruce Van Horn (who has remained one of my closest friends to this day and is a very successful doctor of pathology in Ada, Oklahoma; he would play a huge role in my life later). Clem was a little guy, about 145 pounds, but he could punch you and knock you out of your shoes and wasn't afraid of anyone or anything.

Mom had made a deal with me for a brand-new car — I'd pay for it in the summer, and she'd pay for it the rest of the year. Clem had to drive because I didn't have a license, so we'd double-date. It was a 1954 Buick Special, the same car Mom and I were in when we had the train wreck. Wow, that was really something to have! Our family couldn't afford it, but we got it anyway.

So here we were, in the ninth grade and in downtown Oklahoma City. Somehow Clem and I got into a fight with three thugs. The guy who jumped me was tough looking. I was scared to death. Clem took care of two of them, knocking them out. The big guy and I stumbled around until I was on top, his head against the curb. I held him, screaming, "I'll let you up if you won't hurt me!" That's how scared I was. I was in total control physically but handicapped by my own fear of being hurt or whipped.

Clem came over and kicked the guy's head into the curb two or three times, knocking him out.

I said, "Well, we sure took care of them!"

Clem was disgusted with me and said I was afraid — "chickenshit" was his term for me. For all my sports experience, I was still scared. At that time, I was in the ninth grade and intimidated by the upperclassmen. Some of them, smaller guys who wrestled on the high school team and had a huge advantage that I didn't realize then, had come down when I was in the sixth and seventh grades and beaten the crap out of me. It built their egos, and even at my size, with their experience in wrestling, it wasn't close to fair — they had the advantage of all that wrestling skill. Plus they were more mature, so their muscles were more developed too. Being a bully isn't necessarily tied to one's size.

One time I got chased home by an older kid, and my dad spanked me and told me to get back out there and fight. I went back out there, got whipped again, went back inside, where my dad spanked me again. I was getting whipped both ways. He tried to make me understand. He said, "You shouldn't be afraid. You're bigger than they are. You're stronger than they are. You have to get mad."

"But, Dad," I said, "if I get mad and do something, they might hurt me."

He said, "How could they hurt you any worse than they're doing now? You've got to learn to lose your temper. Most fights are won by who gets there first, with the most. You lose your temper, you won't feel the pain, and as strong as you are you haul off and hit somebody, and you'll win most of your fights. And if you know you're going to get into it, hit them first."

I started learning to get mad, to hit first and to keep on hitting, but I still wasn't totally there. After getting into wrestling, where I learned leverage and skills, and after my dad's talk, I started whipping people's asses. I also learned to trigger my temper. It became my protective shield. When I was angry, I didn't feel pain, nor was I afraid. Learning wrestling only added to the package.

The seniors ran the school, and one of them was Stan Abel, who later became a two-time, 130-pound NCAA champion at the University of Oklahoma in wrestling and then coached at OU for many years. He has remained one of my dearest friends and has always believed in my ability and tried to motivate me, no matter what. Stan, along with three more seniors who were great athletes and tough kids (and I mean tough by anyone's standards) — Eugene Judkins, Eugene's brother Raymond and Forrest McCoy — "recruited" me to wrestling.

Abel came to me when I was a sophomore, right after football season, and said, "You're going out for wrestling. We want you on the wrestling team."

I said, "No, coach said I have to play basketball."

He said, "You're going to wrestle, or we're going to whip your ass."

That closed that case! Stan wasn't an imposing sight physically, but with Eugene, Raymond and Forrest in the background I got the message.

I went out for wrestling, but at that level and at that time they never taught a lot of technique like they do now. You learned things the hard way. We had a great coach, T.J. Snyder, and Putnam City was known for its wrestling. But he was very limited because all he'd do was start practice, then run to the beer joint and drink, come back and run us. Basically, we learned from wrestling the other guys in the wrestling room, so technique didn't advance very fast, and we certainly didn't advance beyond what our coach knew. There weren't any coaching clinics or videos to teach technique. And with all else being equal — strength, desire, heart and so on — the one with the most technique will win.

One of the most embarrassing things my mom ever did to me came during my senior year. I lost a wrestling match in Midwest City that I shouldn't have lost to a guy named Tim Hawes, who later became a good friend and also wrestled at ou. I'd beaten him before but just had an off night. I wasn't aggressive, and he was. He beat me by one point. In her bipolar rage, my mother came right into the dressing room and degraded me verbally right in front of my teammates and my coach. She took me out of the dressing room and wouldn't let me ride back with the team. I had never felt so humiliated.

The coach said, "Mrs. Watts, let Bill ride home with the team. What you do with him, discipline-wise, is your business, but he came with the team, so let him go back with the team."

But she wouldn't. She showed my coach who was boss and embarrassed me in front of the whole team. She took me home, where she and my dad ran me ten miles down an unpaved road in freezing mud and rain. By the time I was done, it was after midnight. The only thing that kept me going was that I hated them so much. The spirit of rebellion was becoming a monster in me.

Another time in high school I hurt my knee on the football field. I was digging my fingers into the ground to keep from screaming, my knee hurt so bad, and I looked up — and there was my mother, right there with the coach, the doctor and the team's trainer.

I said, "What are you doing out here?"

She said, "You hurt your knee!"

I told her, "I don't give a damn, get out of here! Don't embarrass me further."

Later, when I was in college, I came home one weekend to see my brother play a football game for our high school. During the game, he broke his hand. My mother started down, and I grabbed her and said, "Please, Mom, don't embarrass him like you did me. They have doctors and trainers — please don't do this to him."

Her response: "Well, then, you go out there. If you don't go, I'm going!"

So I went onto the field. Bob looked up, and there was his big brother Bill. "Bill," he said. "What are you doing here?"

I said, "It was me or Mom, Bob."

He said, "Oh, thank you."

Between my junior and senior years, my dad took a job in Bakersfield, California. He could always find something, and he'd do whatever he had to do to feed the family. But without him, my mother was really coming unglued.

I came home one day, and she had snapped. All my clothes and possessions were strewn across the front yard, and she was standing out there crying. She took the slacks I'd just received for my birthday from my grandmother, the only slacks I had, and was cutting the legs off with fingernail scissors. She threw me out of the home.

I called Granny, her mother, and asked her to please come and get me.

Mom told her, "If you come get him, I'll never speak to you again."

Granny said, "Emma Lou, this is my grandson. If you are kicking him out, where is he going to live?"

I lived for a while with her and Pappy, my grandfather. I loved Granny so much. Pappy wasn't my biological grandfather, but I sure loved him too. Joe Garrison, the junior high coach who was now my high school football coach, took me to and from school and practice. For all my problems, it was good to know I had a group of people who cared deeply for me. To be loved and accepted is the most elevating of feelings. Too often we don't get that from the right sources. We don't look to our Savior, who loved us enough to die for us on the cross. It is His love that empowers us and attracts our love of Him.

By this time, the football team was basically built around me. I was the defensive star, and on offense I had the right, even over the quarterback, to check his plays if I thought they were the wrong ones. But they didn't elect me captain. I thought the coach had done that, but he said, "No, it was the guys." I was so arrogant that they didn't want me as their captain.

That year we went to the playoffs but were beaten by Cushing. Still, I became the first WigWam Wisemen High School All-American football player out of Putnam City High School. I was also named All State by the *Daily Oklahoman and Times* newspaper as well as Outstanding Lineman in Oklahoma. Later, on November 10, 1975, I was also honored by being selected to the Jim Thorpe "All-Time Greats of Oklahoma" football team for the decade of the 1950s.

I was grateful that I got to see my old football coach, Joe Garrison, before he died of leukemia a few years ago and tell him how much he meant to me. And he said, "Well, you meant a lot to me too. There's not a lot of coaches with 'Coach of the Year' hanging on their wall, and I was Coach of the Year because of you." He had believed in me, and I hadn't given him any crap because I respected him.

One person I didn't respect was the track coach, Carter Burney. I called the track stars "Carter Burney's boys" and called him fat.

One day I was standing there talking with some of my friends. Burney caught me in the hall, grabbed me by the arm, and said, "Come with me."

"What for?" I asked.

"I'm going to resign, and the first thing I'm going to do after that is I'm going to kick your ass."

Well, I never saw him coming, nor did I dream he would take such an aggressive action, but the tables quickly turned as my temper kicked in. I grabbed him by the arm and nearly lifted him off the floor. I said, "Let's get down there, fatass. I can't wait to get you outside and stomp your fat ass."

Burney was screaming, and Principal Leo Mayfield ran out of his office, demanding to know what was going on. I told him the track coach wanted to resign, and I told him to hurry so I could go right out to the front steps and whip his ass. Burney changed his mind awfully fast. He ended up not quitting, although he'd made a fool of himself.

Growing up, I could never please my mother, so I got to thinking I could never measure up. That led me to feeling I was having trouble pleasing God once I hit the age of beer drinking. Also, I was at the point where my sexual hormones were raging.

Remember, in that era too, sex education came from our peers. Most parents didn't talk about it at home, where I believe it should be addressed. What we learned from our peers was minimal and irresponsible. The only "talk" my father ever had with me was about masturbation. He told me it would cause me to "have pimples" or "go crazy." That was it!

And when I hit puberty, with all those hormones and that confusion, and masturbated for the first time, I thought he must be right, because "that feeling" made me think I was going crazy. And of course, about the same time, like all teens, I got pimples, which I felt were a "brand" for my sin of masturbation.

Nobody had ever explained to me that once you're saved you're always saved. God doesn't desert you. He doesn't want you to do those things, but He still loves you. I had been saved as a small child, and I now know that's when your relationship with God begins. The rest of your life is a work in process (not "progress," because "progress" almost seems to say "improvement," while "process" can be either way, like life is) and can have tremendous ups and downs, like any relationship.

However, in the miracle of receiving salvation from Jesus Christ, nothing can break that bond. *We* can break our relationship when we willfully sin against God, but He still is there for us and ready to reestablish the relationship when we repent and confess our sins to Him. Our sins on Earth carry earthly consequences, but nothing can change our salvation.

I wanted to be a testimony, but when my testimony failed I thought I wasn't worthy. I didn't realize that we're all sinners and will continue sinning. If we don't achieve something, or if we fail at some event or don't accomplish some goal, that doesn't make us failures in life or in His eyes! He desires our burdens, and He will take our sins upon Himself. He has already paid for all our sins. In the vicious cycle, you're always in a position of failing, repenting, confessing and then feeling punished for it. We're saved by grace, not by our life performance, and it took me until about 1996 to understand that.

Thus, my guilt ended up turning into anger. Soon I was just shooting my finger at the establishment. It got to the point where, at any function, I would be so bizarre that all attention would be on me, and I would break all the rules. One of the characteristics of insecurity is always trying to be in control of the conversation, acting the proudest, always trying to be the center of attention — symptoms I have exhibited most of my life. I took it even further: I became more and more bizarre or shocking to gain everyone's attention, whether by my language (as so many young boys do by "outcussing" everyone), by my actions (drinking more or faster) or by causing a fight where I could excel by beating someone up. Finally, that antisocial behavior became my perverted, extroverted personality — even though I didn't like "that me."

And once I learned to trigger my temper as I did, it became my safety mechanism. I later gained fame, or infamy, by being the toughest guy around, and it spilled into all of my life. Whenever I faced something I couldn't deal with, I triggered my temper, because my anger kept me from feeling pain, but it also started running me, and it was self-destructive. My dad told me, years later, "I wish I'd never had that talk with you."

It would be nice, an easy way to wrap it all up in a bow, to say I wasn't saved until 1984, but that's not true. I was saved as a child. I was in rebellion, but God was still in my life, even though I was denying Him. My rebellion would last a long time.

BECOMING A SOONER

If you played football in Oklahoma, Bud Wilkinson and the University of Oklahoma were everything. Oklahoma State, it seemed then, got what was left. That's still pretty much the case now, but with more exceptions than there were back then. If you tally all sports, OSU has dominated, but football is king.

To tell the truth, if I had it to do over again, I might have gone to Oklahoma State, because Myron Roderick, the wrestling coach there, had the character that would get the most out of me. He really drove his kids and made them perform.

The OSU football team was pretty bad at that point, but at least they had started to understand the natural growth of a young man, so I'd probably have done better there. Many of the Oklahoma State players from that era went on to have long pro football careers. Not many of the Sooners, especially linemen, from the same time frame did. In my recruiting class at OU, I think Phil Lohman, Jerry Tillery and I were the only ones who ever played pro. In the classes prior to my recruiting class, there were some great pro football players: Tommy MacDonald, Clendon Thomas, Billy Pricer, Jimmy Harris, David Baker, Bob Harrison, Jerry Tubbs, Max Boydston, Dennit Morris, Wahoo McDaniel, Bobby Boyd, Bill Krisher, Prentiss Gautt, David Rolle, to name a few — but most of them were not linemen.

Bud Wilkinson, the football coach when I played at OU, is still so revered that any negative comments about him might offend his legion of fans. That isn't my aim. I don't mean to diminish his accomplishments or any of his athletes' accomplishments. They were truly some of the greatest who played at OU, and Bud's era was considered golden. OU won three NCAA football championships under Bud. But no one, and no system, is perfect. I don't blame anyone at OU for any lack of performance or for my attitudes. But being in the right system at the right time is a huge factor in your success, and that's true in all walks of life.

As you read this chapter, keep one thing in mind — I love OU! But I will be critical of certain things I experienced there. Colleges love success, but "power breeds corruption," as the saying goes. Programs need to be monitored closely, but that really wasn't the case back then.

Let me digress for a moment. Throughout this book, I share my thoughts about life so that you may understand both the choices I made and the consequences of those choices. I'm not trying to justify anything here — I accept my responsibility.

I am neither a psychologist nor a family counselor — not any expert at all. But I am "weathered." At the age of sixty-six, I am still dealing with my own insecurities and "self-installed behavioral reaction mechanisms" — behaviors I adopted early on *to protect myself* from hurt, fear and insecurity. If I sometimes still feel as if I don't measure up, that I might not be loved for who I am, then I suspect most people are also dealing with these issues (even if they don't want to admit it). This is very important to me, and while it may not seem immediately relevant I hope to plant the healthy seeds of deep consideration. Like many people, for much of my life I attempted to control my environment and circumstances. That was a delusion. We're not in control — God is!

Introspection can be painful, but analyzing why we act and react in certain ways can also be the basis for understanding. And, if we're willing, it's also the way to begin changing the things that are most harmful to us. I believe you'll begin to understand this — as I have — as you read about my life.

One of the most powerful forces in our lives is the way we feel about ourselves. How do you feel you measure up to expectations? Are you engaged in a lot of self-criticism? Is there inner turmoil? Do you have real direction in your life? Do you suffer from spiritual unhappiness or insecurity? Many of us feel inadequately prepared to face life's challenges, helpless, without direction — without real inner peace or joy. But we don't have to. I explore this in more depth in the appendix to this book, and I invite you to read more about "the landmine of insecurity" there.

I was recruited by every major college, and I actually had the grades for West Point, so I was thinking about going there — until Bud Wilkinson came to my house. That was just unreal. He was already beyond icon status and to some was almost godlike. So his coming into our home seemed to be the ultimate event!

It was also the only time Wilkinson personally paid any attention to me. The assistant coach assigned to recruit my area was Ted Youngling, so Bud knew he already had me; he was just there to go through the motions of the official signing. In the next three to four years, I never had one private moment with him, not one. His assistant coaches copied him every way they could, so I never had any private or personal time with any football coach there — except for that one short meeting.

When I started college in 1957, I had no idea what I wanted to do with my life. I just figured, if I got my college degree, everything would be taken care of. With my grades, they put me in a petroleum engineering degree program. Well, I had about as much affinity for petroleum engineering as I do for waterskiing.

Bud's coaching dominance was slipping somewhat as things in his life were slowly distracting him. Wilkinson believed in an old Navy officers' axiom: "Fraternize, but do not socialize." We didn't know him. Recently, I spoke with several of my peers at OU and told them I would be making some of these statements. Each had a story too of how he had been ignored and/or made to feel less than a person during his time in the program. None of them remembered having a truly personal conversation of merit or interest with Bud or any of his assistants. And that may have just been a characteristic of that era, but it didn't make it better.

I remember only one football coach who ever seemed to like me, who gave me praise on the practice field and who acknowledged me with a friendly smile and congenial words when he saw me — Bob Ward, who later coached at Maryland. Ward was the *only* coach in football there who ever said he liked my "style, guts and toughness." And he was there only for my junior year, so I really didn't get to benefit from his positive motivation, but memories of his approach have stayed with me all these years.

This lack of positive attention was a tragedy for someone with my parental background. I was attracted to this wonderful school with a great football program run by an icon of respectability, Bud Wilkinson, with his assistant coaches and staff whom I would naturally also respect and want to please. Yet I wanted their acceptance and approval, their encouragement, just a crumb of praise — just a *crumb*. Instead, I got absolutely no personal relationship — no praise except in my junior year when Bob Ward came there as an assistant. In fact, I was demeaned, criticized and made to feel I just didn't measure up.

Recently, I was talking to Wayne Baughman, my friend and an All-American wrestler at OU. He's now the wrestling coach at the Air Force Academy, and during his career he was a great international-level wrestler. He said he overheard several of the coaches talking about my potential to be a great athlete. However, they never shared that view with me. Why couldn't they share with me their hope, their feelings of my potential for greatness? I needed such encouragement desperately! Port Robertson, in wrestling, offered some, in his manner, by trying to meet with George Goodner and me for private wrestling sessions that really challenged us, but by then his administrative load was so heavy he couldn't be consistent, so it never really got going.

Since J.D. Roberts, the main assistant under head line coach Gomer Jones, had won every major accolade as a lineman, while weighing only 195 or 205 pounds (he has since been inducted into the college football hall of fame), he thought every lineman should be small, because that made you quicker. Bud allowed his assistant coaches way too much control over the players, and the concept of "small and quick" allowed Ken Rawlinson, the trainer, and other closed-minded coaches to decide that everyone, including linemen, should be the same weight as Roberts was when he won all the awards. They didn't take into consideration that he was also short — less than six feet tall. Someone six foot three, like me, with a much bigger bone structure and frame, shouldn't be starved down to that size and still be expected to perform at full strength, but that was OU's philosophical mind-set then. This is the same system that had produced Jim Weatherall, an All-American tackle and pro football defensive tackle who weighed over 270, yet somehow, with the influence of people like Roberts, they had bought into a "small and quick" concept and tried making all of us fit their concept instead of taking full advantage of our individual skills, including strength and size.

I believe I played as much as or even more pro football than anyone in my recruiting class at OU, with the possible exception of Phil Lohman and my friend Jerry Tillery, who both played in Canada. And I competed at 295 pounds — not at "around 200," the 215 they made me starve down to my sophomore year or the 229 that I just couldn't get below my junior year. And certainly my twenty-five-year career as a pro wrestling superstar at 297 pounds gives my perceptions some validity.

My normal body weight (prior to my weight training after the car-train wreck) was 245 to 250. Ken Rawlinson called his special diet he put me on "The Mayo Clinic Diet." It was a fourteen-day regimen and consisted of two eggs and half a grapefruit for breakfast, two eggs and spinach for lunch, and two eggs and half a grapefruit for dinner. Once a week I think we got steak. And on the weekend, we got all the fruit we could eat for one meal, which certainly cleaned us out! Later I went on the Internet and tried to research this fourteen-day Mayo Clinic Diet. I found that the diet had never been endorsed by the Mayo Clinic in Minnesota, that nutrition-ists don't think it works for long-term weight management and that it causes physical weakness. It would be exceptionally harmful for athletes because it had so few carbohydrates for energy and fuel.

The coaches destroyed the self-esteem and thus the performance of many exceptional players. Yet, during our freshman year, they lost only one game, to Notre Dame, thus ending a winning streak of forty-eight games, the longest in college football. In 1958, my sophomore year, we again were 10-1, losing only to Texas, and played in the Orange Bowl. In 1959, we were 7-3, in 1960 (by then I wasn't playing there) they went 3-6-1, and in 1961 they went 5-5. Bud never recaptured his old glory, and when Gomer Jones got the head job the system totally collapsed. I don't remember a single coach there who became a successful head coach at the upper levels, except Bob Ward.

Once J.D. Roberts had me in his office (I was in a coach's office only for discipline) reaming me out for some fight I had gotten into. At first, I didn't know what he was talking about, but as he went through the details I realized I was getting chewed out for a fight that had happened over a year earlier. The coaches were so out of touch with the players that they weren't even aware of my "notorious conflicts."

Of course, my behavior was definitely not acceptable for anyone — particularly a college athlete on scholarship who is expected to represent his school and state and be a role model for up-and-coming kids in school. We were held up to a higher standard. This was still the era when athletes were protected by the officials. Even the media cooperated with the administrative arm of the football department. That only promoted an attitude in athletes of being above the law or above the rules governing ordinary citizens or students. Certainly, I wasn't the only one at OU violating social rules, policies and laws. It happened more than you think, and the drinking episodes were not only condoned but also in some circumstances even encouraged.

We didn't even get a drink of water during our two practices a day in the extreme heat! Total ignorance was only topped by extreme cruelty and verbal abuse — which, because of Bear Bryant's success at Texas A&M (and later Alabama), was thought to be the key to motivating athletes. Bryant, another football icon, is still famous for his cruel preseason football camp while he was coach at Texas A&M, where they took seventy-five players off campus and returned with only twenty-five survivors. They are still proud of that! Well, if you were one of the twenty-five, I'll bet you *were* proud — just like if you were a survivor of the Bataan Death March by the Japanese in World War II, where our prisoners of war were brutalized.

But what about the fifty young players they demeaned, brutalized and possibly scarred emotionally for life — for a damn game? Those young men were labeled as failures when they quit. I'm sure they were then labeled failures on campus among their peers, with their families, among their friends and in their hometowns. All of these young men were brutalized for a game, and it was endorsed by an institution of higher learning — with the survivors being given icon status instead of the perpetrators being disciplined. Is that sick or what?

That style seemed to permeate much of the football community. It still exists. It was news recently in Tulsa when one of the coaches had one of those extreme preseason camps and still had a losing season. Some of these "dinosaurs" are still running around loose.

It takes an entire team to win games. Yes, only eleven players get to start the game, but you need more than these eleven to have an effective practice, to cover injuries and to compete during the week to develop the skills and intensity of everyone on that team. That means each member of a team is vital. And if you receive a scholarship, you have performed well enough to earn it, so you become a member of that "family." You should be valued for your contribution and praised for it. That praise will motivate you to perform even better!

But back then, with the luxury of almost unlimited numbers of recruits, the coaches often squandered human assets as they treated those who did not excel or make the starting team like social outcasts and failures. As many coaches bought into the Bear Bryant philosophy, there were even more proponents of this theory who tried to make it even worse for the players in order to prove their bravery and toughness.

I had emerged from a family background that is dysfunctional, and clearly this wasn't the best environment for me at this stage of my life. I'm sharing this not to place blame but to foster understanding. When I am stressed, and have a nightmare, I am back at OU trying to make the team again. I still feel like a failure there because I didn't live up to the expectations of being a starter and earning All-American honors.

For the most part, coaches today have to mentor kids. Major programs have one coach for every eight players, huge coaching staffs, along with graduate assistants, and the position coaches are around these kids a lot. The coaches realize that they've got to be a positive influence in their lives because too many things aren't. They realize that they need to develop a social relationship with their players too, to become a surrogate father, a mentor, a role model for their players, and to encourage as well as guide them. Also, with the NCAA recruiting restrictions on scholarships, these kids are a huge "investment" for the university football program. Coaches no longer have unlimited numbers to replace their mistakes with. Each bad choice they make in recruiting can dramatically affect their success, so they invest more of themselves into mentoring these kids on an individual basis.

Coaches at OU didn't believe in that at the time. I can't emphasize this enough — I love OU, and I am proud of being a part of that team! And certainly the great athletes who excelled in that system earned every accolade they got. I'm not taking anything away from them. I couldn't anyway.

There was a good system at OU in an academic sense. We had grade sheets we had to take around every four weeks, and if you had a C or below in any course you had to go to athletic study hall three nights a week. If you had an unexcused absence, it was ten trips to the top of Owens Stadium. If you missed study hall, it was seventy-five trips, and each trip had to be under fifteen seconds, which was brutal. I believe there were seventy-two steps to the top of Owens Stadium at that time.

This discipline was under the supervision of Port Robertson, a highly respected administrator. Port was the head wrestling coach, but he was phasing those duties out to Tommy Evans as his time was needed more to supervise and administrate the athletes on scholarship — one man for all of us made it a huge task, even as exceptional as he was. Although a tough disciplinarian, he tried to be fair, and he did care.

My roommate, Billy Jack Moore, got ill running the steps one morning and puked. Port said, "Mister Moore, please refrain from regurgitating because you are hurting the morale of the others running steps this morning!"

Another morning there was ice on the stadium steps, so Port gave us eighteen seconds to get to the top, until we had "worn a path in the ice." See? He wasn't totally merciless. And I guarantee you he had our respect. Port remained a person in my life I could look up to, and we had an ongoing relationship until he died.

Port loved OU, and he was a principled man. Here's an example of his integrity. His nephew, movie star Dale Robertson, starred in the TV show *Wells Fargo,* cosponsored by different companies on different weeks — Buick one week, Pall Mall cigarettes the alternate week. On the weeks it was sponsored by Pall Mall cigarettes, Port wouldn't watch it.

Being a football player and a tough guy has some advantages. I had a chemistry class that was the most boring thing I could imagine. Our professor called roll and then started writing formulas on the board, so as soon as he recorded us being there and turned around some teammates and I would go out the back window, down the fire escape. Then, if we could find any, we'd "borrow" parked bicycles and go to the Jeff House (the football dormitory) to eat lunch. I even got to take a nap before football practice.

I'd fill out the lab experiments and turn them in but wouldn't go to lab. One day the lab instructor came to me and said, "Mr. Watts, I know you're filling out experiments that you're not actually doing, so I'm going to fail you in lab. If I fail you in lab, you'll make a D for the course."

I blew him off.

As a freshman, I didn't get to play because of the NCAA's rules about freshmen not being eligible, but we all traveled on our own to Dallas for the annual OU-Texas game. The night before there was a giant rally in front of the Baker and Adolphus Hotels in downtown Dallas and in some of the surrounding hotels. They'd stop the traffic and everything. That year, there was a vicious stabbing of an Oklahoma kid, Charley Messenger, from El Reno. He was almost disemboweled, so they stopped that tradition.

We didn't have any money, so we were running from party to party. If they said, "Yea, Oklahoma!" we'd say the same. If they said, "Yea, Texas!" we'd say "Yea, Texas! Give us a drink!"

We were getting into fights as we went from place to place. We were looking for action, really. We thrived on beating people up, and I was the worst of them all. This anger-driven social dysfunction should never have been tolerated. During the 2004 football season, Bob Stoops kicked Dusty Dvoracek, All-American tackle and team captain, off the team after he apparently demonstrated the same tendency, and alcohol seemed to be part of the catalyst too. That took a serious commitment by Stoops to maintain proper discipline for his team. Subsequently, Dusty accepted his responsibility and made a commitment to reform. Stoops gave him another chance in 2005, and Dvoracek has been outstanding.

I walked into a hotel lobby there and saw a guy beating another guy up. The guy doing the beating had a fifth of whiskey hanging out of his back pocket, so I sidled up to him and snatched the bottle. The guy realized it, turned around and said, "That's mine — give it to me!"

I just knocked him out cold.

The guy on the floor said, "Oh, Mr. Watts! You saved me! You saved me!" It was my lab instructor from chemistry.

I quickly handed the bottle to one of my buddies and said, "Yeah, I saw you there! Let me help you up."

He said, "That guy was killing me! Look, don't worry — you're covered in lab."

I had gotten married in 1957 to Pat. The marriage was an example of my unprincipled life: she became pregnant, and the battle within my principles and my faith was such that I felt obligated to marry her. Morally, I still believe we should be responsible for our actions. If you play, you pay. It takes two to get one pregnant, so it is a man's responsibility to do the right thing. It is not just "the girl's fault," as some claim. We live with the consequences of our actions. God's laws are absolute. You cannot, therefore, break His laws, but you can "trespass" them. You can break yourself on His laws, and when you do you reap the consequences here on Earth.

I was still in high school, and I just wasn't ready to be a father. I sure was ready to be a fornicator and to allow my physical desires to dominate my actions — as a result, Pat got pregnant. We lived in a room in my parents' home, and then her parents gave us her dad's fishing car.

In Norman, we lived in an apartment. The team wanted me to lose weight, but the only thing Pat could cook was Kraft Dinner — noodles and cheese — so I ballooned up. We had a son, Biff, but we just weren't making it. Years have passed, and we can speak to each other and laugh now, so there's no animosity. She has done well in life, but in relationships and marriages she has not been successful, for whatever reasons, like me.

While I was in the hospital recovering from the train wreck, Pat cleaned out my bank account, which I had built up working a summer job, and bought a dress and a cocktail ring. I suppose she felt she was entitled to it, and after being married to me, I don't know, maybe she was. We got divorced during my junior year.

Pat ended up getting engaged to a county commissioner, and I was happy because he loved both her and Biff. They invited me to the engagement party, and her fiancé started baiting me.

We were drinking Purple Passion, this drink made with juice and 190-proof Everclear, along with gin, vodka and grape juice. It made for a lethal mixture that left me obliterated.

He started telling me how he was fleet boxing champion in the Navy and that a boxer could whip a wrestler. I don't know if he really thought a boxer had superior skills or if he felt I was so drunk I'd be easy prey.

I said, "Are you kidding? They haven't made the boxer that can whip a wrestler!"

He kept on and wanted us to go outside.

I kept asking him, "Are you sure you want this? Do you realize how bad you're going to get whipped?"

I think he wanted some sympathy from Pat or thought he was a man and I was just a kid. Often men underestimate young kids they consider boys and aren't aware of their power and ability. I don't know.

He stanced up, but that didn't last. I single-legged right in under him, scooped in under him, and I beat him half to death. Pat was trying to pull me off, but I just pushed her away.

Finally, he looked up and said, "Why did you hit me?"

I just said, "Well, you son of a bitch — *you* started this whole mess!"

I then kicked him in the face and knocked him out. I took some money out of his wallet and went to meet my date. By the time I got to my date, I think I'd already gotten into another fight, in the lobby where she worked.

We were going to the Trianon Ballroom to see singer Hank Thompson and to meet some of the guys on the football team. I'd never paid to get in there, nor anywhere in Oklahoma City for that matter, never had to. The bouncer told me I had to pay to get in, and I knocked him out cold. I went in, and a guy I knew named Bill Boudreau said hello, and I just nailed him in the gut. He was a tough pro football player, and we were friends, but I was still totally obliterated from that Purple Passion.

A deputy sheriff attempted to arrest me, and I bearhugged him over my head. He told my teammates, if they would get me to leave, he'd let me go, which at that moment was his best call.

The next morning I woke up not remembering much of any of this. I was eating breakfast at Town Tavern, and my mother called there, looking for me.

"What in the world did you do last night? You put a county commissioner in the hospital," she said.

They put in the paper that his face was all swollen because he'd had a bad reaction to penicillin. His brother put a contract on me, and we eventually got it straightened out, but I slept with a gun for a while.

I was a kid out of control, made into a superman out of control by the weights I lifted after the train wreck.

Years later I took Suzanne (who is, as of this writing, my wife of six years) to eat at Mike Samara's Celebrity Club in Tulsa. Mike used to have a club in Oklahoma City, and he came up to us and said to her, "Let me tell you about this guy you're married to. I had the only club in Oklahoma City he didn't turn into a parking lot. If he got mad at someone in *my* club, he'd take them outside because he liked me, and boy was I thankful."

A few weeks after the train wreck, I got out of the hospital. My parents wouldn't let me sue the railroad because that was against their principles. The railroad did buy me a car as a settlement — a little, cheap Fiat, if you can imagine me at six foot three in a Fiat.

After the wreck, I was pretty well shaken up. It was massive body shock. Then I ran into a friend of mine, Jay Smith. He was gaining weight and looking really muscular. I asked, "What are you doing?"

He said, "I'm lifting weights."

I said, "They won't let us lift weights."

Yes, as hard as it is to believe now, when I went to OU they actually forbade us to lift weights. Our coaches had only seen guys who were never athletes use weights and become what you'd call bodybuilders, and they were not necessarily very coordinated, because they'd never done anything to *develop* coordination. But the coaches attributed the deficit of coordination to the weights and said they made you "muscle-bound," which is complete idiocy in my opinion but was a prevailing attitude then.

We had an All-American tackle on the Oklahoma team who weighed 195 pounds named Jerry Thompson, who came from Ada, Oklahoma, a major football factory for years. His high school coach, Elvin George, had started the kids lifting weights, and Jerry was so explosive and so powerful. He wasn't even six feet tall! And my roommate was Billy Jack Moore, who was shorter than Jerry was and could come out of the stance and hit you twice before you could move. The coaches, in their lack of understanding, didn't correlate that what made these guys so explosive was the powerful weight training they got in high school, along with the sound football fundamentals there. Combine strength and speed, along with explosion and technique, and you have an awesome athlete.

Jay introduced me to Lynn Hickey. Lynn had played football at Bethany High School, which is right next to Putnam City. Lynn had gone into the Marine Corps at 138 pounds. When I saw him, he was out of the Marines and weighed 218. He was chiseled and massive, and I just said, "My gosh! What happened to you?"

He said, "Come lift weights with us."

So even though the coaches and everyone else said no, I started lifting weights. I was so embarrassed because I couldn't even bench-press 175 pounds that first day.

Before I lifted weights, after spring training, I had to go on the fat man's team and be run every day, because I was too fat. Too fat at 229? I was six foot three! But can you see what that does to a kid's self-esteem? Remember insecurity and that one of the causes is no positive feedback or encouragement?

Racially, things were changing too. Prentiss Gautt, a high school phenomenon from Oklahoma City Douglas, was the first black football player to be given a scholarship to OU, and that was in 1956! Wallace Johnson was the second, also from the same fine high school program.

Remember the Titans, the Denzel Washington movie, showed the racial situation back then but reflected it in the 1970s. We are talking about the late 1950s, so OU and Bud were ahead of their time in this aspect. Still, I felt many situations on the field were racially motivated. Prentiss was such a powerful running back and later starred in the NFL. He was our only "power runner," but, in an era when the quarterback on the field called the plays, I remember games in which he didn't get the call inside what is now called the "red zone." I believe we lost to Nebraska my junior year for this reason. Wallace later served in the Special Forces with honor in Vietnam, and I'm proud to call him my friend. I have a lot of admiration for him too — can you imagine the pressure on these student athletes as they "broke the color line" back then?

They had great athletes at OU, and too often they didn't know what to do with them. The system so demoralized some of them that they never got anywhere near their potential. Some just gave up on football, and went on to other sports to excel, because they became so discouraged by this system — people like my friend Bill Noble, who was one of the fastest on the team but felt he wasn't treated fairly. Another was Stan Ward, a terrific athlete, who blew out his knee, transferred to OSU, graduated with honors and attended law school. He became a great trial lawyer.

Ken Rawlinson was supposedly a great trainer. I had a major shoulder injury, and they took me to Dr. Donohue, a highly regarded orthopedic surgeon ahead of his time in a lot of the ways he treated injuries. However, Rawlinson told me that Donohue couldn't figure out what was wrong with me and said to me, in front of everyone in the training room, "Donohue thinks you're faking it, and you're afraid." Even now I have degenerative arthritis in that shoulder from that injury, which has left it noticeably weaker than my other shoulder — and this "icon" said this to me.

I said, "Why don't you line up the entire football team and ask them which one of them thinks he can whip my ass? I can tell you for sure no one on this team wants to fight me. I can whip everyone's ass on this team. I'm not afraid. That doctor just can't figure it out."

Looking back, I realize that I never got to speak with Dr. Donohue about his diagnosis, so for all I know he might never have said that. Ken could have just made it up to promote his own agenda.

When I started lifting weights with Lynn Hickey and Jay Smith, Lynn worked my fanny off. We lifted five hours every other day. I was at the perfect growth age, and we didn't know what a steroid was. I never took a steroid for weightlifting or size enhancement. We were eating five meals a day, drinking brewer's yeast, even making shakes with desiccated liver. When people tell me they don't like a nutrient because of how it tastes, I think, "You don't even know." Desiccated liver would make you puke just smelling it. You had to hold your nose to drink it. And brewer's yeast? Try mixing that up and drinking it!

I shot up to 315 pounds from 245 in seven months, and everyone saw the change. I was a superman and didn't know it. Lynn Hickey and I put a gymnasium at OU, at Campus Corner, called The Campus Corner Athletic Club. And I lived there.

It wasn't until later that I started to understand what was happening to me physically. George Goodner, a good friend of mine, was a local legend as the stud of our school. He was also the toughest animal I'd ever seen in a street fight. He went into the Marine Corps and was an All-Marine champion, then went to OU and became a national champion, at 191 pounds. The person who defeated him in the state meet his junior year of high school was Danny Hodge, but George took state his senior year after Hodge graduated.

Once, when George was home on leave from the Marines, I met him at the junior-senior prom — I was a sophomore dating a junior, and the guys introduced me to him, saying, "This is the guy who's going to take over your legend. This is going to be the badass from Putnam City." And that was a mantle that had some great history — names like Doc Heron, George Goodner, Eugene Judkins, Raymond Judkins, Stan Abel, Don Adams and so many others. We were noted for having "stand-up guys." If you were the stud of Putnam City, you had to defend it against anyone from any other school. And all I thought, when I saw George and looked into his eyes, was, "Gosh, I just hope this is OK with George. I don't want him to kill me."

After he got out of the Marines, he got a wrestling scholarship to OU and would come back to Putnam City when OU was on break to work out. I got the "privilege" of being stretched, as they say in wrestling. Jimmy Cohn would also come back from college to work out, as would a huge heavyweight who wrestled at OSU named Earl Lynn — and these guys would kill me. But George's ego was such that he didn't have to destroy me when he worked out with me. He knew he could beat me, and showed me he could, but he didn't crush me. He taught me, and we became friends. He was really ahead of his time in developing the single-leg takedown, which they all use now.

Fast-forward to after the train wreck and after I had lifted the weights that totally transformed me. I was at Putnam City High School, and it was the off season. Stanley Abel was Putnam City's wrestling coach at this time. Stan was a senior when I was a sophomore in high school, and he was a two-time national champion at OU at 130. George was also there and had a bad shoulder, but we hadn't worked out together since I'd become this big and strong. We were on the mat, and he shot his patented single-leg in on me. I reached in with my left arm, double-underhooked both elbows and whipped him off the single-leg and had him standing up, his toes barely touching the floor. I was holding him up with one arm.

He said, "Stop the match."

You have to understand that George Goodner wasn't afraid of anything. He was the most fearless guy I knew. I'd never even seen him flustered.

I said, "What's the matter? Did I hurt your shoulder?"

He said, "No. Stop the match!"

I asked why, and he said, *"Stop the damn match!"*

So I let go of him.

He said, "We're not wrestling anymore."

"Why?"

"I just shot my best move on you. You ripped it off with one arm and had me helpless, with both of my shoulders extended. You don't know what has happened to you, and we're not wrestling anymore."

I didn't understand it then. I was confused because I'd been in the roughest barroom brawls in the world with George Goodner, and I knew he had no fear. What he was seeing was that this kid he'd seen since high school had become a superman.

Let me show you the difference even more clearly. Dale Lewis, who later became a dear friend, was a national champion wrestler for OU. He weighed about 250 pounds and had come from the Marine Corps, so he was five or six years older than I was. He was a tremendous athlete with incredible leg strength. He also had maturity because of that four-year age difference. Today it's not as big a deal because kids have more technique in their wrestling, but back then you wrestled only twelve matches a year, or twenty at most, so physical maturity, knowledge and experience dramatically impacted things.

Before weight training, since I would come up from football and they had been wrestling, we had to try out for me to beat him off the team. In tryouts, they didn't count riding time, which they do in matches, and I had to beat him. He didn't have to beat me. Therefore, he would stand on the edge of the mat and be defensive. We went to extension match after extension match, sometimes for twenty-five minutes. When I was in school, a college match was nine minutes, but if the score was tied they'd do extensions. Standing at the edge of the mat was the greatest defensive position in the world because, if I got something on him, he'd step off the mat. They'd break it, but he was in no danger, and he wasn't going to shoot anything in until I finally made a mistake, and he would counter. He beat me by one point after twenty-five minutes and went on to win two national championships. At 245 pounds, I could have beaten him every time if he'd have wrestled me, as I did in our daily workouts, which didn't count. Instead, he was allowed to maintain a totally defensive position and be passive in the match, which is not allowed today.

After I had lifted weights and reached 315 pounds, Dale's workout partner, a dear friend of mine named Dick Benson, got hurt. Port called me and said, "Mr. Watts, I want you to finally do something good for the University of Oklahoma. You've never done anything good for the university. We need you to come work out with Dale and help him come back and win his second national championship."

I didn't tell Port "Screw you," but that's what I was saying in so many words. I said, "I don't owe this school anything. They put me off scholarship, kicked me out of the program." Of course, that was my own fault. I was breaking all the rules, but I told him, "I don't owe this university anything," and I hung up.

Port called me back and said, "You get your little butt over there and work out with him."

With Port, you really didn't say no. Once when Port was coaching, Wahoo McDaniel came running across the room screaming, and he tackled Port. Port was probably forty-five. I thought Wahoo had snapped him in two, but Port reversed him in midair, came down on him and just stretched him. He pulled in flankers on him, and Wahoo tried to claw his way to the edge of the mat. Port grabbed the fat around Wahoo's waist and pulled him back onto the mat. Wahoo was screaming again before Port was done with him.

Anyway, when I got there to train with Dale, there were three or four big mats in the wrestling room, but the whole team was around the first mat. They'd seen how big I'd become and wanted to see the outcome. I hadn't been on the mat in a year, but I'd been on that iron.

Dale and I wrestled, and I pinned him three times in ninety seconds. He tried to wrestle defensively, like before, but he couldn't. I just pulled him in and took him down. I destroyed him. He got up and ran off the mat, and he wouldn't wrestle me anymore.

I didn't like Dale much in college, and yet, when I got into pro wrestling, he was one of those who helped me along, and we became good friends. He had a heart of gold. I have an awful lot of respect for him. He was also a guy who, even though he had a lot of wrestling ability, didn't want to fight. That is almost a paradox for wrestlers, most of whom *love* to fight.

Then Tommy Evans (one of the greatest amateur wrestlers to come out of OU, a two-time NCAA champion and Olympian, an extremely tough individual with an aerobic system that never ran out of gas) officially became head coach as Port got more into administrative duties. Tommy made me wrestle Vaughn Henry, who later became a giant guy too, but back then he wrestled at 191. We were dear friends, but every time he wrestled me somehow something negative would happen to him. It was kind of like I had the Indian sign on Vaughn.

He hit me with a perfect headstill, meaning he snapped under my arm and clear behind my back, but I somehow reached back and caught his chin as he was going under. I was so strong that, as I kicked in a hiplock on him, it crushed him and pinned him in the same move. And then he wouldn't wrestle me anymore.

I had destroyed the two top guys on the team in one short workout, so Port wanted me to go back on the team. We had some great wrestlers on our teams then too. I've mentioned Dale Lewis, George Goodner and Stan Abel, but there was also Paul Aubrey, a close personal friend who recently died; Wally Curtis, who saved my life in a fight in Dallas; and Dick Delgado, a 123-pound national champion who taught me a lot about leverage. And Wayne Baughman, Mickey Martin, Bill Carter, Tony Macias, Earl Secrist, Bud Belz, Gerald Whitfield, Bob Deupree and Sid Terry, among others. They were truly some studs, and I know there are many I have failed to mention.

OSU during this era also had some real studs, many of whom were my friends, even though we were school rivals: Jack Brisco, Bob Johnson and Ronnie Clinton, to name just a few. The rivalry between Ronnie Clinton for OSU and Sid Terry on our team was awesome. Sid was powerful and an excellent mat wrestler. Ronnie was smooth, relaxed, had a tremendous ability to change pace and was awesome on his feet. Their match was decided by whether Ronnie could get far enough ahead by takedowns and then hold on without getting pinned by Sid when he was on the bottom. Ronnie became NCAA champion, and Sid was runner-up. Matches like theirs upgraded the sport and changed its tactics as others learned from them.

After the day I whipped Dale so convincingly, Port said, "We're going to put you back on the wrestling scholarship, but we want you to live off campus somewhere. We don't want anyone around you."

That's how bad my reputation had become. And by labeling me this way, how do you think it motivated me psychologically? It only added to my desire to be even worse publicly. It made me feel ashamed, as if I really wasn't wanted. It seemed that I would be tolerated if they could use me. Tommy was mad that Port put me back on the team, overriding his decision, and called me in and said, "You have to try out with the guy who's going to be the heavyweight next year, a guy named Allwhite."

I thought, "Here's the old political screw again."

I went up for the tryout and pinned Allwhite in the first period, so Tommy said, "No, it's two out of three. Come back tomorrow."

I knew Tommy would be coaching this kid, and I wasn't in wrestling condition at this time, but when you're lifting weights steadily you stay in pretty good condition, especially since I was lifting five hours every other day.

I went up there the next day, and I was right — Tommy had coached Allwhite, who ran from me the whole time. I rode Allwhite the second period, but they still didn't count riding time. The last period I had to go down. In college wrestling back then, you started on your feet the first period. The second period one of you has an advantage. The third period the other one has the advantage. So, in the third period, Allwhite was on top. I escaped in fifteen seconds, and the match score was now 1-0 in my favor.

I looked at Allwhite and said, "Now, buddy, you can't run anymore. You've got to come to poppa."

Allwhite came in, and I forearmed him so hard it knocked him out cold. I covered him and told Evans, "Count him, and you can count to ten if you want. He's out."

Evans was so mad. He asked me, "Did you slug him?"

I said, "Naw, I cross-faced him hard."

I had pinned Allwhite twice, but I saw the deck was stacked, so the next day I signed a football contract with the Houston Oilers and left OU.

To this day, I believe that college football, for all its positives, can be a form of slavery for the athlete. You read about the successful ones who get great honors and glory, and the few who get to the pro level, but you don't hear about all the casualties. A coach can break his contract, take a better job or move on without penalty (unless there is a small clause of damages repaid, which there sure wasn't in my era). But any player who changes schools loses a year of eligibility. If you made the wrong choice as a seventeen- or eighteen-year-old kid and got recruited into the wrong system for you, you were either stuck or penalized dramatically, since you had only five years to compete for four seasons. If a young athlete makes the wrong choice, it can really have long-lasting effects.

Also, NCAA rules can dramatically restrict a player from earning income from a job while on campus, so many players are actually broke. When I visited my son Erik, playing at Louisville, I saw players so broke they couldn't even go out or get something to eat unless they had an "outside source" of money, such as their parents. That restrictiveness contains the potential for cheating and corruption.

The desperation to get money from any source available often leads to well-meaning fans giving money, which is against the NCAA rules and gets colleges placed on probation. But the huge income for the university from its football program is never shared with the players who make it possible. Doesn't it make sense to give players a couple of hundred a month, just to have pocket money?

I benefited in many ways from my OU days, but looking back it wasn't the best choice for me. Years later, after I became a pro wrestling star, I ran into Bud one day while passing through Chicago's airport to catch another plane. We had a short visit, but it was still longer than any during the years he'd been my coach. He admitted they had "made a mistake" with me but limited it to their trying to pull me down in weight and said that didn't make any noticeable difference in my speed, so it had been a mistake. It sounded like he was just throwing me a crumb, but I guess any concession from him was exceptional. It didn't change anything and came years too late, but I guess it validated some of my feelings.

OU has had some great coaching. To my knowledge, Barry Switzer was a positive motivator and a "player's coach." Bob Stoops, the current coach, is also a positive motivator, making the players responsible for playing at the top level. He establishes an attitude of professionalism and tells them they are good, if they have merited such praise through hard work. His expectations of their greatness, along with his encouragement, motivate them to be better.

I hope now that every coach or mentor considers the potential long-term effects of his or her actions. Each athlete is recruited individually, so each is well worth individual time and consideration, just as is each child in a family. Take the time to get to know your charges, and learn what they need and how to positively motivate them. When you give them what they need, you'll get all you need from them and a whole lot more.

GOING PRO

Without a doubt, if I hadn't gotten into wrestling, I'd have ended up in the penitentiary or dead because of the environment I had created for myself.

Was pro wrestling a better atmosphere? I don't know, but it got me out of where I was. As long as my friends were in Oklahoma, I was going to run with them and make trouble. Wrestling changed the environment, or at least my locations and circumstances.

Wahoo McDaniel was the man who got me into pro wrestling. When he was in the mood, he was a hell of a fighter. If you tried to intimidate him on the football team, let me tell you, he was going to meet the challenge.

When Port Robertson was working out to make weight, the legend goes, he ran from Norman to Chickasha, about twenty-five miles. Wahoo said, "Anything he can do I can do," and the news media got wind of it and started following him.

What we didn't know (which he later told me) was that in high school Wahoo had started taking speed. He told me that a pharmacist who was a big booster of Wahoo's high school team and the father of one of his team-mates gave Wahoo a B-12 shot when he wasn't feeling well and then a small pill to take "just before the game." He called it a "vitamin." Wahoo had a tremendous game and gained a lot of yards, so this became his Friday-afternoon ritual. He later realized the small pill was a "benny."

One day Wahoo came in while I was wrestling and challenged me. I got so tickled looking at Wahoo coming at me that I started laughing, and he actually tackled me. You often think a tackle is good, but it's not in wrestling because the tackler is overextended. Finally, I reversed on him, put myself in a dominant position and said, "Now, Indian [realize that I am part Chickasaw, so this wasn't demeaning, merely one of Wahoo's nick-names], I'm going to show you how it really feels." I put a figure-four guillotine on him, with my legs wrapped around one of his and his arms pulled up over my head and shoulder, with my arm under his head. With him facedown, I turned his body, and it was an excruciating hold, with me holding him one way with my legs and turning him another with my trunk strength. He was screaming, and I told him, "You're going to scream, Indian — I'm going to show you how this really feels," but Coach Evans pulled me off him.

Was I mad at Wahoo? No, I don't think I was ever angry at him, but I made sure he knew where we stood.

Wahoo was a tough guy, though. The roughest game OU had each year was at the end of spring training, when we had a scrimmage against the alumni, called The Spring Game. This was before pro teams forbade their players from playing in alumni games, so you had pros in there plus the past All-Americans. Bud Wilkinson loved it because he thought it was a humiliating experience for us. He wanted them to beat us to make us work harder. He thought that having our team destroyed by the alumni would motivate us to get better! What's *wrong* with that picture?

One of the many alums on the team who played pro ball was Jim Weatherall, a 270-pound (which was huge back then) defensive tackle who played for the Washington Redskins. Bud would let Weatherall take the Johnson & Johnson tape cans, cut them in two lengthways and tape them to his forearms, under his shirt. As if being huge and a great pro football player weren't enough, Bud allowed him to have a weapon designed to really hurt his opponents. We wore helmets with one bar going across, not the birdcages they wear now, and Weatherall was knocking people out left and right. Bud loved him being the intimidator, and he loved doing it.

But when Weatherall played Wahoo, Wahoo got busted up, but he fought Weatherall right to a standstill. He rose to the challenge. Another guy who played Weatherall to a standstill was Jerry Durham, one tough man and a friend of mine too.

After I got taken off scholarship, and I believe Wahoo got kicked off scholarship too, once his eligibility was finished, he and I got draft notices from the military, which was the law then, and we had to go to the draft office to be tested and take the military physical. My getting this draft notice was a little more sinister than met the eye.

I'd been in Air Force ROTC at OU and even went to the summer camp between my junior and senior years, at Big Springs, Texas, and got extremely high ratings. I also pulled twenty pounds and made the flight weight limit, so I qualified for pilot training, which meant the Air Force would pay for me to get my private pilot's license during my senior year. But I got kicked off the team. Now, because the colonel who was in charge of the Air Force ROTC had been a former All-American in football there, basically he penalized me for my football problems, which had nothing to do with my ROTC efforts or service, and he kicked me out of Air Force ROTC too. Thus, when I left OU, I was guaranteed a draft notice. So there was mean-spiritedness in all of this, but it didn't work, because in the meantime I had taken up weight training and had experienced tremendous growth in size and weight as well as strength. I'd grown too large to fit any charts for acceptance into the military. At 315 pounds, I was too big and heavy for the Armed Forces, even though I was 315 pounds of muscle.

Wahoo had a bad knee already, so he took a ball-peen hammer to it until fluid built up, so they rejected both of us.

The funny thing was the doctor knew us and said, "Bill, Wahoo — aren't you guys going to play pro ball?" We said we were. Wahoo was already playing, and I was getting ready to play with the Oilers, so the doc said, "Well, you don't want to go in, do you?" When we said no, he rejected us both.

This was 1961, pre-Vietnam, so we weren't dodging combat. But we were both 4-F — I was so big they didn't even make uniforms that could fit me. Of course, the government does everything by its charts, and I didn't fit its charts.

I had signed with the Oilers for a whopping $8,000 contract, with a $700 signing bonus. This was 1961, the second year of the AFL, so they were signing anybody, and I'd never been a starter at OU. I almost made the Houston team, but I had a couple of problems, including punching the coach.

One thing about Bud Wilkinson — he didn't cuss you out, and he wouldn't allow anyone to do that on the field. Whatever else, Bud was a high-caliber guy. Pro football was different — the coaches would cuss us out for anything. Houston's head coach was Lou Rymkus, a former All-Pro with the Cleveland Browns. I didn't think he was very brilliant, and he later got fired. He ran off Walt Suggs and Tom Goode from the camp, and after he left they both came back and had long careers with the Oilers.

If you were a rookie, it didn't matter what you did. It was open season on you. After he ridiculed me in front of the team, I called him outside and told him, "I wouldn't talk to you like that. You talk to me like that, and it's personal. If you talk to me like that again, I'll whip your ass."

He gave me some smart answer, so I smacked him. Later that day, they cut me.

That wasn't even my first run-in with him. He always wanted to show off by demonstrating on guys at practice. He would turn his ball cap around backwards, and get down in his stance . . . But heck, I was in full pads. So, when he fired out at me, I went forward and caught him.

He started yelling, "I didn't tell you to catch me! Get down in your fucking stance, rookie. And when you come up come at full speed! Don't worry about me just because I don't have pads on!"

We lined up and he came at me again. This time I went full speed and hit him with a forearm smash that knocked him on his butt.

By October 1962, I was back in Oklahoma. Wahoo and I were out drinking one night, and Wahoo pulled out a check to cash.

Realize that we had no concept of what it took to earn money. I remember a speech at the student union about what we were going to do after college, where this guy said, "If you get to where you're making $25,000 a year, you're wealthy." That was the difference between the money then and now. I'd always assumed some oil company would hire me to do something. It was the furthest thing from my mind.

Well, Wahoo pulls out this check, and I don't remember how much it was, but it must have been a couple grand.

I asked him where he got it, and he said, "I got it for wrestling."

"For a month?" I asked.

"No."

"For a week?"

"No."

"For what?"

"For one match."

I said, "You got that for *one match?* Who the hell do I have to kill? I could kick your ass in thirty seconds!"

"Watts," he said, "you've got to get into wrestling. You'd love it!"

Jack Brisco had told me the same thing a couple of years before, but I'd never really considered it. Jack had always wanted to go into pro wrestling, and one of the things that helped him decide to go to Oklahoma State was Coach Myron Roderick telling him he could set Jack up with Leroy McGuirk, the pro wrestling promoter for the Oklahoma area. Leroy was a former All-American and NCAA champion amateur wrestler at Oklahoma State, and Roderick knew him.

Growing up, I was never a fan of professional wrestling. I would flip channels, watch a few seconds of it and think, "Aw, bullshit." But this was a chance to make some money.

Wahoo made some calls, and I ended up trying out for Leroy McGuirk. He was a former world junior heavyweight champion until he lost his vision, and then he became the Oklahoma promoter. Oklahoma was all junior heavyweights, though, and they didn't know what to do with someone my size.

Danny Hodge was Leroy's big star. Hodge was a senior at OU when I was a senior in high school. He was the greatest college wrestler I've ever seen, a three-time NCAA champion during the era when the NCAA didn't allow freshmen to compete. If they had, he would have been a four-time champion. I used to race down to Norman to watch him wrestle, but you didn't get to watch Danny long, because nobody lasted long with him. He pinned everybody in the NCAA tournament his senior year. He was so dominant that he never even had a point scored on him that year.

I had met him in college. We were all shocked when he went into pro wrestling, because we didn't watch wrestling.

I really got to know Danny Hodge better once we were both pro wrestlers. He went into boxing before pro wrestling, and he fought Nino Valdez in 1960. He got hammered — I saw him two weeks after the fight, and I'd never seen anyone with that much damage and trauma to his face and eyes.

Danny had such great heart and was one of the greatest athletes I've ever seen, but that doesn't make you a boxer. He just had so much courage he'd let opponents hit him, and he'd eventually wade through them. He had taken the Golden Gloves, but these were the pros, and at this time Valdez was the legitimate number-one contender for the heavyweight championship. But I've never seen a person as gifted as Hodge. He is unique.

His strength was legendary. And Danny would use it in funny situations too. Once, in Little Rock, Arkansas, Leroy McGuirk had booked

Tuffy Truesdale with his wrestling bear. I hated the idea of "booking a bear" for a match, but Leroy felt it drew kids, meaning their parents would buy tickets too. On this particular night, Hodge and I were tag-team partners, scheduled to wrestle in the main event. But the guy booked to wrestle the bear didn't show up, so we had to substitute in the "bear match" since it had been advertised.

I didn't want to wrestle that bear, but back then the cards were small, and there were only three other matches booked, so options were limited. Those bears did not want to be there either, and they smelled bad. Their handlers had pulled their front teeth, declawed them and placed muzzles over their faces and mouths so they couldn't bite. The bears were fed Coca-Cola with honey and whiskey to get them motivated. A bear is a natural wrestler — so powerful that an adult bear can break a horse's neck with one strike of its paw!

I told Hodge, "Let's tag-team this bear for about fifteen minutes so the people get their money's worth, and then we'll have the intermission, and then you and I will come back in the main event and wrestle our scheduled match."

Danny loved it. He *wanted* to wrestle that bear. This was a tough, cantankerous, old bear that, it was said, had bitten wrestler Luis Martinez's finger off. They would get your fingers in their mouths and try to work them back to their molars, which their handlers hadn't pulled, and try to bite off your fingers. This bear was so ill tempered that Tuffy had him on a short collar and chain. What good he felt that would do, I'm not sure.

Hodge decided to "just beat that bear!" And Danny was so strong and agile that he was making that bear nervous. The bear came to the center of the ring, stood up and came forward to wrestle, just like a human on two legs. Danny got behind the bear, put a scissors hold on and squeezed hard. The bear squealed and was getting scared and angry.

Tuffy was telling me to tag Hodge out of the match and take his place "before the bear 'loses it.'" I was trying to listen to Tuffy as I tagged Hodge, so I could go into the ring, and wasn't watching the bear closely enough. It turned to face me, and Hodge went behind it and with his powerful hands reached down and pulled a handful of hairs right out of the bear's anus. The bear squealed, and since I was right in front of him he hit me as hard as he could. I flew over the top rope into the crowd! I was stunned! As I looked up from the lap I had landed in, all I saw was the bear coming over the ropes after me, dragging Tuffy by that chain. Hodge stood in the middle of the ring with a handful of bear hairs, laughing so hard he was crying!

The bear came over the ropes. The people at ringside were running, and I got up to run, but that bear ran right by me and out of the arena dragging Tuffy! That bear wouldn't even go into the ring in our other towns to wrestle because it could smell Hodge's scent. It was sad that this animal was exploited like this — it wasn't Hodge's or my fault; that is just what was happening then.

Another time in Little Rock, after I had started promoting, we were at the Barton Coliseum. Prior to renovations, it was a big, airy place and hard to really heat or cool. It was winter, and Hodge wrestled right before me (I was on last). It was cold and drafty, and I was really looking forward to a hot shower.

The showers had the old-fashioned, hot and cold separate handles to adjust the water temperature. We had six showers in our dressing room. As I went in to take my shower, I saw Hodge with a big grin. I wondered what he thought was so funny. When I got into the shower, all the hot water handles except one had literally been twisted off. I screamed, "Hodge, get in here!"

He came in, all nice and meek, and said, "Yes, Bill, what do you want?"

I said, "Hodge, you twisted all the hot water handles off! Not only will my shower be cold, but I'll have to pay for them to be repaired!"

He said, "Bill, how come when anything happens you always blame me first?"

"Because no one else is strong enough to just twist off the handles!"

He walked to the last hot water handle and twisted it right off the wall too! As he left, he said, "Enjoy your hot shower!" I could hear him laughing.

Many times, as Hodge and I walked through an arena on the way to the dressing room, some fan, generally a cowboy or a farmer (and I've never seen any of those who don't have tremendously strong hands and grips) would come up to us with their girlfriends and want to shake hands. They would try to really "bear down" on that handshake to impress us. Hodge loved it. He would look at me and say, "Bill, this guy is really strong, and he is really hurting my hand he is so strong!" The poor guy would *really* bear down then and kind of look at his girlfriend as if he was such a stud. Then Hodge would kick in with his grip — the same grip that could squeeze the handles of a pair of pliers together to break them or squeeze an apple until it exploded — and squeeze the guy's hand until he went to his knees and screamed in pain, asking for mercy. And Hodge, with that little smile, would just wink and say, "What's the matter, big guy?"

But, getting back to me trying to break into the business, Leroy had me work out with some of his wrestlers. I worked out with Sputnik Monroe, who came out and started his intimidation tactics with me. That was funny. I stretched him quickly and rode him across the mat. Sputnik was a true character in pro wrestling. His background was the old fairs and what they called "ad shows" in small towns, where they would challenge locals to get into the ring, and if they could beat the pro they would make some money. Some of his stories were hilarious! If they got a local who really excited the fans, they'd string him along for the entire week the show was in town, letting him win, without him realizing he was being worked, in order to draw more of the townspeople to their show.

After I stretched Sputnik, they had me come to Tulsa and had all the wrestlers there except Hodge. He was the only one who could have beaten me. I *never* thought I could beat Hodge. I had become so big and strong I didn't think he could beat me, but I sure didn't want to test him out. They told me I'd be "trying out," but those guys were there to stretch me, to work me over. They watched me work out and then told Leroy, "You want someone to stretch *that* big son of a bitch, go do it yourself," because none of them could handle me.

I didn't know all this was going on. I knew they were trying to show me this or that, but most of them couldn't really wrestle. I think a lot of promoters back then didn't want you to have too much ability because then they wouldn't be able to control you.

When I realized they weren't going to do anything with me, I called Wahoo, who got me work in Indiana, a territory run by Balk Estes. Estes worked for Jim Barnett, who owned the territory. I met Barnett after my third or fourth match.

But at first they wouldn't use me. The pro football team, the Indianapolis Warriors, had a defensive coach named Bob Griffin. Bob was Wahoo's best buddy, and Wahoo had introduced us. Griffin said he'd be glad to have me on the team since I had some experience. I enjoyed playing for the Warriors that year and being coached by Griffin. One of my teammates was Bob O'Billovich, who later starred and coached in the Canadian Football League. Griffin was a two-time All-American at Arkansas, played in the NFL for years and was a great football player, not to mention a damn good coach.

Dale Lewis, Bob Griffin and I rented an apartment together. Dale gave me my first tights and my first boots and worked out with me every day.

I was a star on the football team, and that was actually how I met Scranton player Jim Meyers, who was later known as George "The Animal" Steele. Even later we became close friends.

I got my first match because of Art and Stan Neilson, the tag champions. There was a show in Portsmouth, Ohio. Art called and said, "Kid, when you go to the show tonight [because I always went to watch], take your wrestling gear. I'm not going to show up, and they'll have to use you."

About fifteen minutes later, Stan called, and he stuttered, so he said, "Take your g-g-gear to the match, because I'm not going to show, so th-they'll have to l-l-let you wr-wr-wr-wrestle."

I took my gear, and Dale and I rode with George and Sandy Scott. I drove 350 miles to Portsmouth, where they pulled a big swerve on me.

When I got there, the guys gave me another guy's license and told me, "Now, look, this is a commission state. When the guy asks for your license, you don't want to give him ten dollars, because you're only going to make twenty-five dollars, and you have to pay us trans[portation]. Flash this and tell them it's your license."

When a guy came and asked for my license, I flashed it. In the meantime, they had to redo the card, and my match was with "Big" Bill Miller. Miller was a great guy, a great athlete who wrestled for Ohio State while working as a pro wrestler under a mask, which he had to do to retain his eligibility. Back then, if you were a pro in one sport, you were a pro in everything. He was a big, tough German. I was more afraid of having a bad match with Bill, because it was going to be the main event and best of three falls.

Dale saw that I was nervous and came up to me. "Look," he said, "you and I have worked out. Let's go out there, and I'll have your first match with you."

So they changed it and put Don Jardine with Bill Miller in the main event, and I worked with Dale.

Before our match, he told me, "Now, look, you're going to have to heel," which is the wrestling term for a villain or bad guy. I had no idea what to do because they'd been breaking me in as a babyface, or good guy, but Dale said, "Just listen to me out there."

I said I would because I was a nervous wreck.

In the meantime, during the first match, this guy came back and said, "Look, I'm not really the commissioner. I was just teasing you, but that's not a real license. Where's your real license?"

He had driven up with Bill Miller, but I thought he was trying to swerve me. I had him up against the wall, and I was about to knock him out because I thought he was trying to get into my pocket when the boys came in and said, "Calm down! Calm down!" It was just a rib, a practical joke.

I went out there with Dale, and he told me I was going to have to "put him over," which is a pro wrestling term meaning I would let him win.

I said, "Hell, I had to put you over in college. At least I'm getting paid for this."

We went out, and I was just a natural at making the crowd angry with me. We had a good match, and when it was time to "go home," or end the match, Dale said, "Hit me." I did and knocked his tooth out! Here I was, in my first match with the guy who had helped train me and given me my tights and boots, and I knocked his tooth out. I put him over, and on the way home Sandy Scott (a great ribber) pulled so many ribs on me it was unreal, but I really enjoyed the camaraderie.

I think my second match was with Joe Blanchard, and they told us, "You guys go twenty minutes broadway [a time-limit draw]," and Joe said, "Bill, if you get lost, don't worry. I wrestled amateur too, so we'll just work some amateur."

My third match was with Don Leo Jonathan, who was already a super-star. He was six foot eight, about 310 pounds and the greatest natural athlete I've ever seen. He could do nip-ups, walk the top ring ropes and do stuff no one else could do.

He talked to me very slowly before our match, with a big chaw of tobacco in his mouth, and said, "You and I are big men. Brother, when we go to tie up, you tie up with all the strength you've got."

So when we were in the ring and came together, I went in as hard as I could and knocked him to his knees. He said, "Gosh-damn, Bill! I didn't mean to kill me!"

The next week Don Leo said he would ride with me. We were in my Corvair Manza, one of those rear-wheel-job Chevys. With us in there, the back tires looked squat.

Miller and Don Leo were tough guys, but I met another very tough one while wrestling in Ohio named Karl Gotch. The night I met him I was supposed to wrestle Frankie Talaber, a big star there. When I went into the arena, I was carrying Dale Lewis's bag, with Olympic symbols all over it, and he said, "You wrestle amateur?"

I said, "Yeah."

"Where?"

"Oklahoma."

He went to Al Haft, and they changed the match. He didn't want a guy who could wrestle.

The guy I ended up wrestling took some liberties with me in the ring, so I guzzled him (overwhelmed him with wrestling skill). The guy went to Haft, crying about it, and Haft chewed me out. Gotch came over and put a stop to that. He chewed out both Haft and the guy I'd been wrestling. Gotch said, "I watched it, just to see what Bill would do. If it'd been me, I'd have broken every little bone in your little body, you punk."

After about ten matches, I went home for the 1962 Christmas holidays. I was out one night drinking with Stan Abel and some other guys, playing shuffleboard, when three guys got into it with Abel. Well, little wrestlers love to fight, and Abel was maybe 150 out of season and a 130-pound national champion. He was about to clean this guy's clock when this bigger guy stepped up, which got me into it. I went over and gut-shot this one guy. He sat down against the bar rail, sucking air like a guppy out of water. I picked another guy up and slung him down the table like I was bowling a "leaner" (a four-pin shot). The bar owner and Stan grabbed me to get me off him. The sweater I was wearing, which they were pulling, my mother had made me for Christmas. I said, "OK, I'm calm. It's over."

They told the last guy, "You'd better get the hell out of here."

I said I was leaving and went out the back door, where we'd parked. As he was about to go out the front door, it opened. I had just circled the building, run in and hit the third guy on the head so hard that he was knocked out cold, and my knuckle was broken.

We went to the hospital for x-rays. My mother was already there because my brother, Bobby, was there with a knee injury from football. The doctors told us they were worried for a while that the guy I'd broken my hand on wasn't going to make it. Life in the street can be a thin line. If he had died, I would have ended up in prison. I sure couldn't afford a great legal team.

With my hand broken, Balk Estes wouldn't bring me back in, so Leroy McGuirk brought me in to referee matches in Oklahoma. I got over pretty well just refereeing. Al Lovelock wrestled there as The Mighty Bolo. Lovelock was an old conniver, like they all were, and he saw a fresh foe in me. He'd done everything he could do with Danny Hodge. He saw this kid who was fresh and whom people loved. He led me in this program, and we sold out everywhere in the territory. They played off my local notoriety, but Hodge also endorsed me as his partner and friend, and I just had that innate sense of how to get myself over.

Plus they didn't have anybody. It was talent-dry, and here's what happens: you end up with a hardcore fan base, and even *they* get tired of seeing the same thing over and over. Here was a fresh guy who was 300 pounds yet could move, a good-looking son of a gun who was crazy, and they had never had anything like that there, so it caught on.

It also created a huge jealousy, first with Leroy. He didn't want heavyweights because he'd always been a junior heavyweight. There was also jealousy with the other junior heavyweights, who all wanted to be the main event. In wrestling, many would rather be the main event, even if they can't draw money, than have someone else who can really draw money be the main event, which would also make them more money. It was all about ego.

Leroy sent me to "work" (a work is something that's not real, that's part of the story) this gimmick in Amarillo, where I was a fan coming out of the stands who would become a wrestler. It's called the "mark out of the crowd" angle. I was in the stands for weeks, giving all of them a hard time. Dory Funk Sr., who owned the territory, wouldn't tell anyone I was a wrestler, and nobody there knew me.

Fritz Von Erich was wrestling in Amarillo then, as were Ali Bey and Killer Karl Kox, but Dory wanted me pointed at "Iron" Mike DiBiase, one of his top heels and Ted DiBiase's dad, though Ted was just a young boy then.

I insulted all of them, but they didn't know what to do, because here was a pretty big guy in the crowd. I even asked Funk why he didn't tell them, and he said, "No, I want this legitimate."

We finally got to the night where he wanted me to jump into the ring and go after DiBiase, and I asked, "You're not going to tell the rest of the guys?"

Dory still wanted it legitimate, so I said, "OK, but if they come up to me, I'm taking them out."

He also wanted "Iron" Mike to bust me open hardway (drawing blood by punching instead of by nicking the forehead with a razor). He was willing to pay me an extra fifty dollars for that.

I finally jumped into the ring on Mike, and here came Fritz, Kox, Ali Bey and all of them out of the dressing room. In those days, the guys stuck together. Plus they all wanted a piece of me. But they saw me grab Mike with a working hold and realized something was going on. So they stopped, but Mike was trying to hardway me and kept hitting me on the head, but my head's just harder than a block, so it didn't bust — it just got sore.

I saw Killer Karl Kox and started to tee off on him, and he said, "*Kayfabe,* kid," the old wrestling codeword meaning he knew I was working. "I got it!"

The deal really got over. The story was that DiBiase was a star and that I was just a guy out of the crowd, so I had to wrestle someone to prove myself before he would wrestle me. The crowd wanted me to wrestle DiBiase, so we had a natural buildup to "milk the crowd."

Funk told me for my match with the guy I had to wrestle before DiBiase, "When the guy runs over to you, he'll be wide open."

I said I'd give him a good worked shot, but Funk said, "I don't want you to work it. I want you to tee off on him. I want the people in the paper to see his black eye — I want it real."

But I think he didn't even tell the other guy this.

They had me wearing a red, white and blue swimsuit with a jockstrap I had pulled the elastic out of, so it hung down the back of the trunks, and Converse All-Star tennis shoes. No one knew I was a pro wrestler, but they knew about my OU football and wrestling history.

The guy ran over to start our match, and I literally knocked him out. I almost broke my hand on him.

It was a long trip for me on Thursdays to go to Amarillo. On Wednesdays, I would wrestle in Springfield, Missouri, and then drive clear to Amarillo for Thursday, then back to wrestle in Oklahoma City on Fridays. My next time in Amarillo I was set to wrestle DiBiase, and I stopped in Oklahoma City to pick up an old high school football buddy who was out of the Army on a psychiatric discharge. He'd married a Japanese woman while stationed there, and she got raped, so he killed the guy who raped her. He had some mental problems, but he always loved me, so he'd ride with me sometimes, but he always carried a gun.

I was set for my match, but Funk had decided to "shoot an angle" (the wrestling term for a skit or incident to build interest in a future match) between DiBiase and Dory Funk Jr., so he wanted me to put DiBiase over, and then his kid would come in and beat DiBiase.

Dory Sr. and Doc Sarpolis were partners in Amarillo, but they were fighting for control of the territory. I didn't know any of this — all I knew was that I'd been driving in every week from Springfield, 350 miles, for a fifty-dollar payoff. And now I had a chance to make some real money, and they were going to beat me and have some kid beat this guy I was working with?

I told Dory, "Not today. Screw you guys."

We got into a big dressing room argument. I went out for my match pissed off, and they replaced the referee with a real wrestler, Alex Perez. He was a tough guy, and I never held anything against him (in fact, he later worked for me). He was just out there because he had to make a living. Pretty soon I realized the same was true of Mike DiBiase.

We were in the ring, and DiBiase said, "Did you get the message from the office?"

I said, "Yes, but fuck them, I'm not doing it."

DiBiase wrestled amateur at Nebraska and was a Big Seven AAU champion, so he could wrestle, but he saw this big kid who wrestled at OU and knew, if you wrestled at OU, you could damn sure wrestle. Like today, if someone tells you, "I wrestled at Iowa," you know he can wrestle, unlike if someone says, "Well, I wrestled at the University of Tennessee." It was just a different caliber — at least back then.

DiBiase knew all this, so he asked, "You're not happy?"

I said I wasn't, so he asked me, "Would you do me a favor, then? Would you work with me for just a second and let me think?"

I said, "Yeah, but I'm watching you, you son of a bitch. Anything goes on, I'm taking your ass out." I knew he couldn't take me — he was tough and a legitimate wrestler, but he was an older guy by then and not nearly my size.

He said, "Look, kid, I'm getting screwed here too, but I have my wife and kids here, and I'm just trying to make a living. I know they're screwing you, but you're just passing through here. If I give you the whole match, would you put me over, for my family?"

What could I say to a guy like that? I knew I wasn't coming back, so, yeah, I put him over, but he knew I was doing it because I wanted to.

Then he asked, "If I get some blood first, will you do it too?"

I remembered him trying to get hardway juice, and I didn't have a gaffe, so I said no. He said he'd do it, but my answer to that was "Bullshit."

He said, "I promise, it'll be better than you'd ever do it yourself. I promise you."

He got juice, and got it on me, and it was just like he said. We were going great, but we got to the finish and Perez counted me down too slowly, so I kicked out. I kicked out four or five times. The people were about to riot, and they finally did the deal where Dory Jr. ran down.

After the matches, after all the people had left the arena, I went to get paid, and Haystacks Calhoun, a 600-pounder who traveled around as a special attraction, was sitting in Dory Sr.'s office. Dory said, "Kid, you've got the wrong attitude."

I told him, "Fuck you."

He said, "You think you're tough?"

"No," I said, "I don't think I'm tough, but I'm tougher than anybody you have."

He said, "Kid, if you want a fight, we'll go to the ring right now."

I turned around and started to walk out, and he said, "Where are you going?"

I turned back and said, "Let's go to the ring!"

One thing I knew — my crazy, armed friend was sitting down there at ringside, waiting for me, so I knew it was going to be fair, because he had seven friends with him, all .45-caliber. So I didn't care, because if it was fair they didn't have anyone who could take me. I didn't know it at the time, but Wahoo had already stirred that up when he had been in Amarillo. Someone had asked him about me, and Wahoo had said, "Oh, he could take anyone here in thirty seconds or less."

Dory had a tough, old, 165-pound shooter and asked if I really thought I could beat him.

I said, "Let me just give you a clue. There isn't anyone alive at 165 fucking pounds that can beat me. I'm not saying I can beat anybody, but they don't make the 165-pounder who can beat my ass. So fuck you, and fuck everybody here."

He finally said, "Look, we'll bring you back next week and let you beat Perez, the referee."

The bottom line was I didn't want to beat the referee, so I said, "Just give me my fucking money, and I'm getting the fuck out of here."

Haystacks started to get up and say something to me, but I told him, "Look, you big, fat tub of shit — shut up and sit down, or I'll slap you through the wall." Haystacks sat back down. I got to know Bill Calhoun better later on, and he was really a good guy.

From there, I went to Houston. Morris Sigel, the promoter, had called Leroy. Sigel wanted a big white kid to "do a job for" (the wrestling jargon for "get beaten by") "Sailor" Art Thomas, the popular (and black) Texas state champion.

Leroy said, "Bill, you can make more for that one match than we can pay you here all week. Let me tell you about Morris Sigel. His health's not good, but he's a sharp guy. Get a nice suit and go meet him the day before the match."

I did that, met Sigel on May 2, 1963, and he took a liking to me. He had Paul Boesch and two others as his assistants.

In the old days in Houston, you'd work a fall and then go clear back to the dressing room, where they could tell you what to do in the next fall if they chose, and then you'd come back out.

Except for my first match with Dale Lewis, I'd never heeled in my life. Sailor was a giant, and the nicest guy you'd ever meet, but not too swift mentally. Within about three or four minutes of the start of our match, I'd gone through everything I knew to do with him. He wasn't getting it, and neither was I, so all I knew to do at that point was to take him down. Well, he didn't know how to wrestle, so once I got him down he just lay there. With a wrestler, you base up, do some sitouts and at least be busy. I could have fallen off him or something, but he just lay there, so I took him down and let him up repeatedly.

Sigel had apparently told his triumvirate to keep an eye on me, and after the first fall I went to the back. They said, "Well, you've destroyed him. He's never been taken off his feet, and you've taken him down twenty times, so you're going to take the last fall and become the champion."

So "Bruiser" Bill Watts became the Texas champion, completely by accident.

Soon I was having matches with Mark Lewin, a guy I'd met in Indianapolis when I was breaking in. Mark's brother-in-law was Danny McShain, one of the top Houston stars. When I first met Mark, I didn't like him because he and Dale Lewis didn't get along. Dale had tried to zing him, not realizing that Jim Barnett liked Mark better and that Mark was a greater box-office draw than Dale was.

When Mark came into Texas, he was nervous about me, so he came to me and said, "I know you were close with Dale."

I told him I liked and respected Dale but that I was different about the business than he was.

He said, "Well, let me ask you this. I'm going to be the top box-office stud here. I can get rid of you tomorrow, or I'll work with you for a short time, because I'm going on to other things, but we'll have great matches if you'll listen to me and I don't have to be afraid of you."

I said, "Teach me, let me make some money, and you don't have anything to be afraid of."

And he did. Back then I was hungry just to learn, and there were a lot of guys to learn from.

The Von Brauners were a top team there, and I'd met them in Indianapolis, with their manager, Saul Weingroff. I thought that was the finest heel team I'd ever seen — two guys going as Nazis, with a Jewish manager. They were a machine, just great workers. Karl Von Brauner and I became great friends.

He was also a crack pilot and loved acrobatics. Once, when we were in my Cherokee 6 airplane, he took the controls and did a roll — the guys in the back seats never even woke up, it was so smooth.

Leaving Texas was another mess. Morris Sigel wanted me to date his daughter. She was spoiled rich, and he'd take me to the country club. Can you imagine someone as wild as I was going there? Sigel's daughter and I didn't get along, though, and suddenly my bookings changed.

Here was the Texas circuit: Monday night was Fort Worth, Tuesday night was Dallas and Wednesday morning was Dallas TV. They brought me up there and booked me against "Cowboy" Bob Ellis, a big star. Dallas TV had maybe fifteen to twenty-five people in the studio audience. It was Wednesday morning, and nobody cared. They just sat there.

They often tried to swerve young, inexperienced guys. What Marvin Jones, another Houston office representative who refereed and made suggestions to Dallas promoter Ed McLemore, told me was "OK, we want you to get disqualified in the first fall, and then in the second fall Bob will beat you with his flying bulldog. That way you only really lose one fall." In truth, they wanted me to drop two straight.

I said, "You dumb son of a bitch. Fuck you, and fuck Bob. I'm so sick and tired of you bastards I'm leaving."

Marvin said, "When are you going?"

I said, "I'm leaving right now. If you want me to go out and do this match on TV, I will, and we'll just have Bob try to put his best hold on me."

I'd never had a cross word with Bob Ellis, so when he heard me blowing up in there he came in and said, "Bill, I have nothing to do with this. I'll tell you what — if you want, I'll put you over. I'll even get juice for you."

Bob wasn't a coward. He was a man's man. He just didn't want to have to deal with this big kid whom he'd already seen stretch one so-called tough guy named Ned Bartleman, who'd tried to double-cross me in the ring in San Antonio.

I said, "No, Bob, you treated me nice in Indianapolis when I was breaking in and you were a big star. We've traveled together. I'm not mad at you — I'm just pissed at them. Tell you what — I'm going to put you over out there because I'm leaving."

He asked me how I wanted to do it, and I said, "Bob, it's for you. You've got to be here. I'm gone."

He responded, "Well, then, I tell you what. This place is deader than shit. Let's wake them up. You jump me, and I'll get 'color' [another word for juice or blood] on TV."

So I jumped Bob, and he gaffed himself and started bleeding all over the place. I grabbed referee Marvin Jones, tore his referee shirt off and threw him out of the ring. He came back in and disqualified me. Well, while he and I argued about it, Bob nailed me with his running bulldog.

In the end, I did just what they wanted because it was what I wanted, especially considering how Bob Ellis had treated me. They knew then that you didn't mess with me — you'd better ask me first. Get me on the same page. I didn't *have* to do anything, because they didn't have anyone who could have made me.

After our match, the place was in pandemonium. Ed McLemore had never seen anything like it. It was like the dead had been awakened. The fifteen to twenty-five people in the studio were going crazy.

Marvin Jones came to me and said, "Wow! You really caught the boss's attention out there. He's changing the match next week. You are going to be the main event in Dallas! It's you against Bob Ellis, back in a Texas Death Match."

That's how stupid and desperate they were — they wanted to go from one match straight to a Texas Death Match instead of bringing it along. But it didn't really matter how they'd presented it to me, because I'd made up my mind.

"Is that the match next week?" I asked. "Well, it's going to be a little tough."

"Why?" he asked.

"Because I'm not going to be here."

"What do you mean?"

"I'm leaving!"

"When?"

"Right this fucking minute! I did my job, and I'm gone."

A funny thing: years later, when I bought into McGuirk's Oklahoma territory, the referee was Marvin Jones. I never held a grudge against him. He was just trying to make a living in this goofy business. He worked hard and was reliable.

I'd saved my money and bought my first pair of Stacy Adams alligator loafers for sixty-five dollars, which would cost you about $1,000 today. I was getting big-time. I had my Halliburton aluminum suitcase, like the one Lou Thesz carried. I had a couple of nice suits. I was starting to make some good money. Realize that, when I got into wrestling, gas was seventeen cents a gallon, and you could stay in the Grady Manning Hotel in downtown Little Rock for $4.86 a night. If you went to Little Rock and made a sixty-five-dollar payoff, you lived well and banked fifty bucks. So in Houston, making $500 for one match, I was doing great.

The night before the 1963 OU-Texas football game in Dallas, I went with a date, a beautiful girl. She was Canadian, the advance publicity agent for Ice Capades and truly a nice person. Because of all the craziness from the previous years, they'd changed the pregame parties. Now we went to the Convention Center, and in front of it was a street rally.

Thugs always came out for something like this, guys who weren't connected with either school. My date and I were at the rally with my friend Bruce Van Horn. At this point, he was a student trainer for the football team, and I had been wrestling in Dallas for a while as "Bruiser" Bill Watts.

We were on the street — I, my date, a tough little OU wrestler named Dickie Dupree, Wally Curtis (a 123-pound All-American wrestler from OU) and Bruce — and these thugs made a comment to us, so we exchanged some words until the biggest one came out of a car parked there. A fight broke out, which I loved. The big guy had a knife taped to his wrist. He went for my back, but Wally Curtis took the knife for me. It went through his hand and into his chest. I didn't even know the guy had a knife until later.

Now I know it was providential that my friend Wally saved my life that night. Really, I didn't even think about it then. I was just on that euphoric high you get when you "kick someone's ass," along with all the alcohol. But now I see the hand of God in preserving my life.

I decimated the other guys and grabbed the big guy. I bit the top of his ear off. I had read the book *Mandingo* and was actually trying to bite through his jugular vein and kill him. He just happened to turn his head and lost part of his ear instead, which probably kept me from going to jail for manslaughter. I remember holding up the piece of ear, and when I showed it to my date, she threw up, and I never saw her again. Van Horn had another guy down, but the four cops showed up and leveled him with a nightstick. I went to the guy Van Horn had been on and kicked him in the face. His teeth went into my alligator shoe, and I lost one shoe clear across the street, with his teeth attached.

The cops were going to arrest me — I was the only guy standing. I said, "Boys, I'm not going to jail."

They said, "Yes, you are."

I replied, "No, I'm not. Let's just get it on, because I'm not going. Look at them — these guys are hoodlums, and they have nothing to do with these schools."

One cop looked at me and said, "Aren't you 'Bruiser' Bill Watts? Don't you wrestle down at the Sportatorium?"

I said, "Yep, I'm 'Bruiser' Bill Watts."

He turned to the other cops and said, "He's right. He ain't going to jail."

They sized it up pretty quickly and realized these guys had started it.

So I gained part of an ear but lost a loafer and my date. Later that night, after showing the trophy to everyone, I ate it with a beer chaser. I had to go to the game the next day in shower sandals because I'd lost my shoe.

I'd decided to accept an offer to wrestle and play football at the same time. I had a chance to play with an NFL expansion team called the Minnesota Vikings. Norm Van Brocklin was the head coach.

Verne Gagne, promoter of the AWA in the Midwest, thought that it would be great publicity for me to wrestle for him and play football for the home team. Verne, who had started his promotion after winning two NCAA amateur wrestling titles in 1948 and 1949 and being one of pro wrestling's big names in the 1950s, was going to give me some extra money to play football.

I went to the Viking training camp, and Van Brocklin loved me. This was when Fran Tarkenton, Mick Tinglehoff, Jim Marshall, Tommy Mason and so many other great athletes were on the team.

By now, I was making nearly $100,000 a year wrestling, and they wanted me to play football for $7,000 on their taxi squad. I said I would, as long as they would let me wrestle. The general manager vetoed my wrestling, and this was before there was a player's union, so management could really control your life. I wasn't going to play football for a fraction of what I could make wrestling, so I left the Vikings.

I left Bimidji, where they had preseason camp, and every place the airplanes landed or when I changed planes I bought more Scotch. I finally just got off the plane in Tulsa instead of going on to Oklahoma City. In Tulsa, I began looking for Fred Williams, my buddy from OU. He was one tough guy as well as a good businessman, first in banking and later in oil, and we remain the closest of friends. These friendships are true, lifelong ones. Fred was also a smooth ladies' man and as big a sweet talker as I've ever seen. We had some fabulous times with the ladies. At this time, he had a "side venture," a barbecue joint, so I went there, and his brother called him for me.

As it turned out, the state-wide coaching clinic was going on in Tulsa. My brother, Bob, was playing football on a scholarship at Oklahoma State University. They had a coach there who tried to copy Bear Bryant but took his concept too far — they'd slap players, grab them, curse them out, hit them and kick them. They were just bullies! They ruined that football team. Things like this happen when schools and administrations want to win at all costs.

Fred, Stan Abel and I headed out to a bar and ran into the OSU coaching staff, in town for the conference. I was buying them drinks — they knew me, and my brother played there. This line coach went to the bathroom, and I drank his drink and was about to order another round. He came back and said, "Who drank my drink?"

I told him, "I did, but I ordered —"

He cut me off and said, "Well, you're going to buy me another one, or I'll whip your ass."

Wrong thing to say.

I said, "They haven't made the Aggie that can whip my ass."

Now, this wasn't a challenge to all Aggies, because there were some damn tough athletes that attended OSU, but in the heat of battle words get used, and lines get drawn. We got to scuffling, and I nailed him. My punch knocked his teeth out and split his lip. He folded and was down for the count. These guys weren't so tough when they faced a real man instead of college kids who could be intimidated.

Then I had them all lined up against the bar telling them what Sooners think of Aggies. In those situations, the rivalry between OU and OSU always added fuel to the fire. None of them wanted any of me. I told them, "I'm not one of your little chickenshit freshmen, where you hold a scholarship over my head. I'll kick your ass." I was blind drunk, but of all these tough guys none of them wanted to fight someone who could fight back.

My brother saw his coach the next day, with no front teeth and a split lip. He didn't know what had happened, and he asked his coach, "What's the matter? Have you been in a fight?" That sure didn't sit well with this bully — to have the brother of the guy who kicked his ass ridicule him. My brother always said that, when people found out he was my brother, it was either free beer or a fight. Never anything in between.

I started wrestling in Oklahoma for Leroy again, although he really didn't want me. I just didn't fit his niche. Now, there was a lot good about Leroy. But he was blind and had to rely on what everyone else said. He could feel how big I was but didn't know what to do with me. However, I did make a favorable impression on him.

Lou Thesz came through the area and got me booked on the West Coast, in Los Angeles, but I didn't know that Thesz and the promoter there, Jules Strongbow, were having problems. Thesz sent me out there, and they thought I was going to come in and cause problems.

The old promoters loved to get two "shooters" (genuine wrestlers) together and watch them go. None of them ever wanted to put his own ass on the line, but they loved to watch it. Dick Hutton, an awesome amateur who was a former NCAA champion at Oklahoma State University and held pro wrestling's world title in the 1950s, was wrestling in Los Angeles at this time. Hutton was also supposed to be my first match there.

I wasn't there to cause problems, though. All I knew was that I was going to get to meet Dick Hutton! I was excited — heck, he was a legend. I didn't know Strongbow had told him that Thesz had sent me there to cause trouble, so Strongbow wanted Hutton to stretch me, which would really be for Strongbow's entertainment. Rather than being treacherous, Jules was a fun guy, and we later became friends.

Hutton wasn't afraid of me, but he didn't want to be their pawn anymore, and he was married to a wealthy lady who didn't want him on the road anyway, so he quit wrestling rather than do a shoot job for these promoters. When he didn't show up, I was just disappointed I wouldn't get to meet him.

A couple of days later I went to wrestle in San Diego. Red Bastien was there, along with Pedro Godoy. Don Leo was there, living on Santa Monica Beach. Ernie Ladd was there too, as the big star of the San Diego Chargers. I didn't like him at first, because I thought he was really arrogant, but Ernie turned out to be the greatest guy I've ever met. I just didn't know him very well at the time.

My buddy Jay, who'd gotten me into the weights back at OU, was in the Marines, in Force Recon. Force Recon was the elite group of the Marine Corps, and these guys were about to ship out, eventually for Vietnam. I wanted to take Jay and his friends out for drinks before they shipped out, so I got hold of him and said, "Come on — the party's on me." I wanted to take them to Los Angeles, but they wanted to party in San Diego. We ended up going to a Navy bar that, it turned out, was off-limits to the Marines.

The barmaid recognized me, so I was talking to her. These Force Recon guys were in there doing all their "tough guy" shit, in a bar filled with "frogmen," Underwater Demolition Team Navy guys, an elite unit and the precursor to the Navy Seals. The whole bar was doing these singalong songs. Jay and his buddies started singing about a girl who "kisses sailors and sucks Marines." Nobody sang along. It became quiet, and these Force Recon guys became the total focus of the sailors.

Let me make something clear. I love the Marines, and Force Recon was an elite group. I have great respect for all our military men and women, and there are some real studs in each service, and then there are the elite groups. So I am not demeaning anyone, but again, in physical confrontations, there is a lot of "shit-talking," and it can lead to having to back up your mouth with action, which is what happened there.

A group of frogmen went over to them, including this one black kid, who was a stallion, in incredible shape. They confronted these Force Recon guys, and I was still sitting at the bar having a beer and flirting with the barmaid. I looked over and was expecting to see a pretty good fight, but the Force Recon guys backed down. Of course, there were probably 150 sailors in there. It was their turf.

Then the black guy started in on me, and the barmaid said, "You'd better leave this guy alone. He's a pro wrestler."

The guy said, "He's too fat to be a wrestler," but this guy just wanted to fight, because I wasn't fat.

I don't know if he expected me to back down, but I talked trash right back to him. When he started to punch, I came off my barstool and hit him. My punch didn't really have much snap to it, but I had my weight behind it, so it knocked him off balance. He was really agile but stumbled backward about eight feet and hit a wall. He kept his feet under him, but I was on him.

I knew one thing — I was surrounded, and, if I didn't do something dramatic and emotional, I was going to get a bad beating. I popped my left thumb in, because I was going to try to pop his eye out. I missed it but got my right thumb in and popped his other eyeball out. It was dangling by its little cord. I tore the cord and pulled the eye out of his head, and I said, "I'm from Never-Never Land, where the green owls hang." I don't remember if I pulled it off the cord and ate it or not, although that is the story told by those who were there. Whichever way it happened, it got their attention, and I walked out of there. They were in shock because of what they had just seen, and it seemed like Moses at the Red Sea, the way they parted to let me through, so I made it to my car.

I had a little Buick Special, and the Force Recon guys were out there, and we started to leave, but these sailors started shooting bullet holes into my car while we were trying to get out of there. One of the Marines didn't make it, though, and as it turned out he was back there snitching off. But the other three were saying, "We have to go back! The Marines never leave a man behind!"

I said, "Fuck him! You guys didn't even fight, you tough sons of bitches! You're the toughest? The most elite? You chickenshits, *I* had to do all the fighting!"

"Well, we gotta go back and get him!"

"Hell, I'm not going back!"

But they finally talked me into going back — too much alcohol makes for bad judgment. By now, they'd taken the guy I'd fought to the hospital, and the San Diego police got me, and both officers were black. They took me back behind the joint, and these were guys who work the waterfront. These weren't Sunday School teachers.

They started asking me about it, and I said, "Sir, I'm a CPA, and I was here on a vacation, saw my friend and we got jumped. I don't know what happened!"

"You don't know what you did to that guy?" one asked me.

"Well, there was a lot of excitement. I gotta tell you — my parents would really be upset if they knew about this. I generally don't go to places like this. Matter of fact, a good friend of mine is Ernie Ladd," I said, because I'd at least met Ernie. I was trying to think of something, and he was still playing for the San Diego Chargers, so I hoped it would help.

But one said, "We got something for you. We're going to teach your ass a lesson."

They had those big, heavy flashlights, and back in those days they wrapped them up in heavy tape. They were going to beat the heck out of me!

One was a sergeant, and I'm funny like this. You get me to a certain point, and I figure, "If I'm going out, I'm going out as hard as I can." When the sergeant made his move, I snatched him by the belt. As I grabbed for him, I knocked his hat off, grabbed him by the hair and snatched his neck back, drawing him into me. The other guy was going for his gun now — he'd dropped his flashlight.

I said, "When you pull your gun, I'm going to kill him, and then I'm going to kill you. I'm going to bite his jugular vein out and spit it right in your fucking face, and then I'm going to kill you."

The sergeant, helpless, was saying, "Do not touch your weapon! Do *not* touch your weapon! *DO not touch your weapon!*"

I had his neck exposed, and he'd never been so helpless, being held by a guy this strong, and he knew I'd just destroyed another guy and taken his eye out. They let me go. I walked out of there. I figured they'd shoot me in the back, but I got to the car and left.

It was a horrible situation, but could it have been providence? You decide. I should never have made it out of there untouched. But I did. Did I deserve to walk out of there? No, but I am saved by grace, and there was a purpose for my life not yet fulfilled. Back then such thoughts didn't even occur to me.

I hid out at Don Leo Jonathan's house on Santa Monica Beach for three days, and he got me booked in Canada, because I thought it might be a good idea to leave the country for a while until this settled down. Don Leo and I really got close in those days. He taught me to scuba dive, and we ate fish we shot with our spears every day.

I was so far into my rebellion by this time that I'd almost become an agnostic. However, even at my darkest, I could never completely discount Jesus Christ. I could never say that He wasn't real. I just turned my back on Him, pretty much ignored Him. Your heart can harden, and mine had become callused.

Vancouver was promoted by Rod Fenton, with Gene Kiniski as the top star. Antone "Ripper" Leone was there, and they had Waldo Von Erich under a mask as The Great Zim. They dropped the *s* off my last name because they didn't want people to confuse me with "Whipper" Billy Watson, one of Canada's top wrestlers, so I became "Big" Bill Watt.

They were building me up, and I was staying at the Black Stone Hotel. This was a different world. They had men-only bars, and then they had cocktail lounges, where all the hookers were and all the lumberjacks. Lumberjacks, pipeliners and iron workers would come in from wherever they'd been working, with money to spend. They'd get blind drunk and fight the hell out of each other. It was a zoo.

I was starting to get over. Sweet Daddy Siki, a black athlete with bleached blonde hair and a million-dollar strut, was there. I'd never seen a guy who could take bumps like he could. Siki was leaving, so they were building me up as the guy who would beat him on his way out, and then I would go against Kiniski, the big heel.

Siki had impressed everyone, so at a bar the bartender told me there was no way I'd win. I said I'd whip him in our upcoming match. The bartender didn't believe me, so I bet him. I knew Siki was leaving, and I was going over! And I needed some money — I was starving to death with what they were paying.

Fenton heard about it and chewed me out, saying I was exposing the business, letting on that it wasn't real competition.

"You dumb son of a bitch," I said. "If I *didn't* bet on myself, that would be exposing the business! Number one, I knew I was going over, but number two, if I believed in myself, I'd *have* to bet on myself!"

Siki and I had some great matches, and he was the funniest guy — he loved to have me come down to his room so he could let me know he was "banging all these white broads." He was a piece of work.

Leone was really racist and took digs at Siki, but Siki never really did anything about it. Integration was still a new concept in sports. It started in football, I believe, with Tank Younger of Grambling and others. Slowly, it was happening in basketball and baseball, but in wrestling there were still very few black athletes. Today black athletes wouldn't put up with much crap from a racist, especially in the dressing room, and they shouldn't have to either. But back then it happened.

Black athletes had to be careful about being "too militant." As I think back, I respect the black athletes that much more. To take all that shit and keep on keepin' on — is that something I could ever have done? They had to be twice as good and then had to be diplomats.

After I beat Siki, I was over like a million bucks. Then I wrestled Gene Kiniski, the big star. Our match sold out, and he put me over. They were planning to bring in Don Leo to be the big star, so I'd wrestle him and put him over, and they figured then on a long run of business between him and Kiniski.

Guys would go there because the trips were short and easy, and they could make decent money — not super money, but decent money. But I got to a point where I was starving. This was November 1963, and when the news came that President Kennedy had been shot they shut down the territory for a few days. I wasn't making anything. Fortunately, a couple of the hookers in town liked me, and they were giving me money to go party with them. They just kind of took me in because they loved partying with me, so that's how I was eating and living. Plus, for the testosterone-filled animal I was, the "fringe benefits" were awesome too.

I had a match with Kiniski, and it sold out. Six guys on the card made more than I did that night, and I was mad. I called Fenton and said, "What the hell are you doing? The place was dead when I got here!"

It took years before I understood what my charisma was, how I connected to people. All I knew is, whenever I went into an area, it was generally down at first, but it went up. Whatever I did in the ring, because I sure wasn't doing dropkicks and all that, the people could relate to. I just had a way of always getting over.

When I complained about my pay, Fenton said, "Well, go back to Oklahoma. They're worth more than you because they've been around longer. You're lucky to get to be in a main event."

I said, "Then don't put me in a main event if you're not going to pay me as a main eventer."

He said, "You don't tell me what to do."

I said, "Fuck you. The next time you want me to work with somebody, ask them if they think they can beat me."

Don Leo was going to beat me before his big run with Kiniski. Kiniski had put me over, and Gene liked me when we met even though he didn't know how to take me.

Then Fenton and Sandor Kovacs, who helped Fenton book the Vancouver territory, came to me and asked if I was still mad.

"You're damn right," I said. "Don Leo can't beat me, either, so fuck Don Leo, and fuck you. Since he's worth so much more money than me, see if he can beat my ass."

Don Leo was in the next locker room and heard all this. He caught me later in the dressing room and said, "Bill, you mad at me?"

I said, "Hell, no. I stayed at your house; you treated me like a million bucks. This isn't about you — in fact, I'm putting you over in two straight falls, because I'm leaving."

"No, Bill, calm down, and we can make some money here —"

I cut him off. "No, fuck this Fenton. He's a thief and has no respect for any of us. But I'll get some color for you too —"

"No, you're not. No, you're not."

"Oh, yes, I am. I'm putting you over in two straight, big boy!"

Fenton and Kovacs were terrified that I was going to mess up the match and their plans and make problems in the ring with Don Leo, but I put Don over. He remained in Vancouver for the rest of his career, so I never saw him again in the wrestling business, but a few years ago I was in Vancouver and got in touch with him. We had dinner with another wrestling friend named Freddy Baron and their wives. It was great to see them again.

That night I was packing up in the hotel. Antone Leone saw me and asked me, "Kid, what are you doing?"

I said, "I'm making a dash for liberty. I'm out of here. I'm tired of losing my *s* because of that damned 'Whipper' Watson." Watson had also been trying to sign me to a personal promotion contract.

Leone said, "Well, you can't leave! You're in the main event everywhere!"

I said, "It's going to be hard for me to be in the main event because I'm not going to be here."

I called Leroy and told him I was coming home. He told me, "You can't just leave him!"

"Leroy, I'm leaving!"

It was quiet for a second. Then he said, "Can you make Oklahoma City by Christmas Night?"

I got off the phone, and Leone looked at me and said, "You got room for one more?"

We were driving out of there when Leone started laughing, and he yelled, *"In this corner 'Big' Gene Kiniski! And in this corner — where the Hell is 'Big' Bill Watt?"*

We went to work for Leroy, but Fenton called him and said he was blacklisting me. The National Wrestling Alliance, a group of regional promoters in North America who worked together, was pretty powerful then.

Leroy said, "Look, Rod, I'll fly him up there, and he'll apologize."

Fenton said, "No, he'll never work again."

Well, I sold out up there with Kiniski and Jonathan, so I was in pretty good demand, and I was already drawing well in Oklahoma. That "blacklist" threat was pretty empty to someone with ability, because great talent is scarce.

In Oklahoma, I met a nice kid whom I'd end up working with quite a bit. Jim Wehba tried out in Wichita Falls, Texas. I could tell he was already with it, and they asked me to referee his first match. Wehba, who wrestled as Skandor Akbar, was in there with Al "Great Bolo" Lovelock, who couldn't wrestle, and Akbar just wanted to show he could work. Lovelock suckerpunched him. It was the worst nose break I've ever seen. It gushed so bad that I was slipping on the blood in the ring.

Akbar was never any threat to him. Akbar was the nicest guy you'd ever want to meet. I believe the only reason Lovelock did it was because he knew they had me in the ring as a referee, to back him up. But Akbar did nothing to deserve that cheap shot.

I believed in "stretching" new guys, but with wrestling moves, to see if they could wrestle and if they had any guts. Stretching didn't include sucker-punching a person who was sincere and came to be a pro wrestler. And that sucker-punch was the only way Lovelock was going to hurt Akbar. Man to man, Akbar could have kicked Al's ass.

Some time later, after Akbar got into the business, I was at the Tulsa YMCA working out and ran into him. I asked him how much he could bench-press. He said he could do 400 pounds, which didn't impress me, as I had lifted a max of 585 and regularly did repetitions of well over 500 in workouts. We were steroid-free back in the late 1960s and early 1970s, and that was way more than just a "respectable" amount of weight. But Akbar proceeded to shock me in how he "bench-pressed" the weight. He sat the bar with the weights on the ground, not on the bench-press racks, and then proceeded to clean it (taking the weight from the floor to his chest); then he sat down on a bench, lay back and did repetitions with it; then he sat back up and placed it on the floor! I had never seen that done before and haven't seen it done since!

Akbar started as a babyface, and later he "turned" on Hodge to become a heel, and it was a hot angle. He really had heat with the fans! Some of his former fans were so mad that they actually tried to set him up. They invited him to a bar to play some pool and then ambushed him, but it didn't work. He kicked all their asses.

Jim Wehba, a.k.a. Skandor Akbar, was and is a stand-up guy. Also, he was always extremely frugal, so he saved his money and is in good financial shape. He still works out every morning in a gym in his garage. He was a tough guy, strong as heck, but with a great heart, and his word was good as gold. I have nothing but the highest of respect for him, and I'm glad he stayed with it after Al Lovelock's cheap shot, because Akbar became a real success.

THE **BIG BREAK**

Wichita Falls was also where, in 1964, the turning point in my career occurred.

Bob Clay ran Wichita Falls and Joplin, Missouri, for Leroy McGuirk. He was a nice guy, but to show you how backward they were Bob didn't even run television in Joplin. He relied on promoting from a five-minute interview on the evening news on the day of the show. Larry Hennig, a tough pro wrestler I met later in the AWA, said it best: "We're instruments in the hands of fools."

I was working a show in Joplin, and "Wild" Red Berry had come home from New York, where he was managing the Kangaroos, one of the top tag teams in the country. Red had been a big star in the junior heavyweight division, a legend. Every year his wife, Lil, came home to do the census. Bob had me and Wild Red booked in a tag match. We were doing a live interview, and I had come up with a little angle for it, where our opponents confronted Red, and then I came out and ran them off. Bob never did crap — he just had guys come out and talk, but I always had a mind for stuff like that.

Red was finishing up the interview, and he looked at me, thinking of how much he thought I looked like Dick Hutton, and said, "That's right! Me and 'Big *Dick*' Watts are gonna be there, and we're going to take care of those two!"

I used to come out and jump over the top ring rope, to show some agility for a 300-pounder. As I was getting ready to jump over the rope that night, this girl in the front row said, "Well, hello there, Big *Dick!*" I caught my foot and fell right on my face! Yeah, she got me.

Wild Red was really impressed with me. I didn't know it, but he went back and told Toots Mondt and Vince McMahon about me. They were the promoters of the East Coast promotion, the World Wide Wrestling Federation, and McMahon was the father of Vincent K. McMahon, who owns what is now World Wrestling Entertainment.

A few weeks later I was wrestling in Wichita Falls, in that crappy 4-H barn and arena, and the police department came and said, "You have an emergency phone call."

My first thought was "Oh no, something's happened to one of my parents."

They took me to the nearest phone, and it was Toots Mondt and Vince McMahon on the other end of the line. They were both going strong. "We've heard a lot about you! Red Berry told us about you, and let me tell you — you're starting on Washington, DC, TV next Thursday." They had never even seen me — they were just going from what Red had told them.

I said, "I don't know if I can do that."

They said, "*What?* Why not?"

"Well, I don't know if it's all right with Mr. McGuirk."

They laughed. "You just plan on being up here next Thursday. We'll worry about Mr. McGuirk."

When I got back to the office the next Monday, Leroy said, "Bill, you finish up here tonight, and you start in Washington, DC, on Thursday. You're going to like Toots Mondt. This is a bigger opportunity for you than I could ever provide, and you're going to do great there. But you listen to that tough, old son of a bitch. And Vince McMahon is a top promoter. 'Red' Berry has spoken really highly of you." Leroy and Red were good friends because they had gone through the junior heavyweight ranks together.

I was booked to wrestle Antone "Ripper" Leone that night, and naturally the booker wanted me to do a job, but Leroy wouldn't let it happen.

He said, "Are you kidding? There ain't no one gonna believe anyone can beat him? Just because he's leaving, he's not gone — he's still from Oklahoma, and he's not doing a job." They did a deal where Antone Leone got disqualified on me, which got him over like crazy!

When I got to Washington, DC, they looked at me and said, "You know, we were going to bring you in as a heel, but you need to be a babyface. So since we had promised you to Red to manage, you'll give him five percent of your earnings, but he won't be in your corner." At that time, most of the major heels had ringside managers. This was still a big break because Red steered me around a lot of potholes and really was a good guy.

That was also where I first became "Cowboy" Bill Watts. They told me, "Well, you're from Oklahoma, so you're a cowboy." I wasn't a cowboy, but they told me I was going to wear a cowboy hat and boots. I had boots, so I went to the Stetson Hat Factory in Pennsylvania and got my first cowboy hat.

They put us on three to four TV shows a week — Washington, Connecticut, Baltimore and Philadelphia. But the money was in doing arena events. They paid only twenty-five dollars a shot for TV, so I was making only $100 a week and living in the most expensive place in the world. I was going broke, but Red told me to calm down and be patient. "Kid, they're putting you on TV because they like you. You're going to be a star."

He had me move near him in Paulsboro, New Jersey, in these old prewar apartments. Red was the most frugal guy — he was just loaded, and he'd saved his money. He was a guy who'd come up the hard way. He'd invested well and would have me over to his home to eat. He took me under his wing.

Sure enough, I soon started making some money, and when I did Red had me start investing in some mutual funds and started saving my money.

Red Berry was a good mentor, but eventually I didn't think I should have to pay the five percent anymore, and that upset him. To console him, they gave him Smasher Sloan and Waldo Von Erich. It created a rift between us, but he later accepted it. We were never as close again, but it was a business, not a family, deal.

Bruno Sammartino was the main guy in the WWWF, the territory called "New York." Bruno and I took to each other right away. He is a person of tremendous integrity, principle and quality. Just a hell of a guy.

Bruno was a great ring general. A ring general is a guy who can lead anyone through a match, who can have a great match that gets the booking across. A ring general sets the stage, understands the psychological setting of the match and knows where he wants the story to go and how the people should react to it.

Bruno wasn't very flashy, but he had incredible psychology. At 285 pounds, he was so powerfully built that he didn't do a lot of fancy things in the ring. He didn't do a bunch of dropkicks or headscissors. But as far as understanding the match and the picture he wanted to paint in that match, he was great.

I worked out near Paulsboro, where I was living, at the Westville Grove Gym. It was owned by Andy Super and managed by Danny Iacovone, both really nice guys. But when I was in New York City, I'd work out with Bruno, who is still the strongest man I've ever seen in terms of lifting.

Working out with him really accelerated my strength. In fact, at one point, I'm certain we were the only two in the world doing 585 pounds on the bench press, but no one recognized it because we were pro wrestlers, and back then, if you were a pro in one sport, you were a pro in everything. But 585 pounds was unheard of, and we were doing it without steroids and while wrestling, which meant we were banged up all the time. I was never as strong as Bruno. He could put up more pounds and had more endurance on the weights than I did.

Toots Mondt was a tough, old guy and a big gambler — he made and lost fortunes. Vince was always loyal to Toots. They were partners, to a certain extent, but Vince had most of the duties since Toots didn't have a lot of responsibility money-wise. Whatever he made he'd gamble.

I also met Willie Gilzenburg, who promoted New Jersey and was really close to McMahon. Phil Zacko promoted Baltimore and was on Vince's staff. Arnold Skoaland was Vince's office guy, and they usually had him with the champion.

Bruno was the star. Gorilla Monsoon was the top heel when I got there. Buddy Rogers had been the heel star for years, but Rogers and Ray Fabiani had tried to pull something in 1963. I was told they "wanted a piece of the booking office," but before this happened Bruno and Rogers got into it. Bruno didn't trust Buddy because he'd done a giant swing on him once, years earlier, a move where a guy standing grabs a prone opponent's ankles and spins around and around before releasing the guy. Well, when Buddy did it to Bruno, he let him go in a way that sent Bruno out of the ring. He did the same thing to Billy Darnell one time, and it hospitalized Darnell. Sammartino ended up getting mad at Rogers and beat him up, right there at ringside, slamming him into the steps.

Bruno ended up getting fired over it. Then he went to Toronto, a territory that had been dead, and he turned it around and did incredible box office there for promoter Frank Tunney.

Vince then told Tunney that Bruno was a bad guy, so Tunney started knocking him off the Toronto shows, but then he realized, "Hey, I'm killing the golden goose. This kid hasn't done anything here but make money." So Tunney kept using him, and soon Vince was the one with the flat territory. Rogers was pulling some deal where he supposedly had a heart problem. He was trying to hijack McMahon into making him a partner.

McMahon and Bruno made peace, and Vince wanted to make Bruno champion. But Bruno said, "Well, to be champion, I'd have to work with Rogers, and I'm not working with Rogers. If he wants to fight, I'll fight, but I'm going to beat him, and it's not going to take long." Well, it didn't take long, but they didn't shoot — Rogers just put him over quick, and as of May 17, 1963, Bruno was now the champion.

Rogers thought the territory would crash without him on top, but instead it popped. Bruno had them bring in Monsoon as this crazed Gorilla to be the new top heel. Gorilla was Bob "Gino" Marella, a great guy with amateur credentials (so he could certainly take care of himself) and a heart of gold. He was incredibly agile for a guy his size, so he got over like a million bucks. He was nearly 400 pounds and a little taller than me, and he entered the ring by jumping over the top rope.

One of my first matches with Gorilla was in Pittsburgh. I was really over in the WWWF by this point, and he came to me before the match with an idea. "OK, Kid [he kept calling me 'Kid' because he'd been on top with Bruno for about a year and thought he was now a proven veteran], here's what I want to do," he said. He pushed his hands out, which was the signal for me to back off. Then he quickly drew his hands in very slightly, which he said was the sign for me to make my big comeback on him. We had a good match, but the crowd was getting fired up when he gave me the signal to cut off my comeback and I just kept beating on him.

After the match, he came to me and said, "Damn it, Kid! You got everything backward!"

I said, "*You're* the one who had everything backward — didn't you hear the people out there?"

We ended up laughing about it. He really was a great guy.

A lot of people don't know that Marella had studied opera and was a great singer. He'd met and married a girl from New York City when he was young, and they stayed married the rest of his life.

I had nothing but the highest respect for him. He and Bruno were incredibly close, and I saw only one flare-up between them. They argued about something, I don't remember what, until Sammartino told Gino that was enough. Well, he kept talking until they finally got into it a little bit, and Gino found out messing with Sammartino was pretty deep water. But they straightened out that issue, a minor thing, and stayed close friends for as long as I was there.

Sammartino was the one who got Gino a cut of the New York office. Vince offered the percentage to Bruno first, but there were always "trust issues" between Bruno and McMahon, so Bruno decided that whatever percentage it was could help take care of his friend Gino. Gino ended up a part of that office through the time when Vincent K. McMahon took over in the early 1980s. Vince Jr., as he was called, kept Gino in the company until Gino's death. In their way, the McMahons are extremely loyal to their associates.

The crowds were different there. For one thing, the population from which McMahon could draw was much larger. I never thought that the best workers were in the east — I thought you had to be a better worker to work in places where you'd hit the same towns every week. Those people saw you all the time, so you had to keep it fresh. The East Coast had the biggest stars, but it was strictly a formula factory. The TV formula was "big star versus a nobody" and then "another big star versus a nobody." Their theory was you had to pay to see the big stars wrestle each other.

But there were all those major metropolitan areas so close together. They weren't even running Philadelphia regularly at the time, so it was Washington, DC, for TV every Thursday. Then we ran the big show in Washington, TV and a live show in Baltimore, TV in Bridgeport, Connecticut, and live shows in New Haven. Those Connecticut towns were dead. They weren't even running Boston. Pittsburgh was like a little satellite territory of its own, and Ace Freeman promoted it. New York, of course, was the big city.

Bruno wasn't management — he was just a star, but he was smart enough about it that he knew how to get into McMahon's ear about how to handle his programs. Bruno was great at recognizing how to get a guy over to work with him and how to use him best. That was the formula — they'd build you and build you, and then you'd work with Bruno.

In Washington, DC, it was a similar formula, only with Bobo Brazil on top. Bobo was another class guy.

In Pittsburgh, Ace did live TV on Saturdays, and they'd run the arena there once a month. To keep his TV going, he'd book guys for spot shows in the area Friday and Saturday and then do the TV too. He had his own little crew of local wrestlers, plus the stars that came in from the New York or Washington offices.

Luckily, Bruno liked me, so I ended up as the number two babyface — I'd wrestle the top heel to get him ready for Sammartino, and Bruno and I would occasionally be a tag team.

What really got me over with Vince was my series with Walter "Killer" Kowalski, another first-class human being. In his early years, he had a tremendous build, but then he became a vegetarian, which changed his build, yet he developed unbelievable endurance. He was still a big star, so they put us together in Washington, DC, and had us go to a twenty-minute draw — just that I "held my own" against the Killer told the people I was to be taken seriously. We tore the joint down. Wally had that tenacious style, so you let him get his heat, then did your comeback, and you'd have the fans where you wanted them. That match got over so well that Vince booked it everywhere. Kowalski and I became friends. He'd even let me fly his airplane years before I got my pilot's license.

What got me over in Pittsburgh was a crazy thing. Being in the right place at the right time is critical, and if there is an opportunity you need to be ready to take advantage of it. Here's an example. When I first went into the territory, one of the guys I first worked with was named Frank Martinez, a Puerto Rican. They had a couple of Puerto Rican stars, like Miguel Perez, Victor Rivera and Pedro Morales, who became big stars later on. But at this time, the others treated most of them pretty shabbily. Martinez used to be a pro fighter, but I didn't know this. To me, he was just a job guy, so I wasn't going to sell for him, because the stars weren't supposed to sell anything for the job guys.

I worked with Martinez, and I didn't sell anything he did, which was OK until I ignored his boxing-type punches, so he popped me really good. When he did, I shot in on him, took him down and ran his face into the mat. I crotched him and barred an arm. He ate all the canvas that was there, and then I pinned him.

Martinez knew I was hot, but he came to me in the dressing room, and I'll never forget how smart he really was. He said, in his strong Puerto Rican accent, "Cowboy *Beel,* you *beeg,* strong star. You know, I know you gonna be star, but when I box, I box in Madison Square Garden. Only thing I got is my *ponch.* The people believe in my *ponch.*"

Well, they really didn't believe in his punch by then, but I didn't say anything.

He continued, "When I give you my *ponch,* you don't even *fleench.* You don't register my *ponch.* You make me not a man! If you make me not a man and you beat me, then who you beat? So I pop you. But then you take me down, so I know you whip me! But I work with you again? You don't respect my *ponch* again? I *heet* you again. I know you gonna get me, but I *heet* you!"

I looked at him and said, "Hey, I'm sorry. You're right. I didn't know. From now on, when you hit me with your punch, I'll respect your punch."

And he *was* right. You can't be a star if there isn't someone to make you a star. The good "job guys" were very important. I respected him for coming to me, and I think he respected me for admitting I'd been wrong.

Six months later I was a big star, working high on the Garden shows as a babyface. I was in Pittsburgh for live TV. Chief White Owl was there, and he was getting over pretty well as an in-between babyface on TV. He was working this live TV show on Saturday afternoon against Frank Martinez, with Bill Cardille calling the play-by-play and Chuck Moyer directing the show for the station.

During the match, White Owl accidentally broke his leg, right on live TV. My match was over, and I was in the shower. These guys come running in and say, "Hey! Something happened out there! Looks like White Owl broke his damn leg!"

I pulled on my jeans and ran out there. Frank was in the ring, looking concerned. White Owl was on the apron — he definitely had a broken leg. This was live television, so I looked at the clock — I hadn't been in the business three years, but I could think on my feet.

I jumped into the ring, grabbed the microphone and said, "Let me tell you something, Martinez! Anybody messes with my friend Chief White Owl has to deal with 'Cowboy' Bill Watts!"

I turned to say something to the people, and here he came. He jumped me from behind and hammered me. I watched the time on that clock and sold for him, then made a big comeback and beat him just as we went off the air. That incident *made* me in Pittsburgh, and it was because of this job guy, whom I had befriended. We didn't need to communicate or anything. He knew what to do, and I knew what to do. I took advantage of the live television and made myself a star. White Owl went to the hospital and became a star with the sympathy, and I was over like a million bucks in Pittsburgh. They thought I was smart for improvising.

I also ran into Gene Kiniski again while working for McMahon. He didn't have any hard feelings from Vancouver. He was actually the one who'd talked me into apologizing to Rod Fenton. Kiniski had said, "Yeah, I know he's a no-good son of a bitch, but just apologize to him." Gene was a good diplomat, and we became very close in New York.

A few years later, in 1969, when he became the world's champion of the

NWA, we did a deal where I challenged him under a mask in Saint Louis as Dr. Scarlet. Of course, the culmination of that was another deal where I got mad at what they were telling me to do, because they wanted me just to go in and get beat the first time out, after all this buildup.

I came up with a finish, though, and Gene thought what I wanted to do was nuts, but he went along with it. He didn't think we could pull it off, because no one had ever seen it. I'd do a giant swing. But I'd swing him so long that I'd get "dizzy." Then I'd stand him up for a standing suplex but "lose my balance." We'd fall so that his body would hit the top turnbuckle, which would turn him over, on top of me.

He was worried because he was 275 pounds, but I told him, "Just make sure you keep your legs straight, but spread them a little so you don't hit your ankles on the post."

Gene came up to me after the match and said, "Thank God, Bill, you had me scared to death out there."

Four years before challenging Kiniski, however, my time had come to challenge the champion of the WWWF — Bruno. Few people ever knew that the person who inadvertently caused our big run was none other than Bruno's longtime nemesis, Buddy Rogers. I had spent months as the setup man for Bruno and as his tag partner. I would feud with Gorilla Monsoon, who would eventually win to set him up as the next title challenger. By 1965, Bruno and I had become really tight, but we would soon be playing the roles of enemies in the ring.

Red Berry took me to meet Buddy Rogers, who lived in New Jersey. He had a lot of money because he had apparently saved and invested. I learned later that Buddy had contacted Red after seeing me on TV. He wanted to get back into the game. Buddy did everything in the shadows.

Before we got to Buddy's place, Red said to me, "Look, Kid, this is the most brilliant guy in the business. Whatever he tells you, just listen."

Buddy wined and dined me, but he had an agenda. He was really impressive with his diamond pinkie ring, great tan, great house. He also didn't have a lot of trust. One of his favorite sayings was "Watch out for the guy patting you on the back — he's looking for the soft spot to stick the knife in."

Finally, Rogers said, "I've got an idea. I'm going to call Vince, so when Vince tells you about this, don't tell him that you and I have already met." His idea was that he would come out of retirement and manage me against Sammartino. "I think we could make a lot of money," he said.

I didn't really think anything else of it until a couple of weeks later, when Vince called me and said, "An old friend of mine called with a great idea. There's a lot of history with him in this office, a lot of people with different thoughts about him, but I want you to go meet him. He lives in New Jersey, and his name is Buddy Rogers."

So here I was, having gotten close to Bruno Sammartino, a first-class, principled guy. Here was Vince, my boss, telling me to go meet the guy who'd tried to double-cross him, according to Sammartino.

Vince obviously kept an emotional bond to Rogers, a trait I think you see in Vince Jr. with his WWE today. He takes back guys who have testified against him and screwed him. If you are running a business, the bottom line is making money so you can stay in business, and that requires being flexible. I, too, used guys I didn't personally like or with whom I had huge differences of opinion. But back then it seemed so bizarre, a tricky situation I was in.

It had me going crazy, so I went to Bruno and said, "I've got to talk to you. I'm really troubled by this." I told Bruno the story.

He said, "That son of a bitch. Let me tell you what's going to happen. Buddy will come back to manage you, to wrestle me, to get *himself* into a program with me, to get the title. Only I'm not going to put Buddy Rogers over. I'm not even going to work with the son of a bitch."

Bruno came up with another plan. "First of all," he said, "I have to be aware that Rogers wants in on the deal, so I can confront Vince about it, and it can't be you who it comes from." Fortunately, the president of Bruno's fan club, Georgiann Markopolous, was a good friend of Buddy's wife. Bruno sent her to see Buddy's wife and made sure she dropped my name. Buddy's wife told Georgiann about my visit, and then the cat was out of the bag, so the "source" for Bruno was Buddy's own wife instead of me. Then Bruno confronted Vince about what he had heard "from his fan club," and they had a talk about it.

When I came back into the picture, Bruno told Vince he thought it would be a good idea (which we had already worked out) to have me turn on him, but he added, "We're not going to have Rogers in the mix." The feud with Bruno made sense to me, since I was limited in how much I could make as his setup guy, even though it was more than I had ever made. The big money was to wrestle against him.

What they did, though, was put me on contract. It said I had to kick-back twenty-five percent. If I wrestled in Baltimore, Vince would tell his local promoter in Baltimore, "Bill's one of my guys, so he's got to make $1,000," while my opponent, who wasn't one of Vince's guys, would make

$500. So I had to kick-back $250 to Vince, but I was still making $250 more than the other guy. That's just how it worked. It was great for me, because I earned more than my opponents, and great for them, since they made more from their partner in each town, without the partner knowing it.

Because Sammartino and I had become so close, though, we'd settle up once a month with Phil Zacko. He'd have me go through the book and give him Sammartino's dates. Then Bruno would do the books and give Zacko my dates. Zacko looked where the dates matched, figured out the gates and then determined what the kickback should be. Bruno and I would sit there and wink at each other about which dates to give and not give, so we skipped about five dates a month and were picking up the full ride on those days. That was "chump change" to them, but it made a big difference in our monthly incomes.

The contract was one-sided, though. It established a joint account for payment, but if I died they got the money in the joint account. I said, "No, no, my end goes to my parents."

They said, "What's the matter? Don't you trust us?"

I said, "Hey, I'm not the one forcing *y'all* to sign a contract."

They adjusted the contract for me.

When I turned on Bruno, I really felt it from the fans, especially my first night as a heel in Madison Square Garden. That was the first time I'd felt such intense hatred, and I never understood what a weapon it could be if you weren't ready for it.

Prior to our split, Sammartino and I were booked as a tag team for events set after people had seen me turn on him on TV, so I still had to show up and be his partner. I went to the ring with him, and he would start the match, but as soon as he got into trouble and went to tag I'd jump down to the floor and walk back to the dressing room. And that caused riots.

The largest crowd for any event in the old Madison Square Garden was Bruno Sammartino versus "Cowboy" Bill Watts, on March 29, 1965. The fire marshal didn't show up that night, so Vince kept cramming the people in. There had been other big events there, but a lot depends on the limits the fire marshal puts on the building. That match ended in a disqualification as we brawled out of control.

We came back with a "no-disqualification" Texas Death Match for the rematch. That one ended when I kicked him in the balls. I think I may have "potatoed" him (hit him too stiffly) on it — he ended up falling down and cracking his shoulder. When I kicked him, though, the *athletic commissioner* came in and disqualified me to end the match.

Without realizing it, he was made part of an angle. The commission's interfering and disqualifying me, in a no-DQ match, set up another return bout, so we ended up doing yet another round of big rematches.

This might sound ugly, but you have to realize that, in a riot, if you lose your feet, they'll kill you. That's where guys get knifed, burned or whatever. Of course, guys today never have to worry about things like that, because nobody believes in what they're doing. They might have excited fans, but they don't have to worry about getting burned with cigars or being knifed. They generally don't even have to worry about getting hit! We were concerned about all of those things.

Vince hired me a lawyer who wanted $750 just to go to my arraignment. This was a lot of money in those days. I knew an arraignment is where you plead guilty or not guilty and then set a court date. I didn't need to spend $750 for *that*. I fired the attorney and got a recommendation on a good lawyer from the sheriff's deputies at the arraignment.

I testified that, out of the corner of my eye, I saw someone attacking me, so I stuck my arms out, and he must have fallen. The police who testified established that the guy was out of his seat and a troublemaker. Under the law, the floor near that dressing room was *my* space. Legally, I wasn't required to retreat. The only question was whether I exceeded reasonable force in defending myself. A lawyer will tell you that, as long as you're defending yourself, there's no excessive force, but as soon as you win the fight you've used excessive force. If you're a professional athlete, they want you to act as if you have a gauge on each arm to allow you to say, "OK, I need to hit this guy only this hard."

After we won the case, the judge called me back into chambers. She asked for my autograph and then asked me, "I just don't understand where all the blood came from. You said you never hit him, so where did all the blood come from?"

I said, "Ma'am, I'm not sure. I guess some people who aren't athletes are just extra clumsy. He must have just been so clumsy he fell and hit his head on the concrete floor."

It ended up OK for me legally, but, when the case hit, Vince had been planning to switch the title to me for about six months before putting it back on Bruno, because Bruno and I had such a hellacious program going. When that case came up, he got cold feet about it and told us the night we were supposed to do the switch that they'd changed their minds and were doing a different finish — I would lose.

Vince said, "This is what we've gotta do. Is that OK with you?"

I said, "Vince, you sign my checks. I wish it wasn't that way, but if that's what you want to do then I'll put him over."

Bruno didn't like it either, but we did it.

They ended up bringing in Bill Miller as a quick replacement. I endorsed Bill — he was my friend. We had wrestled each other in Pittsburgh, shortly before I turned heel on Bruno, and they picked up Miller based on how well he got over in Pittsburgh.

Our Pittsburgh match came about when Ace Freeman decided to use me to put over Miller on TV, which was a problem. They never used a New York guy to put someone over in Pittsburgh. Miller, at the time, was just someone Freeman was using on the side. Vince wouldn't have let one of his guys put over a guy working strictly in Pittsburgh, but I couldn't get in touch with anyone in the office.

I didn't want to do it, but I knew Bill really well, and I still knew how to watch the clock. He got heat on me, but when it came time to make a comeback I just kept on going until I saw we were off the air. Then I missed the charge into the corner that led to him rolling me up and beating me. Bill didn't even know for five or ten minutes after the match that, unfortunately, his pinfall didn't get on the air. The last image that people saw at home was me beating him up and giving him huge bumps, which he could really take.

Unlike the deal with Martinez and Chief White Owl, not everyone there was thrilled with my improvisation. Afterward, Miller told me, "I guess I'd do better if I wanted to get over by doing the job for you."

I said, "Hey, Bill, I'm sorry. I don't know what happened out there. I just lost track of time." I liked Bill, and it wasn't his fault, but this was a promoter who was trying to screw with my living.

Miller was a good choice to replace me in the program with Sammartino, if someone had to. As Bill and Bruno's series moved forward, they planned a big return match between them in Madison Square Garden. In Washington, DC, Bill and I were booked against each other in a dark match, before a TV taping. The dark match was a nontelevised match just for the live fans, and it always ended in a schmoz, a big double disqualification, just before they actually started the on-air portion of the card. Those matches never having a finish was one of the stupidest things I've ever seen. That was why the TV arenas were always empty. Who wanted to see formula matches when even the main event wasn't any good?

Our match was a battle of two heels, but I was trying to be the babyface in it, to get Miller over as the big heel for his match with Bruno.

Unfortunately, he wasn't selling. Well, not selling anything was turning him babyface, so I hit him with a ball shot, and he didn't sell *that*. He hit me with a ball shot, and I sold it everywhere. I sold everything. Every time he hit me I went down, out of the ring or whatever. So, because I sold, the people reacted, and it showed I still had the most "heat" as a heel or villain. They cheered Bill and booed *me!* The more I sold, the more the crowd cheered him — not the reaction a heel wants. Bill panicked and worked even "stronger," making me more of a heel. He made himself the babyface without even trying!

Vince and Toots were back there watching the dark match, going, "Gosh-damn it, the Cowboy's still got all the heat!" So they changed the upcoming Madison Square Garden match back to Bruno Sammartino versus "Cowboy" Bill Watts. That fifty-dollar TV match cost Miller $2,000 — a Garden payoff. Miller was a big, tough guy, but that night he wasn't the smartest psychologist inside the ring.

After my run with Bruno ended, I formed a tag team with Gorilla Monsoon. We were teaming when I again encountered Haystacks Calhoun. As I said, Calhoun was a good guy, but I'm afraid Monsoon and I destroyed his career there. He just came in at the wrong time, and he wanted us to do his silly comedy. Well, Monsoon and I weren't going to do it, so we turned it all on him and made him look like a fool.

He cried and cried after the match. Gino and I both liked him, and we hated ruining him like that, but it was a dog-eat-dog business. We were trying to get over as serious heels. We weren't going to play "Statue of Liberty" (where he held one heel at arm's length while clutching the other) and all those other goofy routines he did.

Monsoon and I also had a match once with my old Texas opponent Art Thomas and Bobo Brazil. Somehow, after Art died in 2003, Burrhead Jones, another wrestler in the locker room that night, seemed to remember in a newspaper interview that Sailor had backed me down in the dressing room after problems in a match. Well, it wasn't me who'd had the problem with Art — it was *Monsoon*. Art had blocked me on a move, so I'd just tagged out — and Monsoon had slammed him!

I think Art Thomas would have stood up for something he wanted, but don't think I was intimidated because he had muscles. He was clumsy, and I knew he would end up on the ground. When you can wrestle, you don't just stand and fight some big guy like that. Heck, that *hurts*. I didn't care *how* strong he was. If he'd gotten into it with me, he would have been taken down. I always liked Sailor and never had a problem with him. I will never say I would have "whipped" everyone, but no one will ever say I backed down or ran from anyone. That just never happened.

One of my last opponents in the New York territory was Johnny Valentine. Now *there* was a psychologist. JV (as he was known) would hammer you with that forearm smash. He'd try to take your head off. When I worked with him, he hit me that hard, and I said, "Hey!" He did it again, and I took him down and ran his face into the mat. I barred his arm, so he had no way to stop me from feeding him canvas. He didn't move. He knew he was had, so I thought, "Well, that kind of cooled him." I let him up, and we started working. He got me against those ropes, and he hit me the same way again. That's when I understood — that's just how JV was. He didn't mind how hard you hit him, but he was going to nail you. He was a phenomenal worker.

I remember working with him shortly before I left the WWWF, and he said, "Cowboy, would you mind letting me run the match tonight?"

The guy who calls the match is the one who whispers the next few spots, pretty much dictating the flow and pace of the match. Usually, it was the heel's job, but he'd been around for years, so I said, "Sure."

I got in the ring and started wrestling, and he said, "Take me down."

He was the babyface, and I was the heel, so I said, "How? You want me to pull your hair or your trunks?"

"No, do a top wristlock, and power me down."

In New York? No one did anything subtle there, so once I got him down I said, "Now what do you want me to do?"

"Just work the wristlock."

"Want me to pull your hair?"

"No."

"Eye gouge you?"

"No."

"Kneedrop you?"

"No."

He sat in that damn wristlock for fifteen minutes. I was thinking, "Holy mackerel, they're going to boo us out of here in a minute."

Every time he'd start up, he'd tell me to bring him back down, but not using any heel tactics. "Just power me back down," he said.

I didn't cheat once. To this day, I don't know what happened, but about twenty minutes into the match we were about to have a riot. We had people about to get into the ring, they were so mad at me, and I hadn't done anything! That's how much of a crowd psychologist he was. He could emote to people anything he was going through, and damned if I know how he did it, but no one could do it like he did. And he wasn't a little guy — he was six foot three, same as me, so he couldn't get the underdog sympathy that a little guy can get. Today, of course, the crowd would chant "Boring!"

New York was where I again met Ene, who'd become my second wife. Her mother, Leida, was a displaced Estonian. Her father died in a German refugee camp, but her brother, Jaak; her two sisters, Maiu and Ivi; and her mother were sponsored by a Methodist church in Oklahoma, where they went to school at Putnam City. I was in the same class as her sister Ivi, while Maiu, her oldest sister, was ahead of me.

Ene was my brother's age. We dated after I was divorced from Pat. It didn't work out, so we broke it off, and I lost track of her. She had moved to California, got married, had a son, Joel, and then left her husband. She moved to New York to live with her sister, who was dating an exceptionally wealthy man, Manny Kimmel. She eventually married him and was living on Park Avenue. When Ene saw me on TV, she looked me up. We started going together again.

As 1965 came to a close, I left New York on top. I always tried to leave on top. I wasn't staying anywhere if I wasn't contributing. When I left, Vince thought I'd be gone a year, and then they'd bring me back. As it turned out, I never did go back.

I learned a lot there, including what not to do for TV presentation. I never liked the formula of star versus job guy for the whole show. I always thought the Northeast was a jewel of the industry *despite* the way matches were promoted, not because of it.

But Vince and I always got along until he passed away in 1984. He treated me with such class, even later when I had my own territory. I couldn't compete with him for talent because of the money. He'd call me, though, and tell me when he wanted one of my top guys. He always gave me several weeks to finish them up. I never said, "Screw you. You can't take him," because he could, and we both knew it. I just said, "Thanks for letting me know."

And he'd say, "Look, Bill, you've always worked so well with me. Let me give you an extra week on the Giant." He meant Andre the Giant, whose bookings Vince controlled. Well, if you had your territory humming, an extra week of Andre was an extra week of sellouts.

McMahon would always compensate because he knew he could count on me to work with him on what he could have taken anyway. He was smart and smooth, and I never had a problem with Vincent J. McMahon.

SHIRE AND GAGNE: FRUSTRATING GENIUSES

When I left New York at the end of 1965, I was set to go to Japan, but Vince called and sent me to San Francisco promoter Roy Shire. I thought I'd just be there briefly, until I left for Japan.

Shire was a wrestling genius. He'd taken an area that had been dead for wrestling and turned it around. It helped that he had one of the greatest workers in the business — Ray Stevens. Stevens was only about 225 pounds and didn't have an outstanding physique, but he could work with anybody and take the most spectacular bumps of anyone wrestling at that time. He could do it all.

Pat Patterson was there too and worked a lot with Ray. Pat became a great worker but was never the same caliber as Ray. Pat was close to but not quite at Ray's level, but he became great by being around Ray. Stevens was *beyond* good, and when I got there he was at the absolute pinnacle of his career. He could do bumps nobody else could do. And Stevens was another of the great ring generals in wrestling history.

Shire never told you anything. You never knew where you stood. I thought I would be there for only a couple of weeks, but the next thing I knew it was February 1966, and Shire had made me his U.S. champion. I figured he was just doing it to cross people up, so I went to him and said, "I guess you know this is my last week."

He said, "The *hell?* What do you mean?"

"Roy, I just came out here for a few weeks. I told you I was going to Japan. When are you taking the title off me?"

"I'm not taking the title off you! I just made you my damn champion! You can't go to Japan!" He ended up calling the promoter there, and I didn't go to Japan.

In the year or so I was in San Francisco, I became about as close as anyone could with him, and we became great friends after I became a promoter. I kept telling him, "Roy, you're burning yourself out. You can't do it all. You have to get ideas from other people."

It got to where every interview sounded like Roy Shire, because he would tell you word for word how he wanted the interview done. And he did eventually burn himself out. He had a phenomenal mind, but after a while you're going to get stale — I don't care who you are.

Roy teamed me with Jim Hady, another phenomenal worker I knew from New York. There were great workers who might not have been the biggest draws on their own, but they could be placed with a strong drawing partner, and their tremendous ability really complemented the big picture. Jim was one of those workers, and Shire used him to showcase me. As my partner, Hady carried the working load in tag matches so that I could be the star and set up the title matches.

Kinji Shibuya was there too, but we had some problems. Shibuya thought, even though he was a heel, that he would outwrestle a babyface. That didn't sit well with me — if you could outwrestle the other guy, why did you *need* to be a heel? Shibuya hit an iron wall trying that approach with me. Every time he tried to take over, I just guzzled him — but always in a nice way. I never had a cross word with him and always had a lot of respect for him.

Shire sent us to do an hour broadway in Fresno, and the last twenty minutes of that match stunk the world out because I just put Shibuya down and stayed on top of him.

Shire said, "That was a stinkin' match!"

I said, "I *told* you it would stink. I told you I'm not an hour broadway guy. When you design an hour draw for me, it means you don't have the mind to create a finish that will draw some money. And you've got a heel out there who wants to outwrestle the babyface. You've got a mixture for failure because I'm not going to let him outwrestle me."

The entire difference between a babyface and a villain was that a villain had to cheat to win. If a villain can beat a babyface without cheating, then he's not a villain. That was why a heel had to sneak stuff in and do things behind the referee's back. And some villains didn't understand that. Later, when I ran my own territory, my referees got knocked down more than any human beings alive because it was important they not see the cheating.

In the era when I wrestled, it was the sneaky villain who got the heat. Today they do everything right in front of the referee, so all the heat's on the referee, or the promotion, which is ridiculous. Of course, in today's wrestling, the fans all know it's "staged," so there is no real heat anyway. It's all just a show.

Shire would spit, cuss and everything else. He ran a tight ship and did some things that made sense and were different than in other territories. Shire's U.S. champion generally didn't wrestle more than two or three times a week. He didn't wrestle title matches every night, because Shire would be building up a title defense at the Cow Palace, the major wrestling arena in San Francisco. He wanted the championship to be something special, not something you could see just any night.

One night, in San Jose, Jim Hady and I wrestled Pat and Ray. I was in awe of what I saw in the ring that night, what those three guys did. They did moves that were so far beyond anything I'd ever seen that I couldn't believe it. And when the match was over, the people were spent.

When we got back to the dressing room, Shire sat us all down and screamed at us for thirty minutes. *"You,"* he said, "are the dumbest sons of bitches I ever saw! I just had Pepper Gomez, one of my big stars, out there, doing a double countout and looking like an old washerwoman's cunt! You guys go out there and do bumps that should kill any human being, and it's not even the finish! You're killing the business!"

Roy had such a colorful way of ripping you. Actually, Pepper Gomez was a good worker and a well-conditioned one — Roy was just using a colorful example to show the "contrast." And he was right — look at wrestling today. What bump could anyone take that a fan thinks really hurts? It doesn't help that they don't know how to sell. The key wasn't what you did but how you emoted to the people what you were feeling in the ring. The closest a person could come to feeling something was seeing how it affected you, so if you take a bump that should kill somebody and don't sell it right it means nothing.

Ray Stevens was awesome in terms of what he could do. You could whip him into the turnbuckle, and before he even hit it, he would somersault in the air, turn upside-down and backward, go over the top, hit the corner post and gaffe himself on the way down. Nobody had ever done that before.

Logic tells you that Ray should have to go to the hospital, right? Well, the first time he did it, that's what happened. But he did it often enough that soon it became just another high spot. It was like when I kicked Sammartino in the balls — it was the finish of a Texas Death Match to make the commission disqualify me and draw out the feud. The next week *everyone* was doing them as high spots. I called the office and said, "This is bullshit! Get this stopped — it'll mean nothing if it's just a high spot!"

Later we had a match in Honolulu in which Ray and I planned out a spot that Pat didn't know about. Hawaii was one of the few places where throwing your opponent over the top rope wasn't a disqualification, so I told Ray, "I'll throw you over the top, to the floor. Then, when Pat comes in, I'm going to press him, like for a press slam, only I'm going to run over to you, and you'll just be getting up. I'll throw him right over the top, and you catch him coming down, but let's not tell Pat." When I had Pat up and he saw where I was going, he started screaming! Stevens was just getting up when I threw Pat, and he caught him, just like we'd worked out. Pat thought he was a dead man.

That wasn't even the worst of it for him that night. Later he was taking his shower when somebody pushed him out of the dressing room, naked, and locked him out. Often our sense of humor was a bit rough and certainly not "politically correct."

I learned so much in Hawaii. "King" Curtis Iaukea was there, and I'd never heard interviews like his before. "Lord" James Blears and Ed Francis would host, and Francis was the best straight man I ever saw. In a ninety-minute show, they'd have thirty minutes of matches and an hour of interviews, and it was the hottest show on the Hawaiian Islands. They would have a casket, open it up, and there "Handsome" Johnny Barend would be, standing on his head, smoking a cigar, inside the casket. And Francis would interview him. Curtis would do his interviews with his back to the camera, into a dressing room mirror, and they took all the time they wanted. Even psychologists would write in to Ed Francis about the show. It had huge audience appeal.

That was when I realized, when it came to television, what you said was more important than what you did in the ring. The interview revealed the personality of the wrestler and showcased his individuality. I learned that in this business it's the personalities that people are interested in. Selling wrestling was a matter of a fan finding a wrestler to identify with.

Hady ended up moving to Hawaii. Later he wrote to Roy, saying, "I love it over here. I'm getting sun every day, and I've lost 300 pounds." He meant me! Hady lived there until he died of a heart attack a few years later.

Before he headed to the islands, he went to our wedding party after I married Ene in San Francisco. We had two sons together, Erik and Micah, and a daughter, also named Ene. I loved having sons and didn't think I wanted a daughter until I had one — she totally stole her daddy's heart. She is so special. What a blessing to have great sons and a fantastic daughter too.

After Hady left, Joe Scarpa became my partner. I really was fortunate with my partners, because Scarpa was also great. He was from New Jersey and came out west because Vince McMahon had told him, "You'll never draw here because you're just another big-nosed Italian and a local." He went back later, as Chief Jay Strongbow, and made a killing. Joe was a great guy and another one who was very frugal and careful with his money. He was also another teacher, someone who taught me a lot about how to communicate to a crowd.

A few months after my wedding, Verne Gagne called me to work for his AWA promotion in the Midwest. He had McMahon's backing, since Vince was mad at Shire for some reason, and wanted to pull me out from under Shire. Verne offered me his championship, but I said, "It's not about championships, Verne. It's about money. Besides, I'm working for somebody else — if I would just leave him, how could *you* trust me?"

Some time later I decided to stop wrestling and start looking for additional ways to make money because I was always afraid I'd get hurt and wouldn't be able to earn. The first thing I did was save enough money to live on for a year in case I did get injured. I learned that from Red Berry. He was out of the ring for a year after suffering a terrible back injury.

I became interested in a new cosmetics company, Holiday Magic. The idea was to sell healthy cosmetics. I thought it was a great idea. Ern Westmore, the famous Hollywood makeup artist, was associated with it.

I ended up talking to their number-one organization builder, a guy named Mark Evans. He held the world's record for doing the most push-ups in an hour, but he was also an excellent closer. Damned if Mark didn't sell me $5,000 worth of cosmetics for half that, and I ended up signing my name to a piece of stationery as my check, and it cleared the bank! Mark promised me all these Holiday Magic girls to sell my cosmetics, and I'd have it made.

That was the first experience I had with these guys who overpromised and underdelivered, who prey on folks. They are great at hype. Of course, we are responsible for our decisions and should take our time and really investigate any company we consider before investing.

When I took the cosmetics home and showed them to my wife, she said, "You did *what?*" She asked me the company's name, and when I told her she said, "I've never even heard of them!"

The next morning we opened up the San Francisco newspaper, and there it was — Holiday Magic was getting sued. I just about fainted.

But William Patrick, who ran the company, decided to use the publicity to run for governor, creating even more publicity for the company, which turned into a giant success. Also, in spite of being disappointed by the initial hype, I was determined to learn this business and make this a success. It was my first venture in network marketing, but as I learned the business it became successful.

Then they decided they wanted to start an instructor general class for their top producers, where I met Zig Zigler, Ben Gay and others who became very successful in that industry. They taught us the traits of a good salesperson and had beautiful suits they wanted us to wear. They told us to wear alligator loafers. I had alligator cowboy boots, but one of the company vice presidents told me I couldn't wear them. I just said, "The hell I can't."

The strange thing was Patrick loved it when I would disagree or argue with one of his company vice presidents. He'd call me into his office as if he was mad, and I'd put my feet up on his desk after he closed the door. He'd say, "Well, Cowboy, what do you think?" And we just died laughing.

One week out of the month I taught a course and made $3,000 a week for that, plus what I was making for my distributorship. I was making a good living, especially in the 1960s. But then the state attorney general's office started looking into front-end loading and "blue sky" marketing, and the state passed legislation against it. They were right to see it as a problem — I just hadn't seen it because I hadn't been exposed to that side of it.

I saw what was coming, so I got out and went back to wrestling. I had accomplished my main mission, proving I could earn a good living outside wrestling. I called Verne and asked if he was still interested in me. He said, "Well, I'm not promising you anything."

"Verne," I said. "I promised you last time we talked that the next time I was ready to change to a new territory you'd be the first one I called. It's fine. Don't worry — I can get work. I'm just keeping my word to you." And I hung up on him.

Verne called me right back and said, "I want you to come, but I'm not promising you a title."

"Verne," I said. "Quit worrying about your title. If you just open the door to me, to let me do my thing and get over and pay me fair, we'll be fine."

He said, "That's a deal," so I went to work for the AWA in 1968. I ended up staying all of that year and most of 1969.

It was a change in climate, but summers in Minneapolis were gorgeous, and we loved the winters. People were actually more active in the winter, and business was better. Initially, we lived in Christmas Lake, in Excelsior, Minnesota.

Verne Gagne was another challenging guy, a promotional genius in many ways, but he didn't want to be bothered with the details. Verne knew where he wanted the big picture, though, and he was great at keeping things on that course. He had Wally Karbo, a great help to him in the office in terms of keeping an eye on those details, and great people working on his television programs.

One huge thing I learned from Verne, which I applied to my own promotional experience later, was something he had learned from Jim Barnett. Barnett was a powerful promoter in the NWA, although he stayed behind the scenes. Barnett taught Gagne the importance of building personal relationships with the managers of the stations that carried his TV shows. Those relationships would keep you on the air when there were complaints about your show's content, issues with advertisers or some other problem. And Verne was really smooth about building those relationships. He'd take them hunting and fishing, and believe it or not, Verne Gagne was a great partyer.

In the ring, Verne had "Crusher" Reggie Lisowski, a tremendously gifted person. You would look at him and think he was limited because he was just a gimmick, but he could get a match out of anybody. Verne also had "Mad Dog" Maurice Vachon, whose interviews were so intense and ferocious that he was always effective. Verne had the tag team of Larry Hennig and Harley Race — Race could fly like Stevens, while Hennig was a 320-pound powerhouse, so they made for a great contrast.

Verne also brought in Dick Beyer, The Destroyer, put him under a different mask and called him Doctor X. Beyer was fantastic. I teamed for a while with his brother-in-law, Billy Red Lyons.

To me, Billy was one of those great catalysts, like Jim Hady or Ted DiBiase. He could make every match great. He maybe wouldn't stand on his own to be the guy drawing the money, but you would always want him in the match because he could execute. Later he made a great team with Red Bastien, who was the flashy one, while Billy set the tone.

Also during this time, I wrestled in St. Louis, as Doctor Scarlet. It was the only time in my career that I worked under a mask. Saint Louis promoter Sam Muchnick called Verne about me coming in. He wanted me under a mask and didn't want anybody to know. I stayed at a separate hotel from the other wrestlers, and Bill Longson would pick me up and take me to the arena, so no one knew it was me.

It was a full outfit — the most confining thing I ever wore. They also didn't want me using any of my big moves, or anything I was used to doing, so the people or the other wrestlers wouldn't know who I was.

I always thought Sam ran Saint Louis backward. He certainly had his finger on the pulse of that town, but everything moved so slowly. It took so long to get somewhere, and I didn't like the pace, plus I felt that, if I got myself on top, I should get to be on top every week, and it didn't work that way there.

I hated the outfit so much that I came up with a way to get out of it, and they went for it. This was my idea: I was someone whom world champion Kiniski was so afraid of that I had to wear a mask to get at him, but before my match with him I'd unmask and show him and everyone who I was. It caught on like a million bucks, but then they had a stupid finish where I would be hurt and get carried out. I said, "You have got to be kidding me."

Sam said, "Well, Eduoard Carpentier did it —"

"Well, I'm not Carpentier. He could get sympathy on a deal like that because he was much smaller! But I'm six foot three, 300 pounds, and I'm not going down like that!"

The same psychology wouldn't work. For Carpentier, it got sympathy. For a big, tough guy like me, it wouldn't — it would just mean I wasn't tough.

They even sent Lou Thesz down to talk to me. In addition to being a great world champion for years, he was often a "policeman," but he didn't always rely on roughing someone up. Many times he'd play on his reputation and his long-time position in the industry to be a good influence on your decision.

I said, "Lou, did they actually send you to talk to me? What the shit? I mean, Lou, are you worried about what I'm going to do? You've known me since I got into this business. Are you worried? Is Kiniski worried? Get the big, fucking Polack down here."

"Well, Bill, what are you going to do?"

"Fuck him! I'm gonna beat him! I'm gonna take the title! Tell Muchnick I'm taking the title, and that big, dumbass Polack can't stop me, and he knows it!"

I let him chew on that for a second, but then I told him, "Shit, Lou, you know I'd never do that! You know how much I like Gene Kiniski. That would be like me saying I wanted to kick *your* ass. I mean, you've been 'Mr. Thesz' to me since the day we met. I just don't like the office's bullshit."

I snuck down to Gene's dressing room and asked, "Are you worried, you big, fuckin' Polack?"

"No, Bill, no, I'm not worried!"

"Gosh, Gene, we're friends! You straightened out my mess in Vancouver for me. I've eaten dinner with you and your wife. I love you both. I've stayed at your house."

"But, Bill, what are you going to do? They told me you laid out a finish?"

Eventually, I gave him the finish I wanted to do, and it went fine, as I discussed earlier.

Saint Louis was where I met a man who would have a tremendous influence on me professionally. Florida owner Eddie Graham introduced himself to me backstage one night as I prepared to go to the ring. I was in full Doctor Scarlet gear, and even Eddie, one of Sam's fellow NWA promoters, didn't know who I was.

He said, "So, do I know you?"

I said, "No, but I know you."

"What do you know about me?"

"I know you're the thievingest promoter in the South," I said, referring to his reputation for not making payoffs to the wrestlers that were as good as they should have been. Wrestlers always thought promoters were screwing them on money. Of course, they had no real understanding of the "cost of doing business," with TV productions, air times, building rents and commission taxes, not to mention all the ancillary expenses.

Shortly after Doctor Scarlet's career ended, Verne and I got into a couple of disagreements. One was over me going to Japan. He booked me into Los Angeles for a show rivaling one promoted by Charlie Moto, the guy who booked me into Japan in the first place.

I told Verne not to book me there, but he said, "You're working for me."

I said, "It's one match! You're not going to make or break in L.A. off of one match. Just don't insult the guy."

He insisted, so I told him to kiss my ass. I called Moto to tell him about it, but the first thing Moto said was "You son of a bitch! I see you're working L.A. against me! If you're booked in L.A., I'm canceling you in Japan!"

"Well, you slope-headed, squint-eyed, Jap son of a bitch, I was calling to tell you that I just told Gagne to kiss my ass, and you pull the same shit on me? *Fuck you!* Stick Japan up your ass! And I'll be in L.A.!"

Again, the wrestling business has never been politically correct, and if you were in an argument the first things that came out after all the profanity were ethnic slurs. Still, one of my dearest friends for thirty years was Hiro Matsuda, a Japanese man of tremendous character and principle. This was just Moto and me having it out over the phone, and I worked in Japan twice for Moto and got along with him fairly well.

But now I was out of a job in two places, but I told Verne I'd work L.A. I worked the show, and then Moto called and said they wanted me in Japan anyway, and when he did that I knew they really wanted me, so I doubled the price. And Verne didn't want to lose me anyway, because I was one of his biggest attractions.

I still have a note from Bob Luce, the longtime Chicago promoter who worked with Verne, writing about how excited he was with my success among the fans there. The letter was dated March 20, 1969, and Luce wrote,

> Cowboy, Baby!
>
> If my uncanny instinct for "smelling" big box-office material and the mail response I've been receiving and reports of the big impact you made Tuesday nite are not true barometers that your star [here he drew a star around the word and colored it red] is once again on the ascension in Chicago, then a cat doesn't have an ass!
> Prepare yourself, Big Bill, for one helluva house come April 26th!!
> Be here early, so you get in!
>
> "Big" Bob of Chicago

Verne and I also disagreed over him booking himself against me in Minneapolis. I told him it was a mistake because I wasn't going to put him over as a babyface. "You fucking egomaniac," I told the former Olympian and NCAA amateur wrestling champion from the University of Minnesota. "You're only doing this because you've got your friends all telling you that you can't beat me, and you can't. Fuck you. I'm not going to put you over. I'm out of here." Don't get me wrong — I respected Verne, but you had to stand up to him.

He said, "You're wrong. This is not an ego thing. I've looked at this for a year — you and I will draw like hell!"

"You're so full of shit, Verne! This is because of your cocktail circuit friends, plus I'm the one who's been drawing all the money."

He promised it would draw and even said, "I'm so confident in it that you can design the finishes, as long as you don't take the title. I'll do whatever you want, and we'll get as many matches out of it as you want to get."

Well, *that* was a vote of confidence and a real challenge. I mapped it out, and we had a series of matches in each big city. Verne ended up turning heel in our matches, even though he also remained a babyface. He was smaller than me but came off as the heel because of some of his tactics, which made sense — a champion *should* do whatever he can to protect his title. Verne was a fantastic worker and a great ring general. And he really knew how to challenge and intrigue me.

BECOMING an OWNER

In 1970, soon after my series with Gagne, Leroy McGuirk called me, extremely distressed about the shape his territory was in. I agreed to go back, but not just as a wrestler. I would buy into the territory, which covered Oklahoma, Arkansas, Louisiana and a few towns in Mississippi, Missouri and Texas.

Leroy got scared about having me as his only partner, because I didn't have experience, so he wanted Gagne and Fritz Von Erich to buy in also. The deal was that I would get five percent, Leroy would get fifty percent, while Fritz and Verne would divide the remaining forty-five percent.

I told Verne and Fritz, "You think I'm going to go down there, do all the work and miss out on the main-event money I'm making here, to go down to the back end of the world and put up with all that? No way!"

Verne said, "Either you're in, or you're out."

I said, "Fuck you, I'm out."

I gave Verne my notice and then called Leroy and told him, "Look, I'll work out my deal with you when I get there — but I'm coming home to be your partner."

I started making some calls, booking talent. When Verne called me on it, I said, "Yeah, I'm booking talent there. Fuck you — you're out."

Verne and Fritz knew a good thing, so they met and agreed to make me a full partner. The next thing I knew I had seventeen percent, Verne and Fritz each had twenty percent, and Leroy had the remaining thirty-three percent. Leroy sold the other ten percent to Danny Hodge, still his top star.

I'd been excited about my first experience as a part owner, but Oklahoma was nothing but problems. The weather was horrible, the trips were horrible, and the office politics were horrible.

Leroy was difficult because he was blind and, in my opinion, alcoholic and paranoid. He had so many wonderful qualities that had been destroyed over the course of his life. His parents had divorced, which had left him with very conflicted feelings about them. He lost his sight in one eye because of an accident when he was young, but he worked to become a two-time NCAA wrestling champion at OSU, known as Oklahoma A&M when he attended school. He was also editor of the college newspaper.

Years later, while representing the NWA as the world's junior heavyweight champion, and as Sam Avey's top star, Leroy lost his other eye while in Little Rock, Arkansas. They always blamed a car wreck, but I was told by more than one source I considered reliable that he'd lost his eye in a bar fight said to have been instigated by Bob Clay, another wrestler and Leroy's friend, when a guy sucker-punched Leroy. Shards from his glasses had gone into his eye. After that, he had a hard-on about life, which made him difficult to deal with. I tried to treat him like a father-figure, but I never knew where I stood with him.

But because Leroy was always trying to tear things down, and his stooges were always trying to tear me down to get themselves in good with him, I learned to be prepared, to know where I was going and how to explain it. This stress and backstabbing really prepared me for this business, because I had to figure out their swerves and know where I wanted everything to proceed way in advance so that these detours didn't stop me. I also had to slowly get rid of a lot of those stooges.

With some of them, it was easy. The ones I wanted to get rid of who were junior heavyweights I'd put them over Danny Hodge for the world junior heavyweight title. Hodge wanted that title back, and he'd kill those guys! He'd just guzzle them in the ring. I didn't have to fire any of them

— I just put them in a program with Hodge. The first match after they won would be sixty minutes, no falls. The next would be ninety minutes, no falls. Hodge was a machine. He could go ninety minutes, and it wouldn't even bother him. For these other guys, going seven nights a week for ninety minutes with Hodge was enough to send them packing.

I'll never forget Sputnik Monroe's run with Hodge. I put them in Greenville, Mississippi, three weeks in a row. Some of the fans there liked Sputnik and cheered him, even though he was the heel. Danny got really hot when they booed him and cheered Sputnik. So Hodge killed him — he tied Sputnik in knots and was so stiff with him that poor Sputnik didn't get a single inch of any match with him. Sputnik could barely drag himself to the back after their last match, but he made it to Leroy's office, where he dumped the belt at Leroy's feet and said, "Fuck you! Here's this belt! I'm outta here!"

And I liked Sputnik, but at times and due to the "old politics there" he could be a troublemaker. And at that time, I needed him gone. However, I'll always have a close spot in my heart for him.

The roster made some big steps after I got there, though. Verne and Fritz were supposed to supply talent, so Verne sent Billy Red Lyons down there, and I took Dutch Savage from Minneapolis too, although Verne didn't have anything to do with it. I also took Dale Hey from Gagne. Verne was using him only as a job guy, but I saw him as talent, and he came in to fill an opening I suddenly had as a result of a clash with another of Leroy's would-be stooges.

Jack Donovan and his wife (and ringside valet), Verne Bottoms, were two of Leroy's mainstays and had a lot of sway with him, but they also caused a lot of trouble as they tried to run the territory for their own benefit (as would almost anyone who could). Now, I would never let a woman run my matches, and I certainly wasn't going to cater to Donovan, so they were the first two I had to remove. Jack complained about every finish if it didn't go exactly for him, and his idea of a great finish was to pull this phony stuff where he'd win after Verne hit his opponents with her purse. My solution for him was simple. I booked myself with him right away. When I laid out the finish, I said, "Now, we're not using Verne in the finish, and if she hits me with her purse, I'll slap the shit out of her." Of course, I had no real intention of having to do that, but I told Jack, "I'm going to beat you, one-two-three, right in the middle, but if you want to design the exact finish, you can."

I waited a few minutes and then went to Leroy's office because I knew

Jack would go crying right to Leroy. I took Hodge with me because he was a partner, and I wanted him to see how things went. I got to the office, and there was Jack Donovan. I said, "What's the problem?"

Leroy said, "Well, Bill, Jack doesn't like what you're laying out for him."

"Leroy," I said, "I don't give a damn if he likes it or not. That's the way it is."

"Well, but Jack's been with me a long time."

"Well, Leroy, shit changes."

To their faces, Leroy couldn't lay down the law, but Jack was one of the main reasons he'd called me home.

Jack said, "Well, I'm not going to do it. I see what you're doing. There's a new sheriff in town and all that. Well, I'm not doing the job. I'm leaving."

I said, "Are you leaving before or after our match in the ring?"

"I'm leaving before!"

"Let me tell you something, Jack. You're going to do a fucking job tonight. Do you want to do it in this office, or do you want to do it in the ring? In the ring, it'll be a work. In this office, I'm going to beat the fucking shit out of you. Which do you want?"

Leroy was about to flip, and Hodge was just standing there taking this all in.

Jack said, "I'll do it in the ring," but he wasn't happy about it.

I said, "OK, we'll do it in the ring. You try to leave the building, though, and I'll be on you like stink on shit."

We got through that night, and I went over in the match, just like I'd said, and he gave his notice. He was going to work through his notice but then broke his ankle in a match in Oklahoma City, so I had Dale Hey come in to fill his spot. I made him Buddy Roberts, put him with Jerry Brown and called them the Hollywood Blondes.

Buddy Roberts was a great hand. He was real box office, and his chemistry with Brown was terrific. Brown was a good worker too, but as time went by he developed some problems, and we ended up letting him go. I believe his problems had to do with substance abuse, which sure alters personalities and changed a guy who was loyal and a good worker into a real liability. I heard later he ended up in the penitentiary. We all make our choices, and then live with the consequences. It was too bad, because he was a good and reliable worker before the problem.

Fritz sent in The Spoiler and his manager, Gary Hart, a few months after I took over. I worked with them after my program with Dutch Savage. Gary was the best manager in the business and always had a ton of ideas about how to do things, but if you didn't use any of them he busted his fanny to get over whatever the plan was. The Spoiler was a big, mobile guy who was tough and really stayed on you when he worked with you — perfect for my kind of matches. I really enjoyed working with him, and with Hart involved the chemistry was awesome! Gary also became a good friend and one of my "creative consultants and confidants."

But there I was, in one of the worst population centers in the world, with not a lot of talent. We started hammering Dutch Savage over on TV to get him ready, and he was a trooper.

We had some minor problems with an exciting rookie at the time, Dusty Rhodes, who'd become a tremendous asset for me later and someone I'd work with extensively. I got mad at him and chased him off TV in Oklahoma City. He was carrying on and breaking furniture on the set, which was squarely against my rules. Literally, I chased him right out of the ring and out of the TV studio. And he could really move! He might not have looked like it later on, but he was a great athlete — a good football player and a phenomenal baseball player.

One talent change I had to make was the longtime announcer, Danny Williams. To this day, I count Danny as a good friend, but he'd come to the point where he was a bigger star than any of the wrestlers on the show. He was a superstar personality on Channel 4, which produced our show, and that was fine except that he wanted to outshine the wrestlers and had been allowed to do so for years. He wanted to focus attention on himself, even though I don't think he realized it or the cornball effect of when he and Leroy would sit there and just shoot the shit on TV. He wouldn't build things the way I wanted them built, and I had no control over Danny. I needed an announcer I totally controlled.

My solution was to move the production to Shreveport, Louisiana, since Danny was an employee of that Oklahoma City station. Because of the extra travel, he wouldn't be available. I explained to Leroy that we needed to move because Shreveport was more centrally located in our territory, which it was. It was an easy way to let Danny out without insulting him.

I brought in Boyd Pierce to replace Williams. Boyd had been an announcer in Texas for years. He was corny as hell and country as hell, but he was totally loyal and would do the commentary however I needed it done to get things across the right way. Boyd wasn't the most polished announcer, but he *really* loved the business and the guys. And he was a wealthy guy — he didn't *have* to do anything!

One hard thing about announcing was that Leroy wanted to do some

My Aunt, Jimmie Sue, and me, a young Billy Watts.

Putnam City High School football program. Coach Joe Garrison was a positive influence.

Ushering my grandmother, Suzanne Moritz, at Aunt Jimmie Sue's wedding (age 12). I loved my grandmother dearly, and she was always there for me.

THE UNIVERSITY OF OKLAHOMA

NORMAN · OKLAHOMA

January 7, 1957

Mr. William F. Watts, Jr.
5944 N. W. 41st Street
Oklahoma City, Oklahoma

Dear Bill:

I want to tell you how happy we are that you have decided to
attend the University of Oklahoma next fall. Our coaches
are very proud of you and they join me in extending to you
a very warm welcome to our school.

We want you to feel free to contact us at any time concerning
your relationship with the University of Oklahoma. The Athletic
Office phone number is JEfferson 4-6736, and any of the coaches
on the staff will be happy to assist you at any time. We would
also be happy to hear from you from time to time in order that
we might keep in touch with you concerning your future plans.

Again, let me tell you how happy we are about your decision.
I am sure you will find the University of Oklahoma a very fine
institution, one in which you can express yourself fully in
academics as well as in athletics. I will be looking forward
to seeing and talking with you.

Sincerely yours,

C. B. Wilkinson
Director of Athletics

CBW:ch

A letter from Bud Wilkinson about attending OU on a football scholarship.

Air Force ROTC summer camp jet trainer orientation at Big Springs, Texas, after my junior year at OU.

1962 publicity photo with other Indianapolis Warriors — I'm driving.

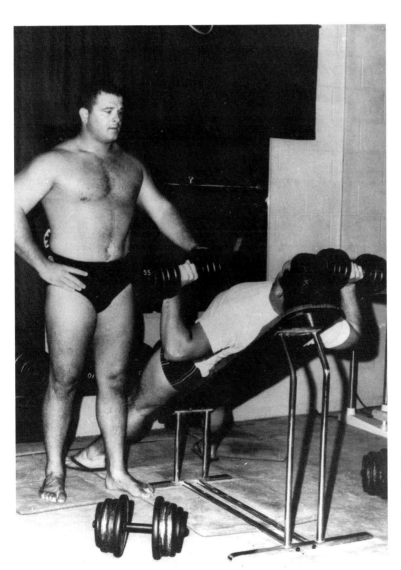

Supervising my brother Bob's workout at Super's Gym in New Jersey (mid-'60s).

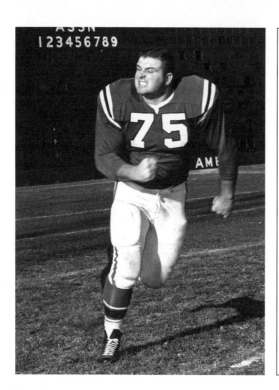

Running as an Indianapolis Warrior.

Wrestling program card for main event in Little Rock – versus World Champion, Lou Thesz. Just in my second year, I was already receiving top billing.

From my first wrestling publicity photos, demonstrating the "standing guillotine hold" on friend and college teammate, Dale Lewis – a two-time NCAA champion (Indianapolis, 1962).

"Bruiser" Bill Watts holding up the Texas State Championship belt I won from "Sailor" Art Thomas in Houston (1963).

Danny Hodge, World Junior Heavyweight Champion: my friend, and pound-for-pound, the greatest wrestler I've ever met.

Wild Red Berry, who discovered and mentored me for the "big time."

A publicity photo featuring Lou Thesz and, yes, Kirk Douglas.

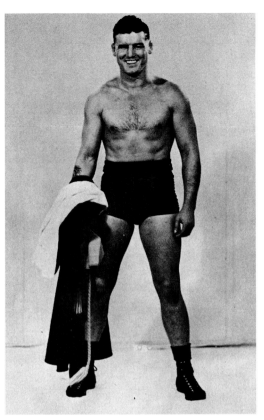

Leroy McGuirk, World Junior Heavyweight Champion – before the loss of his second eye left him blind. A very important person in my life.

In California (1966), with Pepper Gomez and Joe Scarpa (later Chief Jay Strongbow), who was also my tag partner and another fine mentor.

Crusher Lisowski, clowning around in my hat and jacket (Minneapolis, 1968): a true superstar and occasional tag partner.

Jack Brisco: friend, college champion (at OSU), and NWA World Champ – a great athlete, a great "pro," he became an instrumental figure in my life.

of it. Here you had Leroy, blind, calling action in the ring that he couldn't see! Eventually, we eased him into appearances at the beginning of the show, where he could appear as "The Kind Mr. McGuirk." After that intro, during the first commercial break, we took him off the air. He was happy, and so was I, because then we could do the show the right way and still get him airtime to stroke his ego.

One good thing about being in my home area was that I eventually grew closer to my own parents. My mother moved nearby, and my father actually worked for me in the office after I broke away from Leroy and went on my own. It took some doing, and it really wasn't until 1984 that we healed things up.

I wasn't physically at home as much as you might think. We ran two towns a night. For one crew, Monday was Tulsa; Tuesday was Little Rock; Wednesday was Springfield; Thursday was Wichita Falls; Friday was Oklahoma City; and Saturday was Joplin, Missouri. The other crew worked Shreveport on Monday; Monroe, Louisiana, on Tuesday; Baton Rouge on Wednesday; Jackson or Vicksburg, Mississippi, or New Orleans, Louisiana, on Thursday; and Lafayette, Louisiana, on Friday. On Saturday, we did TV in Oklahoma City.

Then we had Loranger and Houma, both in Louisiana, every week on Saturday and Sunday nights. Economically, it was hard to justify running these towns every week. But the Louisiana Athletic Commission, under Emile Bruneau's direction, wouldn't allow a promotion to exploit larger markets while ignoring smaller ones. The entire state had to be covered. Later, when I had proven myself, we could be a bit more selective — as long as we took good care of state's entire constituency. Sometimes, as we changed talent on the cards, we had to book a guy in New Orleans and then have him travel to Oklahoma City on Friday — a brutal trip. Even worse, we sometimes had guys booked in Loranger and Houma on Saturday and Sunday nights, then in Tulsa on Monday night. The guys would essentially leave towns immediately after their matches and drive straight through, arriving just in time to shower, shave and wrestle. It was even worse my first winter back home, because we had horribly cold weather, and the roads were often covered with snow or freezing rain.

The NWA promoters also interviewed me during this time about becoming NWA world champion, but once I told them my thoughts on it I was pretty well out of the running. I disagreed vehemently with how they promoted the champion. I said I wanted to go in and be put over the first two times I was in each territory to get established and then have programs with their top-drawing wrestlers from that point forward. I would not do one-hour broadways every night, especially in the smaller towns, but would do other, close finishes that would draw money. That wasn't going to work for them because the NWA world champion did sixty- or ninety-minute draws every night. My cardiovascular or aerobic system wasn't optimal for these types of matches. I wasn't about to do sixty minutes every night. It didn't challenge me. I liked to set the tone and then have a fabulous finish.

I've sent Jack Brisco and Dory Funk Jr. in hour broadways for the title and sent Harley Race out to do a few when he was champion. But when I did, it was always a special situation. I used sixty-minute draws only to showcase the legitimacy of the athletes involved.

The NWA required each champion to post a $25,000 bond for the title to ensure that he'd be willing to drop it the right way when the members decided it was time. The champion would go from territory to territory defending the title against the top guy in each place. Leroy and I put up the money for Harley Race to first become champion. He was panicking in 1973 because he had the shot at it but didn't have the money to put up. His word to us proved to be good as gold, because he paid us back. I thought Harley was a great champion because he didn't care — he'd go all night long if you wanted him to.

I also thought Dory Funk Jr. was a great champion, but I thought Terry Funk liked to clown around too much in the ring for a world's champion. I liked Terry, but I thought his style wasn't right for the world title. I always thought Dory was a better champion, but Terry was a better character. The guy Terry won it from, Jack Brisco, *was* a great world champion. Terry was great in gimmick matches. I just thought the world's title needed to have a certain class that elevated the sport.

Years earlier, when I was back east, Sam Muchnick and Vince McMahon tried to arrange a big match between Lou Thesz and Bruno Sammartino. They could never agree on a finish, though. It wouldn't have been a good match. Thesz was made to be world champion. He was class inside and outside the ring and a great athlete, but he had a very distinct style. Sammartino's style was so much more slam-bang, while Thesz did more serious wrestling. I know they wrestled before Bruno became WWWF champ in 1963, but I believe that their styles would really have clashed and that the match wouldn't have been a masterpiece. Their personalities might also have clashed. Bruno wasn't one to take any stuff from anyone, and at times Lou could be a bit overbearing in the ring, certainly even forcing his style on the match.

Thesz could be temperamental too, if he didn't like you. I've seen him pick guys apart. He squashed Louis Tillet like a bug in Corpus Christi, Texas, because he didn't think Louis deserved to be there. Well, that wasn't Louis's fault; Louis didn't book himself against Lou — the office did. Louie was a good draw everywhere he worked then. The champion shouldn't get mad at the guy he's working, because the guy didn't have anything to do with putting himself in the match. Although Tillet was a very good worker, he wasn't a legitimate wrestler and didn't have a body that looked like much. Even worse, for whatever reason, Lou just didn't seem to respect him. I don't know what his heat with Tillet was over, but I seem to remember that they became friends later on.

As I recall, Sammartino resented Thesz for just this type of stuff and would have been more than ready to really demonstrate his feelings. Bruno wasn't a technical wrestler, but his power was awesome. He had great endurance and a great heart, and at the time he weighed 285 pounds to Thesz's 220.

But every wrestler had his own idiosyncrasies. Overall, Lou was a great spokesman and representative for our sport. He represented class and was the one wrestler all the newspaper guys would talk to because he was classy, and he could really wrestle a bit. He was a real asset to the business.

Because of the way he worked, Lou was one of those guys who was better with the world's championship than without it. The belt elevated him, even though he elevated the championship.

Lou also had a sense of humor. One night his gear didn't make it to the airport with him, and he borrowed my boots. This was before I wore cowboy boots into the ring, but there was still a considerable difference between my feet and his. Lou was pigeon-toed anyway, so he exaggerated it and acted as if he was tripping over his own toes in my boots, which were two sizes bigger than his.

By the second half of 1972, we were doing OK, but I was becoming depressed about the daily struggles of working with Leroy. No matter how much money I made for him, no matter how well we were doing, Leroy wasn't happy. When you're in a position where you have to defend your actions all the time, you start to lose faith in yourself. So it was good timing when I got a call from Eddie Graham asking for my help in one of the biggest wrestling wars ever. It started in Atlanta.

THE BATTLE OF ATLANTA

For years, Paul Jones, Buddy Fuller and Ray Gunkel co-promoted Atlanta, with booker Tom Renesto reporting to them. Fuller and Gunkel didn't get along, so Fuller stayed away from the promotion even though he was part owner. Like most promotions in the country, the Atlanta group was affiliated with the NWA, a coalition of promoters who shared a common world champion.

Buddy hung out with Florida promoter Eddie Graham a lot. Lester Welch, a relative of Fuller (in the business, they are often called Fullers — all of them — even though Lester's last name was Welch), also owned a piece of Florida, so Fuller and Welch traded stock to make Fuller part owner in Florida and Welch part owner in Georgia.

Gunkel didn't like Fuller, but he *hated* Welch. They had a long history together, and neither was a very lovable character. Ray decided to take over the territory, and he kicked his partners out.

Ray Gunkel had all the talent except one wrestler. He also had booker

Tom Renesto as he prepared to start a new group. His problem was that his ex-partners were the ones with the TV contract to air wrestling on Channel 17, the station that would later become SuperStation TBS, a cornerstone of Ted Turner's cable empire. They also maintained the NWA affiliation. Gunkel became an "outlaw," running opposition.

He was still putting things together when he went to a show in Savannah to talk to that city's promoter. He wrestled a match there, had a heart attack and died in the locker room afterward.

Ann Gunkel, a former Las Vegas showgirl and a real looker, was Ray's widow, and she decided to continue with his plans. I think she saw it as her way of taking the whole thing over for herself. Ann didn't have Ray's TV problem. She knew Ted Turner well and could contact him and get on TV. Ann was an exceptional-looking woman, so you can imagine what the rumors about that relationship were. I do know, from personal experience, that she could call him and set up a meeting anytime she wanted — and she later bragged to me of her "intimacy" with Ted, which gave her certain "bargaining power." Gunkel's former partners had the contract, so Turner put both of them on TV; the two rival companies ended up with sixty-minute shows that ran back to back every Saturday on Channel 17. Both had great ratings, so it really benefited Turner Broadcasting.

Eddie Graham flew me in to appear on an NWA show, but what I didn't know was that Eddie had been keeping tabs on me. Eddie always had an eye for talent. He was the guy who discovered Jack Brisco. Brisco was just a middle-of-the-road guy at best on the cards he wrestled on before meeting Eddie. His talent hadn't been developed, and he was very limited in exposure when Eddie found him, brought him into Florida and started grooming him. Eddie was the one who saw his talent. Brisco, of course, became a great world's champion because of his ability and because he got the chance and the personal mentoring by Graham.

Jack kept telling Eddie, "The guy you need to get down here is Bill Watts."

That first show in Georgia was like working in a vacuum because nobody knew the stars. Some of the top guys in the country — Dory Funk Jr., Hiro Matsuda, Fritz Von Erich and Jack Brisco, among others — were on the card, but we were regional promotions then, and these stars hadn't spent time in Georgia, so the people didn't know them well or how to react to them. The fans just sat there.

The only wrestler who stayed with the old Georgia group was Bob Armstrong. They booked me to go over him that first night, but the people knew Bob. When I saw their reaction to Bob and how over he was, I knew that the best thing for the promotion would be for me to put him over. I changed the match while we were in the ring. We tore the place down, and he beat me, right in the middle. I wasn't planning on coming back anyway — but I didn't know that Eddie Graham had plans for me.

Armstrong became a friend and was a reliable performer. Later his sons worked for me too. They exhibited the best of the traditions of growing up in a wrestling family and were good performers.

Eddie was watching all of this, and he and I talked after the match. "Bill," he said, "I've been following your career. I think you're one of the most talented guys in the business. I want you to come to Florida and work for me. I want you to become a partner in the office."

That sounded great to me, because Jack Brisco had told me all about Eddie — the real story, not the perception I had when I met him in St. Louis as Dr. Scarlet. "This guy's a genius," Jack had said.

I flew to Florida because Eddie wanted to spend a day with me. We had lunch with Jack, and then Eddie let me watch a booking session with him, Leo Garibaldi and Louis Tillet, his two bookers. Jack was selling out everywhere. This was before he won the world title in 1973, and he was over so well all you had to do was put Jack in there with a good heel, and it was like Bruno in the Northeast — money in the bank! But all Leo and Louis could talk about to Eddie was how they wanted to beat Jack.

Eddie kept saying, "Well, guys, wait a minute. What are we gaining by beating him?"

They said, "Well, we'll get heat on the heel."

"But," Eddie replied, "we're selling out with him everywhere. Why should we beat Jack, when we're selling out with him, to build up someone who's not going to draw as well?" In other words, Eddie wanted the heels to deserve their heat by getting over on the usual situations and on their own merits, without sacrificing his star to try to build them up.

Jack had already told me that Tillet had used a blade on him, in one of the few matches where Jack had ever bled. Louis had cut too deep and long, and Jack had bled everywhere. He'd threatened to kill Louis, and Eddie had almost fired Louis over it.

After the meeting, Eddie said, "Well, what did you think of the interplay in the office?"

I whistled and said, "Man! You have a lot more patience than I would."

"What do you mean?"

"You've got the golden goose, and those two fucking idiots are trying to talk you into killing it, and you're sitting there trying to tell them why they shouldn't kill it. I think, after the third time of telling them, I'd have told them to shut the fuck up and get the hell out of my office."

Again my words weren't socially correct, nor did they represent my true opinion of those guys. I later worked closely with both Louis and Leo — there was friction from certain jealousy, but that was rampant anyway, especially if someone felt you got his job.

Eddie started to get tickled and said, "Is that the way you see it?"

"That's the way I see it."

He said, "Well, that's why I want you here, but I need you in Georgia first. But don't worry — I'm sending Leo up to work with you. Georgia is where I'm having to fight the war right now. If they win there, they'll come to Florida next. You'll be my right hand in Georgia, but you are coming here as soon as possible."

I was so unhappy in Oklahoma that, even with Garibaldi as part of the deal, I didn't have to think hard about Eddie's offer. He also bought ten percent of the Georgia territory and gave it to me. He gave Brisco five percent as a wedding gift and gave Tim Woods (a big star as the masked Mr. Wrestling) and Buddy Colt smaller pieces of the office. Over the years, that ten percent was a real gold mine.

Lester ran the office, but I was Eddie's point man. Paul Jones (the "old-timer" wrestler-turned-promoter, not the wrestler by that name in the 1970s) by this time was just a figurehead — an extremely nice, well-respected elder in our business.

I told Eddie, "OK, but I'm only going to be here Tuesdays through Saturdays. I want to fly home every weekend."

He said that was fine, and they kept Garibaldi as the official booker, although I ran the TV and was in charge of the matches.

I saw my family only two days a week, but that was par for the course in wrestling. Even when I was in Oklahoma with Leroy, just prior to going to Georgia, I was gone three to four days a week. I eventually bought an airplane and learned to fly in order to be home more and not have to do all those trips by car.

Eddie wanted me to try to make things agreeable to Leo, and Leo got to think he was still the booker, but I had the say because I was an owner. Lester Welch, the managing partner, would do what I wanted to do. Paul Jones, by that time in his life, wasn't a big contributor on a daily basis, but he had a tremendous amount of goodwill with the fans and local media. He also had a lot of sympathy since Gunkel had tried to "steal" his business.

Leo, though, fought me on everything, which turned out to be good because sometimes, through adversity, you can come up with a better idea. Sometimes the stuff he argued for made more sense than my original idea. I was flexible enough to do what was best, but we were going to do what I wanted to do on TV. His not being a "yes man" was a blessing in disguise because that conflict, or competition, sharpened my skills.

Number one, I was going to get myself over, because I knew I could draw money, and I knew I could count on myself. Because of their ownership stakes, I knew I could get Jack Brisco, Tim Woods and Buddy Colt to come in whenever I needed them.

Woods and I had matches that I don't think were especially good, but he was so over with the people that it didn't matter. We had such different styles, with my power and brawling and his smooth, scientific style. Often, even if styles conflicted, the box-office appeal was still exceptional, but conflicting styles could make maintaining an ongoing series difficult.

Woods was a great amateur, although one time he tried to tell me how he'd tested Danny Hodge, and I just looked at him and said, "Tim, who are you shittin'?" He just smiled, because we both knew he was full of it. But Tim was the hottest star in Georgia during this era and could draw with anyone we put him with.

When he started working more in Florida and less in Georgia, we added Mr. Wrestling II into the mix, and eventually he became even hotter than Tim was. Wrestling II was Johnny Walker, a middle-of-the-road guy who had never really caught on anywhere to that point, but he was hell on wheels under that mask. It became his starring role, and he made the most of it.

And Bob Armstrong remained strong with the people. At the first wrestling show at the Omni, they had a Cadillac tournament. This was Lester Welch's brainchild. We had this Cadillac as the grand prize, and every time I was in town I'd drive it, so everybody who saw me thought for sure I was going to win the tournament. Well, the gimmick with the Cadillac was that, sure, you won, but you had to buy the Cadillac from the promotion at cost. Of course, we got the car at a heck of a good price in the first place because the dealer was getting all of this advertising. Armstrong, a local guy and the only guy who stayed with us through all the defections, was Lester's pick to win the Cadillac. I said, "You're right — he should." We shot an angle with me, as a heel, getting eliminated early in the tournament by Mr. Wrestling II.

The finals ended up in the Omni as Bob Armstrong versus another really great guy, my tag partner at the time, Bobby Duncum. What a great guy Duncum was — just a big, tough, Texas son of a gun! Lester wanted Bob to come out on top, but only after Duncum busted him open hardway. Lester was a big believer in hardways — the Tennessee territories where he had come up thrived on them. I'd seen them work too.

They had done one in Oklahoma where the masked Assassins (Jody Hamilton and Tom Renesto) busted open Grizzly Smith, who teamed with Luke Brown as The Kentuckians. They busted Grizzly open pretty good, and it blew the territory wide open because people were able to see Griz after the match with the stitches and the swelling. They knew he wasn't some faker just pretending to be hit.

I was never a fan of taking those things — heck, they *hurt!* Plus the damage a hardway did to your face and head was unreal. But Lester was a big believer in them, and all those old-timers knew how to bust you hardway with one or two shots.

The idea was to show how tough Bob was by having him come back to win after taking all this punishment. The only problem was that we'd forgotten to school Bobby Duncum on how to do it right. Duncum tried, but he couldn't split Armstrong open. This big son of a gun teed off on Bob's head a few shots, and it was turning Bob a complete flip, but it wasn't busting him.

To bust a guy, you need to have him where his head can't move. You need to have his head on the mat and then drive down and hit over the bone under the eyebrow to bust the skin. You hit him anywhere else around his head and you aren't going to hardway him — you are just going to bruise the heck out of the guy. And if the guy is standing up, his head is going to snap back from the punch, and you aren't going to hardway him. It's just going to hurt! And it can really hurt your hand or even break a knuckle.

Duncum ended up pummeling poor Bob to the point where Bob had a detached retina and a brain concussion after it was over. As I recall, they finally got a gaffe out and cut Bob to get blood that way. Bob was also a firefighter and had to take two or three days off from that job. He was laid up with his concussion, but it got him over as a tough guy.

A few nights later Duncum and I teamed up against Bob and Mr. Wrestling II. By now, the Omni angle with Duncum and Bob had been shown on the SuperStation in Atlanta, plus all over Columbus TV, so when we went to Columbus the joint was packed. I sent the finish over to the babyfaces' dressing room. The finish involved Armstrong getting some juice before they made a comeback and got disqualified for ignoring the referee and continuing to beat on Duncum and me.

Ralph Freed, who worked for Columbus promoter Fred Ward, brought back a message that Armstrong didn't want to get juice because his head was sore, stitched and about the size of a melon.

I thought, "Well, damn, the people have just seen how this guy just got out of the hospital. They know he's stitched up. If we don't get juice on him, then it's bullshit!"

Ralph said, "But his head really hurts, and I think he's right — he shouldn't have to do it."

"I'm tellin' you — I want him to get juice!"

But Fred and Ralph, his son-in-law, said they weren't going to make him do it.

I finally said, "OK, fine."

We went to the ring and were working fine. At one point, I backed Armstrong into our corner and gave Duncum the high sign. Duncum grabbed his arms and locked him in there, held him against the turnbuckles from outside the ring. With Bob unable to move, much less escape, I started picking away at the bandage covering his stitches.

I said, "You just didn't fuckin' listen to me, did you? You didn't want to get the juice with the gaffe, did you? You dumb cracker son of a bitch — who's running this damn territory — me or Fat Fuckin' Freddy [my sarcastic term for Fred Ward when I was mad at him]?"

Then I reared back with my fist and . . . *boom!* I hit him right in his stitched-up eye as hard as I could. That was a *real* hardway on top of all that sore, stitched-up mess he already had. The stitches split — heck, his *head* split! Blood was flowing everywhere, and he screamed as high a pitch as I ever heard him go.

I said, "Let him go, Duncum — I bet he'll make a fuckin' comeback now!"

And he did. He was screaming and cussing me; Wrestling II came in and was cussing me, and Duncum came in. We were just flying for them. They kicked the crap out of us! And it got Bob Armstrong over in Columbus like a million dollars.

But Fred never booked me against Bob in Columbus again — he had the hottest angle in the territory, and the dummy wouldn't book us! This was a perfect example of the local promoter leaving a lot of money on the table because he wanted to book his own matches and ignore the obvious. Due to the political situation in the wrestling war, we needed Fred and his towns, so he sometimes got away with things like this. Fortunately, his greed also kept him pliable.

Another guy I got to work with was Bobby Shane, a smaller guy but with a great mind. He was so talented, and he was Leo Garibaldi's guy, one of the wrestlers Leo wanted pushed heavily. My relationship with Leo wasn't very good at this point, so there was a natural tension between Shane and me, and it showed in everything we did together. But Bobby turned the situation to our advantage because of the way he could convey things to the viewer.

Even when Bobby was my partner, he'd make some stray remark about me, and I'd turn around and say, "You say that about me again, and I'll slap your face."

He'd cower, but then, after I walked off, he'd say, "That's what I like about Bill. He's got a lot of spirit."

And it really became something to the fans, the question of whether Bobby and I were going to cross each other. What a great interplay!

One night we had a deal where I wrestled Tim Woods in an amateur rules match, with Lou Thesz as one of the special judges, as was Bobby Shane. Well, we had Tim just wipe the mat with me. Naturally, Thesz voted for Woods, the second judge, whom the fans knew was "my judge," voted for me, and it was down to Bobby Shane to cast the tiebreaker. He was starting to waffle, and the crowd was going crazy while I glared at him. We really milked it before he finally cast his vote for me. It was a lot of fun.

One thing about dealing with the talent during this wrestling war in Georgia — if it ever got to where someone was going to get fired, he'd often just make a deal with Gunkel and go work for her. And that made sense — heck, the Georgia fans already knew who the wrestlers were, because they had the TV exposure. So that was something we always had to consider, and we hated the idea of giving up guys to the enemy, but sometimes you just had to change your talent.

One example was The Infernos, with manager J.C. Dykes. I wasn't having a problem with them, but I wanted to change directions, so I gave them their notice. They went to Lester, who rehired them! I didn't have any problem with them for doing that, because they were just doing what they needed to do to survive, but Lester should have known better.

I said, "Lester, we're not going to play this game. Hell, I hope Gunkel gets *all* our discards. Pretty soon that'll break her. They're certainly not drawing money for us anymore!"

I knew they'd draw for her for a short time, but when the newness wore off she'd be stuck with them. Lester didn't get it. Dykes and The Infernos were neat guys, but I had to do something, so I came up with an angle involving Curtis Smith, one of The Infernos. We hid him in the crowd dressed as a woman. At a crucial time in the match, he ran in and beat the heck out of the babyface. Well, that nearly caused a riot. It was also funny to see Curtis dressed up as a woman.

The next week I booked the same thing, but this time Curtis never made it into the ring. The fans spotted him, and when he made his move they just started beating the living crap out of him. I mean they kicked his ass, right there in the stands! Curtis then decided to give his notice, and his fellow Inferno (as well as J.C. Dykes) decided to go with him.

I was running the major programs and working with Eddie Graham in this unique situation, which really allowed me to learn and grow in this business. I think what impressed Eddie the most was how flexible I was when it came to booking what was best for business.

There were accusations that the NWA was an illegal monopoly, but nobody in wrestling even understood the concept of a monopoly. The NWA had been hit with an antitrust suit years before I was even on the scene. The stupid thing was they had signed a consent decree to end the case. They'd had bad representation.

Ann Gunkel later claimed that NWA members threatened guys working for her, but we never did that. Leo Garibaldi, I was told, threatened one of her guys, but that was just wrestling talk. There was no real threat — no one was going to shoot anybody or beat up anybody. Gunkel even used a job guy called "Gorilla" Watts as a swipe at me, but I took it as a compliment. We put them down badly in interviews, so that didn't bother me at all.

In fact, Georgia was where I realized that competition made wrestling better. Both companies were selling out Atlanta for a while. Our group couldn't even get into Augusta, and Savannah was nip and tuck, and we were beating them in Columbus and Macon. Lester opened up the Omni for wrestling, which was a gamble, but our success there hurt Gunkel's group in terms of perception of which promotion was really big-time.

Ann began booking some outside talent. One of those pieces of talent was my old friend Bruno Sammartino. I'd contacted him because we'd lost touch, and he told me about being booked for Gunkel. He told me what he'd heard from her about the situation, and I told him our side of it. Bruno didn't like Eddie Graham for reasons that I never really got into, but when he realized that I owned part of the office he'd be competing against he decided to do only the one scheduled appearance for Gunkel.

I didn't want to put him on the spot, so I told him, "Bruno, you do what you need to do. Your word is good, and you're already booked there, but I would appreciate it if you just made your booking and then didn't come back."

Bruno did just that because of our friendship. He had principles and integrity. Anyone who knows him knows he can't be pressured to do anything he doesn't feel is right.

Gunkel finally exhausted herself and wasn't making any money. The funny thing was she wanted to meet, to end the war, and she wasn't going to protect anybody. When they asked her how she wanted to protect her talent or her booker, her reply was "Fuck them." She agreed that the "competition" was over and that her wrestling promotion was finished.

But Lester Welch's "little head" was doing the thinking after we met with her. He took her to dinner and in trying to charm her told her all the promotional mistakes she'd made. She pumped him for information, like you'd pump a station dry. He just couldn't wait until the deal was signed, she was out, and her deal was shut down.

So the "War for Georgia" was back on, and Ann had some success for a while as she "corrected her mistakes." But it didn't last for her, and the pressure must have affected her. She got so mad at me that she once called me and told me she had $10,000 set aside to have me killed.

I really pissed her off when I said, "As good looking as you are, save your $10,000, and try fucking me to death!"

She hung up and never called me again. Again, the verbiage wasn't socially proper. But at the time, I thought it was truly funny — as in "I got *her.*"

Eddie then brought Jim Barnett to buy out Lester. Barnett was a born politician. He bought his way in and schmoozed the TV people in Augusta to get us on the air there. He fought the promotional fight since he wasn't named in the antitrust suit. Tench Cox, Ted Turner's private attorney, handled the case for us.

As far as the NWA being a monopoly — they had their own world champion. Beyond that, well, is the NFL a monopoly? Yes and no. The AFL started, didn't it? Yes, they finally merged, but if you've got enough money, brains and talent you can make it. I don't know what the legal qualifications would be that would have made the NWA a monopoly, because you had the WWWF in the Northeast. They recognized the NWA world champion but never brought the champion into the area. Vince Sr. came to all the NWA meetings, but that was the extent of it.

Ex-wrestler Jim Wilson has made many accusations against me and about the NWA. He claims that he was fired for political reasons or because he wouldn't sleep with Barnett while Barnett was promoting a tour of Australia. Wilson even wrote a book about it, but the truth is *I* fired him in Georgia because he was never in shape. He was a great football player, I guess, but not a good pro wrestler.

Now, don't think this means that Jim Barnett and I were great friends or anything. One time he told my kids, "Oh, your dad's just homophobic."

When I found out, I called him up and said, "Let me tell you something, Jim. 'Homophobic,' to me, means that I'm afraid of you, that there's a phobia there. I don't fear you. I just don't like you. I think you're queer, but that is your choice, and I am OK with that as long as it doesn't affect me or my family. But don't you *ever* again tell my kids that garbage."

But having said all that, I don't believe Wilson's claim that he didn't become a star because he turned Barnett down. Hell, we *wanted* him to be a star, but he was never in shape! In my opinion, he smoked so much dope he couldn't go and couldn't draw. If he had so much star potential, why didn't he get over somewhere? Was he blacklisted? No. Remember, Rod Fenton was going to blacklist me, but I could draw, so that didn't last a day.

I was on top in Oklahoma, Houston, New York, San Francisco, Vancouver, Minneapolis, Georgia and Florida. If Jim Wilson had one bit of legitimacy, he would have at least one place to point to where he drew. When you look at his resumé, it's nowhere. He never drew because he never got over, because he was a lousy worker.

I never heard of Barnett crossing the line and mixing his sexual preference with the wrestling business, so I don't believe Barnett ever hustled him. And Barnett didn't even have a chance to put him out of work in Georgia, because I fired Jim in Georgia before Barnett even came in. Jim is so out there — he must live in a total fantasy world.

He even implied that Tom Renesto, Gunkel's booker, was a spy for us. Bullshit. I used to meet with Jody Hamilton and tried to hire Jody and Tom away from Ann. Jody and I met for lunch one day, and we had a good, careful, guarded conversation, with mutual respect, but he wouldn't leave Gunkel. Hamilton had integrity, and in all my dealings with Renesto, he, too, had principles. He was an opportunist, but he never considered leaving Ann for our side, to my knowledge.

Wilson also claimed that he tried to come after me in a dressing room and that I backed away from him. More bullshit. There's no human being who has ever come after me who couldn't get hold of me. I'm just not a guy who would run from it. Wilson never came after me in his life. Heck, he'd have been out of gas in a minute and a half.

The bottom line on Jim Wilson is that he was nothing. He didn't know how to get himself over, and he was never credible in the business. Since getting out of it, he's done nothing but whine and cry about it. To me, he's a scavenger who never paid his dues and never produced anything.

Another guy I felt was often his own worst enemy was Claude Patterson, whom I first met while working for Roy Shire in San Francisco. There was one huge difference — unlike Wilson, Patterson was box office. By the time he got to Georgia, he was calling himself Thunderbolt Patterson. Since I had known him, he'd worked for a few territories, but he wasn't considered reliable by these promotions. There was a lot of history for him to overcome emotionally. But he sure was talented, and I really liked him personally, so I tried hard with him on more than one occasion.

I wanted Patterson to succeed in Georgia because I was coming to realize that a promotion needed a black star. Just look at the demographics — we had so many loyal black fans, it just made sense. Thunderbolt had been through a lot, though, and sometimes you couldn't count on him to represent your promotional concepts. He was a loose cannon. It got to the point where I couldn't do much with him because I couldn't count on him. What we were looking for was reliability and someone with businesslike traits so that we would know from day to day that he could control his temper, show up and perform as expected. We desired strong personalities who could present their characters, but we also had to trust them not to go off on a tangent totally unrelated to our business, one too sensitive or too racial. I thought Thunderbolt was a talented guy, but his interviews were always so anti-establishment and always had racial overtones.

One thing you have to do to promote a black athlete as a superstar in wrestling is try to help him become bigger than being "just black." Junkyard Dog wasn't just black. He was Mr. American. He was everybody and everybody's hero. He could talk the black vernacular, but he never made things racial. Ernie Ladd was never racial. I was around Bobo Brazil when he was so over in Washington. Bobo was a man's man and a class guy.

Fans aren't ignorant. If a black athlete is wrestling against a white athlete who presents himself as being a racist, fans understand without it having to be overdone verbally or visually on TV or in the arena. This country has really gone through the fires of racism. It has made tremendous progress; it's been painful, there's still progress to be made, but we've come a long way.

I remember after Lyndon Johnson signed the Civil Rights Act. We were in the dressing room in Baltimore, and Don McClarity said to Ernie Ladd, who was six foot nine and 320 pounds, "I don't care what the president says; you're still a fucking nigger to me," with Bobo sitting there too.

I thought Ernie was going to slap him right into the wall, and when he didn't I initially thought maybe he wasn't very tough. But Ernie was thinking so much further ahead than anyone. He was making huge money, and he wasn't going to lose it over a dressing room brawl. Don McClarity was certainly no tough guy. In that era and in that office, he might have lost his job over a dressing room brawl — but it would have been Ernie who would have been labeled a "racial problem." That is just how skewed and biased those times were. Those guys — Bobo, Ernie, JYD — didn't need racial overtones, because they had the charisma, character and presence that overcame all that and touched people's hearts.

Thunderbolt was breaking through in Georgia, but he couldn't go all the way with it because he couldn't get past the racial aspect. His personal rebellion against the establishment created emotional situations that made him too unreliable. But he was a pioneer in terms of elevating the black wrestling star. It was just tough for him to have the patience he needed. Lots of long-held emotions just seemed to boil out. Certainly, if the shoe were on the other foot, I wouldn't have been able to handle it any better.

By mid-1974, things were turning around for us in Georgia, but Eddie could see that Barnett and I were clashing, so he moved me into Florida, which had always been the plan anyway.

On my way out, I wanted to put over Bob Armstrong in Columbus, have him beat me in a Texas Death Match, but Fred Ward still wouldn't book me with Bob after I'd busted him open with Duncum. He switched the match and had me going against Wrestling II. When I cut what was supposed to be the televised promo for the match, my opponent wasn't the one I was talking to.

"Fat Freddy," I said, "you dumb son of a bitch, guess what? I'm not coming to Columbus! You didn't book the match I wanted, so I won't be there."

I'm pretty sure that never aired. And, no, I didn't go.

Since I was leaving, Leo Garibaldi took over as full-fledged booker. He immediately started beating everyone I'd gotten over on TV — the guys who were drawing the money. He even booked me in a Loser Leaves Town Match. Buddy Colt and Tim Woods were sitting in the booking meeting when he trotted that idea out, and they both had the same reaction: "You're doing that to Bill? Have you asked him if he'll do this?"

Leo's reaction? "Fuck him."

They told him, "You haven't even *asked?* You'd better ask."

There was no way I was going to drop a Loser Leaves Town Match. I don't remember whom he had me with, but when I heard about it, I thought, "Leo, you might just have booked that guy to leave town!"

Not only did I own part of the office, but before you book anyone in that dramatic a match you'd best be advised that he agrees to the stipulations. That was what Colt and Woods were saying too, because if they were in the same situation they'd want the same consideration.

I called Eddie and told him, "You won't believe what this guy's done." I told Eddie about Leo beating all of our top guys (which had caused our houses to drop by half) and his plans for my Loser Leaves Town Match.

Eddie said, "Oh, shit." He thought about it and said, "Take the reins of the TV, take back over, and tell Lester to hold down the fort until I can get there and fire Leo."

I went in and told Leo, "You know, Leo, I changed my mind. I'm not leaving. In fact, I'm changing all your plans for TV."

Leo said, "You can't do that! I'm the booker!"

I picked up the phone and said, "Well, let's ask Eddie."

I got hold of Eddie and said, "Eddie, it can't wait."

I handed Leo the receiver and said, "Here, Leo, take the phone."

And Eddie fired him over the phone.

After I left, Barnett hired Jerry Jarrett to be booker. Jerry was tremendously talented and did well in the short term, but eventually he had a clash of personalities with Jim, so Barnett and I began a pattern that would repeat itself several times over the next few years — he would have problems with a booker, and I'd come back in, straighten it out and cover Georgia in the interim until Barnett got a new booker. Since Jim didn't do his own booking, but did run the office and was a principal stockholder, the booker had to have a certain synergy with him.

After Jarrett, Jim brought in Harley Race, but that didn't last long, as I knew it wouldn't. Harley was a phenomenal wrestler but not a very good booker. Then Barnett brought Alan Rogowski in. Rogowski wrestled as Ole Anderson, and I was behind him becoming booker 100 percent because I knew he'd do it well, and he did.

The end for Gunkel really came when Barnett worked our way into Augusta, which had been a cash cow for her because she'd been the only one running it. By the time she was out of business, I was settling in in Florida.

THE **SUNSHINE STATE**

I don't think I was ever under anybody who was as sharp about the business as Eddie Graham, and I worked under all of them.

Eddie was also extremely important in my life because finally I had a mentor who gave me positive feedback and encouragement! He contributed in a huge way to my self-esteem and confidence. His faith in my ability was empowering from a business perspective. However, morally and spiritually, neither of us was a positive contributor, because at that time I was in total rebellion against God, and Eddie expressed no faith. But his influence on me was tremendous.

No more traveling back and forth to Oklahoma every week. Even though we kept our home in Bixby, I brought Ene and the kids with me, and we moved to Florida.

When I first arrived, business was kind of flat. Louis Tillet was still the booker, but he had pretty well burned out. Throughout my experience, it was something I saw with bookers. Even a good booker can run a place only for so long before he starts repeating ideas that had worked the first time.

Louis was having Death Match after Death Match between Dusty Rhodes, a heel, and Jos LeDuc, a tough Canadian wrestler and a nice guy. One week it was Dusty challenging LeDuc to a Texas Death Match. The next week it was LeDuc challenging Dusty to a Canadian Death Match. Well, whatever you call it, such a match should be the blowoff of a feud, but Louis was having one after another, with all the blood and the gore. How exciting can that be? How many times do you, as a fan, want to see the same two guys go toe to toe every week?

When I got to Florida, I started building myself and a few other things. Even though I saw Dusty as my key star, he felt threatened, and he started going to Eddie behind my back and crying because all the focus wasn't on him — he didn't like the "short-term picture," as he interpreted it.

Eddie and I were around each other a lot in the office every day, and we would discuss things. We had tremendous creativity between us. I never knew anyone with more creativity who could analyze an idea better, take things from it and add things to it. And his creativity was never negative.

It wasn't long before Eddie told me about Dusty's complaints. I said, "Well, Eddie, we have a problem, because you've made me the boss. I can't be setting things up and then having Dusty come crying to you about everything, so I'm going to fire his ass."

He said, "You're going to *what?*"

"I'm going to fire the fat prick, because I won't have anybody going behind my back to you, unless you want him to be the booker. And then *I'll* go."

"You thought about this?"

"Yep," I said.

Eddie paused for a few seconds and then said, "Well, then, call him in."

I called Dusty into the office and sat him down. "We got a problem, big boy," I said. "I don't play this game, so you're gone — you're fired."

Dusty looked at Eddie and saw he was backing me on this, and he was shocked. Really, I didn't want to lose him, but I knew I had to get his attention and stop his going to Eddie behind my back. Dusty quickly decided he could work just fine with me being boss. And he did. He transitioned into a true superstar.

Dusty and I always had that kind of relationship, though. His ego was such that he was insecure, which is true of all of us, but he was really unique in this regard. But Dusty Rhodes is a *talented* human being.

I brought manager Gary Hart into Florida and put him with Pak Song

Nam. Pak Song was awesome but needed something added to the package, and Gary was still the greatest mouthpiece in wrestling.

He was also still a great person to work with and a great idea man. And that's what you needed. I never considered myself the most innovative guy around. I just took whatever I had and worked with the ideas of those around me to achieve some success.

Pak Song and Dusty were a top heel team, but Hart and Pak Song turned on him, and Dusty came out on TV and did an incredible interview, one of the best I've ever seen. He talked about being the son of a plumber and fighting his way up, and that's really when he became "The American Dream." I broke out in goose pimples just listening to him. I knew it was hot.

Of course, that brought the challenge of trying to contain the swelling of his head, because as big as The American Dream got, his ego got big right alongside it. That's not a knock on Dusty — you've *got* to have an ego in that position. It's a necessity to believe you're good enough that people should pay money to see you work. But egos must be kept in check enough that others can work with you.

There were certain "gimmick matches" made for Dusty, and other matches he took to the next level and maybe even originated, like the Texas Bullrope Match, where each opponent was secured by one wrist to a bull-riding rope with a huge bell in the middle, which could be a formidable, even dangerous, weapon. I let him do his Bullrope Matches and everything else. I booked him fully until he was ready to drop. And when we'd do the Bullrope Matches, Death Matches, or whatever it was (sometimes, in certain situations, we became partners), he'd get juice every night, and some nights I just wouldn't. I didn't need to — Dusty was bleeding enough for both of us, so I'd just rub some of his on me. That really used to "get" him.

If I did get juice, I'd say, "I think I hit an artery," as if I'd drawn so much blood when it had only been a trickle.

Dusty would say, "Yeah, Gene Artery," in reference to Gene Autry, the cowboy star. It was our personal joke.

I actually hit an artery while blading early in my career. When I did, it really spurted, which you always wanted to avoid. That only happened a couple of times before I no longer gaffed in that area.

Dusty was far from the only piece of talent there. We also had Buddy Colt, who was solid as a rock, and Dick Murdoch, another incredible worker, coming in and out. Plus we had Jack Brisco, who had become the NWA champion and was huge in Florida. He was also loyal to Eddie Graham, who was his mentor and had groomed him to become the champion. His brother, Jerry Brisco, was another great worker in Florida.

We had the Funk brothers, Dory Jr. and Terry, who were great workers, and Eddie had had a long relationship with their father, so they had a certain loyalty to him too. And then there was Bobby Shane, whom I'd had success working with in Georgia. He could really project, and he and I, in both Florida and Georgia, had really been able to work well together. Bobby Duncum, my old Georgia partner, also came in to work for us.

Danny Hodge even came in for some shots as world junior heavyweight champion. Tony Charles, from England, was also a fantastic athlete. He had a dropkick so devastating that it just stood head and shoulders above any I've ever seen. We booked him against Hodge on many occasions and generally sent them twenty or thirty minutes broadway. They would wrestle "clean," with neither being the heel. They almost always got a standing ovation from the crowd.

We also had some young talent coming up — Dick Slater was awesome, and Mike Graham was a chip off the old block. Yes, Mike was spoiled, but that was typical of his situation. But he was a good athlete, a good worker, and he could be a huge asset in the right situations, and that was just where I tried to keep him. Mike has always been a stand-up guy in our business and for me. I truly respect him and care for him; I am just pointing out the "crucible of life" from which he was forged.

So I had many assets to juggle, but that was part of the challenge. The result was the biggest bottom-line profit in the history of Florida wrestling.

But Florida also had its office politics. Buddy Fuller was supposed to be a silent partner, but he was always trying to cause dissension. Eddie Graham tried so hard to be everything to everybody that he just ran himself ragged. Eddie had a lawyer I thought was totally worthless as a partner. Barnett was a partner but totally worthless for Florida. His percentage was a "reward" for his taking control of the operation in Georgia.

Eddie was going to make me a partner, but he realized that he had all the partners he could legally have in the corporate entity, known as a Subchapter S, which they had set up. Barnett had been the tenth partner, the legal maximum. We worked out a deal where I would not be part owner legally or by contract but would be paid ten percent of the profits while I was booking there. That was a great deal for me, because I was getting the financial rewards of being a partner without having to buy into the company. Plus, deep down, I knew I wouldn't stay in Florida long term to do all the work for everyone, several of whom I considered not only dead weight but, even worse, negative influences.

Eddie's brother Skip took care of a lot of the towns and the bookwork. On Monday night, it was West Palm Beach and Orlando. Milo Steinborn, a former wrestling star and legitimate professional strong-man, promoted Orlando, so the office got a booking fee for Orlando, but the office owned West Palm Beach.

All the guys wanted to go to Orlando because it was close to Tampa, and Eddie wanted Milo to have top stars because Milo was his friend. West Palm Beach was doing poorly, and we owned it! That is just not good financial planning — to give everything to a town that paid the office only a booking fee and not to take the best care of the town the office actually owned.

Ron Fuller, Buddy's son, lived in West Palm Beach and had been a wrestler but had quit because nobody would use him. He was good, but the friction of jealousy, whether real or perceived, between the promoters and their sons pushed him out. Ron was selling real estate. Hiro Matsuda and Duke Keomuka were partners in the office and had pioneered Florida with Eddie when he broke in there in the 1960s. Duke, who was older, was now working in the office. Matsuda was still in awesome shape and deeply resented doing nothing, but he remained loyal to Eddie. Hiro was a special person, a very good friend. He got cancer of the liver years later, and I didn't even know until it was too late. I really mourned his passing. I respected him immensely.

Since I was making a percentage, I wanted West Palm Beach to do better, but I couldn't take it out of Orlando because of Eddie's relationship with Milo. I brought Mike Graham in and told him, "OK, Mike, I want you to help. I know your future here, and so do you, so I want to start getting you involved in the actual office and running of this company. So, to start this process, you're going to run Orlando, and I'm going to help bring up West Palm."

When Eddie heard that, we had a meeting, and Eddie was so smooth. He said, "What are you doing?"

"Well, I want Mike to get some experience, Eddie."

"What are you going to take to West Palm? Because I want Dusty, Gary Hart and Pak Song in Orlando."

He wanted our top stars in Orlando, and naturally he would want to be sure if Mike was running it that it did very well so that Mike would get that credit, which was still perfect for my plan. See, I knew I actually had *Eddie* running Orlando, because he wasn't going to let Mike look bad. Mike had good ideas but was young, so Eddie, the expert and teacher, would go each week and make sure Orlando "cooked on high" for Mike's sake and reputation too. This plan let me focus my undivided attention on West Palm Beach.

I brought Hiro Matsuda out of retirement and put him on TV a few times, not many. Then I brought Ron Fuller out of retirement and put him on TV a few times, not many. I took my second team to West Palm every week, including myself.

Bringing Ron in reenergized his wrestling career, and he later became a very successful promoter in the Knoxville area and an owner of a couple of minor league hockey franchises. He became a very successful businessman and a friend I really respect.

Before long, Orlando was selling out every week with a $25,000 gross, and I got West Palm up to $10,000, $15,000, $20,000. Mondays were doing great, and we owned West Palm, so the profit picture for the office was huge. Every now and then we'd bring in Dusty, or world champ Jack Brisco, and West Palm would sell out. Tuesday was Tampa, Wednesday was Miami, Thursday was Jacksonville, Friday was Tallahassee, Saturday was one of many different towns. Plus we'd do a big show in Saint Petersburg once in a while.

I think I learned key things from everyone I worked for. In Gagne, I saw the big picture, and with Shire it was the details. But Eddie Graham had it all. He was the smartest person about the wrestling business and had the most complete understanding of how to make it work of anyone I've ever known. He understood the psychology of how to make a finish work at a big show. His match finishes really told a story — the story we wanted to impress in the minds and emotions of our fans. People would be drained after his shows because they never could figure out when the real finish was going to happen. He was the master of the "false finish," which the fans thought would end the match but instead was just one more emotional twist or turn that would then make the real finish even more effective.

Eddie was also the one who taught me to book a major event, what would lead up to it and what would follow it. When we had our "Super Show" in Saint Petersburg, we still had to have a plan to draw people to Tampa the following Tuesday. It wasn't like the WWWF formula Vince McMahon used, where you knew Bruno Sammartino was going to get two or three matches out of this guy, while the next guy was building, and in their huge population centers they would build to their big shows, because they ran those venues only monthly. We ran weekly, and Saint Petersburg was so close to Tampa that we had Tampa on a Tuesday and then St. Pete on a Saturday, then back to Tampa on the next Tuesday — in effect, three shows in the same TV area to promote. That was a challenge!

Eddie also taught me the importance of maintaining credibility for your organization. When I came in, I was a heel, and I'd figured out long before that I could get over better by talking than I could by wrestling. My wrestling was fine, but I always knew how to put just enough truth into whatever I was saying to get whatever reaction I wanted on a promo. And I'd seen from watching the likes of Curtis Iaukea in Hawaii that what people wanted to see was the wrestler's personality. However, I tried getting myself over by cutting Gordon Solie off on my interviews, putting him down and overriding him.

One evening Eddie called me, and we made small talk for a while, which was what Eddie always did before he got around to the reason he was really calling. Finally, he said, "By the way, let me ask you a question. If you got invited to *The Tonight Show* with Johnny Carson [at that time the hottest talk show around] and every time he tried to ask you a question you interrupted or insulted him, how long do you think he'd stay on the air with you, and do you think you'd ever be invited back?"

"Well, no," I said.

"Bill, you and I know that Gordon works for our office, but we publicize him as the host of Florida Championship Wrestling, and the only thing that gives us credibility is that he can commentate. We know that we lead him where we want his commentary to go, but if we let ourselves portray him and abuse him like he's got no credibility we lose *our* credibility. We also know that you are my booker, but on TV you're a piece of talent. Well, for a piece of talent to go on TV and insult the announcer, demean him and interrupt him, all of a sudden our whole promotion has no integrity."

I saw that Eddie was right, and you never saw a wrestler abuse an announcer in any promotion of mine ever again — ever! That was a mistake on my part, and Eddie Graham set me straight.

But more important than the long-term lessons, the money, the bottom-line profit in Florida, was coming in, and Eddie's eye would light up (yes, "eye" — Eddie had one glass eye). "You son of a gun," he said. "You've got this thing paying like a slot machine. We have never had a bottom line like this." That was a huge compliment and confidence builder, and after three years with Leroy I sure needed it.

When Dusty became booker later on, he knew nothing about the bottom line. He never was a complete businessman and never had the full responsibility of making the talent payoffs or seeing that the company had a net profit. I was given full authority by Eddie to make the payoffs to the talent and to totally control the expenses in each town, because he knew I had "the complete package" and the accounting sense too. I knew that it was not what you grossed but what you netted that you earned.

Accumulating a lot of top talent — main event talent — required a lot of intense juggling to keep them happy and effective. One night Eddie came up to me in the Tampa Armory, and I said, "I've got six matches here that are all main events! I don't have any just simple matches, to warm up the people."

He said, "Kid, I love it. You're knee-deep in talent. I don't know how you do it!" His acknowledgment of my ability and what I had developed was sweet praise to my ears, but it also let me know he recognized the tremendous challenge and would support me totally, which he did.

The "package" show concept also meant that we would never be hijacked or held up by a piece of talent. We had so many guys who were over that no one was completely indispensable. Plus the people never could figure out what the return matches were going to be. The unpredictability of it kept their focus and their interest.

We had Miami so hot that they were scalping tickets. Jacksonville had been a bit of a challenge for a while, until I looked around and thought, "This is a redneck town — this will be the greatest place to hold matches on a Saturday night." Then the place did huge business! It was just a town with that Saturday-night mentality.

Don Curtis was Eddie's front man there. Don was a former wrestler, as great an athlete as he was a person. I still keep in touch with him and his wife, Dotty. Don was also a very good pilot, so I flew a lot with him, and he became a world-class referee in Olympic-style amateur wrestling. Don was a person of loyal integrity.

And Tampa was the base of the whole area. As Tampa went, so went the entire territory. The only town that didn't react like Tampa was Tallahassee. I never could get Tallahassee figured out. It was up in the panhandle, and it didn't seem to be part of the rest of the territory. The only talent I knew that would draw in Tallahassee was Jack Brisco or Buddy Colt.

In Tampa, we were having such a hot run that we were putting billboards up around town with Hart's Army putting up a bounty on Dusty Rhodes and Jack Brisco. Hart was wearing a John Brown belt, a military outfit, a narrow mustache and hair swooped to one side and wetted down, so he looked a little like Hitler.

Eddie loved to show how legitimate his wrestlers were, and personally he loved seeing a shoot. We had a young guy in named Ali Vaziri (who later went on to greater fame as The Iron Sheik), an Iranian who coached the U.S. Greco-Roman team in Minnesota and who had originally been trained for pro wrestling by Verne Gagne. Later Karl Gotch taught Vaziri some moves.

One time we had Danny Hodge in, as the world junior heavyweight champion, and Eddie wanted to see Hodge shoot with Vaziri. Hodge was sick, had lost a lot of weight and had no energy. He would actually be going in soon for serious stomach surgery. We set it up at the office, in back where we taped the weekly TV show. I told Vaziri and Hodge, "OK, when you two go out there, you go full bore. You shoot."

Now, you don't coach the U.S. Olympic Greco-Roman wrestling team unless you are a world-class wrestler. But Vaziri was still no match for Hodge. Hodge, sickness and all, went out there and set him up, slapping at one ankle. Vaziri countered, and Hodge moved as if he was going for the ankle again. When Vaziri started to react, Hodge exploded right through him with a takedown. When they landed on the mat, Vaziri was on his back, and Hodge had him wrapped up like a pretzel. The whole thing was over within seconds. It was as if Vaziri had been hit by a man-eating machine. It was as if Hodge was from another planet.

Eddie and I watched the whole thing from the back. I was so proud of Danny, who was really sick but still had the heart of a champion. Eddie was stunned with disbelief.

I turned to Eddie and said, "Eddie, I'm really sorry. Danny's getting old, and he's really pretty ill right now."

Eddie got it and laughed.

Vaziri worked for me briefly years later, in Mid-South. Even later I was told by Ole Anderson that Ali was having money problems. He was such a good athlete and stayed in top shape. He earned a lot of money working for Vince and had been so frugal with his money. But then he had substance abuse problems and spent it all on that. Addiction is horrible and is no respecter of talent — it is a destroyer of it.

One of my first dear friends in the wrestling business was "Irish" Pat Barrett. He was an all-time great guy. We would party together and have a lot of fun. One thing about Pat, though, his mouth had more balls than his body could back up. We worked out at the YMCA, and I thought he was helpless on the mat. He was a gutsy guy, and he'd fight you, but he didn't have any technical skills in terms of the skill levels of the wrestlers from Oklahoma or the traditional wrestling states — Iowa, Minnesota, California, Michigan and Ohio.

Apparently, as I was talking to Tony Charles later, we were discussing who could really go and who couldn't. Years later, after they were both retired, these two longtime friends, Tony and Pat, got drunk and ended up in a hell of a fight, where Pat beat Tony's butt. It was so heated they actually stopped being friends over it.

Pat later told me, "That was your fault, you son of a bitch! You were the one who told him I couldn't wrestle."

"Well, Pat," I said, "it was the truth. You couldn't wrestle! Just because you couldn't wrestle doesn't mean I was saying you weren't tough. It just means you can't wrestle."

Remember, an all-out fight is no respecter of reputation or technique. A guy who can really punch can sucker-punch you, or just plain tag you on the button, and the fight could be over before you get to wrestle him to the ground. But generally the better wrestler will win because he'll take his opponent to the ground and then defeat him. Pat Barrett wouldn't back down from anyone. And he always had his Irish shillelagh.

Heck, Tony would get half drunk and challenge Billy Robinson (a tough shooter from England). Robinson would stretch him half to death and then help him up, and they'd go right back to whatever they'd been talking about.

I noticed the start of an interesting trend in 1974. It was an era of rebellion, and people liked tough heels. It was the beginning of the "antihero" becoming the fans' favorite. One night I was wrestling Dusty in Miami, and I was the heel in the match. I put him over, right in the middle of the ring. I stayed out there, recovering, while the guys started to come to the ring for the next match. One of them was Don Muraco, and I got into it with him, and he whipped my ass too for all the people to see! Then Gerald Brisco came out, and he whipped me too — I sold like crazy for those guys. Finally, Dusty came back out and gave me another elbow. He whispered to me, "Bill, get out of here! You're blowing off all your heat!"

But guess what? Those fans nearly rioted. The longer I stayed out there, getting whipped, the angrier they became, because I was still in the ring! After all that, I was still the guy in the ring, and people were seething.

I used to tell my heels, "It doesn't matter to a heel if he gets beat. It's all a matter of how you get beat."

In the early years of my career, most babyfaces just barely won after the heel slipped up. As things progressed into blowoffs, the heel really needed to get his fanny kicked. And the more it got kicked the tougher that guy became in the eyes of the people.

Finally, I knew it was time to leave Florida, because I was working constantly, and Ene came to me one day and said she was going back to Oklahoma. "I'm going home," she said. "You come on when you want to."

I'd been working so hard that all I saw was the inside of the office, TV studios and arenas. Our family life was at an all-time low ebb. I was working myself almost until I was ready to drop, so I decided to go home myself.

About that time, a plane crash took the life of Bobby Shane and crippled Buddy Colt. The eerie thing was that I had flown Buddy's plane from Atlanta to Tampa for him. I had my instrument rating, and Buddy was only a student pilot, so with the thunderstorms we were having then, I took the plane into Tampa. When Buddy later flew the same plane out of Tampa, he had weather problems and ended up crashing. Bobby was killed, and Buddy was injured so badly he never wrestled again. Gary Hart was also on the plane and got hurt, as did a young kid named Dennis McCord. Dennis, the least injured of the four, later recovered and had some success wrestling as Austin Idol in the southeast.

Eddie called me in the middle of the night to give me the news, and I couldn't believe it. I still couldn't when I saw it in the newspaper the next morning. Bobby was truly a unique piece of talent who died too young, and it chilled me to think that I had flown that plane from Atlanta to Tampa only a few months earlier.

The next night they announced the plane crash, which, among other things, necessitated changes in the lineup. But the arena didn't feel like an arena that night. It just seemed to take the steam out of the crowd and out of us. The people didn't react to any match with the normal emotions of a wrestling crowd.

It was a tremendous personal tragedy, but it was also a big blow to our business. Gary Hart was the hottest manager around, and Bobby Shane and Buddy Colt were guys you could plug into any role.

Not long after I gave notice and headed back home, but I had learned so much from Eddie about the wrestling business, and I would use that knowledge with great success.

He always used to ask me, "You're a college man. Why are you here working for me, a high school dropout?"

I always told him, "I came to get my Ph.D. in wrestling."

And, working for Eddie Graham, I did.

GOING HOME to STAY

Back in Oklahoma, I finally felt ready to run the show. I'd taken a little from each of the exceptional promoters I'd worked for, and each concept I learned contributed dramatically to my overall perception of and education in the business. Then Eddie had rounded it all out for me, and I had the total package.

Before going on, because I seem to dwell on the "stars" and "events" and might leave out some extremely important people who made dramatic differences in my life and my business, I would love to pay tribute to another providential event — my hiring of Georgiana Seay as our secretary. She became so much more than that. She was and is a very special person. My wife, Ene, went to Jim Elliott, our personal accountant and a longtime close friend, because we knew we needed someone exceptionally qualified to work in our office, to get the books into shape and to stay on top of the money and records.

Leroy and his wife, Dorothy, had always seemed to run their business out of their back pockets. And we had a horrible lack of proper records and control of our cash flow. Our electricity or water would be cut off in buildings we leased in towns, such as Lafayette, Louisiana, for instance, because payment was overlooked or delinquent.

Well, Jim knew a lady who had worked for the State Athletic Commission in North Dakota and was looking for a good position in Tulsa. It was Georgiana. We hired her, and she was a blessing! She had to come into that politically charged office, with all the undercurrents, backdoor politics and things off limits, and begin establishing some order without offending those whose domain this had been for years. What an impossible task, but she did it!

Eventually, she earned Dorothy and Leroy's respect too. And later, when Leroy and I split, she came with me and was my right hand. My books were always exact. She was meticulous and tough-skinned enough to put up with me too. The wrestlers loved her because she loved and respected them, but if they tried any BS with her she was quick to put them in their place. That also added to the respect they gave her. I doubt I would ever have been so successful without Georgiana!

But, getting back to 1975, the first thing I needed to do when I got back to my home territory was kick out Verne and Fritz, who were still "partners" with me and Leroy. I walked in and told Leroy there were going to be a lot of changes. We were going to kick out Verne and Fritz, but we were going to do it the right way.

We immediately began holding all profits and not issuing any dividends or profit checks to them. We just termed them as retained earnings. Then I upped Leroy's and my salaries. Leroy was reluctant because he was scared to take on Verne and Fritz, but he knew I was serious about coming back, so he went ahead with it. It wasn't long before we had $100,000 of retained earnings saved up. Of course, at any time, I could declare a salary bonus to Leroy and me and wipe that money out. A while went by, and our absentee partners hadn't received any money.

That year the NWA convention was held in Lake Tahoe, and we met with Verne and Fritz in a hotel room. I told them I wanted them both out, that Leroy and I were going to own the territory outright.

Verne got mad and took off his shirt and said, "Let's you and me shoot for it."

I said, "Gee, Verne, I didn't know you were just going to give it to me. I was going to buy you out, but if that's what you want to do that's what we'll do."

Verne wasn't afraid — he was a truly tough person and always in shape, but he could never quite figure me out completely, and he knew I'd be a vicious opponent, so it really just wasn't worth taking it to that level. He put on his shirt and said, "Aw, hell, I'll just sell."

We ended up buying out Verne and Fritz for $50,000 each, which was still good for them since they'd been getting payouts for years without ever doing a thing, and they'd put in only $20,000 apiece in the first place. What they didn't realize was that we bought them out with their own retained earnings. Fritz figured it out later, and years after I got a call from Verne.

He asked me, "Is that the truth? You bought me out with my own money?"

"Yeah, I bought you out with your money, but Verne — you weren't doing anything for it. You didn't earn shit! You were a lousy partner."

I still like Verne and respect him tremendously, but business is business.

Leroy was now my only partner, but he was a handful. He'd sit up at night with Dorothy, and they'd pick everything apart. She certainly had her cross to bear with him. In my opinion, they had a totally dysfunctional relationship, but it was also their crutch, as were so many relationships in the corrupt and immoral business of wrestling.

I also pulled the Oklahoma territory out of the NWA. The whole time I ran that territory, whether with Leroy or later, when I formed Mid-South, mine was one of the few territories never a member of the NWA. They let me book their champion as long as I called him the NWA world champion. The NWA didn't give me any grief because they were afraid of antitrust, so I did what I wanted. And I didn't need them. Eddie, in Florida, was still an NWA member, and he always wanted them to work with me. I think they also saw the benefit of me recognizing their champion.

This was also when I first started phasing myself down, and Dick Murdoch became our big star. He was so talented and reliable. Murdoch was a crazy man from West Texas, a tough brawler and amazing talker. His stepfather was Frankie Hill Murdoch, a tough wrestler in his own right. Dickie had been around the business pretty much his whole life, and he'd always had his mouth going.

One of my favorite Murdoch stories was his encounter with Jack Brisco when Murdoch was a high school wrestler. One of Jack's old wrestling friends from Oklahoma State was now Murdoch's high school wrestling coach. Jack was there to see the coach and work out with a few of the kids. The way the story goes, Jack saw Dickie buying a six-pack somewhere and called him on it, and Dickie started jawing at him. Jack said, "Be sure to come to the workout."

Jack wasn't that big, but he was sure skilled. Dick was there, but he knew he was going to get it. Jack looked at him and then really psyched him out by saying, "No, I'll save you 'til last." Jack went through the entire team and then took Murdoch out there and . . . tore him apart.

But Murdoch was a tremendous pro wrestler and really got over with our fans. I knew he was clicking when we were coming out of Shreveport one night. A group of fans saw us and ran past me to get his autograph. It pissed me off at first, because I thought, "Shit, *I'm* the star. I'll show them."

I went to the hotel and had a long talk with the mirror. I said, "You dummy, you *dummy.* Shut your ego down. You've done what you knew you needed to do. You have your first star." However, I also realized I'd need to build another and another — it just didn't pay to have all your eggs in one basket. But that was a key moment for me.

Later we brought in Killer Karl Kox, and he and Murdoch had a great feud. Those two loved each other and loved working together. Killer Karl Kox was a unique guy, and I really enjoyed having him in our business.

Another top guy was Waldo Von Erich, who was not kin to Fritz even though they had worked as "brothers" early in their careers. Waldo was one of the greatest interviewers ever. His snarl, his arrogance, were awesome.

Outside the ring, Waldo was a gentle person with a great sense of humor. He was a crazy, silly guy, one of the funniest people I've ever met. You'd be around him and think, "How could anyone ever hate this guy?" But when he got in front of the camera and turned on his Nazi snarl, he became an awesome interview. He just had that look of arrogance about him. People never knew what a silly son of a gun he was. I can't say enough about him as a human being — he was just one of the nicest guys I've ever met.

We also had a young rookie named Ted DiBiase. He would later be a guy I valued highly, one of the guys I really loved and treasured, but at this point he was a green rookie and so nervous.

One of the first big problems I had was an antitrust suit of my own as Mississippi promoter George Culkin sued Leroy and me. Grizzly Smith had gone to work for George after Griz and I'd had a financial dispute and I'd fired him.

Louisiana was the key to anyone who wanted to run opposition because it was a strong commission state, and the commission was giving out only one license to promote — technically called a "booking license." I started building a relationship with Emile Bruneau, the athletic commission head.

Bruneau was a completely honest guy in a basically monopolistic system. He did what he thought would be best for the people of Louisiana. After I got to know him, he became my biggest ally and a great friend. Bruneau truly wanted what was best for the people living there, and he was the rare Louisiana politician who was impossible to bribe. Jim Barnett had tried it, and so had Dick the Bruiser, because they both saw money in promoting in Louisiana. It didn't work. He ran it with an iron hand.

His son Peppi became an attorney, a conservative legislator in Louisiana, eventually the speaker of the house — and my attorney. We became extremely close, and he is one attorney I fully trust. His sons, Jeb and Adrian, and his wife Brenda (now deceased), became like family. His mother was so special too. Peppi has been a legislator in the Louisiana House of Representatives now for years and is highly respected.

These bonds were built over several years as we all got to know each other and as they understood I was principled and ran an extremely good business. I understood they knew the political landscape in Louisiana better than anyone and would guide me to produce what was best for their state.

I was surprised by George's suit because, even when I was in Florida, I'd occasionally book myself and some other talent for his shows in Mississippi and get him a sellout nearly every time. But he had apparently decided to go on his own and run in opposition to Leroy and me.

Jack Curtis, my right-hand man, was George's nephew. And Grizzly would call me each week telling me how bad it was there. They also had Frankie Cain, the Great Mephisto, going against Grizzly. Now, Cain was five foot six or so, and Grizzly was nearly seven feet, so what a mismatch! And Grizzly was the babyface!

Later Griz said he was doing it to help me. Bullshit! It was his ego — he booked it and wanted it to work with Mephisto. Griz was very talented, not only as a wrestler who'd drawn money in several areas, but also in booking and "talent expediting." He was one of my trusted inner circle and was very integral to my operation, both before and after this little sojourn, but his stuff with Mephisto just was *not* box office.

Well, I wanted that to stay there because I knew it would break George. It wouldn't make any money. But Grizzly was broke. I had compassion for him — he was my friend even though I'd had to fire him. I had Jack Curtis, who lived in Vicksburg, Mississippi, meet with him every week and give him $400 a week to help his family out. The real reason was that I didn't want him leaving, so I paid my own competition to stay there. He couldn't have afforded to stay if I wasn't paying him. I wanted him there with George so that he could keep booking stuff that wouldn't draw.

Curtis was a very important part of my business because he was extremely talented at setting up and running box offices and what we called "spot shows," events at towns that we didn't regularly run. He also began and grew the "souvenir" part of our business. He had years of wrestling experience but also had real business talents. Jack was truly someone I trusted a lot.

George's promotion really just wasn't successful, although he had money personally and had a good political job. When he folded, he filed the antitrust suit, which was deadly because those things are triple damages, and the legal fees are astronomical. George couldn't win because I was competing with him only in the one market. He had the rest of the state, but we were killing him.

Around this time, I had another occurrence that should have made plain to me that providence was shaping my life. I had fired a wrestler (whom I won't name because of the extreme circumstances of this incident) because I felt he'd become unreliable. I believe substance abuse played a huge role in this, because for years he'd been someone I could count on. After I fired him, he started calling me at home, threatening to kill me. He would stand outside my house, follow my car or even terrorize my kids. There were no stalking laws then, so the police would come out, and he'd tell them, "Yeah, I'm gonna kill him," but there was nothing they could do to him. He never had any weapons on him.

Somebody put a clock wrapped up in Christmas paper in my mailbox on Christmas, I guess to show how someone could blow my family up. The guy had gone completely screwy, and I was scared he might actually hurt someone in my family.

One night my wife was with Joel at the hospital because he'd just had shoulder surgery. My little girl, Ene, was sleeping in our king-sized bed with me, and Erik and Micah were asleep in their rooms, when we heard a series of loud pops — someone shot up our home! Our alarm system and the outdoor lighting system I'd installed (due to all the threats) worked fine, and when I looked up both boys were flat on the ground with their weapons ready. But one bullet had gone into the wall of my bedroom near my daughter's head. I was *beyond* livid. I'd always figured if they killed me so be it, but only a coward would intimidate children.

After that, I began hiring off-duty Bixby police to sit on my property each night so that, when I was gone, my family would feel protected.

I also decided to kill him. I'd done a lot in my life, but I'd never killed anyone. Power is the ultimate corruption. Money is just the way of keeping score. Even our struggle or rebellion against God is about power and our trying to either reduce our Creator down to our understanding or to elevate ourselves up to Him. The power to take someone's life would be the "ultimate power" — the highest corruption, unless it was during an act of war, and I rationalized this in my mind as being war.

I had it all documented — the cops had reports on every time he'd threatened me because I'd called them every time. I was going to kill him and plead self-defense. I even had a drop weapon ready.

I got someone to get word to the guy that all was forgiven, for him to come out to the house and talk about me rehiring him. He came to the house, and within a few minutes I had him on my porch, on his knees, with my .357 down his throat. He was crying, strangling on that gun. I was about to blow his brains out when my housekeeper, Virgie, a dear woman and a Christian, drove up with her kids in the car. Their eyes were as big as saucers, and the kids started crying.

How was I going to plead self-defense now?

I took the gun out of his mouth, picked up the drop gun and set it aside. Then I looked at the guy and said, "Let's you and me go out in that field right over there, and I'll just kill you with my bare hands."

He ran, and I never saw the guy again. I heard he later spent some time in prison, so his problems must have continued. That is a shame, because, as I said, at one time I could really count on him. But we all make choices, and our choices have consequences.

But here's where providence came in — it wasn't even the maid's day to work. Virgie wasn't even supposed to be there, but God kept me from doing something that severe. I'm so thankful I didn't kill that guy. He created his own demons and became a slave to the substances he was abusing. But getting him out of my life was a blessing.

Years later, after the Lord had called me back and I realized His providence, I saw Virgie. I hugged her and told her I now knew why she'd showed up that day — that the Lord had kept me from killing that guy and suffering the consequences. She and I both cried because she said she knew that and was so glad that now I did too.

By 1978, I knew Murdoch was the star I'd wanted him to be, and it was time to start building someone else. That someone else turned out to be Sylvester Ritter, who became famous as The Junkyard Dog. Dickie didn't like JYD coming in, but he knew he had to go along with him because I was going to build him. Ultimately, JYD surpassed Dickie, but Dickie was smart enough to ride it out. He was the ultimate worker, but JYD was special.

1978 was also the year that we proved wrestling could be a big draw in the New Orleans Superdome. Ernie Ladd had been working for George Culkin, and I wanted him working for us instead. Ernie had pro football credentials and amazing charisma.

We had Ray Candy, but Ray couldn't get off the step to that next level. He was such a great guy, but he just couldn't get there.

I arranged a meeting with Ernie Ladd and made him an offer, and he said, "But I've already given him [Culkin] my word, and my word's good."

I said, "I can respect that. Now, let's talk about your future. I realize there are a lot of good things we could do. You could be a key guy, someone with a lot of influence on my promotion, and I'd put you in the position to do that."

We kept in touch and talked several times.

Finally, Ernie said, "I've been studying the demographics of Mississippi. There's only one town with even a halfway-decent population. I don't care how much business we do. I can't afford to stay there, so I'm going to do the jobs I need to do there and leave."

His analysis really impressed me. It was a lot more than most wrestlers would ever consider at that time.

I said, "Don't do the jobs."

He said, "No, my word is good. I'm going to give my notice and do my jobs."

That's just the way Ernie Ladd was. He did the right thing for George, then left him and came to me.

When he started with us, we put him over like a killer, and he was really getting over with the people. He came to me one day with an idea for him to work with Ray Candy.

I said, "Shit, it won't draw."

He said, "Trust me. It'll draw."

He finally talked me into it. Then he told me his idea was to have Candy beat him on TV to start the thing.

I said, "You have got to be nuts. I worked my ass off to get you over here, and Ray Candy's going to beat you?"

He said, "He's got to beat me. He's got to own me, like I was his stepchild. Bill, I know me, and I know what gets my stuff over."

Well, by gosh, he was right!

At the same time, a transition in television was making a huge difference for us. Our shows had generally been on local affiliates of major networks. The networks were making so much money that they started booking stuff on their stations for prestige, not for ratings. Ad salesmen for network affiliates didn't have to leave their offices. People came to them and placed orders. Many network affiliates were dropping wrestling shows because, although they got huge ratings, they weren't "prestigious" enough.

Many shows that had been on network affiliates were going to UHF stations. Ted Turner transitioned his into the first "superstation." UHF channels were transmitted at a higher frequency than networks, and the reception wasn't as good. A lot of TV sets didn't even have UHF stations on their dials, but laws were soon passed to make manufacturers put UHF frequencies on sets.

We'd been having trouble staying locked in on our network affiliates, and a wrestling show had to be locked in to its time so that people would get in the habit of watching at that time. Channel 26, out of New Orleans, had a signal that probably covered half of Lake Pontchartrain. Seymour Smith, a tough little Jewish guy from New York who'd been in the construction business, bought the station in the late 1970s, after we'd been on the air there for a while. He was a shrewd businessman, and he became impressed with how well our wrestling show was doing on his station. The previous manager liked what we were doing so much I had a two-year, no-cut contract for the show to air in prime time, in an era when most TV contracts were done in thirteen-week periods. When Seymour bought the station, he inherited that contract, so he called me in to hammer me about it, but he really couldn't. Once he saw the ratings and our value to the station, he was smart enough to want to improve the situation, and he and I started working closely together.

He had the idea of us being partners in promoting the Superdome. This would be a huge challenge, but Seymour understood how to work with the local media, and his son, David, was also very sharp. I learned so much from Seymour about how to approach a huge event.

I also learned more from him on negotiating deals and dealing with businesses and never accepting the "norm," the traditional deal. He taught me, in business, to always push the envelope — primarily in our negotiations with the Superdome. He was awesome.

Leroy was panicked about such a major event, and I was too. To make money, we needed a minimum of 10,000 people to come through the doors. Hell, we'd never even done a $25,000 gate.

We also had to worry about being able to get commission approval to line up the show. When we couldn't get dates in New Orleans, which for some reason we were blocked out of politically, we ran St. Bernard's Parish. It took real political pull for us to get back into the city auditorium. We had to get help from Emile Bruneau and his son, Peppi.

The key to dealing with Emile was to go to him with what I wanted to do and ask him how to do it instead of charging in and telling him what I was going to do. If I went down and *told* him what I was going to do in Louisiana and he didn't like it, it wasn't going to happen. But if I could show him what I needed to do and make him understand it and how it would benefit wrestling for Louisiana, he would show me how to do it.

And when we did have arguments, if I went a couple of weeks without talking to him, he'd call me and say, "Are you mad at me? Get down here!" You'll notice that this was given not in an "invitational" form but as a command. But by then, his bark was worse than his bite because we were friends, and he enjoyed our friendship too. We'd go to his house, sit and talk it over, whatever it was.

Here's an example of how much integrity Emile had. One year I gave his wife a gold medallion as a Christmas present, and he called a commission meeting and made me go down there and take it back from him in front of all the commissioners. I said, "Good gosh, Emile, I wasn't trying to bribe you — it was just a gift for Margaret!"

Emile and Peppi were instrumental in helping us to line up permits for everything we needed to do to promote the Superdome. But we still had to promote it.

Another problem was the group that ran the Superdome. They were not professional then but more "political." Back then it was like the Wild West. There was a different deal for each party. Plus they really "stacked the sheets" on their expenses, it was rumored. They gave free passes to every political hack they knew. We knew they were looking to rip us off, but they were no match for Seymour, the shrewdest negotiator I've ever met.

The show ended up doing huge business. I think our first show there grossed $87,000. Seymour wouldn't take a check that night. I had to fly back down to New Orleans for a Superdome settlement meeting, because he was going to challenge them on everything they charged us for. I learned so much from him in those meetings.

Eventually, the Superdome hired Cliff Wallace as president. He was a real professional, and we had some initial meetings with him and his staff over the same issues. He learned about our concerns and then adopted some policies that kept everything straight. It was a completely different atmosphere from then on.

The show was a huge success, but Leroy wasn't happy. Grizzly and I were in the office in Tulsa with Leroy the next week when Ernie came in.

He came in quietly and sat down, so Leroy, being blind, didn't know he was there. Leroy was puffing on his cigar, bitching and moaning. People who didn't really know him thought he was this nice, gentle, blind man. He wasn't especially nice on this day, though.

"Well, Griz," he said, "what did you think of that fuckin' Superdome? I didn't like it. I thought there were too many niggers in the crowd and too many niggers on the fuckin' card. What did you think?"

Griz said, "Boss, I thought the money was green."

And that was the perfect answer, because that is what business is supposed to be all about.

I jumped in on Grizzly's side. "Leroy, this was the biggest gate we've ever drawn. It put us on the map as a major promotion."

But Leroy kept harping about there being "too many damn niggers" as Ernie stood up and tiptoed out.

A few seconds later he came back into the office, loud enough to be heard. "Hey," he said, "how are you, Bill? Grizzly! Hey, Leroy, how are you?"

Leroy got up and said, "Come here, big fella!" Leroy hugged him and clapped him on the back, but that day Ernie saw another side of Leroy.

Dick Murdoch would do the same thing. He'd come in quietly and listen to Leroy knock him and then act like he was Dick's biggest supporter when Dick let him know he was there.

I think that at one time Leroy was a person of principle, and I know he was a great athlete and a smart businessman. But his bitterness over losing his sight, his drinking, his anger toward his mother and his feeling that life had dealt him badly eventually eroded his character, until he was miserable. Still, he was the only game in town when I wanted to break into the promotional side of the business. I owe him a lot. I just wish he'd been happier, because people wanted to like and even love him — including Dorothy and the daughter he called "Mike."

The Superdome's success gave us a whole new status, and Seymour was very aggressive about promoting more events. We got to the point where we were promoting four shows a year together in the Superdome in addition to our regular shows at the municipal auditorium. At one time, other than the Saints, we were the dome's biggest renter.

Our relations with that station were always strong. A few years later, when Seymour sold Channel 26 to WGN out of Chicago, I was a nervous wreck. Before the sale, he locked me in with a new contract, but I was still concerned, but the new management also liked our success, and we remained strong on that station for years.

THE BEGINNINGS OF MID-SOUTH

Not long after our Superdome success, I knew it was time Leroy and I went our separate ways. Generally, one can take the arrows shot from the front, but it really hurts, and can even destroy you, to get shot continually in the back. And that's what I felt Leroy was doing at that time. In 1979, I told him we needed to split, and he didn't like it.

He reacted by suing me for embezzlement, and it hit the front page of the Tulsa *World* newspaper. He hired some friend of his who was an attorney, but he wasn't giving Leroy good advice.

I called him and said, "Well, Leroy, you've done it now. You've gone public with this and slandered me. Have you forgotten that I never handled the money? *You and Dorothy* handled the money! How could *I* embezzle from *you?* I'm going to countersue you for slander, and I'll end up owning your ranch!" His beautiful cattle ranch north of Tulsa was his pride and joy.

He immediately dropped that lawsuit, and he agreed to split. He kept

Oklahoma, Arkansas, our part of Missouri and Wichita Falls, Texas. I said I wanted Louisiana, and he said, "Then you'll take Mississippi too, with Culkin and that antitrust suit!"

The first thing I needed to do once I was on my own and had officially formed Mid-South Wrestling was go to Mississippi and straighten things out with George Culkin. I called him and asked to meet with him. We talked it out and decided to work together again. It was the best thing for both of us. He wasn't successful in competing against me in wrestling — and the lawsuit wasn't going well for him either.

We met with all the lawyers in the case in Jackson, Mississippi, and his lawyers started blowing up when I told them the suit was over. I went over and shut the door of the office where we were meeting and told them, "You fat, overstuffed, overpriced legal vultures, sit down. George and I are here because we want to be. We're not letting you guys use the big words, blow up and extend this to charge up triple fees. You all are sitting here until you hammer out the letter that ends this antitrust suit and reestablishes George and my partnership."

Emile Bruneau, still chairman of the Louisiana State Athletic Commission, and I had become very close. It just killed him when Leroy and I broke up as partners because he loved Leroy too. Yes, I said "too," because I did care deeply for Leroy and had tried to build a meaningful relationship with him. He just could never trust anyone, and his demons were so destructive. It was an impossible situation. Emile even set up two or three meetings for the three of us to get together in an attempt to get Leroy and me to reconcile. Leroy didn't show up for any of them. That really hurt Emile since he was going the extra mile to help us reconcile. That was when he gave me his blessing to split with Leroy and assured me I'd have the booking license to run Louisiana. Without Louisiana, I couldn't have afforded to split with Leroy.

Buddy Roberts, the job guy I'd brought in from Minnesota years earlier, who went on to become a great star as half of The Hollywood Blondes, played another important role here as the cornerstone of The Freebirds. They were Michael Hayes and Terry Gordy, a tag team for George in Mississippi. Gordy was an incredible worker, and I really wanted to bring him in. Michael wanted to work, but the truth was that, compared to his ability as a manager, he was a lousy worker. He was one of the greatest managers of all time, the greatest mouthpiece going, but he wanted to work. He loved wrestling, and he had that heart of a worker.

I wanted them out of that small Mississippi territory. Gordy wouldn't come in without Michael, though. Finally, I brought them both in. Buck Robley was my booker at the time, but he wasn't clicking with The Freebirds. They hadn't been there long when he was going to trade them to Florida for another team, but I could see that Gordy was special.

I told Robley, "You're not trading them anywhere. We'll get Michael out of the ring, and we'll get someone to team with Gordy to take the bumps."

Enter Buddy Roberts, who made the magic of the team because he was a special kind of heel. You could kick his ass all day long, and he still had heat the next time. Gordy was the tough guy, and he could take great bumps when he wanted to. Michael was an awesome talker. The people *hated* him. Those three combined to make the perfect team. Michael was still screwy in the ring, but the whole package worked. And as I say this, please realize that I love and respect Michael Hayes — this was how I saw it.

I wasn't right on every call, though. Just as Ernie had proved me wrong by making Ray Candy into a big draw for the Superdome show, Bob Sweetan turned out to be more than I thought he'd be. Sweetan was a heel job guy at first, but he battled every one of his opponents and had tremendous matches, even in losing, so that the people hated him more and more every week. With his great matches and work ethic in the ring, he made himself a star. We picked up on it and started giving him a push — primarily on Grizzly Smith's advice — and it worked. Sweetan was all business. He gave 100 percent and earned his position.

One that I did get right was the magnetic kid who became one of the biggest stars I ever had. Sylvester Ritter was a muscular athlete with unbelievable charisma. I gave him a dog collar and chain to wear, sent him to the ring to "Another One Bites the Dust" and changed his name to The Junkyard Dog.

He had a little time in the wrestling business in Calgary working for Stu Hart as "Big Daddy" Ritter when he came to my attention. Jake Roberts had worked against him there, and I believe Jake told me about him. When he got to me, he was still really green! Really, JYD was *always* limited in what he could do in the ring, so initially it was really important that we book him with people who could work with him, emphasize his strong suits and build up his self-confidence. We didn't need anyone tearing him down or trying to show up his weaknesses. I could tell he would become a star. He just had that inner glow.

A few months after he came in, JYD was really starting to get over. Ernie booked him in a New Orleans suburb we ran, called Saint Bernard, when the municipal auditorium wasn't available. It was a house show with Scott

Irwin, the masked Super Destroyer. Ernie had them go twenty minutes to a time-limit draw.

Ernie called me after the show, sounding very proud of himself, and said, "Yes, I just checked out your new star. He ain't got what it takes."

I said, "What do you mean, he *ain't* got what it takes?"

"Well, Bill, I sent him out to go twenty minutes with Super Destroyer. He couldn't hardly stand up. His tongue was hanging out, and he was exhausted. Couldn't do nothing! He was horrible!"

"You just did *what?* This kid, who I told you was going to be our next star, and you had him go twenty minutes to a broadway in the New Orleans market?"

Putting JYD over in the New Orleans area was important since that market had a very significant black audience, which would make it such a good litmus test for JYD.

Ernie replied, "Yep, he couldn't take it, Bill. Super Destroyer ate his lunch!"

"Well," I said, "you're fired, and you can tell Super Dummy he's fired too! I just told you I want this guy to be our next star, to see what your judgment was about how to help get him there, and you send him to go twenty minutes broadway with Super Dummy? You're both fired!"

"Super Dummy" was my twisting of Super Destroyer's handle when aggravated, but as a person and talent Scott Irwin always gave it his all.

"What?"

"I said you're fired!"

"I did wrong?"

"You're fired! He's my next star!"

Ernie said, *"I get the message. Case closed!"* And he hung up.

One thing about Ernie — he would stand his ground if he felt he was right, while still acknowledging I was boss, but when I made my point and he "got it" he really got it!

I knew about JYD's shortcomings and lack of experience — I wanted a booker who would make JYD what I wanted him to be and what I saw in him — an emerging superstar. We would just have to nurture him at this stage of his development. That's the booker's job. Hell, if Ernie could make Ray Candy a star . . .

Ernie and "Bad" Leroy Brown were a tag team for a while, just a big, tough pair of heels. They also happened to be the ugliest, worst tag team in the world. But, damn, they drew money! Leroy never missed an opportunity to tell me how badly he hated my "white, honky ass." Anytime I told Leroy something to do, he'd get furious. He'd throw a fit, talk about "that dumb, fat cowboy who don't know shit" and kick and stomp. Ernie would just stand back and laugh. He thought that was so funny.

One night in Jackson, Leroy went into the ropes, and the top ring rope broke. Our "ring ropes" were actually steel cables with rubber hose as an outer covering and were part of the structural aspect of our rings. They were also used for tactical moves in the ring to generate additional momentum. As you hit the ropes, you turn your back to them so that you can spring off. When he did that, and it broke, he fell back and landed right on top of his head outside the ring on the cement floor — about a four-foot drop. It should have killed him. As it was, he hurt his ankle, got a concussion and split open his head, requiring stitches. He ended up on crutches.

The following Tuesday we had a big match in Alexandria, Louisiana, with me and JYD against Ernie and "Bad" Leroy Brown, but Leroy was hurt. For years, I used a recorder to send my finishes over to the other dressing room because I had a lot of detailed stuff I wanted done. Prior to that, we would "tell the referee," or Grizzly Smith, who then went to the other dressing room with the information. As our finishes and spots became more detailed and psychologically complex, that system stopped being effective because key parts would often get forgotten by the referee or Griz. Really, with the amount of detail evolving, it was beyond the ability of a person to remember and transmit the key points correctly. Even if he could, the people involved often needed it repeated several times to truly ingest it. Recording the finishes also took the "excuse factor" out of the equation. Prior to that, if a participant missed part of what I wanted, I'd get mad at him, and he'd say, "I didn't get that part of it." Well, my new system eliminated that problem.

On this night, realizing that Bad Leroy was injured, I played a joke on him. On his check, I "fined" him for breaking the top rope of George Culkin's ring in Jackson. Only Ernie and Griz knew about the joke. When Bad Leroy got his check, he exploded! He was so darn mad — he cursed and cursed me with invective challenging my breeding and every other aspect of me. He was furious! To add more drama and make it a classic, I designed a scenario to begin the tag match in Alexandria that I knew would drive him crazy. In the way it was sent over on the tape, he would come out on crutches to the ring, where JYD and I would be waiting for our match. I would take his crutches away and hit him on the head, right where he had the stitches, and he'd fall down and get juice.

When I sent over that scenario, there he was, on crutches, head split open, and Griz told him, "I'm sorry, Leroy, but you know how the Cowboy is. He fined you $100 for breaking the top ring rope in Jackson."

I could almost hear Leroy all the way in the babyface locker room: "That fat, white, honky son of a bitch! I'll kill him! Fuck him! Fuck him! *Fuck! Him!*"

As soon as Leroy calmed down, Griz said, "OK, now, here's what the boss wants you to do tonight — since you are injured — before the actual match scheduled begins." And he played the tape of me talking about how I would take his crutch, hit him on the head with it and get blood.

Leroy went nuts. "*Fuck him!* I'm not gonna do — *fuck him!* I'm leavin' this fuckin' shit hole territory — *fuck him!*"

We had a substitute for him in the actual match because, with his concussion and injured ankle, plus the stitches, he really couldn't go effectively. But you know what? When we went to the ring to begin the match, even after he'd ranted and raved and as mad as he'd become, he was a true champion, with a heart for our business, because there he was, ready to do his part!

Of course, the whole thing (including the "fine") was a rib. I wasn't going to bust him open, or take his crutch, and he did get his $100 back. But he was a trooper. He was so mad at me that he wanted to kill me, but he was going to do what was supposed to be done. That was the kind of guy I had a lot of time for. I truly respect guys like that.

Buck Robley was booker during a really great season with JYD, but Buck started thinking it was all about Buck, and he was abusing some substances. The last week he worked for me, he made $7,000. I don't believe he ever made money like that again after he left. He thought it was his genius. He was my booker, but I always controlled things. I used their ideas. I often also used my own ideas, or ones I'd picked up from other places, but I coordinated the final bookings and all the TV tapings.

Sometimes I'd try something I'd seen work elsewhere. The first blindfold match I ever saw was Maurice "Mad Dog" Vachon against The Crusher, in Saint Paul, Minnesota, in 1968. They had designed hoods, from the shoulders up, with masks that covered their entire heads.

The Crusher wanted me to be his second and wanted Paul Vachon, Maurice's brother, to be in Mad Dog's corner. I was embarrassed to be out there, and I told Crusher, "This is going to stink. It's going to destroy the town."

He said, "No, Cowboy! It's going to be great!"

I said, "You are fucking crazy. A blindfold match? It's the stupidest thing I've ever heard of."

Well, I have never seen such a great match. They had the people in the palms of their hands. Crusher and Mad Dog were "looking" for each other in the ring. Of course, the masks were gimmicked, so they could see just fine, but they would just walk by each other, with their arms out, and the crowd would go nuts. Soon Mad Dog put his ear down on the mat to try to hear The Crusher, and I started banging my hands on the mat to throw him off. Eventually, they'd lock up, and one would grab the other in a headlock. All of a sudden, one of them would throw the other one into the ropes and then bend over to deliver a backdrop, but the other guy would just run right by him. It was awesome! Crusher was a creative genius. He really knew his gimmick and the fans — how to deliver to them and to get them involved emotionally.

I was so impressed by how they worked the idea of it that I had Killer Karl Kox and Dick Murdoch do one in the Superdome. We called it a "Jim Bowie Death Match," and it drew fantastic fan interest. You had to learn from other people, absorb ideas about psychology, what worked, what didn't.

The angle that solidified The Junkyard Dog as a superstar in Mid-South was when The Freebirds "blinded" him during a match. That gimmick had been done in Florida, and Dusty Rhodes had told me about it.

For me, the problem was how could I portray wrestlers blinding another wrestler and still allow them to wrestle for me? If it was clearly intentional and they got away with it, if we allowed it, my promotion would have no credibility. That is why so many promotions failed creatively, because they created "heat for heat's sake" and made the promotion a party to it. That becomes distasteful, all hype or stupidity. It kills any real respect the fans have for the promotion and makes it just another part of the show, with no credibility. The promotion should never take the side that's wrong. The promotion should have *a reasonable doubt* about someone's intentions.

Buck Robley's idea was just to have Michael Hayes blind JYD. I said, "No! You're talking about a black kid, our big star who's coming up? Shit, that's *racial!* We have to come up with a way for them to deny it's intentional and to deny that race is involved."

I came up with the idea of having a Hair Match where the loser would lose his hair via this "hair-removal potion" at ringside. In the process, they would get the stuff in JYD's eyes. Although it would be on purpose, we now had some degree of reasonable doubt. As it was shown, The Freebirds blinded JYD on purpose, *but they were able to claim that it was an accident.* We created enough doubt to let them plead their case and deny that it was an intentional act, in a tongue-in-cheek fashion, but to get by without being suspended or even fired. If we "allowed" stuff like that as part of our promotion by giving it our "sanction" when it was so obviously done on purpose, then what was next? Would they try to lynch JYD?

That did not at all dilute the effect of it — heck, to the fans, JYD was blinded. Every week we told the fans we really didn't know if he would regain his sight. That made it even more devious to the fans, that The Freebirds would go that far and maybe have even planned it and figured out a way to cover it up! In that sense, it was just like so many things that happen in real life when the perpetrator tries to get away with a crime by covering it up, denying guilt or even framing someone else.

We even paid JYD to stay at home the next few weeks. We'd take him to malls and film him trying to get around while blinded.

The big Superdome Payoff Match was August 2, 1980, Junkyard Dog, still "blind," against Michael Hayes, with both men wearing dog collars connected by a chain. We had more fans at that show than we'd had for any show in our history.

One of the other matches on that show featured two guys on loan from Vince McMahon Sr., Hulk Hogan and Andre the Giant. Hogan, real name Terry Bollea, didn't want to do a job for Andre. Well, Vince booked the match, not me, so I didn't care. Vince had let me use Andre for my big Superdome show and said, "Hey, I'll send Hogan down there too so that he can do the job for Andre." That was Vince's doing — he was preventing me from having to feed one of my guys to Andre.

When Hogan balked, I told him, "Look, that's what Vince booked you here for. I don't care what you do. *Vince* booked you here to do the job."

He kept saying no, and finally I said, "Well, fine. I'll just go tell Andre you don't want to put him over, and you two can work it out in the ring. I don't give a shit! Beat the shit out of each other if you want to."

I went and told Andre the situation, and he just said, "I'll take care of it, boss."

Hogan was never an athlete in the sense of having a college record, but since he survived Hiro Matsuda's wrestling school he sure had to have ability and courage and a willingness to stick it out. Still, while Andre might not have been a legitimate wrestler, I didn't know many wrestlers who were going to go out and beat his ass. He weighed 500 pounds, was over seven feet tall and was mobile, and I knew what was going to happen when I told Andre what Hulk had said.

Hogan wrote his autobiography a couple of years ago and claimed he'd done another Superdome for me where I'd wanted him to do a job for Wahoo McDaniel. He said he got Vince Sr. to overturn the finish.

That never happened. They never wrestled in the Superdome, and if they had why would I have cared who won? Wahoo was just in and out for me, not a mainstay. I wouldn't have cared who won or lost. I never got to know Hulk well, but history will remember him as the person who drew the most money in the business during his era, so in that sense he was truly phenomenal.

But Hulk Hogan didn't invent "the attitude." When Jack Brisco was NWA world heavyweight champion, I once brought him into Tulsa to wrestle Hodge so that fans would get to see the world heavyweight champion (Brisco) versus the world junior heavyweight champion (Hodge). I laid out the card, with the finish of the main event being that Hodge and Brisco would each win one fall and then wrestle the third fall to the sixty-minute time limit, making the match a draw.

I'd been traveling a lot and was worn out. Plus I was satisfied with the show, and we had everything laid out — I knew Jack and Danny would have a fantastic match — so I was going home. I was on my way out of the building when Jack ran up to me and said, "Where are you going?"

I said, "I'm going home!"

"Aren't you going to stay for my and Danny's match?"

"Jack, you guys are two of the greatest in the business. I don't need to watch you two to know it'll be done right."

Hodge's career was winding down at this point, but my statement to Jack was still true. They were two of the best.

"Bill," he said, "if he hurts me, I'm walking out of the ring."

I said, "Jack, you've been telling people for years that you can beat him."

"Yeah," he said, "but you know that's bullshit."

"Yeah, Jack, I know, but I thought maybe you were starting to believe that shit."

"What are you saying, Bill?"

"Well," I told him, "if I were you, since you're the big world's champion, I'd make the little world's champion look like he owns you. And if you do that, you probably won't have any trouble with Hodge. You all will have a great match!"

And everyone who stayed there told me they did.

As I've noted, Jack Brisco was a stud of an athlete. But he wasn't a stud of the same caliber as Danny Hodge. I don't know of any human being who was ever the same caliber as Hodge.

At that level in professional athletics, even a slight edge is huge. That is also what motivates athletes to take chances with performance-enhancing drugs to get an edge, to increase it or at the least to neutralize their opponents' edge. Hodge and Brisco were just two great athletes who never took steroids to enhance their performance. Hodge was superior, although Jack was also exceptional.

A guy who had to learn about Danny Hodge the hard way, in 1975, was Frank Goodish, who later became known as Bruiser Brody. It was a tag-team match with Danny and me against Frank and Stan Hansen in Fort Smith, Arkansas. Goodish was much taller than Hodge and about seventy pounds heavier. At this point, he was still green and was all caught up in himself and in his body built by weights. Neither Frank nor Stan could really wrestle, but Frank felt that, since he was much bigger than Hodge and had much bigger arms, he really didn't need to sell for Danny. What Goodish found out was that his big arms didn't mean much.

"Look at him and then look at me," Goodish said, right before the match.

I said, "We'll see, in about three minutes."

Hodge ate his lunch, just had him squealing like a little girl. Nothing tickled Hodge more than to take one of those big guys and just take him apart. It was a tag match, and Goodish's partner, Stan Hansen, was smarter than that. He knew he didn't want any part of Danny Hodge.

But I never really had any serious problems with Goodish. As the years went by, and he became a big drawing card, I heard that he became dishonorable in his negotiations. He'd agree to a figure, and then, when he got over and came to the big show, he would look at the crowd and then tell the promoter he wasn't going to make his appearance if the promoter didn't meet his new demands for money. He would just walk out on the show, but first he would circulate around the arena so that the fans would see he was there. Then, if he walked out, the promoter was left holding the bag with the fans! In essence, he was hijacking the promotion. If they refused him, he would just walk out and not appear. That cheats not only the promotion but also the fans, who have paid money to see you perform. And without fans, there are no superstars.

Sometimes athletes' melon-sized, ego-driven heads forget that. They forget that it is the fans who pay their salaries, and without fans they can't be superstars. With today's TV money, pay-per-view money, endorsements, and licensing for toy sales, sportswear, video games and so on that creates such huge money, they really have lost touch with the fact that it is still fan driven and not all about them.

I think that attitude, along with his method of hijacking the promotion for more money than previously agreed, was a contributing factor in his death. It's my understanding that Jose Gonzales, a partner in the promotion in Puerto Rico, stabbed him to death in the locker room in 1988. That was a true shame, because even that kind of business squabble shouldn't cost you your life, but in his case it did. He hijacked the wrong people.

But what drove Goodish away from me more than twelve years earlier was teaming with Hansen. I wanted to split them up because I felt they were holding each other back. Both showed signs of becoming huge stars as singles. I demanded that they split up. We went round and round, and they got so entrenched in their idea of being loyal to each other that they didn't see that, in fact, they were actually holding each other back. They finally gave their notice over it.

I told them, "Since you guys are going to leave anyway, just try it as singles until you leave."

Of course, as singles, they became superstars. Hansen did right away and Goodish a little later. But they were stifling each other as a team and holding back each other's development. When you are young in the business, sometimes you need a certain security, and theirs came from being teamed together. Sometimes you need something to force you out of your comfort zone, something to really push you to take chances and grow.

I worked a lot with Hansen. He was a quality guy in and out of the ring. Once I was working with him in New Orleans, and I forgot my own high spot. Completely my fault, not his, and I paid for it. I forgot to duck, and he hit me with his clothesline, knocking me clear back into the ropes. You could hear it go off like a shot all over the building. It would have killed an ordinary man. He leaned in and asked, "You OK, boss?"

I said, "You kidding me? They haven't made the fuckin' Texan that can hurt me."

Well, I was lying. He'd just about scrambled my brain. Stan couldn't see well, so you'd better not be there if you're not supposed to be! But that, too, was the way we responded to tough situations, by being macho and making it fun! Yes, you got hurt, but even hurt you needed to try to find the humor in it.

After promoting Mid-South by myself for a couple of years, I decided it was time in 1982 to go back into Oklahoma. I was kicking ass in Louisiana and Mississippi, but I lived in Oklahoma, so I finally said, "What the hell am I doing?"

Leroy's group was going downhill. He had George Scott booking for him, and George had a reputation for being a good booker in the Mid-Atlantic states in the 1970s, but I thought his concept of booking and his finishes were about as exciting as watching grass grow.

I checked on how Leroy's TV shows were doing, and I found that they were in arrears with every television station they had. Leroy owed those stations a lot of money. I got his Little Rock station and then Tulsa, where they liked Leroy but saw that my ratings were much higher than what he was getting for them. When I got Oklahoma City, that meant I had the territory.

I didn't want to hurt Leroy, but I was coming in one way or another. I called him and asked him to meet me. When we met, I told him, "Leroy, it's passed you by. You're not doing well financially. You've had your day, and it's time to go. I've already got your television, and I'm coming. That's going to finish your ass. You're barely hanging on anyway, so wouldn't it be a lot better for you to sell out to me and retire than to have me come up and take it away from you?"

I wanted Leroy to have a graceful way out. Despite our differences, at one time he had been great, and I never forgot that he was the one who gave me my first real start in the promotion.

He was offended by my offer, but he saw the logic of what I was saying. "Well," he said, "I've got to talk to George Scott about it."

"Why do you have to talk to George Scott? He's just your booker."

George didn't own any part of the business. He couldn't even get on as a booker anywhere at that point. He finished up in the Carolinas but was successful there only because he had Johnny Valentine, who maneuvered the Carolinas so well that George was able to coast on the momentum for years. He also continued John Ringley's (son-in-law of Jim Crockett Sr. who took over briefly after Crockett died in the early 1970s) concept of changing the Carolinas from a tag-team territory to one featuring individual stars. The Carolinas had been a tag-team territory for years, and the established stars had "homesteaded" there, so their talent had become stale, with no turnover. In the transition, they obtained great talent, such as Wahoo McDaniel and a young Ric Flair, who was becoming a superstar. Ringley lost his job because it took a while for this "new approach" there to click. By the time it did, George Scott was the new booker, but Johnny Valentine was the real genius behind Mid-Atlantic's success. To me, George was smart enough to ride the momentum, but he didn't take it further, and it grew stale too, until they eventually replaced him as booker.

Leroy's wanting to "discuss it with George" was just typical Leroy — stalling for time. He finally agreed to sell out, but part of our agreement was that we would take what he owed the television stations out of the sale price, and that money went to the stations. I had the goodwill of the TV stations after that because they were all thrilled to get paid.

And I took in a lot of the talent that Leroy had. The guys he had whom I wanted — such as Skandor Akbar — I didn't hold anything against. They were just trying to make a living.

I had Leroy in for a show a few years later, kind of an old-timer's appreciation night. His memory was really going by then, and I had to tell him who people were, but he really enjoyed the evening.

From there, Mid-South expanded into Houston, then promoted by Paul Boesch, whom I had known when he was Morris Sigel's assistant. Boesch had been working with Joe Blanchard's Southwest Wrestling group out of San Antonio, and we worked with Boesch to put on some shows in Houston. However, Joe's son Tully, one of the top wrestlers there, appeared to be so messed up on cocaine (it was becoming a huge problem in the business) that I finally got fed up and got rid of him. I called Joe to set up a meeting in Houston to talk about it, but he wouldn't come — why, I don't know. Both Joe and Tully ended up mad at me, but it had to be done.

Now Tully has turned his life around completely and done some wonderful things in the ministry. I haven't seen him in twenty years. Still, in life, it's how you run the whole race, and what your life stands for, that count. There can be some real valleys along with the peaks. I am so glad Tully found the Lord.

There was no question, between Joe Blanchard and me, that I was going to be the one calling the shots. Between that and my problems with his son, there was no way we could coexist in Houston. Boesch and I reached an agreement where I would provide the talent for his shows, and I bought a percentage of the office.

Another kid from there I got to work with some was Gino Hernandez. He was so, *so* talented, but he had a tragic end too when he overdosed on cocaine in 1986. Boesch also liked to use José Lothario, which was never a problem with me because José was always a good hand in the ring. I respect José.

Working with Boesch wasn't much of a problem except that Paul had a bad influence, I believe — his nephew, Peter Birkholz. Peter helped Paul to make some really poor decisions, and I think he cared only about maneuvering things to where he'd take control of the Houston promotion himself.

Boesch also announced his local bouts that aired on his TV shows, which showed some of our matches in Houston, plus the hour-long "Mid-South Wrestling" show. Like Danny Williams before him, Boesch had become a bigger star to people in Houston than the wrestlers, so it became a struggle for us to get him off the air, or he would dominate the show.

It became a fine balance. By the time my working relationship with Paul ended, he was barely doing any of the play-by-play. He got to do his little segment at the start of the show, and that was it. Still, we had a tremendously successful run in Houston.

CHAPTER 12

LAND of THE TOUGH GUYS

Things were going strong in 1982 when I got a call from my old friend Stanley Abel, now head wrestling coach at the University of Oklahoma. He has been a true friend ever since we met in high school. He always believed in me as a person and in my ability, accepting me warts and all. But on this day, he had something specific on his mind.

"Bill, you have got to come down here and see this kid," he said.

"This kid" was Steve Williams, an amateur wrestler at ou who'd been called "Doctor Death" since high school. He'd broken his nose in a match, and the next time he came out to wrestle he had to wear a hockey mask for protection, and one of the kids said, "Here comes Doctor Death!" The name stuck — and Doc loved it.

I liked Steve from the first time I saw him. I watched him wrestle for four years in college, and he was a four-time All-American in wrestling and a two-time All-Big Eight in football. He also played pro football in the short-lived USFL. When Abel told me Steve wanted to get into pro wrestling, it was a done deal.

It took some time for Doc to learn how to work, but he was a tremendous athlete. Steve was never what I would have called a great ring general, but he was so damn credible as an athlete that he was a top-notch guy to have on your card. He was money in the bank because of his credibility. He commanded respect.

I used to work the heck out of young guys. I'd make them work five, six, seven nights a week. It was hard, but they learned. You weren't going to learn to work doing four- or five-minute TV matches every week. You learned to work by getting in front of a crowd and going fifteen or twenty minutes or more every night with someone who could carry you for that long.

I had always believed in using guys with legitimate wrestling credentials. In 1981, I brought in Bob Roop, whom I'd met in Florida. Roop was a former U.S. Olympian and AAU college Greco-Roman wrestling champion. He was a good wrestler, whether you're talking amateur or pro, and a very intelligent guy.

Roop worked a lot with Bob Orton Jr., who was blessed with so much natural ability for working in the ring. His dad had been a big star, and was a big influence on his life, but to me it was a negative influence since he would really screw up Bobby's head. I don't think I'm the only one who thought that either — anyone could see that, whenever his dad would come to visit, his attitude would be pretty screwed up for a few weeks.

Many wrestlers complained about the way I managed my companies. I've been called a bully, a tyrant and all kinds of other names. In other words, I was *boss.* There was no doubt about it — I paid the bills. And mine was the tightest ship in the entire industry. No one else fined guys for being late. No one else made the wrestlers get to the arenas an hour before the matches began and made them stay until after the last match was over, unless the booker personally okayed their leaving. No other territory held back two weeks' pay in case a wrestler left the territory owing money.

We ran it like a business. It was structured. It had discipline. It also created an era of personal responsibility for the wrestlers, which was definitely needed. The tail wasn't wagging the dog. If the promotion wasn't successful, the wrestlers wouldn't have a place to work.

When I was a wrestler, I often got presented with things I didn't want to do, but I found a way to do them. I did what I was supposed to do to accomplish what was needed. I never packed my bag and walked out of the building without performing. I didn't like the finish Sam Muchnick had for me as Dr. Scarlet against Gene Kiniski, so I devised a better one, but my finish still put Kiniski over, right in the middle of the ring. When I got into it with Rod Fenton, I put over Don Leo in two straight falls and bled for him on my last night. In that Bob Ellis situation in Texas, I put *him* over in two straight falls.

I would disagree and let them know they couldn't control me, but I never hurt the business. I always left an area better than it was when I got there and always did what was traditionally expected of guys on their way out.

The closest thing to a no-show I ever had was in Georgia, when Fred Ward booked me in that match without my permission against an opponent I didn't approve, even though I was the booker, resulting in that interview I sent telling him I wasn't coming. If a wrestler ever told me he didn't want to do my finish, all I wanted from him was another idea to get us where I wanted us to go. I was always willing to talk to a guy who had another idea. I think I got along well with top talent on finishes because, if they had any ability to do so, I let them be a part of designing things. Now, there were times I had to put my foot down and say, "No, this is definitely what I need to have tonight."

There had to be an authority, and in my companies I was it. But I'd often negotiate to get things done. The difference, maybe, was that I knew I had the ability to get over that would make me a coveted piece of talent, so I felt bolder about telling promoters what I wouldn't do than a guy without that ability.

In the 1960s and 1970s, what had been local offices had become regional territories. The old alliance of promoters had never wanted wrestlers running things, but over the years things had transitioned to the point that almost all of them were being run by guys with wrestling backgrounds — Verne Gagne owned Minneapolis, Dick the Bruiser and Wilbur Snyder owned Indianapolis, Roy Shire in San Francisco, Eddie Graham in Florida, the Gunkels and the Fullers in Georgia, Ed Farhat (The Sheik) in Detroit and the trio of Harley Race, Bob Geigel and Pat O'Connor in Kansas City.

Back in the Strangler Lewis era of the 1920s, the wrestlers got most of the gates, and promoters got what was left over. Then the promoters consolidated power, with a lot of them cooperating, and began taking in more of the gate. Many of the top wrestlers started to realize that the way to have some future, some longevity, was to own their own businesses.

One thing I knew was that it was my company, my business. The wrestlers were just passing through. Therefore, it was very important to make sure they conducted themselves as businessmen.

That was something Emile Bruneau impressed on me. He once told me, "We got tired of dealing with different promoters and different wrestlers. We finally decided to appoint one booking license for the state and held that person accountable for everything. We could monitor you instead of keeping track of thirty wrestlers or having to monitor more than one wrestling booking office."

With that system in place, I made some changes of my own, starting when I first came back. Leroy had been paying the guys nightly. After the matches, they'd call him and give him the gate. He'd figure up the payoffs and have the boys paid. I moved to a weekly check system.

All I wanted a guy to do was fulfill his notice. I wanted each wrestler to come in and leave as a businessman. I also wanted to discourage the wrestlers from walking out on us (and the fans) after we'd invested TV time and effort to get them established as stars. We held back two-weeks pay on every wrestler, and we required two-weeks notice before preliminary guys could leave. For main-eventers it was four- or five-weeks notice, depending on what we worked out. Conversely, we protected every wrestler with this too. By contract we had to give them at least two-weeks notice if we wanted to terminate their services (unless they violated our policies.) The two-weeks pay we held back gave us a potential pool of income to draw on should we need to fine them for something — including walking out on the promotion. This money could also be used to cover hidden problems — like a wrestler walking out on apartment or motel or telephone bill — the kinds of things that plagued an industry perceived as unreliable. When I started as Leroy's partner, it was a huge problem. In essence, we cleaned up irresponsible behavior and instituted business policies. There had to be some consideration and, hopefully, mutual respect. The professionals who honored their word didn't give us any problems, but we had to have something we could reduce to writing in a contractual form.

We also had a system of fines to ensure you were in town on time and handled yourself like a professional. If you didn't show up, you got fined. If you were late, you got fined. If you stiffed a motel, I took it out of your money. I used to tell guys, "I can't fine Delta Airlines for you being late, but I can fine you. You should have caught an earlier flight. I can't fine the motel for not giving you your wakeup call. I'm not paying the motel to wrestle, so I'm going to fine you." If you got into a fight at a bar, I didn't care, but if you lost I fired you. It was that simple — if you were going to go out and make an ass of yourself, you'd better win.

Guys bitched and moaned about the fines and the structure, but they respected it. They learned to operate in a structured atmosphere treated as a business. I had rules, and the guys understood them. But I couldn't control everything the wrestlers did twenty-four hours a day. I would talk to the guys about life and what I expected of them.

Guys who watched me lay out a show for the first time were amazed because there was no question about what anybody's role was. Even if you were a top hand, if I needed you to put a guy over, I expected you to do it, and I expected you to do it the way I wanted it done, but I had enough respect for you to tell you why I was doing it. There was never any doubt about what one of my wrestlers was supposed to do. I didn't leave room for interpretation. However, allowing those with ability to help design these things made them a part of this process and showed them I valued them. As long as it accomplished my goal, they often had great ideas for things they could execute even better or things that maybe no one had done. Their creativity was also stimulated that way, and they felt they were an integral part of the big picture. Again, being accepted and feeling valued are two powerful motivators. I also rewarded those who performed or participated more and at a higher level with a system of bonuses on their checks, so they would know their input had value and was appreciated.

A lot of guys became unreliable because of cocaine addiction. When guys started smoking grass in the early 1970s, it wasn't an issue. I know many will cringe at this, but to me anything that alters one's personality is a drug and therefore can be addictive. I know many say marijuana is a "threshold drug" to cocaine or heroin, but to me alcohol is a horrible drug too and is the real threshold drug. Certainly, more death and destruction occur under the influence of alcohol than from grass. Also remember that, in my life then, everything was "relative." I'm not trying to legitimize grass, and I know I can't get alcohol made illegal. Remember, it boils down to choices and consequences.

But when a guy was on grass, he wasn't getting into fights — he was happy. It was when cocaine took off that guys had real problems. I always thought that it was a stupid drug to take, although I have never tried it. Listening to guys who did, it seemed to take away everything they normally wanted to do. If you're on cocaine, eventually it gets to where you can't have sex, you don't want to eat, and you can't sleep! Well, what three things drive a wrestler? Eating, sleeping, having sex! Another thing about coke was that it seemed the guys who used it never had enough. They would keep buying and using it, and that vicious cycle perpetuated until they ruined themselves.

And when crack cocaine became prevalent, that was even worse. JYD was never the same after getting hooked on that crap. He smoked up millions of dollars, and he'd been the greatest kid, such a great star. Buck Robley, who was open with me about his usage, would get on cocaine and become so completely paranoid I couldn't even deal with him. It was as if, no matter what your relationship with him or what you said, in that drug-induced paranoia he thought you were trying to screw him. I knew so little about it back then that I didn't see the long-term effects. We tried to deal with the symptoms and didn't even understand the cause.

So, yes, I was very strict where discipline was concerned. Even Ted DiBiase, whom I love dearly, has called me a bully as a boss. But Ted is a nice guy, not a tough guy like Doctor Death or Hacksaw Duggan. What Ted saw as bullying Doc and Duggan just related to, because I didn't get into Doc's face and call him a dummy. I would cuss and scream and raise hell about things, but it was always about the issue. It was never personal. I couldn't have gotten away with that even if I'd wanted to. No one's tough enough to stand in all those guys' faces and berate them like that! *No one!*

It was amazing how guys, even the ones who griped the most, would leave and then call me from another area just to say, "I didn't realize how much you were teaching me until I got here." One of those calls came in 1984 from WWF star Paul Orndorff. I'd met Paul a decade earlier in Tampa. He was a friend of Mike Graham's and an exceptional athlete who wanted into the business, so Roop and some others stretched him. In Florida, to get into the business, you had to go through the stretching. Paul got his ass kicked, but Eddie wouldn't let anyone injure Orndorff. Eddie just wanted the guys to put it to Paul enough that he could check whether he had guts enough to come back. Orndorff was a great athlete and a tough kid with a lot of guts. He didn't have any legitimate wrestling skills, but he tried. He didn't give up that day, and he sure proved himself to be a fighter. He made the grade.

I hired Paul in 1980. He was never happy with his money or, it seemed, with anything. I even changed my method of doing payoffs because of him. I used to do weekly payoffs when we were taping local promos, which were all done at the Shreveport TV studios. I quit handing the checks out until after the interviews, because Orndorff would see his check and be so mad it would spoil his whole afternoon of interviews. Every week, after he got his check, he'd be on the phone trying to get booked somewhere else.

He and DiBiase were both babyfaces in 1980, and I was getting ready to turn Orndorff heel. They were doing a babyface match for DiBiase's North American title in Jackson, Mississippi, and I wanted them to go an hour broadway. DiBiase was upset about it, and Orndorff was so mad he couldn't see straight. They both griped about it. "You're going to kill us dead. We can't go out there for a solid hour in a babyface match."

It wasn't the hour-long match they were worried about; it was doing an hour while both being babyfaces, which does take a lot more ring general-ship. In a heel-babyface match, the psychology is much easier since you have more give and take, and it is easier to execute and to maintain the fans' intensity. A babyface match was a real challenge. Remember, though, to grow you must get out of your comfort zone.

I said, "Well, you guys *are* pussies. You're right. You probably can't do it. I'm going to give you a finish, but I don't want you to do it until five minutes before the end of the hour. Then, if you don't feel like you're man enough to do the hour, then you can do the finish."

Seemingly, I'd given them an out, but knowing their ability and their pride really I hadn't. I had pushed them up a notch and put them to the test.

Sure enough, they were so mad at me that they did the hour and had the people standing. It changed both of them because they realized they could do it. They both really grew that night. I know neither of them will ever forget that defining moment. To be a leader, you sometimes have to challenge people.

The thing about Orndorff was that, no matter how mad he was at Bill Watts, when he went into that ring he gave 100 percent. I still talk to him now and then. We had our philosophical disagreements, but we established mutual respect.

Orndorff's attitude made him the total opposite of Mike George. Mike was always upbeat, always had a great attitude, just a great kid. He would bust his ass to do a good job. He was never one of my biggest stars, usually in the middle of the card, but he was reliable and worked hard, and I have a lot of respect for him.

Junkyard Dog had really become a superstar. In 1982, we did an angle where JYD was unjustly forced to leave Mid-South for ninety days. It was a match where Junkyard Dog and the masked Mr. Olympia (Jerry Stubbs, a nice guy, very reliable and a good worker — I can't say enough about that guy) faced DiBiase and Matt Borne. The story was that "Hacksaw" Duggan, DiBiase's regular partner, was missing.

The loser of the fall in this particular match would have to leave Mid-

South for ninety days. The Louisiana State Fair was going on, and I said on the broadcast that they must have brought in a gorilla, who was at ringside passing out balloons to kids. He was out there for pretty much the whole show.

The big tag match was going on, and Junkyard Dog was cleaning house on both heels, who'd been working over Olympia. All of a sudden, with the referee knocked down, the gorilla jumped up on the apron and unmasked. It was Jim Duggan, and he hit JYD with his finisher, the spear, making JYD easy prey for DiBiase. The people were stunned because they'd seen JYD go through so much and couldn't believe he was being forced out. But that wasn't the end of the story.

We still had Junkyard Dog — he returned under a mask as Stagger Lee, with the gimmick being that Ted DiBiase couldn't prove JYD and Stagger Lee were the same man. We all knew it was JYD, but in order for the DiBiase side to prove it they'd have to beat him and unmask him. We stated that, if they did beat him and unmask him, and it was JYD, we would ban him from Mid-South! They did unmask Stagger Lee once, but it was Porkchop Cash (another black wrestler we had substituted in JYD's place) wearing the mask, so JYD was outsmarting them.

DiBiase was an awesome heel but had been a good babyface too. Outside the ring, he was a nice guy with a great heart but not a tough guy like Hacksaw Duggan, Danny Hodge or Steve "Dr. Death" Williams. DiBiase wasn't a killer. I'm not saying he wasn't a man or was afraid — he just didn't have a mean streak. But he was a great worker.

I always liked Matt Borne. His father, "Tough" Tony Borne, was one of the guys (along with Leo "The Lion" Newman) who took me right in when I worked in Houston in 1963. I loved Tony Borne, and Matt Borne was always a neat kid when he worked for me and just busted his butt in the ring.

DiBiase and Borne ended up feuding with Mr. Wrestling II and Tiger Conway Jr. Tiger had a lot of talent, and his father was a heck of a guy. Tiger Sr. came up in the 1950s and 1960s when it wasn't very easy for a black man to thrive in such a white-dominated business. He was a good businessman who started a fencing company and did very well for himself. I'd met him in Houston in 1963, and he was a quality human being. I didn't get to be around him much, but just from the limited time I knew him I quickly grew to respect him.

Tiger Jr. was a product of all the rebellion of the times. He had a big Afro and everything, but I always liked him and don't remember ever having a problem with him. He was one of Paul Boesch's stars in Houston, and when I went into business with Paul I had to integrate those guys into my stuff. There were some natural tensions because the Houston guys who didn't go full time for Blanchard were worried about maintaining their positions, and my guys didn't want to lose their spots either.

A great opponent for Junkyard Dog in 1983 was King Kong Bundy, a 440-pound monster of a man. We did a gimmick with Bundy where he demanded referees count to five when he had an opponent pinned, instead of the usual three, to show his dominance over his opponents. Of course, this played out when he challenged Junkyard Dog for the North American title and pinned him one-two-three but demanded that the referee keep counting to five, and JYD kicked out before then and came back to win the match.

Bundy was really impressive but had no cardiovascular conditioning, which really isn't much of a surprise for a guy that size. He wasn't even very strong, really, but his look and his size were very imposing, and he really got over with the five-count gimmick. When he went to the WWF in 1984, Vince ended up doing the five-count gimmick with him there too. But it was done first in Mid-South.

One young guy I wish I'd gotten to spend more time around, because he was such a quality individual, was Merced Solis, who wrestled as Tito Santana. He worked for me briefly in 1983 before going to Georgia for another brief period and then to the WWF, where he had a lot of success. I remember watching Merced play at West Texas State. He could outrun anyone on the field, but he couldn't catch a thing. He had hands like skillets! Tully Blanchard was the quarterback on that team, and Ted DiBiase played for them too. Dusty Rhodes, Stan Hansen and Bobby Duncum also played there prior to these guys, as did Mercury Morris of NFL fame. But in wrestling, Merced was *quality* — very reliable and a great athlete.

He played his heritage a lot smarter than many of the guys did. Many wrestlers with the potential to be ethnic stars tried to hide their ethnicity. Even dumber was when a promoter would try to create a "Mexican" star for the Mexican-American fans by sending a Puerto Rican to the ring and telling people he was Mexican. Let me tell you something — you weren't going to fool those people. When it comes to someone's heritage, they know who's real and who isn't. I always thought the smartest thing you could do for most guys was to let them be who they were.

Every now and then someone would want to challenge another guy. John Nord wrestled for me as The Barbarian in 1985, and he got into it with Butch Reed once in the locker room after an afternoon match in Oklahoma City.

Butch and Nord had some problems in the ring. Their match was just awful. The problem was that Nord wanted to call the match because he thought Reed wasn't calling the right match. Usually, the heel called the match, but Reed had so much more experience. Nord was a good kid, but he thought he knew more than he really did.

After the match, they were having some heated words, blaming each other for the performance. I don't recall what it was, but Nord finally said something to Reed that set him off, so Reed walked up to where Nord was sitting and said, "Get up, you son of a bitch, and let's get it going!"

Nord started to get up but sat back down and said, "No, I got the flu, but I'll fight you next week."

Dr. Death Williams and I were there talking about something else entirely, but we stopped and just watched these two. When Nord sat down, I said, "Butch, he don't want any of your ass. Him's too sick. He'll get your ass next week."

Nord, with one boot off and one on, got so mad that he stood up and popped Reed about as hard as I've ever seen someone hit a guy. It backed Reed up about two steps, but he fired back. And the two of them just stood there trading blows, just popping each other. They weren't rolling around, tussling for control. They were toe to toe, just blasting each other.

I looked at Steve and said, "Doc, how many of those shots would you take?"

He just laughed and said, "I wouldn't have taken but the first one, and then that son of a bitch would have been on the ground."

I nodded and said, "Gosh, me too."

Finally, Butch started breaking through, and he was banging and banging on Nord. Then Butch picked up a sixteen-foot piece of PVC tubing, and I went over and grabbed it.

I asked him, "What in the fuck are you going to do with *this?* It won't hurt anybody. You can't even swing it!"

He dropped it and popped Nord a couple more times, and Nord finally said, "I've had enough."

That was that, but now they had to wrestle each other that night in Tulsa. When I ran Oklahoma City in the afternoon, I wold run Tulsa that night, so we often had some of the same main events scheduled. On this night, one of those was Butch versus Nord. I knew I had to motivate these guys to work together.

We loaded them into the cars and got them to Tulsa, where they had the Hurricane Room at the Tulsa Fairgrounds, our venue that night. So I had Reed and Nord brought into the Hurricane Room. By now, they were sore as hell — their eyes were puffy, their mouths were puffy, their faces were completely swollen up.

I came in and said, "Well, guys, you know, I loved it this afternoon. By the way, you know there's no bonus for that, right? You do understand that I don't pay you to do that?"

They both looked at the floor and muttered, "Yeah."

I said, "Well, since we're going to do this again tonight, I just want to film it, you know? I'd actually rather have you guys fight here than in Oklahoma City, because I've got cameras here. That way I can film it and dub it off. Then I'll have it on tape, because I love watching you guys fight! So, would y'all do that again for me? I really want you two to kick the shit out of each other. Now, I bet your faces are pretty sore, and your hands too. If I felt like that and I was pretty smart, I'd probably figure out a way to work this damn match."

Then I looked at The Barbarian and said, "Now, Nord, if I were you, I'd let the old veteran lead me through it. *You* don't know shit from Shinola. But if you guys want to just beat the shit out of each other, the pay's the same, but you'll make this old man happy!"

Of course, the crowd won't really understand what you are doing. A great "work" is always better spectator entertainment than a "shoot."

"Well," Butch said, "I think we can go work this out."

Nord nodded his head in agreement, and off they went. And they *did* work it out. They ended up having a pretty good match.

I believed strongly in handling those issues and conflicts head on. I didn't believe in being circumspect and letting resentments build. You weren't going to find anyone in one of my dressing rooms saying "I backed him down" if it wasn't true. You sure weren't going to find someone who said, "He's just lucky they wouldn't let us fight." They also knew that, if you started one in the dressing room, no one was going to bail your ass out.

The way to circumvent all the trash-talking and backstabbing that went on in a lot of places was for everyone to know that everyone had the same opportunity to fight it out. Now, if you were a bully in the dressing room, picking on everybody, I wasn't going to put up with that.

Jim Duggan wasn't a bully, but could be so intense that I had to step in and deal with him. In 1985, I had what I thought was a hot angle — the "Best-Dressed Man in Mid-South" feud between Duggan and Ted DiBiase.

They had a contest to see whom the fans thought looked better in his tuxedo. The fans chose Duggan, and DiBiase went out to the parking lot to argue with Joel (my son, directing the show in the TV truck) about the sound-measuring equipment they were using to determine which one had gotten the best crowd reaction. While he was out there, he saw Duggan's car in the parking lot and smashed in the windows, using the bat he'd been carrying to "protect" himself against Duggan during the contest. It was an awesome TV angle, and we had really "milked it" over the buildup, so we had great ratings too.

But I was having some problems with the towns going down each show, on the return match with those two on top, and I couldn't understand it, because it was such a strong angle, with Duggan looking for revenge over his car. I figured it out once I watched one of their matches. Duggan was guzzling DiBiase! DiBiase wouldn't do anything about it because he knew he couldn't physically stop Duggan. And Duggan wasn't guzzling him to be a bully. He was doing it because he got too caught up in it — that was the level of his intensity.

I finally took Jim aside and said, "You dummy — you're killing him! You're not giving him anything! There's no heat! You have to trust him to engineer the match. You can't just guzzle him out there, Jim. The gates are going down because you're taking too much of the match, and it's killing the angle!"

There has to be some mystery. If a babyface just guzzles the heel, no matter what he does, the people really don't want to see it. They want a contest. Now, if the heel also adds some subterfuge, or cheats to take advantage of the babyface, then they really get into the match and get riled up, but there has to be the right mix.

But I could always talk to Jim. I related to tough guys.

People used to ask me things like "What do you think Duggan would do with Doc in a shoot?"

"Well," I'd say, "Duggan and Williams would be hell for two or three minutes, and, if neither of them scored a really devastating kick or blow, then I think Doc would overcome him, because Doc is in shape, and Duggan has never been in shape."

As tough as Duggan was (he was a state champion in high school), a better legitimate wrestler would have the advantage. Doc was a four-time All-American at OU, plus he had better conditioning. Doc was not only a big guy — he was also in tremendous physical condition. You weren't going to wear out Steve Williams.

Again, this is all speculation, the kind wrestlers love — and maybe Duggan knew that too. But it never happened — they were good friends, but I doubt Jim would ever have challenged Doc. Doc, knowing that Jim "sits on ready," would never have wanted that either. Jim Duggan isn't a guy *anybody* would ever want to fight head on, because he's a hard-headed son of a gun, and he's not afraid of much. He could be ferocious.

And as tough and rugged as the guys were, I wasn't getting in as many fights as when I was younger — although it still happened. Inevitably, we'd be in a bar somewhere, and some idiot would recognize us and try to impress his girlfriend by showing up a wrestler. Here's the mentality: "If I can sucker-punch this guy and knock him out, then I'll be a real stud since he's a tough guy on TV. And if he whips my ass, then I'll get a lot of sympathy." The problem is that it doesn't take into account how badly the guy is going to get whipped.

One main reason the number of fights with nonwrestlers died down during the late 1970s and early 1980s was the emergence of the litigious society. A guy would come up and spit in your face and then sue you for clocking him. You had to be careful. Sometimes, if a guy insulted us, we'd wait until he went into the bathroom and follow him in, with another guy stationed outside the door to keep anyone else from going in. The other wrestler would go in, beat up the guy, stuff his face in a toilet and walk out.

Once I became a promoter, I didn't have to deal with that so much. Another thing I allowed, even encouraged, was stretching the marks. If a mark wanted to try out a pro wrestler, we made him sign a waiver absolving Mid-South and the wrestler involved of any responsibility for what happened to the guy in the ring, which we had set up before opening the arena doors for a live show. They also had to put up some money, which I gave to the guy who stretched them.

One time Doc was stretching a guy, and I wasn't happy with how he was doing it. I ended up in the ring with the guy and put him in the "sugar hold," which cut off the blood in his carotid artery, so he "fell asleep." The guy was out, and if I hadn't let up he'd have been dead.

Our mentality was that, whenever we were in public, we were representing the business. Sometimes that meant having to convince people. They might not believe in wrestling, but they'd sure believe in whoever they tried on for size that night.

One night in Kansas City, Dick Murdoch got into a beef after the matches with a boxer who was supposed to be on some big, televised boxing show the next night. Murdoch beat the heck out of the guy — I mean just whipped him up and down that bar — and they had to cancel the guy's fight.

I always felt that tough guys were going to give you 100 percent. Rick Steiner was another stud. He came to work for me in 1985 and was really green, but he was a guy I really enjoyed being around, and I loved watching him develop. He was my kind of guy.

Doc and Rick Steiner were driving from a show one night near Lafayette, Louisiana, when they came upon an emergency. There were some people around a burning car, but there was ammunition in the car, and rather than risk their own lives these people were going to let the guy in the car burn to death. Doc and Steiner just walked up, ripped the doors off the car and pulled the guy out. He didn't make it, but Doc and Steiner did more than anyone else could have. They just got back into their car and kept driving. I didn't even know about it right away. The station manager in Lafayette called me days later and said, "These guys are heroes."

THE **TRADE** THAT MADE A **BANNER YEAR**

In 1983, "Hacksaw" Jim Duggan went from being a mid-level heel to one of my top babyfaces. He became a very popular star who would do great for me in 1984, my most successful year. I saw him as a guy with tremendous explosiveness and a great character. He was a tough man who always gave it his all.

At the tournament to crown the first UWF champion in May 1986, he had his head run into a post in Houston, with the ring buckle bolt on the back side almost penetrating his skull. It was a horrible wound, but tough guy that he was, he kept making his bookings, until his wife called me and said, "I don't think Jim can work tonight. He can't even close his eyes."

I said, "What?"

"His face is swollen!"

I told her to get him to the hospital because he had blood poisoning. Heck, he almost *died*, but he was still making his bookings.

The tradition of "accountability" is what separates real men from boys, and it's evident in all pro sports: the best play hurt. I remember what Bobby Layne, the NFL Hall of Fame quarterback, once told me: "You know why my marriage has lasted so long? Because I tell my wife it is like the NFL — you have to 'play hurt.'"

Another guy who started to become a difference-maker in 1983 was Magnum T.A., Terry Allen. He was a kid who had worked in Florida and San Antonio and had been a sort of protégé of Dusty Rhodes. Although Magnum started for me in 1983, 1984 was the year his star really took off. We slowly built him up, and then I decided to make him a sort of sex symbol. We bought him motorcycle leathers and changed his whole look. He was really getting there when Dusty took him to the Carolinas, where he became a big star, until he had a terrible wreck in 1986 that crippled him and ended his career.

Dusty himself worked some shots for us in 1983, as he had on and off for years. He usually just came in for a few weeks at a time as a special attraction. But he was still a character. He had so much charisma! The people loved him. He was a true superstar.

One day I had Dusty out on an airstrip trying to turn the propeller of my plane by hand to start the engine. My battery had gone dead, and we had to get the plane started so that we could get to a show in Houma, Louisiana.

Dusty said, "You know you've got a million dollars worth of talent here trying to turn a prop on a fuckin' plane? That prop is gonna take off and cut my arm off!"

The plane started, and Dusty was still in one piece, so he got in, and we took off. By the time we got to Houma, it was getting dark, and the airstrip (like much of the area around Houma) was swampland and woods. There were no landmarks or lighting for me to see where I was landing, nor at that time was there any instrument landing system for the airport. I think I clipped a tree as we descended. Dusty acted as if he was having a heart attack, but we landed safely. I think I had two of my children with us too. Again, that's providence.

Once, on a trip in the same area, after the matches we were driving back to New Orleans in a rental car. We stopped off in some Cajun bar and ordered a case of beer. In that era, wrestlers measured the trips by how many beers were consumed. I realize that it's against the law and totally irresponsible, but that is just how it was. The guy at the bar started drawing drafts, filling up twenty-four paper cups.

I said, "Shit, I don't want that! I want cans!" But he didn't have any there.

We finally found a place that had cans, so we were going down the road, drinking our beer, behind Jack Curtis, who also had our gate receipts in the car with him. We decided to push Jack, who was already doing about seventy miles an hour. We locked bumpers with him and pushed him up to where we were both doing about 100 mph. Jack Curtis was about to have a puppy, but Dusty and I were laughing like crazy people, which is about what we were.

And then there was Buddy Landel. Landel had been a job guy for me in 1981 and 1982. By early 1984, he'd bleached his hair blonde and was calling himself "Nature Boy" Buddy Landel. Buddy was another kid who was self-destructive. He was one of the most talented kids I ever saw, but he always struggled with substance abuse.

It seemed I was always chewing his ass out about something, but he worked his butt off and gave his entire heart in the ring. How could you not like a kid like that? I still love Buddy Landel and have kept in touch with him. He just has that thing about him where one day you want to smack him, and the next you want to hug him. Ric Flair was his idol, and he emulated Flair in the ring, which wasn't bad because Ric always gave it his all in the ring. That is the pride of a great performer — to always try to set the standard for being the best in the ring, on interviews or in whatever you do.

A lot of these guys were like my kids, and my real kids grew up with all these guys. What a childhood they had! It was exciting, but there was also something else that I didn't see then. Being so "immersed in the business," they were learning a truly dysfunctional lifestyle in this fantasy-filled, selfish, ego-driven business. Being around wrestling put them around all the things that were beginning to influence our culture — including the drugs and extremely loose morals! There is no way that could be good for children.

My son Joel ended up coming to work for me after flunking out of college. He had been a straight-A student in high school but got into that partying mentality when he went to college. Ene had me give him my Porsche 928, a state-of-the-art sports car, to drive. Three tickets later I took it back and bought him a Caprice. Finally, I said, "This semester, if you don't have a 3.0 grade-point average, your ass is out of school."

He went right back to the University of Oklahoma and partied his ass off. He wasn't cutting it, and he knew it. He came home and said, "Look, I'm wasting your money. I'm just not ready for school yet. Let me come work for you."

Joel did production work for us and was unbelievably artistic. In 1983 and 1984, the idea of doing music videos for wrestlers was new, and Joel was perfect for it. Jerry Jarrett had started those videos in Memphis in 1983, but Joel really took it to the next level. He was so talented, and years later he went on to win several awards at one of the major network affiliate TV stations here in Tulsa.

In 1983, Joel was twenty-one years old and just totally took over our TV trucks. He was very hands-on but had a bit of a problem delegating. In trying to do everything, he would sometimes screw up. When he did, I yelled at him — which he hated. I once told him, "The difference is, when I yell at you, you're not fired. You made a $50,000 mistake [which he did once], and I might kill you, but you're still my son!" But words hurt — especially words from your parents or other authority figures. Often those "injuries" last a lifetime.

I had a lot of talent on board by the end of 1983, but what really made the next year a big one was a talent swap I made with Memphis promoter Jerry Jarrett. At the time, my business was flat. Sometimes it doesn't matter how sharp a businessman you are; you can't see your own problems because you're too close to them. I asked Jarrett and his top star, Jerry "The King" Lawler, to come to one of my television tapings and watch, then tell me what they thought was wrong.

We had what I thought was a hell of a taping, and I sat down with them after it was over. One of them, I can't recall which, said, "Bill, where are all the blowjobs?"

I said, "You guys came all the way here for blowjobs? I thought you guys in Tennessee had all your relatives to do that!"

We all laughed, but then they said, "You're missing the point. Where are all the *blowjobs?*"

I was getting exasperated. "What do you mean? I flew you guys all the way here so you could ask me *that?*"

They said, "Bill, your crowd is made up of old, hardcore wrestling fans. You have the toughest wrestlers in the world, but you don't have anyone who's going to draw young girls. Because where the young girls are the young guys will be too. You need a youth movement. You don't have anybody on your shows that the kids are going to give a shit about."

Jim Ross, my announcer and someone who was working increasingly with my television stations, picked up right away on what they were saying. Ross was a *smart* kid and my right-hand man by this point. In fact, he is one of the most talented, dedicated men in wrestling. He loves it. He survived and thrived under me, and he survived and thrived at WCW until that idiot Eric Bischoff fired him to promote his own agenda — but by then Vince McMahon had seen Jim's talent and hired him. By the mid-1980s, Jim had become the best play-by-play announcer in the business, and he's been that ever since, in my opinion. He's an incredibly talented individual with a great love for and knowledge of what he's doing.

By contrast, Bischoff was, to me, a "popcorn fart" — all noise, some smell but little substance. He sure took WCW to a position of dominance in our business (for a short time — like a popcorn fart), but he also ruined it. I'm told that, under his last year of management, TBS lost some $62 million! It takes a real genius to lose $62 million at *anything*. I don't think someone could even do that without planning it. But he did! What a dumbass! I love it. What a thing to be remembered for — the guy who broke the will of TBS to have a wrestling company. Vince is probably getting a kick out of having him go get coffee for him. Vince loves to make his former competitors into his "stooges." It's like having a trophy around for a while, until he gets tired of it. Bischoff will be a glorified "gofer." And that may be more than he has the ability to be really good at. Sure looks like Jim Ross got the last laugh!

But back to late 1983 — Jarrett said that he had some guys he was looking to get rid of who could fill the bill for the demographic I needed to create a "more youthful audience" and that we might be able to solve each other's problems, so I went to one of their shows in Memphis.

I saw a young manager there named Jim Cornette working a lot of undercard stuff. He was so obnoxious that *I* wanted to slap him, and I knew he was only working! I knew he was instant box office if he could get *me* that riled up! He was a natural heel with an incredible mouth. Cornette has become legendary in this business in his own right. I have tremendous respect for him and consider him a true friend. I am proud to have had a positive influence on his perception of our business.

There was also an undercard babyface named Bobby Eaton who could take incredible bumps and a veteran heel named Dennis Condrey, who was spinning his wheels in the middle of the card.

Jarrett also had Ricky Morton and Robert Gibson, two smaller guys, in a midcard babyface tag team called The Rock & Roll Express. His main tag team was a similar sex symbol team called The Fabulous Ones, Stan Lane and Steve Keirn. The Fabs, as they were called, were great, but their success meant Morton and Gibson weren't doing much in Memphis. Gibson was good, but Morton was just phenomenal. But that's why they worked together. You can't have two equals on a team, and Gibson was the perfect fit because he knew his role.

One look at The Rock & Roll Express and I knew I'd found the perfect act to appeal to kids and girls. Stan and Steve, The Fabulous Ones, were a great team, but they were already to the point that they were satisfied with being on top and were already into themselves as top superstars. I liked guys who were hungry.

It all worked out. Jarrett wanted to keep The Fabs, and I wanted The Rock & Rolls. He wanted to keep Jimmy Hart, the one I'd have gotten rid of if I was him. Hart was talented as hell, but he'd been there so long.

We also got a young babyface named Terry Taylor, who was a real babe magnet. The girls loved him! Taylor worked really well with Barry Darsow, who had come to be known as Krusher Khruschev. He came to learn because he didn't have a lot of experience. A lot of my crew, over the years, had come to learn, and I think my territory was a pretty good training ground for a lot of guys. The big offices couldn't create a star — they had to inherit stars. We created stars.

Darsow got the Russian gimmick after he wrestled Nikolai Volkoff. The story was that, after Volkoff beat him, Darsow became a heel "Russian sympathizer" by aligning himself with Volkoff so he could learn the strength and conditioning techniques of the Soviet athletes.

Volkoff was a nice guy. He was an incredibly strong man and a great athlete. His only problem was that he was almost *too* nice a guy, which made it tough for him to be a very convincing heel. You have to let that sniveling nature come out in you to be a good villain.

I was always a good villain because I was able to tap into my own cowardice, from the days before I learned to "trigger" my temper. As a heel, I was a treacherous foe because I would figure out some way to beat you that wasn't fair. My psychology as a heel was that I was afraid of getting hurt, or getting whipped, so I would find some way to foul my opponent to gain the upper hand.

Volkoff, on the other hand, was such a great athlete, so strong and such a nice guy that it was hard for him to emote the viciousness that a heel needs to exude. But he was a great guy to have around. He was always in a good mood and always tried hard.

As 1984 dawned, these younger guys became part of a package, with the tough, rugged ones people could believe in. But in putting The Rock & Roll Express in with my big guys, we had to be able to explain on TV how the much smaller Morton and Gibson could hang in there. In doing commentary, I would note their quickness and say they were tag-team *specialists*. And they ended up having the perfect opponents in the two Memphis midcarders we paired up as The Midnight Express — Dennis Condrey and Bobby Eaton.

Having that variety made our demographics explode. Mine was probably one of the first wrestling companies to really study demographics.

Jerry then came down to another of my TV tapings and picked whom he wanted. He decided on Rick Rood (who became Rick Rude), Masao Ito, Hacksaw Higgins and Jim Neidhart. He was completely happy with our talent trades — only later, when our business exploded, did he allow his mind to create this illusion of my "stealing his talent."

Jarrett spent years swearing that I stole all that talent, but he was *begging* me to take them, as a favor to him, because he had no room for them. He had them doing jobs, and none of them was featured. In early 1984, Mid-South was becoming incredibly successful with this new mix, but Jarrett was having troubles because he'd kept guys he'd had around forever and who were stale. Years later, though, he called me when I was running WCW to apologize.

I told him, "Jerry, I understand. I've never harbored any ill will. I never understood where you came up with that shit, but I thank you for being man enough to call me."

We've had a good relationship ever since. I think Jerry saw that I never did anything to retaliate or to hurt him. In fact, I ended up solving one of his biggest problems.

Jarrett had been in a promotional war with Angelo Poffo's group, which was also operating in Tennessee. Jerry was beating them economically, but it had become ugly. Angelo's biggest star was his son, who wrestled as "Macho Man" Randy Savage, and Savage had pistol-whipped Bill Dundee in one altercation. Poffo's guys would also challenge Jarrett's on TV. Jerry was scared of Savage. Of course, if you had a crazy guy with a gun running around threatening you and your guys, it would be wise to "be very apprehensive of him."

I was the one who finally got the Poffos and Jarrett to work together. Randy called me, at his wit's end. I'm not sure what made him call me, except that he knew me a little from working as a masked guy for me in Florida while playing minor-league baseball (his team wouldn't allow him to wrestle, so we just placed him under a mask, and he wrestled without them knowing). He'd also worked for me in Georgia briefly, during one of my fill-in stints (but by then he had really grown and developed, possibly due to some chemical enhancements that were becoming the rage), and I think we had built some mutual respect.

When he called, I told him, "Your problem is you've become a loaded gun. You're unreliable, and people are afraid of you. You're threatening to either shoot people or beat them up! You can't do that shit. And you're getting your ass kicked economically. You've got to bury the hatchet with Jarrett and come on into the mainstream."

We talked for a while, and he agreed with me and asked me to help him get this resolved. Then I called Jarrett to set up a meeting between them. It worked out, and they did a big deal where Savage and his brother, Lanny Poffo, came into Memphis as invaders against Jerry Lawler. They did some great box office before Savage went in 1985 to the WWF, where he became one of the biggest stars in the world and made his fortune.

My compliment to Randy Savage is this: at the height of his run with Vince, he took the time to call me and thank me. He had no reason, nothing to gain. He just wanted to say thanks for helping him work things out with Jarrett. "I wouldn't be in the business today and making all this money if it wasn't for you," he said.

That, to me, is the measure of a person — the way you touch other people's lives. You know, I've done a lot of shitty things in my life, but I did good things too and made some positive differences.

Jarrett also had a wrestler named Bill Dundee who alternated as a booker with Lawler. Jarrett was looking for somewhere to send him, because he'd been at or near the top for years, and they'd done everything they could do with him as a wrestler. The fans had seen him as a top baby-face, teaming with Lawler; they'd seen him as a top heel, fighting with Lawler. He needed to get away because he was becoming stale. The dynamic between him and Lawler was played out, and Lawler was part owner of the territory, so he sure wasn't going anywhere. I talked to Dundee and to Jarrett and agreed to hire Dundee. It wasn't part of the talent trade, though — just a chance for Dundee to get a breather.

I didn't want Dundee as a wrestler, but I could tell just from talking to him that he had a keen mind, so I offered him a spot as booker. Make no mistake — I was still the main booker, or at least the "last word," but I always wanted someone with a fresh perspective, and Dundee had a ton of original ideas.

He was booking his own programs in Memphis, and he had a lot of good ideas, but I knew I would have to keep him from wrestling because of his ego — he was about five foot four, and I didn't want a much smaller guy beating my big studs. Dundee's ego would have had him doing just that. I loved Dundee, but I wanted to channel his drive and talent into building my business, and not have it compete with his ego as a worker, so I "disarmed that missile" and channeled and challenged his mind into just booking. The results were awesome!

Dundee's finishes and ideas for gimmicks made me a fortune. But I had to control him. It was no different from what Vince does today. Everything in that company goes through Vince, and he's got an unbelievable mind. Other people might give him ideas, but he fine-tunes them. With Dundee, I had to tone him down. He had tons of ideas, but if it had been up to him there would have been gimmicks in every match. He would have had the guys throwing powder in each other's eyes in the dressing room, just to warm up for the opening match! I mean he could have thought of a different gimmick for every match on every card.

I did end up letting Dundee work some, but in the bottom half of the card, and even then I pulled the plug on it pretty quick, because I could see him trying to position himself.

So, by early 1984, we had The Midnight Express, The Rock & Roll Express and Terry Taylor. Add those guys to the mix of Junkyard Dog, Butch Reed, Magnum T.A., Nikolai Volkoff and the rest of my crew, and we were really cooking.

And then came April and The Last Stampede.

I had kept myself out of action for a few years. Instead, I wore the hat of Mid-South's president and CEO because I wanted out of the ring and into more of the business side. Jim Ross and Dundee, however, were so in tune with the crowd they realized, in addition to these tremendous new pieces of talent we had, that there was a way to make money by putting me back into the ring on a short-term basis.

The angle was that Cornette's team of The Midnight Express had just won the tag-team titles, and Cornette had bought time on television to throw a party in celebration. He had a cake, noise makers — the whole deal. While he was cutting the cake outside the ring and his boys were on the opposite side of the ring, taunting the fans, The Rock & Roll Express ran out and smashed his face in the cake.

Later on the same show, I explained that we had a few minutes left of air-time but not enough to have another match. Therefore, I had opted to show Cornette's face going into the cake again, because I thought it was funny.

Cornette came out to ringside and had a fit over his "humiliation" being shown a second time. He was dressing down Jim Ross when I went out and said, since I was president of Mid-South, if he had a problem with anyone, it should be with me. He started threatening to sue me and was jumping up and down, but then he started talking about my "goofy-looking son," which ended the talking. I shouted at him that no one was going to insult my family. I said this was twice I was letting him leave with his skin intact (we'd had a confrontation on TV a few weeks earlier). This would be the second and last time I would walk away, I told him.

When he grabbed my shoulder to try to turn me around, I spun around and smacked him. And I give Cornette credit — that kid had *guts.* He stuck his face right out there for it, and I slapped him so hard it almost turned him a flip. The audience just exploded because he'd been interfering in his team's matches constantly and hadn't yet received even a little comeuppance.

The next week Cornette's Midnight Express attacked me while I was conducting interviews and left me a bloody heap. From there, I had to "get my revenge," so I recruited Junkyard Dog (back under the mask as Stagger Lee) as my partner.

That was an incredibly successful run of matches. We did a "Last Stampede" in every major town, and it was pretty much two straight weeks of sellouts, or close to it, grossing well over $1 million in my small-population territory.

They were also very trying matches, because as good as Cornette and The Midnight Express were JYD definitely had limitations in the ring. In one match, I kicked one of the Midnights so hard I blew out my hamstring. There's nothing as excruciating. It's like an electric shock going through your leg. As you are falling, you try to look around to see what hit you, and then the pain is so excruciating you want to die. I lay there, hardly able to move, but I finally worked my way over to the corner, where I tagged JYD. Well, he made his big comeback, cleaned house and then tagged me back in. I couldn't move! He forgot I was hurt, and I had to get back in there and gut it out.

Over the rest of that series, hurt or not, I had to do most of the work. That also fit in with how I wanted JYD portrayed. I never wanted him in a situation where he was getting beaten down for long periods of time. But JYD was having more problems than I fully realized. I knew he was getting high, but I didn't know until later he was hooked on cocaine. He was also involved, I was told, with a woman who was into voodoo. She would do things that scared him half to death, such as burying his clothes in the garden. He was terrified of her — that she had "the mojo" on him or something. I'm sure the cocaine only aggravated his delusion. We had been so close, but he and I were soon to have a bad parting.

Around the time of The Last Stampede matches, we really kicked into gear the angle that was going to take Magnum T.A. over the hump. His coach and mentor, Mr. Wrestling II, was going to turn on him, forcing Magnum to defeat the guy who'd taught him about being a star.

Wrestling II had a hell of a run as a heel years earlier in Georgia, feuding with Tim Woods, the original Mr. Wrestling, and II loved working as a heel with Magnum. If you could make the transition and work both ways, it gave you a double life in a territory. And Johnny Walker, as long as he understood where you were going with him, was a great participant. A quality son of a gun, he was dead serious about his matches. And if I ever gave him something that didn't make sense to him, he'd think about it and come back to me. "Well, now, wait a minute, Bill. I've been thinking about this, and. . . ." He was *that* passionate about what he was doing. He really cared about doing good work and giving the fans something that made sense.

His wife, Olivia, made all his robes for him (she also made a lot of Ric Flair's famous robes) and was a great companion. The last time I saw her was in 2003, just shortly before she passed away, which just devastated this man whom I'd always known as such a tough guy. But that was how much he loved her.

Wrestling II was never what I would call a great interview, but he could say just enough. However, he could emote his character and personality through his actions.

That strong stretch continued until around the fall of 1985. By then, The Rock & Roll Express was gone, The Midnight Express and Cornette were long gone, and Bill Dundee was returning to Memphis. Dundee and I didn't have a bad parting, but after more than a year it was time for both of us to change gears. Dick Slater came into Mid-South as his replacement, and I tried Dick as both a wrestler and a booker.

Business wasn't as strong as it had been, but I don't think that was because Dundee had burned out the territory with too many gimmicks, which was something I've heard. I think "holding back" so that you don't burn out the territory was an antiquated concept even twenty years ago. I think excitement is excitement. Every booker had a different style, but, if you get a guy in there who understands how to get across his vision, it'll never miss a beat.

VINCE McMAHON AND THE
WRESTLING WAR

Vincent K. McMahon, who bought the World Wrestling Federation from his father in 1982, had planned for some time to use cable television to become America's first national wrestling promoter. He had $1 million set aside to do it, but Vince later told me that he nearly went broke.

Vince was ambitious and wanted to make his mark. Many of the old promoters hated him because he was driving them out of business, but he was hard working and, really, a brilliant man. He had a far-reaching vision — and it wasn't that far from my own.

When I saw what he was doing in early 1984, there wasn't much I could do about it except fight it out when he came to my area, which we always did. I think Vince himself would admit that every time he came to my territory he got thrashed. We kicked the living crap out of him in Houston, Oklahoma and Mississippi.

He was locked out of Louisiana altogether for a while. Heck, *I* was the one who helped to break the booking license restriction in Louisiana that had meant only one office could run shows there. We encouraged them to change that in 1986, which meant I also no longer felt I had to make political contributions to the governor, as it became free enterprise. Vince had hired a lawyer to try to breach that regulation, but he wasn't tuned in to Louisiana politics. Finally, I told one of Vince's agents that the lawyer whom the WWF was using there had been dead for over a year.

Corruption is rampant in political systems everywhere. In Louisiana, it just seems to be more openly embraced ever since Huey Long made "political patronage" the catalyst for good government. Governor Edwin Edwards, in office for most of my promotional career, was tremendously charismatic, smart and charming. He seemed to have everything one could possibly wish for except character and integrity. Remember that old saying "There's no honor among thieves?" Believe it.

I started backing Edwards before he was even a front-runner. I just had a "feel" for him. My feelings about him turned out to be correct. He often told people when we were together that I had told him he would win and become governor when he was a longshot. Edwards became another example of money being just a way of keeping score. I once figured it cost about $350,000 a year to do business in Louisiana due to this "system."

Emile Bruneau, the athletic commissioner, had tremendous integrity, but the governor still "appointed" his political supporters in special interest positions, whereby they benefited from the hard work and success of our operation while never sharing in any losses for any event. So we had "our towns," which we totally controlled and kept all profits from, except maybe for fees to a figurehead licensee. In other towns, Edwards appointed his supporters to be licensees. They got the profits and just paid us for "talent" and "a booking fee." As time went by, we were so successful that we encouraged them to help out on our transportation costs, TV production costs, plus any airtime costs for their market, and we raised the booking fee percentage.

Edwards also required our "political contributions" to be in cash — naturally! I've seen suitcases full of money by his desk, so I thought that surely I wasn't the only one being encouraged to give support. I think a lot of his contributions were possibly "invested" in gambling in Las Vegas, where, I was told, he was notorious — a real high roller!

Emile's son, Peppi, was also a person of integrity and thus was always opposed to the governor. As Peppi became more influential as a state legislator, he would accompany us to our "meetings" with the governor. This allowed him to witness any "requests" made, which at least was a positive step. It also allowed us to make our "contributions" by check instead of cash — to the governor's chagrin. Finally, when I felt Edwards's demands had gotten totally out of control, there was a colorful confrontation between the governor and me, and a couple of his "political operatives," in the governor's mansion.

Peppi was standing by at the legislature, and if the governor had continued with his demands I was prepared to go on TV and expose him, and I let him know it! That didn't happen — Edwards realized how harmful that could be since I was on the air in every major town in Louisiana every week with our show, and the governor was already under indictment. It was another in his series of trials, and he won *that* one.

The administration's total lack of scruples grew as time went by. Edwards once chartered two 747s to France to help pay off his "campaign debt." The top political operatives personally called each of the big supporters they were encouraging to give more political contributions to tell them they expected them to be on this trip — at $10,000 per seat! They tracked me down in Memphis, visiting Jerry Jarrett. We were at the TV station in Memphis, and they told me they had reserved two seats for me on this airplane. By that time, I was getting pretty stubborn about anything beyond the norm of our past agreements, and I refused their invitation. When the caller tried to intimidate me, I told him to call Peppi Bruneau, my attorney, because I sure was! And I hung up on him. They called me back and said that they had checked, and "everything was fine" on my account.

One of the governor's supporters got in serious trouble for being a bookie in Louisiana, and the governor pardoned him. In the supporter's local newspaper, an editorial cartoon depicted him with angel's wings as the paper reported how the governor had pardoned him — and he was one of those "special people" I was encouraged to work with as the "promoter" in his town, and I had to run his town every week.

Edwards is now in federal prison. You can win several of those criminal trials, but you have to lose only *one*.

In 1984, Vince McMahon took over Georgia Championship Wrestling, including the spot on Turner's cable Superstation, which had been Channel 17 in Atlanta. Shortly before that, I had sold my shares in the Georgia company to Ole Anderson. Ole, who was booking Georgia at this time, and I had been friends for a long time. He did a good job in the early 1980s and was in a tough spot, with Barnett being the boss. He ran a good business, and we had made a lot of money.

The only time I ever needed to go in was when Ole got bogged down, which could happen to anybody. When it happened to me, I would just change bookers. Ole couldn't do that because he *was* the booker. So, sometimes, I would go in and help him get back on track. It wasn't that I was a miracle worker. It was like when I had Jarrett and Lawler come in and look at *my* business. Sometimes you need someone to come in because you're among the trees and can't see the forest.

Ole was a good hand in the ring and had a pretty sharp mind, and he and Barnett made for a successful partnership. In 1982, Ole asked me about buying my shares. I agreed to sell them, but I ended up having to sue Ole to get my money. Eventually, however, I got what I was owed.

Even afterward, we were always able to help each other out with ideas. In 1983, Ole had me come and look at what he was doing. I saw these two awesome bodybuilders he had working as The Road Warriors. I told Ole that they would stand out even more by shaving their heads and painting their faces. They were awesome but uncontrollable. They got to the point that they really believed in their own gimmicks. They truly believed they were supermen. And they relied heavily on pharmaceuticals for those awesome physiques.

I remember Hawk once telling me that he was shooting straight monkey hormones. He said, "The first thing I want to do when I wake up in the morning, I want to kill somebody."

I just looked at him and said, "What a way to live."

Still, they were great kids with great hearts. Ole put Paul Ellering with them as their manager, and unlike most he *really* managed their business affairs.

McMahon got the TBS slot when Jim Barnett and the Briscos sold their shares to him, giving McMahon majority interest in the Georgia promotion. He shut it down and started running WWF tapes on TBS, giving him a lock on national cable television, because he also had the USA Network at that time.

Ole tried to fight the WTBS takeover in court, but he lost. In my opinion, there were two territorial promoters who could have won an antitrust suit against the WWF in the 1980s.

I was one of them. By 1987, I had documentation of McMahon's predatory business practices in terms of getting arenas and his tactics in getting his TV shows on in my markets. I had the top law firm in Louisiana ready to go, but I decided not to file because I would have been fighting that one for years at a cost greater than what I could afford in 1987.

The other promoter was Verne Gagne. Vince taking his talent en masse and forcing Gagne's AWA off some of the Midwest TV stations was clearly predatory. When Vince was first starting to go nationwide in late 1983, he took not only top stars such as Hulk Hogan and David Schultz from Gagne but also Gagne's commentators. He really targeted Verne.

It was a different story in Georgia. The Briscos and Ole had never gotten along. I mean they always disliked each other, so it wasn't like the Briscos had to weigh out a smart business move against their loyalty to their good friend Ole Anderson.

I heard from a fairly reliable source that they went out and did this deal where Ole and the Briscos reaffirmed their faith in each other, shortly before the Briscos turned around and sold to Vince. They all got drunk, and knowing Jack and Gerry they were probably also smoking a lot of dope, and they did a blood oath by cutting their hands open and mixing their blood.

After I heard about it, I used to tease Ole: "A Polack and two Indians in a *blood oath?* What a deal!"

Selling to Vince turned out to be the best thing the Briscos could have done. Gerald is still a road agent for Vince, twenty years later. They made the right decision if you weigh everything out. They had no allegiance to Ole. And Vince already had Barnett's shares in the office, because Ole had uncovered how much Barnett was spending on himself, and he pushed Barnett out of a position of control. So Barnett had no reluctance about selling out his stock to McMahon.

Not long after that, though, Vince fired a shot at Mid-South that definitely got my attention — he snatched away The Junkyard Dog. It was a devastating blow. The worst thing was the way we found out. One night in August 1984, JYD just didn't show up. And he never showed up again. Years later Vince told me that he'd never told JYD not to show up for us, and I believe Vince — at least I think I do. Still, JYD walked out after all those good years. . . . One might think some serious money changed hands, wouldn't they?

I had loaned JYD $10,000 in cash and $10,000 more that I recorded. I ended up suing him, and the Louisiana Athletic Commission suspended him because he owed me $10,000. So he had to pay that back, but the half I loaned him in cash I never saw again.

It was a real loss to the territory because we had built him up as the key guy, but what hurt me the most was the loss of that personal relationship I felt we had. Another sad thing to me was that he was a true superstar in our area, but when he went to Vince he was just another guy there, even though Vince did make him a lot of money.

I've seen it happen to a lot of guys, and I'll tell you — when a guy gets hooked on drugs, there's no way for him to think logically. That person sees life only through the filter of whatever drug or substance he's abusing. And if you're not a drugger, you can actually convince yourself that you can help someone through a problem like that.

I believe JYD never recovered from cocaine. He made millions in his three years with Vince, and he ended up with nothing. He told me it all ended up getting smoked or going up his nose.

I even tried to bring JYD into WCW when I was running it in 1992, but he had gained a lot of weight. I told him he needed to get down to 250 or 260 pounds and get off that junk. We were actually on amicable terms at that point, but I had to refuse him work after a few shots because he couldn't get his life in order.

When JYD left Mid-South in 1984, I tried several times to replace him with other charismatic black athletes, but no one could fill his shoes. They didn't have his universal charisma. New Orleans had a huge black population, and those fans never fully came back after JYD left.

Many of the other cities remained strong because of The Midnight Express, The Rock & Roll Express, Jim Duggan and some other guys, as well as the "package show" concept I'd first seen in Florida. The package concept was not to control the wrestlers; it was to maximize the number of dollars we could draw at the box office, because if you had packaged your show right you had all the demographics covered.

One of the guys I tried to have fill JYD's role was "Hacksaw" Butch Reed. Reed had been my top heel, as JYD's main rival, and I turned him babyface. People reacted well to him, but it still wasn't the same. I want to tell you, though, Butch was a hell of a guy. He was a good athlete and tough as nails. He was also a hell of a heel and did everything that was ever asked of him.

What ended up putting Butch out of my territory was the travel. Mid-South always had the reputation of having the roughest road schedule, and a lot of it was on two-lane roads. Butch's wife lived up in Missouri, where he was from, and the grind really got to him.

Then Butch got on cocaine. His wife called me once and blamed me. I guess she thought he was doing that stuff to himself to keep up with the pace, but she was really letting me have it.

I finally told her, "Let me tell *you* something, honey. I'm not the one putting that powder up Butch's nose."

She finally yanked Butch out in early 1986. She gave him an ultimatum

— give up that stuff and come home, or stay on the road and forfeit his marriage. Well, he was gone, and I had to fine him because he walked out on a lot of bookings. I respected him for choosing his family, which was the right thing for him to do, but he shouldn't have walked out without notice.

But if I looked Butch Reed in the eye today, I'd offer him a handshake and a hug, because he was a man's man. I still have a ton of respect for Butch. A lot of people who didn't start out respecting him learned to respect him. Just ask John Nord.

But after JYD left, whether it was Snowman, Master G. or Reed, they just didn't have it at the level JYD did. He transcended black or white. He just had a special charisma, and he was a great-looking kid.

That intrinsic thing JYD had was hard to define and just about impossible to replace. Terry Taylor was a babe magnet — the girls loved him. He was also a smooth worker in the ring, but on his own he couldn't draw serious money. I could put Terry into a situation with someone who could draw, and it would work, but I felt I could never build my territory around him. I do not say this vindictively but to point out that special thing, that certain quality, that just a few had. Every "top guy" feels he has it, but the proof is in the gates drawn and the places he fills while in the top spot for a length of time.

And I tried. I pushed Terry into a big program in the spring of 1985, challenging NWA world champion Ric Flair, but it just never clicked. He just couldn't carry things on a main-event level. However, I respect and like Terry and am most proud of his becoming a follower of Christ.

About two months after the WWF's war with the regional promotions had cost me JYD, my top babyface, it indirectly brought Ted DiBiase, *always* a welcome addition, back to me. DiBiase had left for Georgia after his feud with Duggan in 1983 and was the top heel there when the WWF took over the company's time slot on WTBS. Ole Anderson started up again with an early morning slot on WTBS, but it was a smaller operation, and Ted wasn't able to earn what he had, so he came back to Mid-South.

In 1984, some of the old NWA promoters, along with Verne Gagne, tried to work together and promote in McMahon's home base of the Northeast under the banner "Pro Wrestling USA." They could never cooperate, though, and Vince was far ahead of them in presentation and TV production values, so I didn't stay involved in Pro Wrestling USA very long.

I fought the war in my own territory. Vince didn't really try to come into my territory until several months after he started his national push. When he did come into my towns, he found himself up against a promotion that was going to put up more of a fight than he was used to.

Jim Ross came up with a lot of great ideas to fight the WWF. One was "Fan Appreciation Night," where we ran a free show opposite McMahon in Oklahoma. We took a little bit of a financial hit on those, but when McMahon saw what his shows were drawing he apparently decided it wasn't worth it to run Oklahoma, in the short term anyway.

I fought back by booking shows to go head on against Vince when he came into my area and by showing matches on TV featuring one of my current stars beating a guy who was now with Vince, especially if it was someone he had in a featured role.

Anywhere I was I always emphasized that my guys were the toughest guys there were. I did the same thing in WCW in 1992. I emphasized that we were "the real deal." I had to stop using that phrase because boxer Evander Holyfield had a copyright on it, so I changed it to "Let's hook 'em up!"

What better way to show that my guys were better and tougher? Showing one of my guys beating a guy that McMahon was featuring on WWF television was a freebie. It didn't mean I had any animosity toward the WWF guys I was showing.

In 1985, less than a year after JYD went to the WWF, I lost The Rock & Roll Express to Jim Crockett, whose NWA group got a WTBS Superstation slot that had been promised to me. Their feud with The Midnight Express (who also ended up on WTBS by summer 1985) ended with a series of scaffold matches in November 1984. After that, Ricky Morton and Robert Gibson worked with Ted DiBiase and Hercules and then moved into a feud with the Guerrero brothers, Chavo and Hector. The Midnight Express went to work for Fritz Von Erich in Dallas for about six months before joining Jim Crockett's promotion.

Terry Taylor also went to work for Jim Crockett's group on WTBS in 1985, around the same time The Rock & Roll Express went. As big an attraction as The Rock & Rolls had been, their gimmick had pretty much run its course here. We had a great run with them, and Crockett's group was red hot when they went, so I couldn't blame them.

One thing I understood, if a guy had a chance to go to an area where he could get himself a better financial deal than I could offer, I wasn't going to be able to keep him. One guy I couldn't keep was Jake "The Snake" Roberts. Jake was Grizzly's son, so he had grown up in the business. He understood it and always had talent and psychology. He had worked for me in 1980 and came back in 1985, starting out as a midlevel heel. He really caught on with the fans, to the point where he was soon a main-event babyface. As talented as he was, it was fine with me when he decided to go to the WWF in early 1986. My problems with Jake weren't nearly as bad as they would be later on, but he was already showing signs of being a shifty guy who liked to cause chaos and capitalize on it. But he gave his notice, like a professional, and we parted on good terms.

After he gave his notice, we had an unusual deal in Houston. A newspaper columnist named Ken Hoffman wrote that Jake (wrestling Dick Slater for the North American title that night) would definitely not be winning the belt because he was WWF bound. Paul Boesch showed me the clipping, and we knew there was only one thing to do — cross him up. Jake won the title that night and dropped it back to Slater in Oklahoma City a couple of nights later. We made sure Jake mentioned the columnist by name in his promo with the belt after the match.

Paul and I capitalized on the situation in Houston. And the fact that we did it was really a testament to our trust of Jake and his professionalism. But he was soon off for the WWF to make the big money. I just couldn't compete with the WWF or Crockett for money. I couldn't compete with Georgia when things were good there, because the Georgia trips were short, and the money was pretty good.

In 1986, when Terry Taylor came back from Crockett, I made him booker, replacing Dick Slater. The first thing he did was book himself to beat every top heel in the company. I had to put a stop to that real fast.

A guy who can do all the things in the ring is always going to think he should be in that spot, but there's an intangible thing, a unique charisma, that draws money. I can't tell you what it is, but I can tell you who had it and who didn't. Dusty Rhodes had it. Dick Murdoch had it, and so did Ernie Ladd, Bruno Sammartino, Dick the Bruiser, Hulk Hogan, Ric Flair, Gene Kiniski and Fritz and Waldo Von Erich, among others.

And, in all honesty, I think "Cowboy" Bill Watts had it, because I got over in every territory I worked. This, to me, was the true test — whether a guy could draw money or get over in every territory he worked. Some guys got over only in one territory and couldn't in others; their popularity was more a product of a unique situation or special handling. Some, when they had that success, never left the areas they were in, but the guys mentioned above got over wherever they went because they had that charisma. JYD was truly a superstar in only one area — Mid-South. Jerry "The King" Lawler was a tremendously talented performer, but he stayed primarily in Tennessee, except years later when he went to work for Vince, and he became more known for his commentary.

Ted DiBiase had plenty of charisma, and he was *so* talented, but he would make the match at his own expense. At times, that worked against him, which seems to be a paradox. Could "Cowboy" Bill Watts make a match the way Ted could? Hell, no. "Cowboy" Bill Watts could get "Cowboy" Bill Watts over, and if I could have a good match with you at the same time that was wonderful, but if I couldn't I would come out of the ring with the fans believing in me.

There was also something to having a mean streak. My son Erik, as a pro wrestler, is *too* good with people. He gives them too much. He's a great athlete and a tough kid, but he lacks that killer mentality. He won't take control if the person he is working with isn't giving him his fair share of the match. He's not afraid — he is just kind hearted and would rather make the match. Well, I had no problems — if you messed with *me* in the ring, I'd put you down, and those people would believe in me. If you tried to stiff me, or didn't do what I wanted, I was going to get it one way or another. That doesn't mean I was tougher than everybody else. I just was able to figure things tactically. The Bill Miller matches from the mid-1960s are examples of that.

And I had that "something" that is hard to describe. I can't put my finger on what it was, but I had it as a wrestler even before I got into power. I just had a way where, no matter what I did, it went over with the people, and the people left my matches remembering Bill Watts.

KEEPING IT REAL

I came from a position, from day one of my wrestling career, that you'd better respect me. I couldn't change your mind about the business, but you'd better respect me. In the promotions I worked in early on, protection of the business, or "kayfabe," was an important aspect of wrestling.

Roy Shire in San Francisco was a stickler for it. Once Ray Stevens and I wanted to go out and have some fun, so we went to Los Angeles, far outside his territory. Well, when he heard about it, he fined us both for going out together in public while Ray was a heel and I was a babyface. But, oh, what a party. Stevens was an all-time partyer — an earlier version of Ric Flair.

A couple of years later, when I was working for Gagne, I went out with another wrestler (I won't mention his name, because he's married) after we wrestled each other one night, and we picked up a couple of gals. We went out partying with them, and they asked us about Verne Gagne. We both said Verne was in the old folks' home — we really laid it on him. Well, we didn't know that they knew Verne, and they went right back and told him. He confronted us separately at the TV tapings in Minneapolis the next morning and was just livid.

"So you two worked against each other in Duluth, and then broke the kayfabe, and even took these two broads out. What the fuck's the matter with you?"

I said, "It's my fault. [The other wrestler] didn't want to do it. It was my fault."

Well, that got him even madder. "Damn it!" he said. "I just blew up at [the other guy], and he said it was all his fault!"

I think what he was really mad about wasn't that we'd broken kayfabe — he was mad about what we'd said about him.

But we had to protect the business because no one else was going to protect it for us. Were we getting any positive press? Heck, no. Anything that came out on wrestling in the newspaper was derogatory or tried to expose it, but we had one thing the newspapers didn't have. We had an hour-long commercial about our business that aired on TV every week. That meant we could set the tone for whatever context we wanted our business to be seen in. Our main restriction was that we had to put on a show that generated ratings so that the TV stations would keep us.

I always emphasized the athleticism and toughness of my wrestlers, and I always treated the sport like a sport. Yes, it was a "work," but it could still be a very athletic and tough event and not for the weak hearted or "sissies." And back then things could get out of hand, or someone might refuse to "do business." Some might even try to double-cross an opponent in the ring, although that was rare. The bottom line was that you had to be prepared to deal, physically, with a situation that might pop up in the ring.

I even made tongue-in-cheek remarks in my interviews with newspapers: "Look, we know they shave points in basketball games. We know at least one team has thrown the World Series in baseball. We know football is fixed, because Karras and Horning got suspended, and Bobby Layne retired rather than get suspended. The only legitimate sport I know of is wrestling! There are no scandals in wrestling, are there?"

In every case, the reporter would look at me as if to say, "You've got to be daft."

Of course, the reason there were no scandals in wrestling was that the media didn't consider it a sport! But I would use that just to mess with their heads. And it at least gave their readers something to think about.

In 1985, one of the most notorious media reports on wrestling of all time aired. The ABC show *20/20* did a major "exposé," with my old "friend"

Jim Wilson and another ex-wrestler named Eddie Mansfield talking about matches being rigged and how wrestlers draw blood by cutting their foreheads with razor blades. I always thought it was funny that the main figures in the piece were Mansfield and Wilson, two guys acting like experts in the field when both were failures.

The reporter, John Stossel, ended up getting slapped dizzy by David Shults, one of Vince's wrestlers. I always figured Vince had set that up. And if he had, good for him. What do you think a smartass reporter should get when a guy's out there sweating and busting his butt in the ring and then the smartass sticks a mic in his face and says, "I think it's all fake"? I'd have slapped him too.

Announcers were key components of maintaining that reality. The thing about an announcer is that the people can't feel the moves in the ring. They can only see and hear them, same as any form of entertainment. I always tried to verbalize for the fans "what the wrestler is feeling" from the hold or maneuver in the ring.

In 1992, the movie *Unforgiven,* with Clint Eastwood, ended up being a big award winner. It tried to present that western period as realistically as it could, but you still couldn't smell the pig manure when they were down in that pigpen (and that might just be the worst smell in the world). *Saving Private Ryan* is the most graphic war movie I've ever seen, but you still can't taste it, smell it or feel it. You can only react to the visual elements and the sounds you hear.

We tried to get the feeling of wrestling across by making a picture in words. I didn't want my commentators talking about who was sleeping with whom or about politics. That's what Vince has his announcers doing today, that "funny banter" dialogue. It's almost like a cartoon series come to life, with two guys doing a comedy routine. My commentators knew they'd better be talking about what was going on in the ring and helping the people at home to understand how each maneuver affected the other guy. If one guy was applying a wristlock on his opponent, I explained the kind of pressure it created. Then, when people saw the same hold at a live event, they understood how the physical effects were playing into the story they were watching unfold in the ring. The only better way I could have made people understand those holds and moves would have been to bring them into the ring, one by one, and put the holds on them.

Also, as an announcer, I had to think on my feet, to cover for the occasional, unplanned moment and to be able to quickly explain why something unexpected had happened. Sometimes that meant covering up for blown spots, but in a way that didn't insult the audience's intelligence.

There was a segment in 1984 when The Rock & Roll Express wrestled The Midnight Express. At one point, Jim Cornette jumped up on the apron, and Robert Gibson threw a dropkick that was supposed to connect. Cornette, bless his heart, threw himself back to take the bump early, and Gibson missed him by a foot. I was on color commentary, and instead of trying to act like Gibson had connected I just said that Cornette saw it coming and must have practically fainted from fright. You can't make chicken salad out of chicken shit, and you couldn't make something real if it missed. Some guys, like Cornette, made it easy for me. Because his onscreen character was such a coward, I was able to say that he was overcome with fear. The one thing I couldn't do was insult everyone's intelligence and try to say it took his head off.

That certainly wasn't the only time a wrestler missed a move only to have his target still take a bump. Sometimes one guy would throw a punch and miss, and his opponent would sell it. I would rationalize that with the fact that, in a boxing match, you seldom saw the knockout punch. The opposing fighter was moving, trying to get out of the way, "rolling with the punch." And often it was the accumulation of punches that determined a knockout. When Muhammed Ali beat Sonny Liston, there was no definitive knockout punch. When Oscar De LaHoya lost to Bernard Hopkins in 2004, Oscar took a body shot over his liver, causing a sort of "delayed reaction" knockout. As a wrestling announcer, I'd point out that, if you stood into a dropkick, it could really hurt you, so you might try to roll with it to "reduce the shocking power of a direct hit," explaining why a guy was taking a bump even though the actual kick missed — same with a missed punch.

So, as a sports reporter once said about wrestling, "If you get hit, it is an accident." Well, *no shit!* Do you think a boxer gets hit on purpose? Do you think he sticks out his chin so his opponent can knock him out? Do you think a football player gets hit like a freight train collision by a downfield block because he sees it coming? Do you think Joe Theisman allowed Lawrence Taylor to snap his leg? No, these were *all* accidents!

Generally, it is said, the punch that knocks you out is the one you don't see. In boxing, you see a flurry or two, and at some point you might see the knockout punch. But, if you break it down and look at it in slow motion, how many of those punches actually land? If a guy throws twenty punches in one flurry, one hit or maybe two. Does that mean boxing is all fake?

You might remember, years back, that kick all the sports reporters got on where they all wanted to try the sports they were covering and tape their efforts. Some of them wanted to try out wrestling moves. I couldn't begin to guess how many TV reporters I put out with the sleeper hold. Done correctly, that hold is a legitimate "naked strangle," cutting off the blood to the brain by crimping the carotid artery in the neck with your forearm across the throat while the opposite arm leverages the head to provide pressure for the crimping. It's extremely fast and effective.

We had a guy in New Orleans once doing one of those stories, and he kept trying to show me up by surprising me while he had me talking to the camera. It was kind of ridiculous because this guy weighed about 180 pounds and couldn't even lift up one of my legs. I finally slapped the sleeper on the guy and held it on a little too long. Maybe I just lost track of time.

Maybe.

Anyway, he started going into convulsions, with drool streaming out of his mouth and his eyes rolled up in his head. The news cameraman (who'd filmed matches for me and was a heck of a good guy to work with) got a nice, tight shot of the reporter, helpless as a kitten.

Then I let him go and woke him up. The way you wake a guy up from the sleeper is to whack him between the shoulder blades or slap his face really hard to shock him into coming out of it. Danny Hodge often "dropped" smartasses with it and then just sat down and waited for them to regain consciousness themselves.

When the reporter finally went back and saw that footage, he couldn't believe it. We weren't even on this guy's station, but he played that piece on the prime-time news show multiple times. The highest price for any commercial with a local outlet was for a spot on the evening news. What I got out of doing that segment, and clamping on that sleeper, was a free two-minute commercial at the best possible time.

The difference between that and what Hulk Hogan did to Richard Belzer right before the first Wrestlemania in 1985 was that I woke my guys up and made sure they didn't get hurt falling while they were out. I knew wrestling holds and applied them. Hogan knew *nothing* about actual wrestling. He had Belzer in a front facelock so tight it shut off the guy's carotid artery, and Hulk let him go. Belzer fell on his face and injured himself. I would never have dropped a guy like that. I would have set him down, because I wouldn't have been trying to split him open.

Twenty-five years after Roy Shire drummed kayfabe into my head by fining Stevens and me, I was telling the dumbass executives at TBS, "You know, John Wayne didn't really kill all those Indians in all those movies, but he sure didn't stop killing them and ride off into the sunset with his arm around them either." When you take the mystery out of wrestling, you kill the business, which is what the WCW guys did when they started making all the big TBS money and the Hollywood types and actual scriptwriters started coming in. All the mystery was gone! The average fan didn't want to know it was all a work.

A guy named Larry Heinimi, who wrestled as Lars Anderson, always wanted to make wrestling like a ballet. He wanted to announce that it was all fake.

I said, "Well, then, who the hell is going to come see it?"

It was like a few years ago when my wife Suzanne said, "Let's go see *Titanic*."

Well, what the hell do I want to see *that* movie for? I know the outcome. The friggin' ship sinks!

Eddie Graham took it to a different level with me, but I was always ingrained with the idea of protecting the business as being real. From Danny Hodge on down, each territory had tough guys who would take on the "marks." Heck, I even did it in Pittsburgh.

Promoter Ace Freeman stuck a ringer in there on me one time. I'd been out drinking the night before and was healing up from a big gaffe job. I still had butterfly stitches on my head. This mark was an amateur wrestler out of the University of Pittsburgh. As soon as we tied up, I knew he had amateur skills, so I clamped down on him when he shot in for the leg, and I beat him senseless.

Afterward I went up to Freeman and shook him by his lapels. "You no-good son of a bitch," I said. "You snuck a ringer in on me, because you don't like me, because I'm with the New York office. But you could hurt the business! You ever do that again, I'll beat the shit out of you too!"

In Joplin, Missouri, when Leroy and I ran shows there in the 1970s, we would try out the marks. It often got a little rough as we made examples of them, and we had to buy corn meal or flour to put on the canvas mat cover to soak up the blood so that we could work!

In Little Rock, a martial arts expert wanted to challenge me, but I wasn't at the arena yet, so Griz sent Hodge in to deal with him, which was probably the best thing that could have happened to the guy because Hodge was so good — he could slick you and beat you before you even realized you'd been beaten. And that was how Hodge was trying to handle the guy without hurting him. He had the guy in a keylock, a submission move that had the guy so wrapped up he could barely move. But the guy made a mistake — he tried to reach up with his free hand and claw Hodge's eye. Hodge just snapped his arm in two places, like it was nothing.

By the time I got there and heard what had happened, the guy was in a cast and getting loaded onto a stretcher. He looked at me and asked, "Who's going to pay for my broken arm?"

I told him, "You'll see him when you look into the magic mirror."

"What do you mean?"

"You've got a mirror in your house that's magic. Go home, stand in front of your mirror, look closely and say, 'Mirror, mirror, on the wall, who's the dumb motherfucker who's gonna pay for this broken arm?'"

In Florida in 1974, Eddie decided that he wanted to make some film clips showing the people just how devastating these maneuvers were. As I mentioned earlier, Tony Charles threw one of the most unique dropkicks I'd ever seen. He could be lying sideways on the mat and just launch himself up and throw that dropkick. It looked like it took the top of his opponent's head off. In fact, if his opponent didn't take the bump, it would have taken the top of his head off!

The move looked so devastating that we made it part of a segment where we would film moves being done and then show them again in slow motion, to show people the impact. But we were having a tough time finding someone who was willing to take Tony Charles's dropkick. It was one thing to do it in the ring, where a worker's instincts would take over, but to just stand there in the ring and know that burst was going to catch you was another thing altogether. Bobby Duncum finally said, "I'll do it, by gosh."

Duncum got in the ring, and as he was coming off the ropes he somehow tripped and lost his balance. He started to fall forward just as Tony's dropkick was connecting. Tony just about decapitated Bobby! But it sure looked awesome to the fans at home when we showed the demonstration of that move.

John Heath, who recently passed away, narrated these filmed segments. Heath was a smart guy who had so much credibility in the community. He had a long career in the business and later coached amateur wrestling. He really knew his stuff, and he was announcing for Eddie.

Heath started out by saying, "For you to walk in off the street and tell me you want to be a wrestler would be like me walking into an operating room and telling a brain surgeon I want to conduct a lobotomy. It takes years of training to be a doctor, and more to be a specialist, and more before you become a brain surgeon. Well, let's look at wrestling." He talked about the years of training in amateur wrestling, and how someone had to work his way up into pro wrestling, before showing the clips. Then, as the regular clip and slow-motion follow-up played, Heath painted a picture with words, describing the impact on and harm to the body.

Florida was also the place where many of the guys learned the sugar hold, one of the most dangerous holds there is. I learned it later from Bob Roop. He and many others had learned it from Gordon Nelson, a tough shooter.

One time a mark in Florida wanted to try the wrestlers on for size, so Eddie let him get into the ring with Gordon. As Gordon was about to get into the ring, Eddie yelled, "Kill him, Gordon!"

They locked up, and Gordon guzzled him almost instantly. Then he locked in the sugar hold. The guy was passing out and started gurgling.

Eddie, watching, said, "Is he going out?"

Gordon said, "Well, yeah."

"Well, let him go, Gordon!"

"But, Eddie," Gordon said, calm as could be, "you said to kill him."

The sugar was an awesome hold because, even if you were facing a guy with amateur wrestling skills, all you had to do was snap in a three-quarter nelson when he went in for a leg and turn him over into a reverse half nelson, which isn't a dangerous hold to an amateur wrestler. But you can put on pressure from that position in a way that will put the guy out right away.

Learning those holds and showing fans how dangerous we could be was all part of defending the business. And in 1986, I made my own version of Eddie Graham's demonstration film clips. We made a video montage of some of the stiffest, most brutal, moments in matches we could find. We showed the stitches in Jim Duggan's head after he went into the corner post in Houston. We showed hard chair shots and punishing moves from the likes of Terry Gordy and Steve Williams. We sold the brutality, the physical aspect, of it. We were trying to sell our guys as the toughest guys you could find.

Pro football did the same thing and still does. When you see a highlight package on an NFL show, what do you see? You see the hard hits, guys flipping through the air. They don't show you the guys sitting on the bench scratching their asses. They show you the tough stuff! Same thing with auto racing — do people go to see the cars go around in circles, or are they there to see crashes?

In wrestling, fans didn't come to see the science of matwork. They came to see the excitement — the mud, the blood and the beer.

Being real also meant stressing that wrestlers were athletes, not entertainers or showmen. We were in a business that everybody thought was a farce to begin with, so we had to build the credibility of the guys we had. That's why we were constantly reminding people that Steve Williams was a four-time All-American from the University of Oklahoma. There was no denying his credentials.

And generating that excitement sometimes meant creating some scenarios that might seem far-fetched. But I was often an announcer on my own shows, which meant I could get something across exactly as I intended. When we formulated ideas, I had to know where I was going with them. I didn't just go out there with an idea for this week, and only this week, like some real-life soap opera where I didn't know what was going to happen next. I often showed surprise, but only as part of the show.

I also understood that we could lead the viewers to the conclusions we wanted them to make. Later, when I was in wcw, that became part of my problem with the wrestling newsletters or rags. They were always trying to figure out what we were going to do. With every other promotion, it was easy to figure out what they were doing. But, to me, that was part of maintaining that sense of mystery — you had to come and see it happen. That was why people were crying when we made Ron Simmons wcw world champion in Baltimore. Heck, when's the last time you heard about people *crying* at a wrestling show, in modern times, after being taught it's all a farce? And Baltimore was a pretty tough crowd. A year before I took over, the same audience spent an entire pay-per-view chanting, "We want Flair," in reference to Ric Flair's recent split with wcw.

Even with Eddie Graham's finishes, he always had a moment of anticlimax before the actual finish because he didn't want people to figure out what was going to happen. And it always fit the wrestlers involved and the situation, which was what I always strove for in Mid-South and the uwf. If you watch those old Mid-South shows, you'll notice that one event would have almost a ripple effect on multiple other things going on. I felt that we had to make everything have an effect on everything else, because that's how life works! Nothing happens in a vacuum.

Another thing that was a key to believability for me was to have tv that was never formulaic. Yes, Mid-South had matches with the star beating the job guy, but we booked more main-eventers against each other on our tv than any other promotion. My concept was, since I was in such a low-population area, in order for me to attract a television audience, I had to make the tv so exciting that fans would want to tune in. Once I had them watching, I had to excite them so much they wanted to see the continuation of the story in the arena.

I didn't have a huge pool of people to draw from as in New York. In an area with that many people in it, you could throw the most boring stuff on TV, and there were enough people in that huge city to support wrestling anyway. Compare that to the population in Arkansas or Oklahoma. I never thought the WWWF was a great promotion, and I think that's evidenced by the percentage of people going to the matches there.

In some of my TV markets, I had a sixty percent share, which meant sixty percent of all TV viewers were watching Mid-South during the hour it was on. Memphis was the same way — they had a hell of a show and got incredible ratings. No one in New York *ever* got those kinds of ratings. And it was because our fans believed, or at least buried their disbelief, and wondered at the mystery of what they were seeing, and they couldn't wait to see what would happen next.

Not to go on patting myself on the back, but our success in small-population areas made our bottom line even more dramatic. Our net was within the top three in the United States for most of the years I ran Mid-South; in truth, we probably outnetted everybody. I remember in 1984 what Jim Crockett told me he was making each year. From that, it was easy to figure out what the profit was, because all three members of the ownership family got the same amount. Their total wasn't even close — I was kicking their butts. And they had bigger towns with stronger economies.

With me, everything that happened had to be logical. The thing about what Vince does is, if they're out there fighting in cars or someplace, how come the whole camera crew's out there? It's so bogus — there's no legitimacy. Two guys are going to fight and wreck cars in the parking lot, and you've got four cameras out there? They started going so far that, if they weren't satisfied with the angle, or even one portion of it, they would just reposition the people involved and do it again so that they could retape it on video. I would *never* have done that. They were totally destroying any mystery and credibility for the fans.

Every time I had a camera film something away from the ring, there was a reason for the camera to be there. We'd be filming a scheduled interview, or a postmatch celebration, and then the camera would "happen" to catch this other thing.

When I was in Florida and Georgia in the 1970s, videotape wasn't conducive to portability — the cameras were big and super expensive, and we used 3M tape, called "three-inch." Editing was a tough and not surgically correct process prior to computer editing, so we used film to shoot our angles, and everything from the arenas that was shown on TV was done on film (Gordon Solie's son, Greg, and Jerry Prater were truly masters at this). All our angles were done on-camera, and of course we couldn't edit film closely as they can now. When they had the first digital editors for videotape, that was huge! So we had to work around what we had and be able to explain what was shown in a realistic manner.

And I carried that philosophy into my own matches, where it was as real as you could make it without killing somebody. In the business, they called me "stiff." Whatever I did, it was going to get there, and it was going to be solid.

A lot of my success with Mid-South hinged on the way we presented the matches on television. I carefully monitored the TV content. I didn't let anyone say "balls" or "kiss my ass" on TV, and if something got "too violent" we'd throw slides up and tell people it wasn't suitable for home viewing, which was a great gimmick to make people come to the live shows and see what they couldn't on television. Back then there was no pay-per-view, no licensing, no selling toys and souvenirs. Those things have been huge changes in the wrestling business! We made our money off live, nontelevised events.

For our TV shows, I had some great announcers who could get across what we needed to with believability. Reiser Bowden was a booth announcer for Channel 3 in Shreveport, and I needed someone to handle interviews. Shortly before I bought into the territory, there was a huge case where wrestling fell under the FCC's scrutiny, as an hour-long commercial, because the athletes worked for us and we were promoting house shows through the TV. Since we had total control over the content of our shows, and our shows were promoting our events, it was decided that, in actuality, we were "program-length commercials." Stations were kicking us off the air.

Duane Harm was manager of the CBS affiliate in Tulsa. He spent a lot of time trying to work with us to get the FCC off our backs. He finally got to where he couldn't do much more, and he said, "We're going to have to take you off, but let me tell you what you need to do to clean your show up."

One key thing was that our commentator shouldn't be the guy conducting the interviews for promos. We needed some separation — the shows would have our "wrestling content," and then we would have our actual event promotion in a separate segment, in my shows actually in three separate segments, which the stations could log as "commercial time." There was to be clear separation from the wrestling content, and that's where Reiser came into the picture. Aside from occasional ring introductions, he only did interviews, which were our "commercials" promoting our actual live events. Plus it was clear we weren't going to interject his personality into the interview. All we really needed him to do was read the card and hold the microphone straight. It was the wrestlers' personalities that were going to sell the thing.

That was one thing about Gordon Solie. As great as Gordon was, he never tried to upstage the wrestlers. Jim Ross, back then, learned to emulate Gordon's concept and became the best play-by-play announcer in the business. They knew the wrestlers were the stars.

Reiser was perfect for interviews because he was the perfect straight man. He suffered from migraine headaches and had to change his diet to get them under control, but he was reliable, and doing the interviews gave him an easy source of extra income, because he worked for Channel 3 anyway.

I actually had some great, long-term relationships with people in local media. Oral Link was our production manager for years, and what a precious guy he was! He was so sharp about television production. Edwin Wray's family owned Channel 3 in Shreveport. Edwin was a stand-up guy, and they were a real quality family. Ray Brown in Little Rock kept me on the air there and was just fabulous. Bill Ritchie and Wally Dunham of Channel 2 in Tulsa were special friends. When Bill left, his replacement, Ben Hevel, a class guy, became my friend too. Dennis Fitzsimmons became the station manager of Channel 26 in New Orleans, and we developed a great business relationship. Since then, he has proven himself by becoming CEO and president of the Tribune Company, which owns the cable station WGN and the Chicago Cubs. There were others too, whom I fail to mention here, but TV was our life blood.

Wednesday was our day to videotape localized promos for the individual towns' shows. I never gave explicit instructions to my guys as to what to say, the way Roy Shire used to do. We would do the promos with a cutaway. Reiser would read the card, and then it was over to the heel, who'd talk about what he was going to do. Then we'd come back to Reiser, who was with the babyface, who would answer it. Both guys would talk about what they were going to do at the matches. If one of the wrestlers wasn't doing it right, emphasizing the key points we'd been stressing as selling points, I'd stop the promo, correct the guy and make him do it over. Some guys got great at it, but some guys never could get it, and those were the guys who made managers an important part of the business, because it was a waste of talent not to use a guy who was good in the ring just because he couldn't talk. You put a manager, a mouthpiece to do his interviews, with him, and you had a winning package.

And some of the great interviewers were lousy workers, but they still drew money because they could tell the story to people at home. "Mad Dog" Maurice Vachon, one of the AWA's top stars for years, wasn't what you would call a great worker. He was as unorthodox as hell, but his interviews were such a deadass shoot about how mean he was, how ferocious he was and how he was going to tear you limb from limb that no one watching his promos doubted him. It wasn't the fact that he was a great worker that got him over — it was his real-life toughness and the fact that he was able to project, in promos, just how tough he was. Outside the ring, he was the nicest, most gentle guy you could ever hope to meet, unless you crossed him. But his interviews were ferocious! He would growl and snarl through every one.

When we had matches with special stipulations, usually to settle or continue a grudge or feud, the key thing for the people to know was what those stipulations meant. That usually involved a visual element. If we were promoting a Coal Miner's Glove Match, I'd have one of the guys wearing the glove and talking about the damage it could inflict. If it was a Cage Match, I'd have a guy standing behind a section of cage banging on the bars to show it didn't have any give.

The bottom line was to keep people believing in what they were seeing or at least leave them with that sense of mystery intact.

THE UWF

I actually had the concept of going national before McMahon started his campaign by taking over the NWA stronghold Saint Louis on Christmas 1983. I even approached Kinney National Services (my sister-in-law Ivi's husband, Manny Kimmel, had a son, Caesar Kimmel, who was a huge stockholder), a media conglomerate, with the concept. My vision just wasn't as big as Vince's, and I didn't understand how big an undertaking it really was, so the time just wasn't right for me in this.

The other thing is that, when Vince was trying to expand, he had a built-in advantage. The territory he took over from his father was based in New York and the Northeastern cities, the prime population area and the base of most of the nationwide media. Starting from a base of Oklahoma and Louisiana, I didn't have those advantages, although at one time I thought I'd have a media juggernaut on my side.

In 1985, during the last weeks of his deal to run Vince McMahon's WWF shows on Saturdays, Ted Turner ran a few weeks of Mid-South on TBS on

Sunday afternoons. It started when I got a call from Ted. He'd become disenchanted with what McMahon had been putting on the air since taking over from Ole Anderson's group in July of the previous year, primarily because it was a tape instead of live bouts in the studio, which Turner was used to having and which had better fan appeal than videotape, which generally had already shown in some other markets.

Ted's original pitch to me was that he would buy me out, and I would continue to run the wrestling side of the company for him. He was also going to kick McMahon off WTBS since his lawyers were telling him he'd be able to break that deal with no problem.

I countered with an offer for him to buy half of Mid-South Sports-Wrestling after which we would co-promote. Turner thought that was a good idea, so he put my show on WTBS, his cable Superstation, and told me we had a deal.

In those few short weeks, Mid-South was bouncing around different times on Sunday afternoons and was still getting better ratings than anything else on that station, because the show was so good compared to the "squash match" of McMahon's shows. I thought this would be a great thing because we knew what the power of the Superstation was, we knew we had a built-in market, and we knew that we produced a more exciting TV show than McMahon or anyone else. I even bought a $750,000 plane, a much better aircraft than I'd been flying, because going back and forth to Atlanta weekly with my staff required it.

The problem was that Vince's contract for the time slot hadn't ended yet, and he was refusing to get off the air. In fact, he was threatening to sue Ted over it. While this threat of legal action held up the deal Ted and I had shaken hands on, *I* was told that Ted and Mid-Atlantic promoter Jimmy Crockett had bumped into each other at a yacht club and had started talking about the situation. Crockett had said he'd offer Vince $1 million for the WTBS time slot and take over, thereby getting McMahon out of Turner's hair. Whatever happened, all I know is that Ted accepted and reneged on his deal with me.

Sometimes I wonder if powerful people come to believe it's OK for them to do anything they want, no matter what they've promised, but everyone's word has to be good to them. One of Ted Turner's attorneys once told me he thought Ted was sitting around waiting for someone to nominate him to run the world. You think someone who thinks like that is going to consider himself on equal moral footing with a normal person?

A year later, in 1986, I decided to make a go of it on my own. I knew I had to try to expand nationally, or my company would die.

It was important not to seem "too southern" as we began this push. The first thing we did was move our TV tapings out of the Boys' Club in Shreveport and into arenas to give them a bigger feel. One of the worst parts of the change was the next thing I had to do — let Boyd Pierce go. I hated losing Boyd, but in our big national push the syndicators wanted us to get away from that regional twang that he had. Boyd was such a good person, and he loved the wrestling business so much that he would have been on the air for free. Boyd had money. He stayed in it because he loved the business. He loved being "Boyd Pierce on the TV." I know that leaving the business that way hurt him dramatically, but he was like a trooper falling right on his sword.

Jim Ross was not only an excellent announcer but had also become my right-hand man. So we replaced Boyd with Jim, which hurt Boyd's feelings, but that was the way things were as we tried to keep pace and survive. I haven't been around as many people as brilliant as Jim. And he was the kind of guy who, even when he was mad at you and would cuss you in private, would always give you his all and remain loyal. Jim had a tremendous impact on my life.

I'd hired him right out of college, where he'd been a 4.0 student. He started in Mid-South as a referee. As history has shown, though, he became much more. Jim is on the ball and has always been a tremendous asset for any company he's worked for. If not for him, my run at going national would never have gotten off the ground.

By 1986, Jim had established one heck of a national syndication network for us, so Mid-South Wrestling became a thing of the past, replaced by the Universal Wrestling Federation. We were trying to do what Vince McMahon had done two years earlier. Jim made deals with stations and changed the way we arranged our contracts with them. In the old days, we used a barter system. The barter was that we gave the stations the show, and we got to keep seven or eight minutes of time to plug local interviews and our house shows. Jim wanted to try a new way of doing it. He and I talked about it, and we decided to experiment with a "per inquiry" system, where we got to keep some commercial time to sell, which became a money-maker for the company.

Then Jim found a guy in Dallas to work with us on syndication, and he was backed by a multimillionaire who owned a chain of hotels. We were off on a tear! We were syndicating our show into about seventy percent of the United States, and you had to reach that certain percentage before you were eligible to have the big companies start buying commercial time. We were getting there.

We also made another deal that brought some extra cash flow into the company by signing a talent-booking deal with Antonio Inoki's New Japan Wrestling. They paid me a fee to use my guys and paid them to be there, which made it good for all of us. When it came time to renew the contract, we set up a meeting in Tulsa. They had a woman who was one of the vice presidents of their company; she was bilingual, but I found her bitchy and incompetent, and I couldn't stand her. It wasn't because she was a woman. It was because she was lousy at her job.

I told them I didn't want her in the meeting.

They told me, "But she's our vice president!"

I said, "I don't give a shit! I'm not dealing with her."

When they came to Tulsa and I walked into the room for our big meeting, there she was. Jim Ross and Ken Lusk (Ken Mantell) were with me, and we exchanged all the pleasantries, and then it was time to start the meeting. But I had a point to make first.

I said, "Wait just a minute. I told you I wasn't dealing with her. She can serve the tea, or do whatever the hell else you want her to, but she's not going to be a part of our meeting."

Here is my understanding of the Japanese. First, with them, it was all about control. When a Japanese guy does business with an American, he might not show that he understands English, but he does. The gimmick is that they run it through an interpreter, which gives them a delay. While you're listening to the interpreter, they're watching your reaction. That's the psychology. Second, Japan is a male-dominated society, so the woman being there was nothing but a gimmick, something my "serve the tea" remark was designed to let them know I was aware of.

But they still played it out and were screaming, and she was screaming loudest of all. Finally, one of the other ones said, through the translator, "I'm sorry, but she's our vice president, and she is staying."

"Well, then," I said, "fuck you. This meeting's over."

I shut my briefcase and stood up. Jim and Ken were sitting there in shock. I guess they must have been thinking, "Holy cow, all this money is flying out the window."

I turned, looked at them and said, "You guys, shut your briefcases, and let's go."

"But, Cowboy —"

"*I said let's go!* The meeting's over!"

They had stunned looks on their faces, but they shut their briefcases and started getting up.

Well, these guys had come from Tokyo to meet with me! Do you think they were going to let our whole deal fall through over this woman? Heck, no!

We were just going out the door when all of a sudden, from inside the office, "Wait! Just a minute! Just a minute!" They went almost into a huddle and chattered for a few minutes, and the woman was out! So now the meeting was back on.

They had a professional international business interpreter with them, and he took over those duties. His presence told me they knew my thoughts on working with her, but they wanted to try to force me their way. It just didn't work, and the meeting proceeded, but with one small difference — my price just went up because I saw how desperate they were to close the deal.

But I'll tell you one thing. I got a few more bucks out of them, but let me assure you — no American businessman, myself included, is ever going to beat the Japanese at a deal. You might get a better deal than you had, but you're not going to beat them. If you want insight into their business philosophy, just read *The Book of Five Rings* by Miyamoto Musashi. You can call it their corporate bible. And I don't mean that in a negative way — that's just how they do business.

I timed it so that I was making the big announcement about switching the name to Universal Wrestling Federation while we were promoting a big event — The Jim Crockett Senior Memorial Cup. It was a tag-team tournament, with teams from most of the remaining American promotions (except the WWF), plus teams from Canada and Japan, and it was held in the Superdome.

Our partner in that deal was Crockett, but I wasn't worried about any friction or that my guys were going to come out looking second best. First of all, who was going to antagonize me? It was my town. And they certainly didn't have anyone who was going to stand up to my talent physically, if it came to that. Heck, they sure didn't have anyone who could whip Duggan or Doc. But at the same time, I wasn't out to embarrass Dusty or Flair or any of them. In a situation like that, it only works if you accommodate each other's stars.

Soon after the Crockett Cup, I started bringing in new talent, and a lot of it. I even brought back Kamala, after a less than perfect departure in the fall of 1985. Kamala, Jim Harris, was just a natural talent. He'd been a journeyman wrestler as James "Sugarbear" Harris until 1982, when Jerry Jarrett in Memphis turned him into the Ugandan giant. Kamala came to me from Jarrett in 1982. I put him with Skandor Akbar as his manager, and Akbar was a tremendous stabilizing influence. Akbar was the kind of guy who, even when he got pissed off at things, wasn't going to miss his shots. We had Frank Dalton as "his man Friday" too.

Akbar was a tough, tough guy, but he had his moments. One time he was doing an angle where he was going to "burn" me by "throwing fire" (he was very secretive about his gimmick, but I heard this was done with a Bic lighter set to flash paper, like a magician uses). Well, he burned me so badly that it cooked all the hair off my chest. He knew what he was doing too — he got me! I chased his ass all over the building! He sure could truck it when he needed to.

Kamala was an awesome piece of talent, but he needed that stabilizing force. He'd left for a group in Texas in 1985 without notice, and Akbar even had to fill in for him in some matches. It caught me by total surprise, because I never thought he would be that way. But Kamala worked his gimmick as well as anyone I've ever seen.

We also brought back another great gimmick guy — The Missing Link. He'd been Dewey Robertson, and I'd tried to get him over under his own name in the 1970s. He was exactly what I was looking for in a babyface, and I made him my champion. He looked good in a suit and tie and was good in the ring. He just couldn't get over as a babyface. He just didn't have "it." But after he became The Missing Link, it was like a complete transformation. It was like when Johnny Walker became Mr. Wrestling II.

Another one like that was Dick Beyer, a fabulous athlete who played football and wrestled for Syracuse University in the 1950s. But Dick Beyer, as Dick Beyer, would never get over. He was balding and had a big, round face and protruding teeth. He just wouldn't be a big draw on his own. But when he put that mask on and became The Destroyer, in the 1960s, it released his inhibitions, and he became someone totally different, someone who could draw money. Don Jardine was the same way. He couldn't draw a dime until he put on a mask and became The Spoiler.

Well, Dewey Robertson became The Missing Link. When you get a gimmick and it takes off like that, it can control you. Dewey sometimes had a problem separating the gimmick from reality. He'd just get dingy, from time to time, and the gimmick all but took over. Dewey was fine, though — he just had to work that gimmick, and he did very well, although he also battled substance abuse.

One who really broke through and was becoming a star, as well as a hell of a good worker, was George Gray, who wrestled as One Man Gang. George had wrestled for me off and on, and I usually had him with Akbar. He was a big, fat guy who didn't have a reputation for being a great athlete, but he had a knack for being able to work, and he was hard working. He also had an intimidating look, with his head shaved into a Mohawk and skull tattoos on the sides of his head. He was always an asset to me.

One Man Gang and The Missing Link had been part of Fritz Von Erich's group, and they came to work for me, along with The Freebirds, when I brought in Ken Lusk, who used to wrestle as Ken Mantell. I made Mantell a trusted lieutenant, but my trust in him would ultimately prove to be a big mistake.

Ken had worked as Fritz Von Erich's right-hand man for a long time. Fritz's Dallas promotion had been hot for a long time because his sons were so hot. Anyone Ken threw in to work with the boys drew, even though the boys were usually so obliterated by their substance abuse that they didn't know where they were. I initially brought Ken in because neither Slater nor Taylor had worked out, and I was looking for that new booker.

Ken's problem was that he was totally undisciplined — he wanted to stay up all night and sleep most of the day. I let him get away with that stuff because I had so many new things to deal with in my national effort that I couldn't juggle all of that plus the booking.

The Freebirds had really polished their act since they had worked for me in 1980. They were always business. Gordy was a loose cannon, and he already had some of the substance abuse problems that would cause him some real health problems later and may even have been a cause of his early demise.

They had a car and kept having problems with it, so Gordy finally drove it into the dealership — and I mean *into* the dealership! He drove right through a window and ended up getting arrested, after pissing all over the service manager's desk. He surrendered peacefully when the police showed up, but after they cuffed him, when they were trying to get him into the car, he jumped up and smashed the siren lights with his head! Gordy was just . . . Gordy. That's the only way I can describe him.

And Buddy Roberts drank a lot, but I'll tell you what — they showed up every night, for every match, and they were always great in the ring. And Michael was still a brilliant guy. It was almost like Michael was Gordy's alter-ego. Gordy spoke through Michael. To the fans, it was almost as if Michael was the Charles Manson of the Freebird clan.

And they were the perfect package. Michael loved to create controversy but had a tremendous drive to succeed that went along with his creativity. Gordy was a phenomenal performer in the ring. And Buddy would give you everything he had, physically, every night.

I still had Michael in the ring as little as possible. My position on him hadn't changed, but his position on wanting to work hadn't changed either. And it wasn't just the quality of his work. I believed that, if we had Michael, essentially the manager of the team, out there getting his fanny kicked, it was taking the heat off the whole team. You want your manager not to be touched unless it's the blowoff or unless it's to set up a major angle.

The Crockett Cup Superdome show didn't do as well as I thought it would, but the first real sign of economic trouble was the next Superdome we tried, in the summer of 1986. I knew there was trouble before we even went for the show.

One of our advance publicity guys liked to call escort services when we were in town. He called me before the summer show and said, "I have called every escort service in the book, and they're all closed." These escort services had page after page of huge ads in the Yellow Pages of the New Orleans phone book — ads that cost a lot of money — and every one had gone out of business. On the face of it, you might not see the significance and might be wondering, "What the hell does that have to do with wrestling in the Superdome?"

Well, that was the first clear sign of the megatrend that swept through our oil-states area and devastated all businesses, especially anything to do with entertainment, as people in those states no longer had that disposable income to spend. We hadn't yet realized the impact, but we were about to experience it in full!

When I next flew to New Orleans, I went down to Bourbon Street, and there wasn't a single hooker there. And I didn't want a hooker, but I knew that, if the hookers weren't there, the entertainment dollars were gone. I mean you're in New Orleans and can't find a whore? That's scary.

Sure enough, our advance ticket sales for the show hadn't been all that much, and we did our advance, with practically no walk-up sales the night of the event. Generally, we did two or three times the advance as a walk-up.

That show was also a co-promotion with Crockett, who'd brought Dusty, Ric Flair and some of his other guys in. Crockett didn't understand why the gate was so bad. He thought we'd done a lousy job of promoting it, but we'd busted our asses, Jim Ross in particular, to promote the show. Heck, it was the most loaded lineup we'd ever had! But attendance was poor. And I was blaming Seymour Smith for the failure, while he was blaming me.

Not understanding that these outside forces were the cause made it a huge emotional disaster too. The conventional barometers we used to measure our business were no longer valid. But we blamed each other in desperation.

Meanwhile, in Shreveport, we had an altercation. I'd whipped Sting and the chickenshit he was teaming with, Jim Hellwig. They were a tag team called The Blade Runners, and it was in a Lumberjack Match. In such a match, the ring was surrounded by wrestlers with belts, and the idea was that, if one of the wrestlers tried to leave the ring, the other wrestlers would whip him until he went back in. I guess this treatment was too much for Hellwig, because he whined about it afterward. He and I had words, and he left, and Sting was going with him. I sent Griz to bring Sting back, because I saw something good in Sting. He was very nervous and tentative, but he is a quality person, and he came back. History has proven his ability.

When I booked Sting in a match with me in Tulsa, he was scared to death. I think he thought I was going to beat him up, but I really just wanted a chance to work with him, to see firsthand what he could do. He came up to me before the match and said, "I have a couple of high spots I'd like to do with you. Do you mind if we do a couple of them?"

I said, "Yeah, you go ahead and call them when you feel the time's right."

I did a move where I whipped him into the turnbuckle, then took his legs and spread them across the bottom turnbuckle with the ropes acting as a support for his legs, which were stretched fully open. The idea was that his "family jewels" were completely exposed. Then I backed up and ran forward and kicked the heck out of the turnbuckle he was resting on, which made for a great visual moment as he bounced up and down to sell the spot, and it looked like I had kicked him in his balls — we were becoming pretty extreme too. The thing was he thought I was really going to blast him in the nuts.

Later, when he told me (in a story he has repeated to me several times since) how he thought I was going to beat him up, I said, "No, Sting, I wanted to work with you because I saw something special in you. Now, your partner, I think he's garbage, but I think you have some good, intrinsic qualities."

And I was around Sting a lot in wcw in 1992. He and I haven't always seen eye to eye, but I'll tell you one thing — if he told you he would do something, you could count on it. His word was good, and I have nothing but respect for Sting.

As The Ultimate Warrior, Hellwig actually turned out to be a pretty big star in the WWF for a short time, but I saw him as another popcorn-fart kind of guy who couldn't really stand prosperity, and he was never anything again after he screwed up his relationship with Vince. And I understand that, after steroids were banned by Vince during his legal problems with the government, Hellwig's weight and muscle tone dropped so dramatically that he wore a "body suit" with "painted-on muscles."

A DYSFUNCTIONAL BUSINESS AND A CHANGE IN MY LIFE

During this mid-1980s period, I also ended up becoming partners with Fritz Von Erich again, in Tulsa and Oklahoma City. At the time, his World Class Championship Wrestling was red hot, and he had some of the top talent in the country, so we worked out a deal for him to provide talent on those shows. David Von Erich, who showed the most promise of his sons as far as understanding the business, was lost in 1984 to a drug overdose, I am told, in Japan. What a tragedy.

The problem was that Fritz's sons Kevin, Kerry and Mike were so zoned out on drugs that they'd become unreliable. When I tried to tell Fritz about the problem in 1985, all it did was piss him off. After that, I just wouldn't use his boys anymore, so he sued me, claiming I'd breached our deal.

Well, I knew how Fritz thought, and I had anticipated his reaction. Before I told him about his sons' problems, I did a few interviews with Kerry in Oklahoma City and had them videotaped. I had a segment where he was showing my son Micah how to throw the discus, since Kerry had held the discus record at the University of Houston. He was so zoned on drugs that he would go around and around in the discus motion but lose his balance and go tumbling into a pile of boxes. He would get up slobbering, with snot running out of his nose. Kerry also had a *Playboy* playmate with him, and we did an on-camera interview where he talked about how much he loved her. One problem — Kerry was married, and not to the playmate! And his family was very visible in their church in the Dallas area.

Another time I had Kevin booked for an arena show but couldn't find him just before he was supposed to go out for his match. We ended up finding him in the bathroom. I was told he was sitting in the lotus position with his wife. They were telling each other how much they loved each other when he was supposed to be in the ring! I recently saw Kevin and would have loved to have visited with him and talked about that period of time and how he saw it. He is really a fine person who was also a product of the "anvil" on which we were all being formed.

When Fritz sued me, I told him, "I'm going to send you a video that I'm going to enter as evidence in the trial, and you may not like it because you're a big Baptist and have your wonderful, Christian kids. How's this gonna fly? Plus Kerry's wife might divorce him." Fritz dropped the suit, but he could never come to grips with the fact that those kids were substance abusers. Kerry and Kevin didn't know what day it was half the time.

I went to David Von Erich's funeral in February 1984. I was told drugs had killed him too. Even though we were on bad terms when his son Mike killed himself by overdosing in 1987, I called Fritz to offer my condolences. I also called him about his youngest son Chris's suicide in 1991. I've never talked to a person in as much denial as he was by then.

After Chris's death, he said, "Well, you know that wasn't drugs. The boy was asthmatic."

I said, "Jack. The older boys have had him high since he was eleven years old."

Two years after Chris died, Kerry was on probation after getting caught with drugs when he got caught again. I was told that he didn't want to go to prison, so he borrowed his dad's gun and killed himself.

It was all drugs. The only one who hadn't died as a result of drugs was his first son, Jackie, who'd died in the 1960s as a child. Fritz had just bought the boy a new bicycle and found it left outside as he returned from a wrestling trip. Fritz woke Jackie up and said, "Get your butt out there and put your bicycle up!" The kid went out to put it up and was struck by lightning. He fell into a drainage ditch with water in it and drowned. What a traumatic thing for a parent to endure, especially since he was disciplining his kid. Fritz did what was right! I have no doubt that the boy's death haunted Fritz for the rest of his life.

The Von Erichs were great kids and great athletes, but they were self-destructive, and most of them didn't make it. The ironic thing was that Fritz was a very stern father, and the boys' hearts were good. Gosh, they were good kids, and Doris was a good mother to them. She was a Christian; see, you can be a Christian and still lead a defeated life spiritually — not that I'm labeling Doris that way or even Fritz or the boys.

Of course, we can all talk about the Von Erichs, and they might have been one of the most premier, vivid examples of a family that had everything and just fell apart. But it wasn't just a matter of them being a dysfunctional family. They were a family in a dysfunctional business. They were in the corrupt, immoral world of pro wrestling. There was no moral fiber, no measuring stick for morality or integrity in a family. When your kids grew up in that business, they were going to grow up to do what Dad did, not what Dad said. Dad can say, "Don't do this. Don't do that," but the kid says, "But, Dad, I want to be like you."

Of course, if I'm going to talk about the Von Erich family and all their tragedies, then I have to be responsible and address this issue in my own family. This is very painful and sensitive, and I wish there were some way to "sugar-coat" it, but there isn't. And the purpose for writing about it is, if only one person's life is helped by something he or she reads here, then it is well worth it. Life is precious, and God has paid the dearest price for each of us.

My divorce from Ene occurred in 1989, and my children certainly experienced all the anguish and crap that a split like this exhibits. Our relationships have really been through some ups and downs — these kids are all grown now and have families of their own, so "Dad" isn't the guiding influence in their lives now. In fact, in some ways, they might believe I am to blame for their lives not living up to expectations. There are those "expectations" again, with their desires based on the wrong model, instead of choosing to be all that the Lord desires for them to be. And for that, I do share a large portion of the guilt, because children will do as you do and not as you say.

Some of my own children have been involved in substance abuse. Recently, one had a close brush with death because of substance abuse, overdosing on "Somas," a muscle relaxer that is deadly when combined with alcohol. Too often as parents or family members we might be under the delusion that we can rationalize with a substance abuser about the problem — we think we can fix it. Too often the drug abuser's response is to "attack the messenger" and remain in denial.

It creates tremendous stress. Of course, without proper understanding of this situation, we are soon defending ourselves instead of confronting the substance abusers for their terrible choices and pointing out the consequences of addiction on those they love. We mustn't allow ourselves to be their "enablers." They are the perpetrators, and we should never lose sight of that. Any consequences are their responsibility, not ours.

I also believe we need to seek professional counselors to help us in this, even if we attempt an intervention to get them to face the truth of their addiction, because I believe that, until the abusers admit their problems to themselves, and make a conscious choice to accept full responsibility for their choices and to seek help, nothing positive will happen. Studies and information are now available that just weren't that well known back then.

In 2004 Ted DiBiase told me that since 1993, when he stopped wrestling, there have been over forty wrestlers or ex-wrestlers who have died where substance abuse was a contributing factor — and that pain pills (especially muscle relaxers) and alcohol combined are deadly. Mike Graham tried to intervene with the sons of two dear friends of mine in this business, and they got angry and told him they didn't have a problem and to butt out — and both of them are dead, with substance abuse a key factor.

My weakness or, as I sometimes refer to it, my drug of choice was sex. Illicit sex, sex outside marriage, is against God's law. But, in the wrestling business culture, it was a way of life, with all the consequences. And I wallowed in it until finally it destroyed my family. How foolish of me to think my own children wouldn't be influenced while I was on the road being an adulterer. I even deluded myself that I had my life "compartmentalized" — I separated my home life from my life in the business and on the road. What a crock! Another delusion was thinking they wouldn't find out. The worst offshoot was men in this business initiating their sons into this morally bankrupt way of life like some ritual of passage. I recently saw sociopaths described as those who could "compartmentalize their lives" in such a detached manner.

When your children find you have no moral fiber on one issue, they feel you are deceitful on all issues. And, if they still look up to you, they will want to emulate you! And then there are the drugs and alcohol to help them escape reality even more.

The first thing they understand from going out on the road is all the whoring around. They might not want to accept that their dad is doing it, but once they get involved they become proud of their dad doing it. And Dad is often helping them get laid!

Gene Kiniski hired a hooker at one of the Las Vegas NWA conventions to service the Von Erich boys. He thought it was funny as hell. Fritz just about fainted when he heard about it. And one of the boys ended up getting a sexually transmitted disease! It was a big, funny story to all of us.

And I even told my wife Ene, "I can't wait until my boys get old enough — maybe one of my buddies will buy them a good-looking hooker too!"

She was aghast! What a moral standard that was. It was all about how much you could cheat on your wife, how many laws you could break. The height of pride is to consider ourselves above the law. We see this way too often in our society, even in the highest office of the land, where we've seen lying under oath coupled with public denials that getting a blowjob is having sex.

But whether we are good examples or bad ones, we are always examples for our children, and they will follow those examples. And those of us who are tremendously successful also burden our children with huge expectations. They feel they are expected to carry on or surpass our careers. This can be subliminal but more often is reinforced by actions and words. And then they are compared with each other, with all the destructive messages that sends, creating huge insecurity.

I have lived with the consequences of my acts here on Earth. They cost me my family plus a lot more, and they are still paying the price for my trespassing against God's moral law. It seared the hearts of my children — those blessings from God, given to me to love and honor, whom I did not appreciate enough to even stay married to their mother. My selfish desires overrode my faith. I hardened my heart in rebellion for years. Thank God, He penetrated the calluses of my heart and called me back to Himself! Still, I'll live out my life on Earth with the consequences of my choices, my sins against God.

How can you expect moral behavior from a child who sees a different example in his own father?

"Son, you really shouldn't drink."

"Why, Dad? You're drinking a beer right now, driving 100 miles an hour. How come you don't worry about it?"

"Well, I can handle it, plus all the cops know me from TV."

With that kind of moral fabric, I never saw a family in wrestling that was normal. I thought mine was until I started really taking a look at things. I thought I was a guy with a great big white hat. I really thought I *was* "Cowboy" Bill Watts! What I really was, was a lying, cheating son of a bitch. My children didn't grow up in a Godly, moral atmosphere, except for a brief period of time when God shone a light on my family. Even then I was too undisciplined to follow consistently His illumination and His love. As a result, my family was dysfunctional.

And I'll tell you something else — women are smart. They are blessed with what some call a sixth sense. These wives all understood their husbands were cheating on them. They didn't confront them if it wasn't thrown in their faces, but they damn sure knew, and they bore that burden. Think about it — do you think women are stupid enough to go to the matches, see all the other guys cheating and think you're the only guy in the crew who isn't? Well, to show you how stupid we men were, that's exactly what we convinced ourselves of. And you should have seen some of the extremes we went to to convince our wives we weren't cheating.

Oh, I had boundaries. I didn't screw around in Tulsa. *That* was my boundary, but eventually I broke that one too. When you set boundaries in sin, you'll violate them because they're not set on any solid moral ground. They're set on your worldly standards, and those are fickle because they're all self-centered. Anything based on self-centeredness is going to change to fit what the self wants, because the self can convince a person that he deserves anything he wants. And using your peers as the source of your self-esteem is another trap along the same lines, because they too are fickle, worldly and carnal. Only God's laws are absolute, righteous and suitable for training, instruction and discipline.

Just as wrestling was a work, we let our lives become works. The philosophy we espoused was that we would "sacrifice" ourselves for the business by sleeping with the arena rats (girls who were groupies for wrestlers) so that they'd keep coming back and buying tickets, thereby helping the business. And in some cities, you just wouldn't bring your wife to the matches because it was only going to cause problems. The guys with the happiest marriages were the guys who kept their wives totally isolated from the business.

And the arena rats all aspired to get a wrestler to marry them. Why, I'll never know. If a guy is such a disloyal son of a bitch that he'll cheat on his wife, why did those rats figure the guy wouldn't cheat on them too? I guess they didn't think that far ahead, and I think that, if they'd had their way, the wrestlers' wives would have found out about the affairs.

The rats and the wives all hated me, so when I took my wife Ene to the matches they'd follow her into the bathroom and start talking about some made-up deal to implicate me in something, making sure they were talking loudly enough for her to hear, just to cause me problems. Ene would confront me about these things, and I would become very indignant. Well, the incident she was asking me about might have been false, but the activity she was asking me about was true, because my lifestyle was that of a wrestler on the road. I finally got to the point where I just didn't take Ene to the matches because I didn't have time to deal with her blowing her stack while I was trying to run a major show. See how we justify our sin, our selfish desires, our pride of life? I was blaming my wife for her reactions to my actions. I was just like substance abusers, attacking the messenger who confronts them to switch the blame away from my bad choices, to deny responsibility and thus not accept the consequences as mine.

Look at families in wrestling. Eddie Graham, whom I loved and from whom I learned so much, committed suicide in 1985. It was just a combination of the business going down and Eddie battling alcoholism and having marital problems. It all got to be too much for him.

Eddie always had a dysfunctional marriage — hell, his son Mike even knew Eddie's girlfriend! She had the same seat at the Armory in Tampa every Tuesday night and was often on TV in the film clips. Her little girl called him "Daddy."

And what do you think Eddie's son wanted to be? The kids want to be like their dads. They want the fame. They want to be the tough guys. They want to be the center of attention. And they see that the way Dad gets it is by breaking all the parameters and rules.

I'd gotten so deeply into my rebellion against God I thought that whatever I was big enough to take was what I deserved, whether it was your wife, your territory or whatever. I convinced myself I deserved it because it was a dog-eat-dog world. And that might have been the biggest work, the biggest lie, of all. It was a corrupt way of life.

When you are in rebellion against God, there is no peace. Money, fame, sex, drugs — nothing of this world can fill our need for, or substitute for, having peace with God. That is why none of those material things is ever enough. We only want more. Things of the flesh never satiate or totally fulfill us. Some successful people who do not have God in their lives seem to have peace, but they don't. They are never totally at peace. For one thing, whether or not they admit it, they don't know where they will spend eternity. For all their wealth and power, death will still reign in their lives.

And I was fully involved in this world by 1984, my biggest year ever in the business. But 1984 ended up being a crucial year for me in another way

— it was the year God got involved in my life again in a deeply personal way.

I'd been working on a real-estate deal with my accountant and friend, Jim Elliott, a principled, moral guy and a Christian, who introduced me to one of his clients. This client, a man named Gene Griffin, headed a small ministry.

Jim and I played football against each other in high school and were both on the all-state high school football team. We also competed against each other in college when he attended OSU and I went to OU. We liked each other from the day we met, and he always accepted me the way I was. He was a quiet testimony to me of God even when I was in total rebellion and didn't realize it. Jim had a quiet influence on my life, when I saw how he lived his, because of his faith. For some, our lives are the only Bible that will be read. In Jim's instance, it was a good testimony.

We were working on a deal where I was going to buy a house and then rent it to Gene's private ministry. This meeting, without a doubt, was providential. Here was this devout man meeting me at a time when I was making $2 million a year, had a $750,000 airplane, the hottest sports car, plus a Rolls Royce, and a 20,000-square-foot home on forty acres. I had all that, but the pressure was unbelievable, and I think I was wishing to escape from my responsibilities and just run away. My life was that frazzled.

Those of us who have been born again, who have gone far enough into that relationship that we start understanding things, can look back and see where we were weak. Back then all I could think was that I wanted to go to an island somewhere, smoke dope and have illicit sex. I think it was the pressure-cooker of a business I was running. In wrestling, there was no equity. No matter how big your business is, you have no equity. Eddie Graham used to say, "It becomes unbooked every night at eight o'clock." Once that bell rings, that town becomes unbooked. In other businesses, you built up a value, some equity. In wrestling, what did you have? Your talent changed, and if you didn't match your talent right you had no income. You either won or lost, and it was a daily grind. It was the highest-pressure thing you've ever seen.

I was also getting to an age where I couldn't do physically what I once could, and that probably brought some fears about my own mortality, so I had a lot of bad influences in my head.

So that's where I was internally when I sat down to finish the deal with Gene Griffin. I was trying to argue some last points, just to beat him a little on the deal.

He was so calm and said, "No, we're not going to change the deal."

Then he looked at me, and I'll never forget what he said: "You look like you're about to explode."

Here's a guy I was trying to beat up with my mouth and my high energy, because I was Mr. Big Shot, and he was just a little pissant. The whole thing was just a $75,000 deal, just pocket change. And when he said that, it was as if he'd slapped me.

And I just said, "You are right. I am about to explode."

He said, "When we finish this deal, if you want to meet, I would be happy to meet with you."

"Hell," I said, "I don't want to meet with you. You Christians are going to inherit the Earth — six feet of it, and don't get too close to me. I don't want to get infected by your disease. I don't want it!" That's how deep my rebellion was — I was in total denial.

Gene said, "What is your problem?"

I started reading him my litany. "I went to the church," I said. "It's so hypocritical, so cynical. I remember every building fund, it would go right to the last week, and Mr. Big Bucks would be sitting there saying, 'How much do we need to send the fund over the edge? I'll contribute that.' And he got to be the great Christian, while he's the same guy trying to fuck your wife or your momma. The pastors are screwing the parishioners. All it is is money. They're taking your money to build bigger and bigger monuments to their 'success' under the cloak of religion — and it's so hypocritical!"

Still calm, Gene said, "Yeah, that goes on," and "Yeah, I see what you mean," to everything I was saying.

I continued my tirade of complaints against the church for some time.

Then he asked me the question I will never forget until the day I die. "I've listened to you. Now, can I ask you one question? *What has Jesus Christ ever done to hurt you?* I see everything you're saying, but what has Jesus Christ ever done to you to hurt you so much, to make you so angry?"

His one question penetrated my heart like a shot! I couldn't answer him; I couldn't even speak. Christ had never done anything except love me enough to die for me at Calvary, and I'd never even considered it the way Gene phrased that question.

I stormed out of that office and was driving 130 miles an hour down a two-lane road, in my 928 Porsche, when the thought entered my head that I needed to go somewhere and buy a Bible, which I hadn't read in years. As soon as that thought hit, it was like a load lifted off me, and I started crying uncontrollably.

I bought a Bible and read it cover to cover. And it blew me away

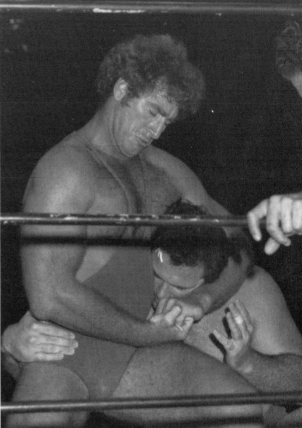

Bobby Shane "going over the top rope" (Atlanta, 1973). Lost in Buddy Colt's 1974 plane crash in Florida, he was unique, and left us far too young.

Bob Armstrong, a quality person and big star in Georgia, squeezing me in a headlock (circa '73–'74). As time went on we became good friends.

Cowboy Bill Watts.

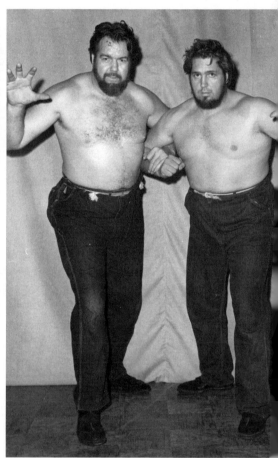

The Kentuckians: Grizzly Smith (left) and Luke Brown. Grizzly became one of my trusted and loyal Mid-South "inner circle."

Facing Mr. Wrestling II, with Klondike Bill as "special referee."

Skandor Akbar in his early wrestling years: a formidable man, someone I worked with for years and respect.

Celebrity Home Run Derby, Shea Stadium (1964): Bobo Brazil, Hall of Fame Manager Casey Stengal, me, and Arnold Skaaland.

Cowboy Bill Watts versus "The American Dream," Dusty Rhodes (Florida, 1974). Our lives and careers intertwined – Dusty became a true superstar.

With "lots of hair" in the mid-'70s. Note the trademark bandages of the "biz." (Remember, "blood red means green dollars.")

Standing with Ivan Putski, one of my early "box office sensations." (While I was a partner in Leroy McGuirk's Championship Wrestling.)

Jerry Brown and Buddy Roberts, The Hollywood Blondes: my top tag team in the early Championship Wrestling years, both excellent workers.

The Big Cat, Ernie Ladd: an awesome man, a great athlete in both pro-football and wrestling, my dear friend, and now brother in the Lord!

Battling Stan "The Lariat" Hansen – who became a big star after I "broke up" him and tag team partner Bruiser Brody (who also became a great star).

Barry Darsow with the mic at a Shreveport TV taping – beside Reiser Bowden, one of our announcers – after Darsow had "gone over" to the Russian camp to become Krusher Kruschev.

"A daughter steals her Daddy's heart." With my Ene (1975).

Marrying Suzanne. Pastor Bob Bender officiates at the Ada, Oklahoma, home of my dear friends Dr. Bruce and Sherry Van Horn (1998). Words cannot express my love.

because I had lived that life of sin it addresses. It was so much more compelling than when I'd read it as a young child, or even as a young teenager, because now I'd been seasoned, immersed in life with all its worldly, carnal desires and pride, and I'd "excelled" on life's stage to become "someone" — at least in my own delusional mind. So, when I read the Word of God, it struck me to the very marrow of my bones. The truth, His light, broke through my calloused heart.

That was my beginning, and I started meeting with Gene once a week. He was so gentle, so patient. One day he was listening to me go on about every problem I had, and this gentle, meek, little guy finally said, "I don't understand why God doesn't just snuff you right out off the face of the Earth."

When I told him about it years later, he said, "I don't remember that, and I cannot imagine saying that to you."

Well, it wasn't Gene telling me that — it was God.

Gene conducted a Bible study in my home and baptized my children. My friend Jim Elliott was also used as a vessel by the Lord in this. There is no denying that he was brought into my life for a purpose.

I didn't understand the impact all this was having on my children in the short time before I went crazy again. As the Bible says, "Raise your children up to God." Well, I hadn't really raised mine that way. Their mother, Ene, had tried to teach them certain values and ethics as best she could, but it was such a tumultuous family.

Ene was such a good person, but by the time God got me to where I was trying to straighten my life out, our relationship was destroyed. I'd come to understand that the most devastating thing that can happen to kids is divorce. It's also the most devastating thing that can happen to an individual going through one. When you break your trust with the person joined to you in matrimony, you don't believe strongly enough that your children are blessings from God (as the Scripture states); you are sinning against God, and it has consequences.

I even tried to justify the divorce in my mind by thinking that our splitting up was better than the kids being around us when things were bad. But I bet, if my kids had it all to do over again, and the other choice was to listen to Ene and me argue every night, they still would have wanted us to stay together. Even though the kids were high school or college age, it devastated them because children look at their dad as the fixer. This was especially true in my case, because I had convinced myself I was some kind of hero. I should have been able to fix anything, because I was "Cowboy" Bill Watts! I controlled the world! I was on television every week, saved everyone from the Russians when they attacked and was Mr. Superman. The kids thought, "You've done all that, so fix this marriage! You're our dad!" They were actually trying to patch Ene and me up themselves, which was a terrible position to put them in.

I think Ene had some real hope when I started becoming more devoted to a scriptural life, but the bottom line was my previous actions had torn my family apart. I maintained the marriage for a while, but I'd just done too much damage to the relationship for Ene to move past it.

Ultimately, I wasn't man enough to allow Ene to get over this injury I'd caused. I wasn't willing to ask for forgiveness as many times as required to salve her wounds; I wasn't willing to swallow my pride, to change my ways — finally and forever — and to never cheat again, no matter what. I couldn't do it, even though God had shown me the error of my ways. Our pride is our biggest stumbling block and the biggest challenge we have between us and God. At the root of all sin is our pride. Lust appeals to our pride.

Remember all this when I talk about someone having a drug problem or being an alcoholic. Every time I do that, I should also be looking at myself in the mirror.

If there is one thing that I could go back and do again, I'd never hurt my children like that. They deserved to have their parents accept them as gifts from God, nurture them, love them and do right by them. If I couldn't do that, I shouldn't have helped to bring them into this world.

The first impact the scriptural change had was on my personal life. I quit screwing around. I started living a cleaner lifestyle. After the matches, I'd go back to my hotel room, read some Scripture and go to bed. It's a funny thing about your spiritual life — you can go through a period of real peace when the Lord is trying to show you how good it can be. But then He's going to test you. Your faith is going to be tested. And mine failed a lot. I'd revert back to the wrong decisions.

For one thing, I was still in a business that was against God. I didn't come to that awareness until right around the time I was trying to sell the UWF, in 1987. That was when it hit me that I was promoting sex and violence.

It's like when I hear a pro football player say, "I'm playing football for God."

I heard that from a player I knew, and I said to him, "Explain to me how you're playing football for God. Do you think Jesus Christ would have played in a football game?"

And this is an introspective question, not an indictment. It is meant more to get someone to really meditate upon his life and think about what part of it he is really living for Christ and what part is really self-serving. I'm not advocating against football. But I am questioning it being anyone's mission in life.

So many now wear a bracelet with initials standing for "What Would Jesus Do?" Well, would he have played in a game where the object is to physically destroy your opponent? The player's reply was "Well, but I'm a quarterback. I don't play to hurt anybody." Well, heck, when I played pro ball, if you could knock the quarterback out of the game you got a bonus. Lawrence Taylor even alluded to that in his book and on TV interviews. Do you think Jesus Christ would have played that game? Life isn't a "game" to Christ. And certainly He wouldn't participate in a game or social activity with so much violence and injury.

For you to get up there and say you're playing for Christ means you haven't really thought about what you're doing. Now, if you want to say, "I play football so I can get enough fame and notoriety that I can talk to you about Jesus Christ," then I can buy that.

Football and Jesus Christ are at opposite ends of the pole, and I know there are many athletes out there who are wonderful Christians who might not have arrived at that point yet. I applaud the players who go out and do God's work, but don't tell me they're playing football for Jesus Christ. They're playing football for themselves.

Being a gladiator, centuries ago, was different because those men didn't have any choice. Going to war is also different because a soldier goes when his country sends him to war. God said He would raise up the rulers anyway, so you have to respect your government.

But when you choose a game or an occupation that has physical damage, or even the possibility of death, as part of the competition, I think a person who says he's doing that for God is using a thought process that's a little shallow. But, then, who am I? This issue is between each person and the Lord — as is everything.

THE **MEGATREND**

By 1986, many of the remaining regional promoters were still having a hard time adjusting to the fact that the wrestling business no longer had borders. My moves toward national expansion had included getting a lot of talent from Fritz's World Class Wrestling as well as his booker, Ken Mantell. Soon we were running shows in the Dallas–Fort Worth area that he'd owned for so long. Naturally, Fritz was ticked off. He called me and was threatening to run opposition to me.

I told him, "Hey, we're trying to survive here. Run wherever the hell you want. It's a whole new world out there."

I had a similar conversation with Jerry Jarrett, who wasn't happy about the UWF running live shows in Memphis. I told him I was sorry, but since we had TV in Memphis we were going to run there.

Now, we hardly ever made any money there. It was almost like when McMahon had tried coming into my cities in 1984. He was competing with the home team, us. Now I was competing with the home team, Jarrett's group.

Business tapered off more and more in late 1986, but the bottom fell out in January 1987 as the oil crisis hit home. I remember years earlier, when the auto industry went to crap, and Detroit promoter Ed Farhat (who also wrestled as The Sheik) couldn't draw anymore, I was thinking, "What are they crying about? It's just the car business." Well, in Detroit, the car business was everything, because everything else was ancillary to it. When the car business went into a slump, the whole economy went into a slump. In 1987, the same thing happened to me.

And a lot of people didn't, and some probably still don't, fully understand what the price of a barrel of oil had to do with my business. Well, when the states go down to nothing, and there are no jobs, there is no extra money for entertainment. People quit going out.

Leroy McGuirk used to say that movies during the Great Depression did better than ever, but back then movies were a dime. Entertainment was cheap, unlike in the 1980s, when you're talking twenty, fifty, or even a hundred bucks for a ticket. That's not cheap, even allowing for inflation, and ticket sales will stop really quick when you enter a major recession.

My strongest cities, the ones that made up my base, were in Oklahoma, Louisiana, Arkansas, Mississippi and Texas. Their economies were basically supported by the oil industry, but their economies were planned around oil going for at least twenty dollars a barrel. When it reached eight dollars a barrel in late 1986, it was a major crisis. Refinery jobs and related jobs dried up, and when they went a lot of the local service and entertainment industries went with them. I mean entertainment just *died*. There was a period when top musical acts stopped coming to Oklahoma, Louisiana, Mississippi and much of Texas. Country music shows, rock & roll — it all died, and pro wrestling was no exception.

It was a devastating ripple effect, and it kept coming in waves, getting worse every time. By the end of 1986, we had gone from averaging a gross of $100,000 per show in Oklahoma City and $60,000 a show in Tulsa the same day to averaging $14,000 in Oklahoma City and $26,000 in Tulsa. We could barely afford to keep the doors open for those shows. Banks were going broke, real estate crashed, and even airlines, like Braniff, went broke — it was a disaster. Hotels were going broke and being repossessed. The oil crunch took people out of businesses they had been in all their lives. People lost everything.

The timing, with us trying to expand the UWF nationally, couldn't have been worse. Vince had solid markets in New York and many other cities, so while the crunch hurt his business too he wasn't dependent on the oil states. The only way I could afford the expansion effort was to rely on the strong revenue sources that the towns in Oklahoma, Louisiana, Arkansas and Texas had always been for me.

None of us could read the data correctly. We were caught in a megatrend the likes of which none of us had ever seen. A megatrend is a course of events that has a huge ripple effect, and this was a bad one. I can't tell you how devastating that was, because I blamed myself for the UWF's failure to draw a lot of fans. I didn't understand a force bigger than me was at work.

And Ken Mantell, my booker, just didn't seem to have it, but looking back I don't know that anyone could have had it. His ideas sounded good, and the TV ratings were strong, but the live shows were killing me. Ken did as good a job as he could, and a lot of his stuff made solid sense. I can't really say it was his fault.

It was heartbreaking for me and for many of my guys. For a while, I thought things would improve, but payoffs got bad for a lot of guys, except for the top stars, who had big "bilateral contracts," which required me to pay them well, no matter what. I *had* to have them — the only way I could keep my stars from jumping to McMahon or Crockett was to have them on contract. The only contracts these guys were going to sign were ones that guaranteed something. So I was paying these guys, feast or famine. It was devastating for me as a businessman because I didn't realize that, no matter what I did, I couldn't have changed it, because nothing about the way I promoted was the reason that my business was upside-down.

By January 1987, the net result of all this was that I was losing $50,000 a week. It got so bad I refinanced my home. By the time I did that, my goal was to keep things running, even at that level of loss, long enough for me to sell the business. Of course, I was going through that money like Grant taking Richmond, and my new house payment was $20,000 a month.

Even my syndication partner in Dallas, the one whom Jim Ross had found and who had done so well with us, went broke. Heck, the multi-millionaire backing him, who owned all those hotels in Houston and Dallas, went broke! Can you imagine? A guy who owned several hotels — and these weren't Econo Lodges or Motel 6; they were some of the biggest hotels in Dallas and Houston. And the syndicator was a heck of a nice guy, but I was so wound up by all of this that I was threatening to kill him over $80,000 he owed me (I never got it).

And while I was breaking myself to pay the contracts, the chance at even bigger money was still a lure to my top guys. In early 1987, Duggan gave his notice and was headed for the WWF. I was losing my top guy again, but he gave notice and left the right way, and I don't recall a cross word passing between us. To this day, I consider Jim Duggan a good man.

And we were starting to push Steve Williams as the next big star. He had become a really valuable talent, although he never became what I would call a ring general. He got over just by being so physical. The things Doc did didn't always have the greatest timing or finesse, but his intensity was unparalleled, and people picked up on that. He was definitely a 100 percent guy. He gave me his all in the ring, and that's all I could ever ask of him. And his performance had improved tremendously, and I think some of that polish came from teaming a lot with Ted DiBiase, who was a great partner and a great friend for him.

But no amount of star power, from Doc, The Freebirds or anyone else, was going to keep me in the wrestling business. The money wasn't the only issue. I also got to the point where I realized the business I was in was against God.

I planned to sell to a group of investors who wanted to purchase the company in a stock deal. I flew to New York to meet with them. The negotiator for the deal was a guy named Daniel Skouras. He used to be Barry Gordy's right-hand man at Motown Records. In fact, Barry and singer Diana Ross had been the best man and maid of honor at Daniel's wedding. (I later met Barry Gordy in L.A. and went to his home with Daniel.)

Skouras had put the group of investors together and was getting a finder's fee on the deal. But we also became friends, so he helped me to hire a team of lawyers in New York to meet with the buyers to analyze them and see if they felt they were honorable and if their deal would fly. Since Skouras was getting a finder's fee, he wanted to know too. They charged me $3,000 for an afternoon's work!

But those lawyers tore the investors apart, and I saw that this deal wasn't exactly what it had been cracked up to be. Once they had my company, all I had was this stock, and there was no proof of value to their stock. I was willing to accept a portion of the sale price in stock, but I wanted some of it in cash too. That demand caused the deal to blow up, so I'd apparently gone to New York for nothing, although I did make a new friend in Daniel Skouras. He was really a neat guy, a member of the same family that owned the Skouras Brothers theaters that were all over New York at one point.

I had a great dinner with Skouras and met actor Jose Ferrer at the restaurant we went to. I asked the lady who owned the restaurant to see if he'd be willing to sign an autograph for "Cowboy" Bill Watts after he was done eating, as I was a big fan of his. As it turned out, he was also a fan of mine! Daniel and I spent the evening at his table, and we all got drunk on Sambuca and had a great time just laughing our butts off.

That story has a sad ending, though. A few years later I tried to get a hold of Daniel, but I couldn't find him. I called Barry Gordy's people, and they didn't know where he was. I even called his son, who had no idea. And that was strange, because Daniel and his son had always been very close. It was like he'd disappeared from the face of the Earth. I've often wondered what happened to him.

Even though that New York deal didn't pan out, I was becoming convinced that God wanted me out of the business, so each time someone came to the table I jumped right up, because I thought it was meant to be. When you're struggling in your faith, you have no discernment. Patience is not a gift. It must be learned, especially in your relationship with the Lord. We see example after example in the Old Testament of the saints trying to "fulfill" their understanding of God's will, in their own way and time, with all the disastrous consequences. Waiting upon the Lord is not easy to learn.

My last-ditch effort came after Jim Ross had a great idea. "You've got two ways to go here, Cowboy," he said. "Let's call Vince and tell him that you're going to file a federal antitrust suit against him but that you won't do it if he'll buy the territory. And then we'll call Crockett and tell him you're getting ready to sell to Vince, and since he's the number two, if Vince gets us, Crockett won't stand a chance. Then we'll just see who comes to the table."

The antitrust suit was something we'd been researching. I'd met with Vince a year or so earlier, and he had me meet with George Scott, Leroy's old booker who was working for Vince at that time. Vince is good for that — he'll always run you through your paces and put you through a bunch of BS before you get to him. That's how he tries to demean you. And having to meet with George was about as exciting as his booking was, but I finally went in to see the big man. And Vince's concept was that he wouldn't buy the company; rather, I'd close it down and go work for him.

Yeah, right.

If I closed it and went to work for the WWF, I wasn't going to make any money from it. I was just going to have this job, which I didn't really want anyway, but no guarantee of security or stability. And Vince knew that —

his counteroffer was just his way of telling me to go screw myself.

But then Crockett came to the table. The price we agreed on was more than $4 million. I got a huge down payment, and then he was going to pay me the rest on a monthly basis, as a consultant's fee, which was smart on his part because that way he could write it off.

For all my success, I really wasn't very sophisticated in transactions. What I should have done was buy insurance to cover the sale, and I didn't even know anything about that. Crockett's books certainly would have passed muster in the spring of 1987, and I never would have thought he'd be broke a year and a half later. After all, they'd been operating for years, had a great year in 1986, were on WTBS and had a great brain in Dusty Rhodes. I just didn't realize how inept Crockett was. Of course, that is just my opinion.

He also got the lease on a fabulous set of offices we'd just gotten in Dallas. In making my national expansion, I had wanted my company based in a better media center than Tulsa and settled on Dallas, which was central and near where we were taping our weekly *Power Pro Wrestling* show at Billy Bob's, in Fort Worth. Crockett wanted me to sublease the offices to them, but I said no — if they were buying the company, they were taking over that deal directly, because I wanted to be through with it. Thank goodness I got him to take over that contract.

The deal went down pretty quickly, and a lot of people seemed surprised by it. I don't know that it was ever possible to keep anything of that magnitude a secret in the wrestling business, but several people appeared to be taken aback.

Paul Boesch was one of them. I owned a percentage of his Houston promotion as a result of the deal we had in 1982, but he owned none of mine, so he didn't have any say in what I did. We weren't drawing any money in Houston anyway, and I was actually slowing down on the number of shows we were running there, because if our shows weren't drawing fans I sure didn't feel the need to continue running there every two weeks. Well, that didn't sit well with Boesch, because he'd been running shows on that schedule forever and ever. Plus he had Pete Birkholz in his ear all the time, griping about how badly they were being treated. I thought Pete was a self-described genius who'd been leeching off Boesch for years.

Boesch double-crossed me and went with Vince McMahon and the WWF in 1987 when I sold my company. I said, "Well, that's fine. Just give me my money for my percentage of the promotion, and buy me out."

He said, "Well, you've been making money all along on this, so I'm keeping your initial investment. I'm not going to give you your money back."

But I was an owner in his business, with equity in his promotion, and under the terms of our agreement I was the provider of talent. That meant I got my ten percent booking fee for each show there, plus my percentage as part owner.

Boesch and Pete thought they'd been pretty smart about it and wouldn't have to pay me back what they owed me, but I'd been pretty smart too.

I remember saying, "Paul, you know how you guys have raked the gate every time, which cheats the state out of their sales tax, and the athletic commission out of their full cut, and also falsifies your records and thus your personal income tax reporting — and I wouldn't participate in that stolen money with you? And because of my honesty and refusing to do this illegal skim with you, how you would bonus the money, on my report, to reflect what my share of it should have been? Well, I'm going to go to the state athletic commission and the IRS and tell them what you've been doing."

He said, "You can't prove anything."

"Paul, I got my percentage of the gates, but it was based on the actual gates, and it's all accounted for. I have the figures there on every single report, and I'll be sending out copies, unless you give me my money back."

The discrepancy between my figures and their figures created a paper trail that proved they were skimming off the gates at the shows. They'd been in violation of every level of tax law there was for years.

"Now, when they see the extra percentage that I've declared, it's going to be pretty apparent that you guys have been fiddling with the gate," I told Boesch. "And once I tell them that's what you've been doing, they will sure as hell investigate your operation. Now, which would you rather have?"

They decided it would be cheaper and easier to give me my money back. Here is the kicker — Paul ran only a few shows with Vince, and then he retired. Vince didn't need him.

None of this means that Paul Boesch didn't do some wonderful things in his life. After his first wife died, he remarried and adopted his new wife's son, Joey, who was blind, and Paul just doted on Joey. Boesch was just caught in that megatrend, just like I'd been. We were all guilty of bad judgment. We were all trying to read things based on what we knew, but one thing that experience taught me was that, when you're in a megatrend, you might not really be able to read what your input or output is going to be. You're in a situation that's bigger than your business can handle. Paul passed away in 1989, just about two years after he and I parted ways.

The business collapse also strained my relationship with Joel. I think he might have felt I should have consulted him, as my son, but, heck, he didn't understand how to run the business. He was running one isolated department and was struggling with that.

Joel either didn't like the sale or just didn't like the Crocketts, and it's possible that Vince McMahon saw a chance to disrupt things, so he hired Joel to work for the WWF, and Joel ended up doing a good job for Vince. I was really disappointed because he didn't even show up even once to meet with Crockett. I had arranged for them to offer him a contract paying about double what I'd been paying him. All he had to do was show up and listen to what they had to say. If he didn't like it, he could reject it. He told me he'd meet with them, but he never did, and I guess the fact he lied to me that way bothered me more than anything. After he no-showed the meeting, I called him and agreed to pick him up at the airport so we could talk about his situation, but he never showed up for that either.

Joel went to live in a condominium in Vail, Colorado, with his mother, after Ene and I split for good, more than a year later. I don't know exactly what happened, but they didn't get along, and she ended up buying him out of his half of the condo. He later took on his biological father's name, Armstrong, even though that man never did a thing for him his entire life. I barely saw Joel for the next seventeen years.

My other two sons, Erik and Micah, were also disappointed in me, both for the problems with their mom and for selling the company. I think there was a sense that it was their birthright, and they both had designs on working in the company someday. But they accepted it, in a way, because it was all they could do. The bottom line was, as I explained to them, it didn't matter what I'd promised them, what they wanted or what I wanted for them. The business was going down the tubes. I was trying to survive.

The megatrend had devastated my business, my self-esteem and many of the relationships in my life. I'd been blaming other people for our problems, and they were blaming me. I fell out with George Culkin, whom I'd been through thick and thin with since we got back together after Leroy and I split. It split Paul Boesch and me. It split Seymour Smith and me, as much as I'd learned from him. Seymour's son David and a guy who worked for them named Skip Weller were also people I'd become close to, but we ended up thinking each other had been failing to perform. These were all great people, but it wiped us out.

Jim Crockett Promotions just didn't have a clue what to do with the

Universal Wrestling Federation. I felt that Dusty was out of control as booker and that Crockett didn't know how to rein him in. As part of the sale, they paid me to be a consultant, but Crockett wouldn't even talk to me. I wrote him a couple of letters trying to point out some things they could do. I even tried to set up a special deal on fuel for their airplanes through my Phillips dealership. He wouldn't even answer my letter about that. Just because I offered advice didn't mean he had to act upon it, but to totally ignore me and my years of experience in the business when he was going down the drain was ludicrous and extremely revealing. But that was fine with me. At that point, all I cared about was getting my checks, but I could see what was happening.

When we were closing the deal, I told Crockett he had a potential gold mine, based on the lessons I'd learned from the war with Gunkel in Georgia fifteen years earlier. "You start a deal where it's the Universal Wrestling Federation coming in to feud with your NWA, and you've got a ready-made program," I said.

Crockett seemed to like the idea, but Dusty never did anything with it.

Crockett did hold a meeting with the talent, or tried to. They tried to meet with Doc, but Steve kept putting them off, which wasn't very smart. I finally called him and said, "Doc, let me give you a clue — I just sold all the assets to my company. One of those assets was your contract. You don't get your next check from me — Crockett now owns your contract. You've got a hell of a contract, and Crockett wants you, but if you don't do a deal with Crockett then, in effect, you're a free agent." He finally got it straightened out with them, but they had no idea how to use him.

They ended up pushing the UWF guys to the bottom of the cards to show that the NWA guys had been better all along. By 1988, the only ones from my entire company who were still with Crockett were Sting and Rick Steiner. Because of ego, Dusty had completely squashed what Crockett had bought. By late 1988, Crockett had become a victim of what I saw as Dusty's inability to have a feel for a bottom line — and Crockett's own inability to make the tough management decisions to control his business and get it back to operating within the revenue it was generating.

I feel that Dusty's fiscal irresponsibility was a critical factor. Dusty always pointed to what he grossed, but he didn't give a lot of thought to what he netted. His run in Florida as booker brought a lot of big houses, but the company was losing money because he couldn't manage a bottom line. With me, everywhere I went, it was always about the net, because it's a business. I had an accounting background from college, and I applied it to the wrestling business. It's not what you gross but what you retain! At one point, the Crocketts bought a six-passenger jet and named it *Stardust.* Why would you need a *six-passenger* jet in the wrestling business?

Dusty was very creative, and so talented in the ring, but if he became disinterested in something he was booking he'd just drop it. With me, the thing I learned from Eddie Graham was how to bring each thing along and develop each program and issue.

I don't want anyone to think I have bad feelings for Dusty, because the truth is I love Dusty, and I've got all the time in the world for him. I'm not trying to down him, because he was one of the most talented guys I've ever been around — he married a tough, little gal named Michelle, who has been a true blessing in his life because she has stayed with him and keeps him grounded.

Dusty and I used to talk angles all the time. The Midnight Rider gimmick that he did in Florida came only about two months after we did Stagger Lee in Mid-South in late 1982, and of course I later did the Midnight Rider angle myself.

Nothing had to be original. It was all in how you put it together. I was always great at taking an idea that worked somewhere else and fitting it into what I did, in a way that I thought made sense.

After the demise of Crockett's company, when Turner Broadcasting bought the promotion, Dusty ended up with practically no control. He ended up quitting and went to work for Vince, who dressed him up in polka dots and turned him into a buffoon. Vince loves to take people who have been adverse to him and demean them a bit when they inevitably end up working for him, as I would see firsthand in 1995.

OUT OF BUSINESS

By the middle of 1987, I was finished with wrestling, but the megatrend that crippled my company wasn't finished with me. My other business venture was an airplane dealership and fueling station called Tulsa Piper. Because of the economy, that business was also going down the tubes. To "make it" at an FBO (fixed base operation), you needed "corporate aircraft" basing with you — turbine powered or jets — because of their expensive maintenance and high fuel consumption. You also needed a very successful aircraft sales department and charter department.

I knew nothing about the airplane business, and my partner was a great guy named Dick Scott, a medical doctor, but he was going through something I was about to experience — a big divorce. He needed capital, so he sold forty percent of his interest in that company to me. At one point, my youngest son was working for us.

Micah, while playing football, broke his neck and suffered what was called a neurological concussion. He took a bad hit, and when he got up I could tell it was different. At the doctor's advice, he took some time off to let it heal. When he went back out, the first hit he took he experienced the same horrible and scary situation. As before, I could tell it was more serious than the usual hit.

We took him to a neurosurgeon, who told him, "You're playing Russian Roulette. You've suffered some possible brain damage from this neurological concussion, and the next one could make you into a paraplegic."

The news broke his heart. This kid had planned to play with his brother and was just becoming a powerful amateur wrestler. Oklahoma assistant wrestling coach Jerry Stanley even came to work out with Micah one summer. He was amazed by Micah's ability. Micah was just awesome, with great strength and an unbelievable ability to throw, which meant he would have been great in either freestyle or Greco-Roman wrestling. Those words from the doctor were like his life had been taken from him. But we had him sit out for a year in the hope that he could heal up over that time. He wanted to go back out so badly that we finally checked in with the school, and they gave their blessing for him to play again.

Micah was doing great. It was like he hadn't missed a week of drills, much less a year of them. But then he had a head-on collision with another player, and it was the same thing all over again. At that point, we said, "No more," and that meant no more wrestling either.

Micah became really depressed over it and ended up with some substance abuse problems. Everything he'd worked so hard for was no longer available to him. To me, that was the kind of dysfunction you can have in a household with a star athlete father, because there's so much pressure for the kids to live up to, whether it's the parents putting that pressure on them or the kids putting it on themselves, along with the comparisons.

I put Micah to work at Tulsa Piper, and he was doing a marvelous job, except he wouldn't show up for work on time. I pulled him aside more than once and told him, "You have to clock in and out, like everybody else. I can't dictate to people that they need to be here on time when you won't do it."

One time he said, "Well, you don't come here every morning on time."

"Hell, Micah, I own the place! You're doing wonderful work here, but I can't have my son coming and going whenever he wants."

I finally had to fire him.

But I had even more problems at Tulsa Piper. We were having problems with our manager, so Dick hired a guy who was in the National Guard and politically active as well as a prominent churchgoer. He had all the credentials you could want, but in my opinion he just wrecked us. He sold a plane to one of his sons at cost and did a lot of other things that made me wonder if he wasn't actively trying to put us out of business. Then he hired a new accountant, one of the most disorganized people I'd ever seen. We later found statements in drawers and everywhere else. Our manager was telling us everything was fine, but when Dick and I actually got an accurate accounting we found we were $50,000 in the hole.

I finally took it over myself and told Dick, "We've either got to shut the doors, or we've got to remodel and make it a sellable asset."

We got a bank to float us a loan because they liked my proposal for remodeling the place, but we were still in this fuel crisis. If I thought it had hit the wrestling business hard, well, I was about to find out the worst business to be in during that kind of recession was the aircraft industry. When major corporations have to tighten their belts, the first thing they get rid of is their flight program.

The entire aircraft industry had been turned upside-down. I wasn't even having much luck selling my own airplane, which I didn't really need anymore since I was out of the wrestling business and didn't have to travel so much.

We sold Tulsa Piper, and Dick and I are still friends to this day. He was a man of tremendous principles and integrity, but we were getting wiped out while pumping every dime we had into this business.

But I was having more than just business problems. While away from the business, I was also putting the final nails in the coffin of my marriage to Ene. It was hard because we were fighting so much but still wanted to be good parents to our kids.

After all I had done, it didn't take much to bring things to a head. A friend of mine from my wilder days, Fred Williams, turned fifty, and I was planning on going to his birthday party.

Ene gave me an ultimatum: "You go to his birthday party, and I'm leaving!"

My attitude was that, if she was asking me not to go because she wanted me to stay with her instead, I wouldn't have gone. But when she put that ultimatum on me, I was going to go just to show that I was the one in control of my life. Big-shot pride is disastrous!

So I said, "Don't let the doorknob hit you in the ass on the way out."

And I went. I even wrote in the register at the party, "You son of a bitch, I've come to this party, and it's going to cost me my marriage."

The party was an all-day, all-night affair, and I was back home by 8 p.m.

to find Ene still there. Just to show you where my attitude was by this time, I asked her, "What are you still doing here?"

Soon after, she finally left. She had always said, "If I tell you the marriage is over, it's over, and I'll take the kids, and you'll never see them again."

So when Ene finally said it was over, that was that — I believed her. I called a buddy of mine and said, "My marriage is over, and I'm ready to party." They fixed me up with a good-looking woman, but I didn't want to go out in Tulsa, because if it came out it would hurt my children. It was a sick idea, really. Here I was, ready to sin against God, but I wanted to take it to a different town so the sin didn't affect my kids. Remember, when we trespass God's laws, His moral principles, there are consequences.

She and I went to Dallas, and I ended up not even doing anything with her because we got into an argument, and I left her there. Still, my intent had been to sin with this woman. When she got back to Oklahoma, she was still pissed about what had happened, and she called me demanding $1,000 not to tell my wife about it.

I said, "Go fuck yourself" and hung up on her.

Not long after that, Ene and I started talking and slowly working on the process of trying to make up, so I wanted to tell her what had happened. "Ene," I said, "I'm telling you this so you don't get embarrassed, because she'll be looking for you to tell you this since she's mad at me." I told Ene the whole story, and she went ballistic. I told her she shouldn't be so upset. "I was operating on your edict that the marriage was over," I said. "You always said it was over when you said it was over, not when it went to court or anything else. I'm telling you this, but nothing happened with me and this girl."

That's what happens when you are living a life with no moral values. I had already been called back to God, but I was still trying to control my own life. I didn't surrender myself to Him on a consistent basis. Of course, I'd never been consistent with anything in my personal life, going all the way back to my childhood — and by that point, I'm sure the mixed messages I was sending Ene had reached the point where she'd react with complete disbelief to anything I said.

My wife moved out with my daughter and rented a condo for them to live together in Tulsa. Our marriage had finally come to an end. Then she moved to Florida but left our daughter in that condo alone. The girl was just a junior in high school! I went over there and worked on repairing the bridge between us, and I found out who the manager was at that condo.

It turned out he was a former athlete from the area, and he knew who I was. He was a really nice guy and put some extra security on that condo to keep an eye on her until I could get her out of there.

Another family event happened prior to our split — I was at WattsAir, our airplane business, and I got a phone call from her. "Bill, what are you doing tomorrow?"

"I don't know. Why?"

"Well, Micah would like for you to come and be the best man at his wedding."

"The best man at his *wedding? What?*"

Micah had gotten involved with this girl, and she was pregnant. With my faith, I couldn't tell him not to marry her, even though I knew she had some emotional baggage, nor could I tell him to have her get an abortion. They got married, and I stood up for him, as his best man, but their marriage too didn't work out. Of course, my son had me as his role model, and I surely wasn't an ethical or principled example.

About a year after our divorce became final, I met Sandy. I was in small-claims court on a case where a guy owed me some money, and she was there on a case of her own. I thought she was beautiful. She said she'd been living in Chicago but was going through a divorce herself and was moving back to Oklahoma. We kept talking and found out we had a mutual friend.

We really seemed to hit it off, but I thought it was just a passing deal and told her, "Well, call me when you come back to town," not really expecting that she actually would.

A few months later, our mutual friend called and said, "You're not going to believe this, but Sandy's moving back here, and she's coming to work for our company."

We started going out. She was exciting, vivacious and good-looking, but we had a stormy relationship. We had great sex, and I still had my big estate, which I think was a big attraction for her. In retrospect, I think she was pretty calculating.

A few months after we started going out, she figured we had reached the point where we should get married. I was so racked with guilt over my split with Ene and still struggling with my faith so badly that I just said, "You're right." So we went to Europe to get married, but we got to fighting so much there that I almost called the whole thing off and went home. It was constantly up and down with Sandy.

A couple of years after selling Tulsa Piper, I went into a business called

Omnitrition, a multilevel marketing company with a unique product line developed by Dirk Pierson, a bona fide genius from MIT. He had developed a line of nutritional supplements that controlled cholesterol, boosted energy, made you lose weight and kept your mind sharp. My involvement in that company would come back to haunt me later.

WCW

When I sold the UWF in 1987, as far as I was concerned, I was out of the business for good. I never went looking for a way to get back in — the business ended up coming to me.

WCW was Turner Broadcasting's wrestling company. TBS bought it when Jim Crockett was going under in 1988. WCW was never a moneymaker because all it had to show in terms of proceeds were the gates from the live shows and pay-per-view. Pay-per-view was a big change in the business, allowing us to put on huge shows for nationwide audiences.

Tench Cox, Turner's attorney and someone I'd known for nearly twenty years, contacted me in early 1992 and asked if I'd be interested in taking over WCW, as executive vice president. Tench was one of Ted's personal lawyers, not a network guy. He had represented us in the antitrust suit with Gunkel when I was working in Georgia, and apparently he was impressed with the way I did business. He later told me he had said to Turner, "You know, there's only one guy who can come in and straighten out this mess." He still is someone I have a lot of respect for.

Tench and I talked, and shortly after that Bob Dhue gave me a call. Bob was the guy they were going to have running the wrestling division. He was managing the Omni when Ted bought it and changed it to CNN Center. Bob was always successful because he was a good people person and a sharp guy. But when they cleared out the old WCW vice president, Kip Frey, they had Bob take his position. Bob wasn't a wrestling guy, though, and after we talked he asked me to run the wrestling end of things. I thought about it and decided to accept the WCW offer, even though I wasn't really doing so wholeheartedly.

I'd grown stronger in my faith, but getting back into the wrestling business got me back into the mind-sets I'd been trying to get away from. All the anger, and the obsession with sex, returned. I fought it, but it just kept creeping into my consciousness. I didn't "cheat," but my marriage to Sandy started falling apart almost as soon as I started with WCW, although I don't think it would have ultimately survived anyway. Coming back to wrestling was like taking a recovered alcoholic and making him a bartender.

I knew I'd be making trouble for my faith, but this was the industry I had spent most of my life in, and the offer was $7,000 a week. In the previous five years, I hadn't really found a role for myself. When I got out of the business, in 1987, I thought I was smart enough to make money at anything. But by 1992, I was wondering if I was competent for anything but wrestling. I was making a living at the things I was doing, but I certainly wasn't setting any records. I sure didn't consider myself successful, and I was getting really disenchanted with Omnitrition. Plus I was in a very mercurial marriage.

But here was a business that I'd always had a knack for, and WCW was offering me a lot of money to come back. They were also offering me autonomy. That's what they said anyway. A lot of how we react to things is based on our own self-esteem. My self-esteem wasn't very high at the time. I might not have known what I was doing with Omnitrition, or with Sandy, but one thing was for sure — I did know the wrestling business.

But I was still eaten up with this inner conflict about whether wrestling was a business for me to be involved in, which made it even harder for me to function as WCW's leader, a job meant for a Superman, something I certainly wasn't. WCW was the most screwed-up company in the world. Here's just one example of how bad it was. Before I got there, they spent $30,000 on a survey to find out "what wrestling fans wanted to see." The fans wanted something more serious, more believable. They wanted the tough wrestling, the old NWA style they'd been educated on — in other words, the total opposite of Vince McMahon's cartoonlike characters and soap opera. Jim Herd, TBS's head of WCW, responded to that by trying to copy Vince's gimmickry instead. Vince was the "originator" of his concept, so for WCW to attempt to copy him was ludicrous and an expensive failure.

When I came into WCW, Jim Ross showed me that survey, and I couldn't believe what I was reading. I thought, "My gosh, this is exactly what I'd do." And even in 1992, I don't think it was too late to restore some believability to wrestling or at least that old sense of mystery.

There was no reason WCW should have been trailing the WWF. Vince had only his wrestling company, while Turner Broadcasting had thirty companies to sustain it. I wanted to use those resources to win the war for fans. We had free specials called *Clash of the Champions* that aired periodically on TBS in prime time. I wanted to run those shows directly opposite Vince's pay-per-views and make people choose. Turner Broadcasting's legal department told me we couldn't do that because it was unfair competition and could be considered "restraint of trade." Isn't it amazing that, after I left WCW, they later put on a show directly opposite *Monday Night Raw,* Vince's flagship program?

In 1992, I was already saying, "If we're going to compete with McMahon, then let's compete! Everything we can drain off of him will hurt him a lot more than it would hurt us. Since we're going to give away the *Clash of the Champions* shows anyway, for the sake of television ratings let's put it where it'll do us the most good — directly against his pay-per-view events." If we could have knocked ten percent off the number of pay-per-views he sold, it would have hurt.

Initially, my primary objective was to cut losses and stop the bleeding. One thing that was different from later, when Eric Bischoff took over and had his run, was that when I was there the revenues from all our TV shows aired on TBS went to TBS, not to WCW. This meant that WCW was always a money loser, and one of my mandates was to cut losses as much as possible.

But I also saw some other areas where I thought I could effect some positive change. The key venue for World Championship Wrestling on TBS had always been the Omni, but by 1992 it had fallen on hard times. The gates were down to about twenty-five percent of what they had been in previous years. Things had become so bad that WCW was only rarely running the Omni, and that was the company's hometown arena. There was no excuse for WCW to have lousy attendance at the Omni.

In wrestling, you always had to find the town that was the base of your promotion. In Florida, working for Eddie Graham, it had been Tampa. We ran Tampa every week, and as I wrote earlier, as Tampa went, that was how the territory went. That was generally the case. There was always a town that was your flagship town, and you could gauge what was getting over and how hot business was by what was getting over in that town and how hot it was. In Louisiana, it was New Orleans for Mid-South. In Mississippi, it was Jackson; in Oklahoma, it was Tulsa. The same thing applied a few years later when I worked for Vince McMahon. I always told him, no matter what, he had to keep Madison Square Garden strong.

But here we were with the Omni's attendance in the dump. We worked on some things to rebuild attendance in the Omni, and we were successful.

I knew there was no use copying Vince because no one was going to outdo what he did. Vince was a genius in his own right, extremely creative. No one was going to make a copy that was better than what he originated. The only way to have a truly viable, competitive product would be to do something different.

So we started doing things differently. What I wanted to do was what I'd always had success doing — showing that my guys were the toughest guys around, so I made some changes. I got rid of the foam mats around the ring. They really didn't do any good anyway. To me, having those mats was a good way for the guys to get hurt by hitting the crease between the mats and twisting an ankle. Heck, we wrestlers had been hitting concrete from the ring our whole lives.

The response to the move was "But the wrestlers could get hurt on the concrete."

My response to that was "Well, yeah, but our guys were tough guys."

It made for a great talking point. And I was actually making the ringside area safer while selling the *idea* that it was more dangerous.

"Oh, my! That Bill Watts is going to make someone get hurt!"

Well, golly! We put a little danger back into wrestling! How about that?

Another change I made was to make moves off the top rope an automatic disqualification, which had always been the rule in Mid-South.

The reaction to that one was "Oh, no! He's just eliminated all the high flying!"

No, I just wanted the guys to sneak it, not to do it right in front of the referee. Wrestling always needs rules, or there's no heat. Everything a heel does means nothing if it's totally in front of the referee. If there are no rules and anything goes, you're not going to be able to create controversy, and you have got to be able to create controversy. Having rules and opportunities for guys to break those rules puts some strategy into it. Emotionally, you can capitalize on them. Wrestlers had done that for years with great success.

In wcw, I found myself having to deal with corporate people. I'd always had differences with other people in every company I was in, but dealing with nonwrestling people in a corporate environment was another world altogether. One of the few good ones was Bob Dhue. If we'd been allowed to do everything that Bob had told me we would, I think we really could have turned wcw around. But there was one dominating factor that negated any amount of good that Bob or I might have wanted to do. That factor was Bill Shaw.

Bill was a TBS executive in human resources, and he was the guy Bob and I both had to report to. He, in turn, was the guy who reported to Ted Turner. But, in my opinion, Bill Shaw had no integrity and no principles, and he didn't want to see Bob Dhue or Bill Watts do well. You see, when Turner took over the Omni, he also inherited Bob's contract, which was based on performance. And he'd done a heck of a job, which meant he was getting paid well.

I didn't immediately realize what Bill Shaw's problem with Bob was. What I figured out later was that Bill was constantly undermining Bob and me because he was resentful that each of us made more money than he did — at least that is what I was told. Ultimately, I think, he wanted Bob's job, and I was just a guy in his way.

Bill Shaw knew nothing about the wrestling business, but he was the guy we had to report to. At one point, I felt that Shaw tried to turn Bob and me against each other, telling Dhue that I had complained about him. That was when I figured out Shaw's agenda. I told Bob, "That's bullshit. You know that, if I had a problem with you, I'd come confront you about it face to face. He's after your job, Bob."

I tried to talk directly to Ted about it, but every time I did he'd say, "Tell Shaw what the problem is, and he'll get it to me."

I wanted to scream, "Ted! Shaw *is* the problem."

But the corporate politics didn't end there. I also got into it with a Turner Broadcasting accountant who reported to another guy in another department. This accountant was trying to tell me what we could and couldn't do, and it was amazing to him when we brought in the losses to such a small amount. I eventually made some progress with him, but not a lot. And the corporate structure kept me from firing people who simply weren't doing their jobs, because every one of them had a "daddy" some- where in the corporation to protect him or her. The daddy might not even be in wcw but in cnn or wherever. It was such a convoluted place.

In many ways, it seemed as if wcw was the red-headed stepchild of Turner Broadcasting. We got equipment that was left over from the other stations in the company, from cameras to editing equipment — even our production people told us we got the short end of the stick in this. How was a company with that mind-set going to take on Vince McMahon, who had the absolute best of everything? He spared no expense on his production, whereas Turner Broadcasting was strangling its wrestling company.

I felt that the tbs station manager had an obvious bias against wrestling. He always wanted to replace wrestling with a movie package. One thing Ted Turner understood, though, was wrestling's appeal to the masses. He'd built the Superstation from a tiny uhf channel in Atlanta, and a lot of that success had come from wrestling. It always had the highest overall and consistent ratings of anything on his station. I remember the World Series, with the Atlanta Braves in the finals, drew bigger ratings than the wrestling shows, but that was about it. Year after year, wrestling was above the station average. And they had us producing a lot of hours of television each week. The amount of production was just unreal, and that also diluted the product, because you can mix things only so many ways.

But they had us producing so much because our ratings were awesome, which translated into commercial dollars for the station. Despite the success, we had these "geniuses" coming to the station with either no understanding of wrestling or a disdain for it. They wanted to replace it with movies, figuring they would be cheaper. But I'm here to tell you that movie packages run out too — once you play the same thing 900 times.

Here's something else I never understood. Vince merchandised wwf events so well as home videos, but Turner Broadcasting was a media empire with incredible resources, and, in the unlikely event they made a wcw show into a home video, the packaging looked amateur to me. tbs should have excelled at that kind of thing, but Vince kicked our ass at every aspect of merchandising and, for that matter, in every other department. There were entire affiliates in Turner Broadcasting that could have made wcw into a real powerhouse, but it seemed as if the money wrestling made wasn't as good as money made from a baseball game or a movie. There is no other excuse for why wcw shouldn't have been beating the wwf at everything from international syndication, to videotape sales, to merchandising.

And to me, the things they did spend money on were ludicrous. They did one video trailer to promote a pay-per-view with Sting and Vader where they helicoptered the guys in. It was in Vader's "mountain chamber." They spent $80,000 on this trailer. They had a casting call for *midgets!* The way I remember it, this was all the brainchild of Sharon Sidello, one of the vice presidents, who later became Mrs. Ole Anderson.

Yes, if you wanted to see fiscal irresponsibility, Turner Broadcasting was a great place to look. When I was leaving, they were having an independent guy come in and conduct a company-wide investigation. I don't know how it came out, because I was gone by the time it was done (although I'd bet Shaw managed to castigate me as much as he could), but when I talked to the investigator he said to me, "I have never seen a company with so many different divisions where all thirty companies are more interested in fighting for their own spots than in cooperating." And he was right. There was no real cooperation between the companies within Turner Broadcasting. Like I said, I don't know what the consultant put in his final report, but I'm fairly sure he did what most of them do — tell the bosses what they want to hear so the consultant can get the next contract.

As it turned out, the only person I could fully trust in wcw was Jim Ross. Without Jim, I'd never have gone into wcw in the first place. I just wouldn't have wanted to be there without him. Jim had stayed on as an announcer when I sold the uwf in 1987 and had gradually become one of wcw's key people. He was invaluable because he knew production, announcing, booking, syndication — he ate, slept and drank the wrestling business.

The bottom line was that we were wrestling people reporting to people with no understanding of wrestling. Not long after I got there, we had a main event, a Cage Match that ended up being pretty bloody. I immediately got the edict from Shaw — no more blood. I guess if somebody got busted open unintentionally and started bleeding, we would have had someone running into the ring and ordering the match to stop while we went off the air. That was just insane. Sanitizing wrestling took the drama out of it, the thrill of the physicality and the element of danger in it. I wanted to take it back to the days of tough guys and try to make people care about what they were seeing. Their excuse was the fear of AIDS. And although that fear may have some validity, we still see bloody boxing matches, football players getting hurt, but the referees and trainers stay safe — what a charade. I guess boxers, football players, basketball players and so on can bleed all over each other, but we'll have the referees wear rubber gloves.

What made things worse was that it seemed to me that Bob Dhue was having some personal issues that were taking away from his time with wcw. When Bob was there, things were great, because he could look at a situation and not only know the answer but also know how to handle it politically. But I felt that Bill Shaw was trying to use Bob's absences as a way to have Bob fired.

When wcw hired me in the spring of 1992, one of the first things Bill Shaw wanted to know was whether I would fire Dusty, who'd been the booker for about a year.

I said, "Sure, I can fire him, but that's not the issue. I want to find out if he can work for me, because if he can work for me I can control him. He respects me, and I respect his talent and ability. For me to walk in and fire Dusty for what he's been allowed to do here would not be fair. He was doing what the system here allowed him to do."

Dealing with Dusty was nothing new for me. Just like in 1974, when he was going around me to complain to Eddie Graham, I had to make sure he understood how serious the situation was. I walked into Dusty's office at wcw and said, "Dusty, here's the deal. I'm taking over, and part of the deal is I'm supposed to fire you. What I want to know is can we work together? I know your abilities and your weaknesses, and I want to work with you. But you have to understand — I'm the boss."

He got up from behind his desk, walked right up to me and gave me a hug. "Let's do it," he said.

And Dusty did terrific work from then on. He is one of the most creative guys I've ever known, but he has a lot of demons in terms of taking responsibility and setting his ego aside. I knew Dusty could be a real asset, but he needed strong leadership.

One time I had to fine him $1,000 for violating procedures in one of my booking committee meetings. He told me, "You can't do that!"

I said, "The hell I can't! I've already told Bob Dhue and Bill Shaw I'm doing it."

He came into the office later crying about how he couldn't tell his wife, so I ended up loaning him the $1,000 so he could pay the fine. He paid me back, of course.

I also saw a lot of familiar faces from Mid-South and the uwf in wcw. I'd been one of Rick Rude's first employers in wrestling when he came to Mid-South as a preliminary boy in 1983. Nearly a decade later he was a star and had several pretty successful years in the wwf. He was a talented kid, but he was a product of steroids. In my opinion, he wasn't a good ring general because he was selfish. He was a little guy trying to be a big man. He didn't understand that a heels gets more heat by being sneaky and doing devious things than by overpowering his opponent.

Rude's manager was Paul Heyman, or "Paul E. Dangerously." Paul E. had a lot of energy and creativity. However, he'd been influenced by a leadership that didn't believe in discipline, so he didn't want to be disciplined. He would take things in a direction I didn't want to go, so it must have seemed to him that I was always coming down on him. I also fined him quite a bit for missing shows. He and I were just like two opposing forces, but he was so talented that it was unreal. He just wouldn't work within the bounds of what I wanted. Eventually, we tried to break his contract; lawyers got involved, and it was a big mess.

You want creativity, but there has to be a positive flow. I'd have loved to talk to him after he got to promote his own company, ECW, for a few years. I would haved asked him, "Did you ever have to instill some discipline, some structure?" It's a choice: either you run your business, or the tail wags the dog.

We got a lot of charisma out of Rick Rude, but we just couldn't get him to take that next, great step toward becoming a true ring general and developing as a personality. I think Rick's attitude caused him to miss the mark on becoming one of the top stars in the wrestling business.

Another Rick had really blossomed into an awesome piece of talent. Rick Steiner was still a tough guy and awesome in the ring. His brother, Scott, was a tough guy too, but I just couldn't get through to him. To me, Scott was a living example of what happens to a guy on steroids. No one's ever really done a study of steroid addiction, but when you're on a substance that changes your personality, and steroids do that, it's drug abuse. Scott Steiner was so blown on that stuff that he had what I call "roid rages." Once you added them onto his ego, he became impossible. I also thought he was a bully. He'd hurt job guys for no real reason, getting mad when they couldn't execute something like he wanted them to.

More than once I called the guys together to make sure they understood what a key role those job guys played and to ask for some patience with them. I said, "Listen, these guys doing jobs, most of them are only working on TV, or on the weekends, strictly on a part-time basis. They are not full-time professionals. They're not going to be able to do everything you might want. For you to get mad and hurt them is terrible. The mark of a good worker is that you can execute great-looking moves on your opponent without hurting him!"

Wrestling is a "work," and it requires trust. You give your body to your "opponent" in so many maneuvers, trusting him to protect you, and he returns that trust when he gives his body to you. It would be different if the business were a shoot, or on the level as a true athletic contest, where you take or initiate the maneuvers by skill and ability, regardless of your opponent's defensive actions. Then hurting an opponent with a legal maneuver would just be part of it, like in pro football, hockey or any other contact sport. But, in a work, hurting the other guy because of your own negligence is totally irresponsible and uncalled for. It shows a total lack of respect and, even more, a total lack of integrity! I don't care who you are — you can't "press-slam" even an average athlete without his cooperation. And certainly dropkicks, backdrops, arm whips, headscissors, beals and many other moves require an opponent's cooperation. Generally, hurting someone is a violation of that trust.

wcw ended up with a bunch of lawsuits as guys injured their backs or knees because their opponents were working too stiffly or weren't even trying to protect them or, worse, got angry and hurt them on purpose, without any warning whatsoever. I finally told the guys, "This is going to stop, or none of you guys is going to be on TV, because you can't be stars if you don't have someone making you stars."

If you look at the star system, a star is created by a series of bouts on TV, and in the arenas that showcase them some job guy does the jobs for the person being built. Without the job guys, no one gets to be a star, which ruins the purest concept: the "money matches" created by booking star against star.

Was Scott Steiner a great athlete? Hell, yes! But he was so arrogant and aggressive that he created a bad atmosphere. Now, Rick Steiner was a great guy. I liked him from the first day I met him, back in 1985, and I never had a cross word with him. To a degree, he kept Scott in check, because Scott knew who the boss was — Rick. But Rick was always loyal to his brother and pretty much agreed to go in the direction Scott wanted to go.

Scott's other problem was that he wanted to outshine Rick. On that team, Rick was the one who was the box-office attraction because he had the great personality. With a great tag team, you've got to have one partner who's the main star and the other who's secondary. With The Rock & Roll Express, for example, the main star was Ricky Morton. Someone has to be the primary one who draws emotion out, who makes people care when he gets in trouble, which makes it a big deal when he tags his partner in to clean house.

I had an idea for Scott Steiner that would have turned out great, and actually did turn out pretty well, years later — I wanted to turn him heel on his brother. And he didn't want to do it.

I told him, "You'd be the best heel in the world because you're the biggest asshole in the world. You're a natural heel."

I thought it would be a great feud because brothers turn on brothers all the time in real life. A lot of people could identify with the concept of a family feud. And Scott had the right personality to make himself the top heel in the business. Rick was all for it, but Scott wouldn't do it.

I felt that Scott was also milking his contract, sitting out and collecting his money with minor injuries. He was going to show me that he didn't have to do what I wanted, and as it turned out he didn't! It could have been huge box office, but Scott was just so against me at that time that he wasn't going to like anything I said. And with the structure of the contracts, no one could be made to do anything.

Instead, Scott stayed babyface and was just another muscle-head good guy. But as a villain, he would have been so hot that the whole thing would have revolved around him. And when he did turn heel, years later, he was better than he'd ever been. He was an awesome heel . . . because he's a prick.

Vader was another guy who was brutal to the jobbers, and I had to talk to him as well. Overall, Vader was an interesting guy. I was impressed with him — he could cut a great promo, and he had a great gimmick. He'd been an All-American football player at the University of Colorado, so he had that athletic background. He had great presence and was a pretty good guy to have in the ring.

I also saw Magnum T.A. again. He was getting around on a cane and working in the front office. Talk about a guy who'd had a hard shake! To go from being an athlete to being partially paralyzed after a wreck and still making a go of it, I have nothing but the highest respect for him.

And I brought in Jake Roberts, which turned out to be a real error in judgment. Jake had become a big star in the wwf since he'd last worked for me in 1986, but his fame wasn't the only thing that blossomed. His substance abuse problem had too, and it had made him really unreliable by this point. I didn't realize how bad he'd become. It's really kind of sad because Jake was a smart, talented guy who had everything going for him. You know, he hates my guts now, and the only thing I ever say about Jake is that he's aptly named. "The Snake" suits him well.

I always knew that Jake was a guy who needed to be watched. He was what we called a "dressing room lawyer," meaning he knew how to stir up turmoil and then become kind of the spokesman behind the scenes. A dressing room lawyer never had the guts to stand up and say things himself.

He would tell another guy how that guy was being wronged and then build his own following around that.

But I was open to the idea of bringing Jake into wcw since I'd never had any major problems with him, but we didn't sign him to a huge contract. We were already working with a system of contracts that had windows where we could cycle a guy out based on performance, and this gave us much more control. To me, this system would keep them aggressively proving their worth, just like in pro football or other pro sports. Also, I was very conscious of guys becoming stale.

Jake made an impressive debut. We had managed to keep his hiring a secret and hid him out in a hotel until we were ready for him to run in and attack Sting. The story was that Jake's attack took Sting out of a title match with Vader, our champion, so we held a drawing to see who would take his place. The name drawn was Ron Simmons, and he ended up taking the title that night. Well, there were several names on slips of paper, but ring announcer Gary Cappetta knew what name to say.

Simmons was a great athlete, and we made him the first black world champion of a major promotion. By then, the only major promotions left in the United States were wcw and wwf. Sting had been a key guy for a long time, but I wanted to bring a black athlete to that top level. Ron Simmons had a lot of legitimacy as an athlete (his was one of only two numbers retired by Florida State at that time). His Florida State coach, Bobby Bowden, cut some interviews for him and put the business over.

Besides, Sting himself was a gimmick, and he didn't need a title. His gimmick was like a title — it elevated him and created "an identity awareness" with the fans. I would liken him to Dusty Rhodes, who always wanted to hold titles when he was working, but it hurt him because he was such a character that he exceeded the title. When we put him in that box of holding the title, we put him in a spot where he had to win or lose in straight matches.

Plus, to me, the world championship on Dusty Rhodes looked ridiculous. I mean here was a big, fairly fat guy, and he's the world champion of your *sport?* But as a character, he exceeded that. Sting was the same way, except that he had a great body. He was beyond the world title. What I was looking for in a world champion was someone who would elevate the title and be elevated by holding it. It had to be someone with athletic credentials. Conversely, having a gimmick without the ability and personality to back it up was like putting the cart before the horse. Very few of those who became a gimmick for the sake of the gimmick had long, successful careers — the fans could sense that difference, and they are the final judges. So, in the "pre-Vince WWF era," we encouraged a new wrestler to develop his ability first and allow the gimmick to come to him instead of trying to find a gimmick and then trying to grow into it. Steve Williams got the "Dr. Death" name while wrestling in high school, and he carried that forward in college, so he was the real deal — this wasn't some marketing title.

Ernie Ladd would have been a great short-term world champion, even though he was almost too big, because at his size he could still make every match a contest. Ernie would only have worked as a short-term champion, though, because if you don't beat him how many fans are going to believe that a guy six feet tall and 230 pounds is going to beat a six foot nine, 320-pounder who's turned back challenges for six months? There has to be something to create unpredictability. You can't offer up something where everyone knows the world champion's going to win, and then he does. It was the promoter's job to put together matchups and scenarios that allowed for different possibilities to play out, to keep every match from being a cookie-cutter thing.

The NWA, in retrospect, was smart. Lou Thesz was a great world champion. He wasn't flashy or that colorful. He epitomized respect, wrestling and being an athlete. He didn't punch you or kick you. Dory Funk Jr. didn't either. He used wrestling moves to beat you. He epitomized a wrestling champion. Terry Funk, however, was ultimately a gimmick. He'd cartoon, show his ass, get tangled in the ropes and get the people laughing. As I said before, I never thought he was a great world champion, although I thought he was a great character who, used right, drew lots of money.

Harley Race, Vader's manager in 1992, had also been a great world champion. Harley could go out and take bumps all night long. Even though he really was a tough guy, he made people believe he could be beaten. Jack Brisco was a phenomenal champion — clean-cut and not the biggest guy in the world, but in shape, and he could wrestle. Jack didn't throw a punch or a kick, especially if he was in there with someone who could wrestle. He could go out and just wrestle and have the people in the palm of his hand.

WCW also needed a black athlete who was a legitimate box-office attraction instead of just playing a "step 'n' fetch it" role. Wrestling still had a lot of black fans, and if you looked at the demographics of every major sport black athletes dominated. Well, here was a manipulated sport where few black athletes truly dominated. Mid-South was the only place in the 1970s and 1980s that had black wrestlers as the true stars around whom the business was built.

I didn't make anything racial out of it — it just made sense from a dollar standpoint. When I looked and saw I needed to get more teenagers at the matches, I put more young wrestlers on top. When I wanted more girls at the matches, I knew I'd better find some good-looking guys to draw them there. So what was I going to do for the black fans, the biggest part of my television audience? It was just that basic.

Once that was settled, I looked at who was on the roster and went with my best athlete, the guy I thought could do it. Ron Simmons had all the credentials in the world — he was mobile, strong, had a great look — so I went with him. And stop and think, who else did we have at that time who could have been world champion?

I believed the championship would elevate Simmons to that elite level. And Ron tried his heart out, but he just didn't seem to have that knack, that intangible "it" factor, necessary to take it to the next level. And as athletic as Simmons was, he wasn't the greatest worker. I hate to say anything negative about Ron, because he was a great athlete and a great guy, with a ton of heart and a great work ethic. He was a credit to the wrestling business, but he was just missing that intangible thing that you can't bottle and is so hard to identify — that internal charisma, that innate sense, that lets someone turn any situation into excitement. So few have it, and Ron just wasn't one of the ones who did, at least at that time in his career.

Charisma is such a strange thing because you can't make a guy have it, but it is possible to have it and then lose it. Junkyard Dog had it and lost it, I think, because of his substance abuse. It was heartbreaking to see what happened to him over the years, because even when there were bitter feelings over his departure from me in 1984 I always had a love for him. And JYD was another guy who never would have made a great world champion, because he was a gimmick and because he was very limited in the ring. But he was the kind of guy who was instant box office if you put him in with the right people and in the right situation.

The angle that led to Simmons winning the title also sparked what could have been a hot feud with Sting and Jake "The Snake" Roberts, but we were having problems with Jake showing up for events and showing up in any condition to wrestle. I finally just let him go.

When you're dealing with a drug addict, the substance filters every one of his perceptions, whether you realize it or not and whether he realizes it or not. When you're talking to someone involved in substance abuse, there comes a point where you're talking to the substance, not the person. And that substance can't allow that person to be truthful or logical because the substance alters his personality.

Having a black superstar wasn't the only promoting principle of mine that I tried to apply in WCW. I also wanted to instill some discipline because there was none. Athletes need discipline — just look at the NFL, the self-anointed paragon of virtue in sports. The league lets its stars get away with murder. Look at the Saint Louis player who killed somebody while driving drunk. Then, in 2004, he got another DWI. And the league didn't even punish the guy! Look at Major League Baseball in 2005 and the tremendous problem it has because its players' union is so powerful it prevents the owners and the league from enforcing a truly comprehensive drug-testing policy with real consequences — and that includes steroids. What you have today is players becoming bigger than the game in their own minds. Look at basketball — recently there was a fight that went into the stands at Auburn Hills. The players' union actually filed legal challenges to the fines and suspensions levied by the league. The consequences haven't kept pace with the salaries, and the sport hasn't made the tough management choices to maintain structure and discipline.

I tried to institute the same system of fines I had at Mid-South to create an atmosphere of some discipline. I think, if you're a professional, there's more to it than just working in the ring. You have to show up and be on time and conduct yourself as a responsible citizen in our society — not be above the law.

I wanted the guys in the dressing rooms an hour before the matches started. If I had a huge show to lay out and my stars wanted to come walking in whenever they wanted, it would have made planning impossible. What if one of the stars didn't make it, or was injured, and I had to change the card? If guys weren't showing up until the last minute, it was like trying to bake a cake without having any sugar in the kitchen. I needed the guys there in order to craft the performance we wanted. Unfortunately, the guys had gotten into the mentality that they could show up whenever they wanted and leave whenever they wanted. Of course, they always had excuses, and I don't know why any of them thought they had excuses I hadn't heard before.

The bottom line was that I wanted to pay based on performance, because that was the way it had always worked, and that system had worked well. I was trying to make the wrestlers personally responsible, but they were all on these contracts that were written to make Turner Broadcasting responsible for everything.

To me, Jesse Ventura was a classic example of the foolishness of Turner Broadcasting's contract system. He was a very talented announcer, but they signed him to a contract for $400,000 a year just to commentate pay-per-views! He was not only talented but also extremely smart. The thing was he had his own agenda, and he was there when I came in, and we didn't have much of a relationship at first. I finally had to tell him what I wanted him to emphasize in each match, because Jesse liked to just go out and extemporaneously do the match. He didn't want to sit in the booking meetings to see the directions we were going and how we wanted the people at home to react.

I think Jesse also wanted to promote Jesse. He wasn't tied to anything else in the company — his incentive was in how valuable he could make himself as a character. Well, I wanted Jesse to be the character he was, but I wanted the wrestlers to be important too. I couldn't have Jesse be a bigger thing than the event he was out there commenting on.

He just kept doing his thing, though, and I finally told him, "Jesse, you're going to collect your contract. I can't stop that, but I can take you off the shows, and I will, if you don't start doing things the way I want them done." I told him to meet with me before each show he was announcing to get a sense of the matches and where they were going. I also said, "I still want you to get your shtick in, but I want you to build the issues that I want built with the wrestlers."

Jesse was smart enough to realize that I wasn't a threat to his $400,000 a year but that his value could be hurt if I took him off the air. And after that talk, he became a big asset, because he was a great personality and talented enough to communicate all those ideas and points of emphasis. I don't know what he thinks of me, but I think we had mutual respect. And, without a doubt, he was a notch above most people in the business — heck, look at what he's done since then.

Becoming the governor of Minnesota was an amazing thing. I saw his election as a commentary on the American political system. Things had got to the point where everything had to be whittled down to a thirty-second sound bite. Do we really know the people who are running for our major offices anymore? No. All we know is what they put in their commercials and what the TV stations put in their sound bites on interviews. Well, heck, why can't a wrestler be anything he wants to be in politics anyway? That's what a wrestler does — he projects his personality the way he thinks it will create the biggest box office in a promo that's often thirty seconds long. The key to our political process is what you make people think, how you communicate with them. The only difference is that the wrestler doing the promo is trying to build up the numbers of fans in the seats, while the politician is looking to build up the number of people voting for him. So here comes Jesse Ventura, one of the great "stick" men in the business. He makes a great interview, so why can't he be governor? Most people sure didn't know much about his political record up to his gubernatorial campaign.

I'm not a Minnesotan, so I don't know well what kind of governor Ventura was, although I thought he stayed loyal to everything he said he wanted to do. I do know he was an excellent announcer, although I still wouldn't have signed him to that contract.

Ventura's wasn't the only contract I thought exorbitant. The wrestlers had injury clauses that guaranteed full pay but didn't require any rehabilitation or testing by an independent doctor. Those things were just licenses for the guys to get paid full contracts and sit on their asses.

It seemed as if all the wrestlers had agents, and the Turner Broadcasting legal department called those agents and said, "Just write up the contract for whatever you want, and we'll sign it." There were certainly no performance-based incentives. And these guys were making so much money, no matter what they did, that they had no incentive to show up on time or work a show they didn't want to work. And many guys didn't want to work the towns. They wanted to work TV and pay-per-view, and that was it, so it was a constant battle.

Vince McMahon certainly wasn't writing guaranteed contracts for anyone. From the job guys to his top champion, he didn't guarantee anybody money. His contracts didn't have provisions to pay guys even when they didn't work. His contracts were based on a wrestler's performance.

An athlete can't operate in a total comfort zone. He has to have some fear of loss, and no one had that at WCW. Turner Broadcasting guaranteed everything. I was later told by some of the guys that their contracts were signed with TBS directly — not WCW. Their money was guaranteed even if wrestling was dropped by Turner. Once again, the "suits" were bested by the wrestlers they considered beneath them.

Vince was also a genius in merchandising his guys. A guy who was over was going to make a lot of money in the merchandising of his name and image, but that also gave a wrestler an incentive to work, to get over. It wasn't that way in WCW.

One time Sting came up to me and said, "Well, Bill, the business has changed a lot since you've been away."

I said, "Yeah, Sting, we used to get paid based upon what we drew at the box office. We used to have to earn our pay. You guys get paid no matter what, and you're the highest-paid guy we have here, so you're going to have to set the standard."

And he did. Sting was a guy who was going to give his all, guarantee or no guarantee. He had a lot of principle. There were times I had to challenge him, but he always stepped up to the plate. I admired Sting for keeping his head when he suddenly got this huge contract, even though I felt he'd never really drawn money or been proven as a top box-office attraction in WCW.

When I got to WCW, Sting was in a program (or feud) against a kid named Mick Foley, who wrestled as Cactus Jack. Cactus Jack was an absolute pleasure to work with. He had no regard for his own body, just taking horrible, dangerous bumps, that often he shouldn't have taken, but he wanted to make the match. I had a lot of time for him because he was so dedicated to doing memorable matches and promos. I was actually trying to do more with him during my last months in WCW. We turned him babyface, and I think he was just starting to catch on when I left in February 1993. He was like Sting in that the best way to motivate him to succeed was to challenge him.

"OK," I'd say, "here's where we're going, and this is what I want. Why don't you give me your ideas for what we can do and how we can get there? How would you do it?"

That really put them to work, and the creative guys, guys like Cactus Jack and Sting, really responded.

A lot of guys couldn't respond to that challenge, though, and they seemed to have the notion that, if something they were involved in didn't work, it was because the booking was lousy, and if it did work it was because they were so great.

It reminds me of Hollywood. Look at what they pay those actors! The people they ought to pay are the director and the writers, because to take a story and condense it to an hour and a half, or two hours, if the director doesn't get it right, it doesn't matter how many great actors he's got — it's going to be a lousy movie and probably a flop. How many top stars have been in total flops of their own making?

A lot of wrestlers were like that. They didn't have a clue unless a strong booker was there to guide them. Some of them, though, were ring generals, and the way to get the best out of them was to ask them to contribute ideas so that they could feel as if they were a part of making something special. The idea was that they knew their gimmicks better than I did because they were living them.

One guy I thought a lot of in WCW was Ricky Steamboat. I'd never had much of a chance to be around him before, and he was classy. In a sense, he reminded me of Ted DiBiase, because Steamboat could make any match a great one. He was a great ring general. Like DiBiase, he wasn't the greatest stand-alone box-office draw, but also like DiBiase he could have a great match with just about anybody. If Ricky Steamboat was in the match, it was going to be a great match. I found him a pleasure to be around, and he was serious about his craft.

One thing I actually managed to do in WCW was bring back the NWA name. In 1991, when Flair left WCW because, I was told, Jim Herd drove him off, Flair technically held both the WCW world title and the NWA world title. The NWA title's lineage traced back to the 1940s, when the National Wrestling Alliance was a loose-knit group of local promoters. Herd made Lex Luger WCW champion, but the promoters who made up what was left of the NWA voted to keep Flair as NWA champion. It became a big mess, but the end result was that fans who had watched the NWA stars for years on TBS suddenly never heard about the NWA anymore.

My first NWA world tag-team champions were Steve "Dr. Death" Williams and Terry Gordy. Since they had last worked for me in the UWF, both had gained a lot of stardom in Japan. Steve was really an excellent relationship for Gordy to have. Gordy was one of the all-time great performers, but he had an awful substance abuse problem, and on one instance in Japan, I was told, Doc saved his life. Gordy had collapsed and was the worst shape he'd been in, and Doc got him into the gym and was really a wonderful influence on him. He was a stabilizing influence on Gordy. Unfortunately, he was fighting a losing battle. It was tough for Doc, because he got mixed up in a little bit of that stuff too, although not to Gordy's extent. I know Doc's been very proud of his sobriety the past few years, and he should be.

But when he came in with Gordy, it didn't take long for Doc to get over. And just like before, Doc got over by his own personal force. Fans could see, without a doubt, what a great athlete he was and how unbelievably strong he was. Doc might not have had the subtlety to paint the picture exactly the way you wanted it painted, the way a ring general could, but Steve Williams was always going to get over by his intensity. The force of his personality made him a valuable hand, as it had in Mid-South and the UWF.

The other half of that team, "Bamm Bamm" Terry Gordy, was a great ring general. He had a tremendous knack for the feel of a crowd, and his timing was perfect. When you put Gordy in with Doc, you had a great team because they complemented each other so well, and they could do it all.

Unfortunately, Gordy also became unreliable while working for me, and I had to stop using him, but I will never be able to express how much I respect Steve Williams. Here was a four-time All-American and star football player. He was reliable, accountable and a tough, tough guy. We didn't agree on everything, but, heck, if you get along with anybody 100 percent of the time someone's lying.

I wanted to bring back the NWA world title and the NWA world tag titles because that NWA name had been established for years in fans' minds as the most legitimate championship ever in wrestling. That was also true in terms of international recognition. Having the NWA titles made our athletes much more valuable to the Japanese offices. I found myself working with New Japan again, mainly through New Japan President Seiji Sakaguchi, although we also worked with Masa Saito, a tough wrestler, and referee Tiger Hattori.

And New Japan was just what a lot of our guys needed. I don't care how talented a guy is — there are times when you've just got to get him out of your area for a while, or he becomes stale. This is even more true today. Vince McMahon owns the whole industry, and there's pretty much nowhere else for his guys to go. When you have the same stars for years and years, eventually you run through everything you can do with them, and people get tired of them. I like chocolate cake, but I don't want it every day of every week of every year. Once you go through every conceivable matchup with a guy, soon you've got the fans saying, "I'm gonna barf if I have to watch that guy one more time." But what was I going to do with a guy who was stale?

Hiring Doc meant there were two guys named Steve Williams in the company. The other was a blonde-headed heel who was using the alias "Stunning" Steve Austin. He was a young guy who seemed to me to be a real student of the business. I corrected some things he was doing in the ring after the first few times I saw him, and he really studied things because he really cared about the business and about making himself better. He came along so much in terms of his timing and the psychology of being a heel.

I did try to bring in some new wrestlers whom I thought could be rising young talents. One of those hires got me some heat.

Erik, my son, and I had maintained a good relationship even through my divorce from his mother. He went to the University of Louisville on a scholarship and actually got it after Coach Howard Schnellenberger found himself sitting next to Jim Ross on a plane. They talked football, and Jim told the coach about this talented kid in Oklahoma.

Schnellenberger figured it was fate and came out to the house. He told us, "Well, I've seen Erik's stuff, and I don't know if he can make it at this level or not, but he's a quality kid."

Erik had red-shirted his first year, which was really beneficial to him because he developed a little late. But he ended up starting only one year at quarterback, which both he and I felt was a bad choice by Schnellenberger. The bottom line, though, was that the quarterback when he got there was Jay Gruden, whose brother runs the Tampa Bay Buccaneers. Jay has played arena league football for years, so he was a pretty fair quarterback.

And the quarterback who beat Erik out after Jay left was Browning Nagle, who turned out to be a number-one NFL draft pick after tearing Alabama apart at the Fiesta Bowl. The next guy who beat Erik out, Jeff Brohme, also eventually went in the first round of the NFL draft, to the San Francisco 49ers, but during that year in college he got injured, so Erik played his senior year. I was there for just about every game he played for Louisville.

Schnellenberger might have been down on Erik's talent, but Erik got to start a whole season, and he had his entire schooling paid for plus nine hours toward his master's degree. I always tried to encourage him to focus on his success instead of moaning about what might have been. Most kids who try out for college football never get to play, and few graduate. In his last year, Erik got to start at quarterback, the position requiring the most but also receiving the most recognition, and he received his college degree. He did a lot better in both departments than I had!

Regardless of my personal feelings, Erik was a guy I'd have taken a chance on. Here was a young guy who was six foot five, beefed up to about 280 pounds, who had played football, could really wrestle and had grown up in the pro wrestling business. It created a lot of animosity among the wrestlers, but the truth is that I never put him over anybody who was a star. He ended up being a victim of the corporate nonsense at Turner Broadcasting and the "sheets" or wrestling newsletters.

The sheets were turning against me anyway. They'd been crying for someone to come in and do something different, and then, when I did it, they had to pick that apart. Of course, if I did everything they wanted the way they wanted it done, then these self-appointed critics wouldn't have had anything to write about. You could never please these guys. After a while, I started to wonder what these guys had ever done that made them authorities on anything in our business. It was amazing to me how people would lift these writers up as if their opinions meant more than anyone else's.

In my opinion, the closest Mark Madden and a bunch of the other "sheet" writers would ever have gotten to being athletes was catching athlete's foot. They wanted to belong, so they made themselves the big sticks, but the only way having a big stick meant anything is if they used it to tear down people who had some credibility.

And certainly, one of the things a lot of them criticized me for was Erik's push, but they didn't know the whole story. Dusty and Jim Ross both wanted to push Erik a lot harder than I did. I kept holding him back. Dustin, who was Dusty's son, was pushed harder, and Dustin had no legitimate wrestling skill — none whatsoever, and I don't believe he ever played any football either past the high school level. But to his credit, Dustin was a good hand who worked hard.

I didn't even give Erik a particularly good contract compared with the ones being handed out in wcw at that time. The way people acted you'd think I had hired him at $1 million a year and made him world champion.

I had some problems with Rick Rude about how he called his matches with Erik. I didn't want Erik to beat him, but I wanted certain things done in the match, and he just wouldn't do them. Dusty and Jim wanted me to have Erik beat him, but I didn't think that was necessary. I just wanted it to be a good contest, but Rick didn't understand that concept.

I got over in New York, as a rookie, by Vince Sr. putting me in a twenty-minute broadway with Killer Kowalski. Kowalski was such a star that going to a draw with him made me a star. Now, if Killer Kowalski had gone out there and eaten me up for those twenty minutes, I wouldn't have gotten over. What got me over was that I let him get his heat, and then I cleaned the ring with him. Actually, the more I dominated him in the match, the more heat he got, while at the same time the more credibility he transferred to me. The people got angry at him because he "escaped being pinned" by me, and they believed in me because he was such a star — yet he allowed me to "own him" in that ring. Killer Kowalski was a great ring general; he was tenacious, and he made the match.

Rude didn't want to make the match with Erik — Rick Rude wanted to make Rick Rude. To this day, Erik doesn't fully realize all I went through over that situation, but if I had it to do all over again I'd still bring him in the same way. Erik was a better hand than most of them and was certainly worth every dime he made there. He loved the business and still does.

Unfortunately, Erik was less than a year in the business when I left wcw, and I love Erik, but I don't know that he ever developed that innate sense of how to make people pay to see him — a lot of guys never do. Erik always went out and tried to make the match, which is a great concept, but often it doesn't get the individual over. I think he has gone out with the goal of getting the match over, sometimes at the expense of getting himself over, because he loves the business.

Finding new wrestlers to be the next superstars was just starting to become a problem. wcw had set up a training program where we had some very qualified wrestlers, such as Jody "The Assassin" Hamilton, teaching the basics to young guys, but you can't duplicate the crowd noise in a training gym. You can't duplicate the timing that a guy develops only with maturity and experience.

To address this, we started a new program. We started setting up shows at high school gyms and small venues within a drivable area, kind of like a mini circuit, where we'd let these kids work in front of a crowd for fifteen, twenty, twenty-five minutes. They had to learn to do something besides choreograph every move. They had to develop that instinct, that timing, which all the great ones had. Then we brought Ole Anderson in and started taping every match. His job was to sit the guys down after their matches and go over the tapes with them, just like a football coach goes over game films with players to make them see what they were doing and to help them improve. Ole was a great wrestler and a good booker, so he was perfect for that role. Hamilton was a great one, and so was Mike Graham, because they understood the business and had such a sense of tradition that they knew what worked.

And having the matches right there for the guys to look at was key. If I was chewing out a guy for something he did in the ring, he might not have seen it the way I did, but if I have it right there on tape we can both see how it looked. It was a huge thing in terms of developing talent.

I tried something similar with the TV production people. After every major TV show or pay-per-view aired, I would have a postproduction meeting with all the production people. It had never been done before. They seemed to be receptive to things at first, but I knew I was getting the corporate screw from somewhere above when they started responding to my points by saying, "We don't have to do that. You can't make us." Trying to get things done there was like being in quicksand, because someone was always sabotaging me for his or her own ends.

I worked on restructuring contracts with a bunch of the guys on long-term deals. When a guy's contract expired, I tried to sign him to a deal that had twelve- or sixteen-week windows. Within those windows, we could either renew the guy or not. That was a way to encourage a wrestler to give it his best and not to become complacent. We also needed a way to churn talent, to allow us to move along guys who were getting stale, which was something the NWA promoters were always able to do, because they could circulate the talent.

A huge problem in the business at that time was a steroid scandal, which was getting a lot of publicity, most of it centering on Vince McMahon's WWF. McMahon even went on trial in 1994, but he was exonerated. Later he told me it had cost him millions. I found it ironic that Hulk Hogan, the guy McMahon pushed to the moon and, I was told, one of the biggest abusers, was also one of the prosecution's witnesses against Vince.

Personally, I was strongly against steroids, but they were one of those things I thought was a personal choice. Still, I didn't have any problem going along with testing if Turner wanted a steroid-free environment. They told me they wanted these guys to be clean. We put in a drug policy, and Sting came to me and asked, "Are you really going to enforce this?"

I told him we were serious about it because that was what Ted Turner wanted.

He said, "Well, I've been on steroids most of my career, and I'd rather stay on them. But as you've told me, I'm the premier guy in the company, and if that's what we have to do then I'll get off them. But if you're not going to enforce it, and it's just another one of these political deals that we see all the time, let me know so I can go back on the juice."

I told him we planned to enforce the testing, and Sting went off the steroids, because that was the kind of guy he was. He understood the responsibility of being the top hand in the company.

We instituted a random-testing program. We had it designed and administered by an outside agency to give it more unbiased credibility. Five of our top guys flunked that drug test, and I was going to use it to "renegotiate" some of their exorbitant contracts and add certain performance parameters that made business sense. I figured that would at least wake everybody up. But the agents started bitching and threatening, and all I know is that Ted didn't sign off on it, according to the people I had to report to, so it became a nonentity and another political deal. I wish I'd realized they were just going through the motions and weren't really serious about cleaning it up.

One of the test failures was Rick Rude. We had a blowup over the testing. I believe he'd have weighed 180 pounds and been out of the business without steroids. And, of course, tragically, he died early, and I was told the coroners pulled an enlarged heart out of him. And then there was Brian Pillman, who was thirty-seven when he died. Unlike Rude, Pillman beat the test. Afterward, I told the testers, "You guys have got to watch the urine come out of their penises and into the bottles, because this guy who beat the test I believe is on them." You could just look at Pillman, with the acne and the water retention, and know he was on the steroids. When he tested negative, we all thought he'd beaten the test. I liked Brian, and he busted his ass in the ring.

Pillman was a tough kid. When he came out of college, he was one of the top-rated middle guards in football, and this was the same year William "Refrigerator" Perry was drafted by the Bears. Brian played special teams for a few years in the NFL. He was just a free-spirited guy with a lot of guts — and a substance abuse problem.

But, again, he died so young, and you can't point the finger at any one thing. However, I can't help but believe, every time I hear about one of these guys dying so young, that narcotics or steroids had something to do with it.

Vader got out of the steroid testing. He brought medical records showing his doctor had prescribed him a certain steroid to help him and his wife conceive a child. I was flabbergasted — here was a monster who weighed 400 pounds, and he was taking steroids! But he was sharp enough to "cover his tracks."

Along with bringing back the NWA name, I saw another way to bring back some sense of the tradition of the company — Ric Flair. Flair had gone to the WWF after his split with Herd in 1991. Flair was another great world champion. He had the charisma, and he always gave it his all, in the ring. No matter what else was going on, regardless of any philosophical disagreements he might have with the promoter or booker, he was going to give it his all in the ring. And Flair had that charisma, that character, to the point where he could have been a gimmick, but he was also small. His size meant he wasn't overpowering, and he carried that air of beatability.

Flair had a good run with the WWF, but it was winding down, and Vince always was smart about not signing guys to long-term contracts. With McMahon, it was simple — if he wasn't using you, you weren't making the money. In Flair's case, Vince had given his word: he'd release Ric without question if asked. And Vince kept his word.

Ric and I had always got along. He was a young boy breaking in for

Verne Gagne in 1973, when I would occasionally fly in to do a show. Years later I loved to kid him, "You used to carry my bag, champ," and he'd just laugh. Ric's a fun, personable guy.

And I was anxious to bring him back in because of what he represented. wcw needed guys who would perform as advertised. We had a pay-per-view in October 1992, *Halloween Havoc,* that drew a strong buy rate. Unfortunately, it was the worst stinker of a pay-per-view I'd ever seen. None of the matches lived up to expectations — they were all complete flops. We had all this hype and all these expectations built up, and nothing worked out right.

Terry Funk had been scheduled to appear on that card but no-showed, and this was after I'd helped him settle his lawsuit with Turner Broadcasting over money he was owed. To this day, I don't know why he didn't show, but he never called ahead to say he wouldn't, and we haven't spoken since. I was surprised that a guy who grew up in the business, as he had, would do something like that. It was such an insult. If there was some reason he just couldn't do it, you'd think he could have called a guy he'd been through thick and thin with to let him know.

After the *Havoc* show, I was realizing that, if we wanted to compete with McMahon, we needed guys who could go out, give it their all, make the match and deliver a performance that was worth the pay-per-view hype. Flair was that kind of person. If I was going to build around a core group, I needed to make sure that it had some solid workers.

I was also working on bringing in Eddie Gilbert, whose mind had really impressed me when he worked for Mid-South Sports in the 1980s. I wanted him to come in and do a little of the booking, but Eddie started announcing it before it happened, and he ended up getting a little heat on me with the company (as if I needed any more).

Eddie had been fighting some substance abuse problems, and I kept telling him, "Eddie, I like you, and I want you on my creative committee here, but you're going to have to be straight."

Jim Ross was for it, and so was Dusty, but Eddie just couldn't hold his tongue. He was really out of control by that point, but he had an awful lot of talent. With Dusty's creativity, adding Eddie to the mix would have been fantastic. The more creative people you have throwing ideas out there the better. That was how I always had success, by incorporating other people's ideas into what I was doing. I was never hung up on one idea. What I wanted was to keep things moving, because I knew the way to keep people watching your television was to have a lot of stuff happening. But it was hard to produce a winning product when there was corporate interference with everything I tried to do.

Management at TBS wasn't my only conflict. The whole time I was in WCW I was also struggling with my faith. My problem was trying to come to grips with my life as a Christian, as my personal relationship with Christ developed, and wondering how to reconcile my participation in wrestling. There was a spiritual war raging within me.

God had given me my salvation, and going back into wrestling was a problem I created for myself. But I'll have problems until the day I die. Going back into wrestling meant going back to the anger, the foul language, the sex — things that were part of my nature that I needed to deny myself, not out of fear, but out of love. I wanted to try to live a good life, because I wanted to try to repay just a tiny fraction of the gift of salvation.

Finally, I got fed up. My anger was full blown, and my language had completely reverted back. I had no peace. And I was sick of the corporate fights. Spiritually, I was realizing why I got out of the business in the first place.

I'd been negotiating pretty hard with Flair to come in, but I talked to him shortly after I'd made the decision to leave WCW. "Champ," I said, "they really want you. I'm leaving, so I'm not going to be in the negotiations anymore, but I'll tell you this: take it to whatever level you want, and get whatever you want out of them. They'll give you anything you want to come back. Make sure the contract you get is the contract you want."

That call was one of my last acts as head of the wrestling division. I'd had enough of the politics and backstabbing. I called Bob Dhue to tell him I was quitting. Later the same day Bob got another call. It was from Bill Shaw, who wanted me to report to his office in what they called the North Tower. I think Shaw had decided to push me out and thought he finally had his excuse.

I'd done an interview with the *Pro Wrestling Torch* newsletter, for an annual special that came out in 1991, in which I talked about some of my political views. One of the writers for the *Torch* was Mark Madden, also a newspaper columnist in Pittsburgh. I'd never met Madden, but he was one of many writers who went from being thrilled I was hired in 1992 to wanting me to get fired in 1993. He decided that the way to do that would be to fax part of that interview, in which I talked about racism in America, to Hank Aaron. Aaron, the legendary baseball player, was a TBS board member at this time.

Madden, to me, was just another jerk in the media exalting himself. Our media have such influence in society. They influence how court cases are decided, how wars are fought, and they can hide behind the power of whomever they're writing for. I understand Madden had been vilifying Bruno Sammartino for years. I saw him as just a guy with a pen who would slander people without accepting any responsibility for what he wrote.

I was saying that I was against racism in the interview, and that if Lester Maddux felt strongly that he shouldn't have to serve blacks, then at least I respected the stand he took by closing his restaurant instead of following the government's equality laws. Did I agree with his politics or how he was doing his business? No! I never said his politics or his morals were ethical or right, because I was (and still am) against racism. The only respect I had for Lester Maddux was that he believed so strongly in his right to discriminate that, rather than bow to the legislature, he closed his business. His convictions were wrong, but at least he had convictions and believed in them.

I just wished that his discrimination had cost him economically to where the market would have put him out of business instead of it having to be legislated into our culture. But, looking back, integration has been so important that I'm glad it was legislated — anything to get our cultural conscience to have to deal with it.

I hate that our nation is at a point where we have to legislate against racism or to legislate morality. I believe in free enterprise and think that the market ought to determine what businesses do. If a businessman is abusing the market, then free enterprise ought to dictate that he goes out of business. Unfortunately, it doesn't work that way. I've come to realize that we *have* to legislate morality. The laws against murder and theft are moral. We also have to legislate against racism.

The funny thing about that interview was how people used it to make me out as a racist. I was the one guy in the wrestling business who had used black bookers and a black man as the top star in my territory. Heck, in wcw I promoted a black woman, Brenda, to the post of office manager, and not because of any racial consideration at all. I did it because she was sharp, the best one for the job. So I find it ironic that I could get a "racist" label after that, not to mention my history with my own company, Mid-South Sports.

And I can't even tell you that I'm 100 percent not a racist, because, unfortunately, I think everyone in America grows up learning to think racially. Anything you don't understand you learn to fear. If you haven't been around any black people, the first time you see them you're going to be afraid because they "appear different." The same thing's true for a black person who grows up never seeing a white person. It's inherent.

What made sports so great was that they provided a great place to meet people of all different colors and creeds. I made friends with Wallace Johnson, a great athlete who was black, in college and all my life have had black friends.

Ernie Ladd is one of the dearest people I know. He was a huge influence on me. He taught me about being "black" as much as a white man can learn, because a white man can never truly know what it is to be black. The closest I ever came to understanding it personally was when I inadvertently walked into a black bar in the panhandle of Florida. The guy at the bar told me to get out — they didn't serve whites. That showed me the rejection attached to it. I was going to flare up and get mad, but I looked around. I was the only white guy in there, and there wasn't a friendly face in the whole bar. I just turned around and left because it was all I could do.

So, unlike many of my critics at the time, I actually experienced what it's like to be on the receiving end of racism, if only in this minute and isolated instance. Even though it was just a taste, it was bitter.

But we were in a time when everything had to be politically correct. And I think that's atrocious. Why can't you say what you think? We've got to get back to being able to say what we think, because that's the only way you can have an honest dialogue. We need to get beyond people going crazy if someone says something a little bit racial. Gosh, we're made up of all these different races. There needs to be a little honesty in how we relate to each other. I'm not talking about viciousness, but I remember guys getting fired for saying black people are better athletes. Well, is anyone watching sports in America today who feels that this statement is wrong? Why else are black athletes dominating every sport they're in?

We live in such fear of terrorism, yet the security people at the airports can't use racial profiling? One time I got picked for one of those random security screenings, and I said, "Do I look like a terrorist? Is there an alert out for sixty-five-year-old white grandpas?" None of the guys who hijacked those planes on that awful day was a fat, bald, sixty-five-year-old Anglo-Saxon. Every one of them was an Arab and a Muslim, but because we're so politically correct we can't profile, even though profiling, in this case, makes sense. Racial intolerance in this country still needs to be confronted. We, or course, *shouldn't* be able to use race as a way of stripping people of power or, even more important, dignity.

I also got labeled a sexist because I didn't want Sharon Sidello in my booking meetings. Well, heck, she didn't know anything about booking wrestling. What was she going to do — create a new idea for another $80,000 wrestling trailer? They had stuck me with her, though. I did everything I could, bending over backward, to get along with her. But I felt she was still stabbing me in the back to Shaw.

Shaw had been undermining me almost from the time I got there, so it was really only a matter of time. I'm pretty sure he had already made a deal behind the scenes with Bischoff, and I'm also pretty sure they had already decided to get rid of Jim Ross.

The thing that made it such BS was that this "race card" that Shaw had always known about became his excuse to fire me. This interview had been done a year before they hired me, and they knew all about it before I ever stepped foot into a TBS office. Shaw even asked me about it before I was hired. I guess he just forgot when Hank Aaron got a letter from Mark Madden about that interview. I never did know what Ted Turner was told, because those corporate buffers kept me from getting to him, not that I really care anymore.

That prior knowledge was one problem with Shaw's plan. When Shaw tried to call me on the carpet about it, I thought, "What an idiot." Another problem with his plan was, while he might have been ready for me to go, I'd already decided I was ready to go. I'd been there for about nine months, which turned out to be longer than I really wanted to be there. Bill didn't know that I'd already told Bob Dhue I was quitting. So, when Shaw had me in his office and tried to call me onto the carpet over this interview he already knew about, I just smiled and said, "Well, Bill, I hate to steal your thunder, but I've already quit, you idiot. I'm going home!"

I'll never forget the look on his face. It was like he was a little kid and I'd just cancelled Christmas. He looked at Bob Dhue, who'd also come to the office, and Bob said, "Yeah, that's the reason I came over here — to tell you he was quitting and going home."

My only problem left was that I'd been such an optimist when signing with WCW in 1992 that I hadn't sought to have anything put in my contract as far as severance pay or to ensure WCW would pay for my move back to Oklahoma. Heck, my move to Atlanta had cost $20,000! Of course, Shaw was so eager to be rid of me that he agreed to pay me both severance and the move, almost as soon as I could tell him that was what I wanted. So I walked out of WCW with a check for $49,000, seven weeks' pay, plus $20,000 to cover my move back to Oklahoma.

When I went to WCW, it was said that division was losing over $8 million a year. The question to me was could I bring it in with less than an $8 million loss? I brought it in with only a $400,000 loss that year! And if we had been allowed to count TV commercial revenues for WCW, instead of TBS, it would have been a considerable profit. But do you think I could get Shaw to give us a letter of commendation for that?

Of course, $400,000 is a far cry from the $62 million lost in one year under Bischoff's leadership!

* * *

My new marriage ended up not lasting much longer than my stint at WCW. I had always been very passionate about Sandy, but I was also very guilt ridden. I think I tried so hard to make that work because I felt so guilty about my marriage with Ene falling apart. But we just couldn't satisfy each other's needs emotionally. And Sandy had her own emotional baggage. I finally reached the point where I realized I could never give her enough to make her happy.

Sandy's children, Cherami and Jeremy, were exceptional kids, though. Both graduated from college and have done well. I am sorry their experience had to include this roller-coaster relationship Sandy and I had.

I stayed involved in Omnitrition even after I left WCW. The two guys who owned it turned out to engage in some questionable practices, but my old friend Ken Lusk (Mantell) came to me and said, "Look, we can own the market in Australia for this stuff. All we've got to do is take the product down there." Well, that sounded great to me. I'd been looking for something new to do. Ken and I even moved to Australia!

What I didn't realize was that, even though I'd put up all the money for him and me to be equal partners, he was selling me shares in the company at $30,000 a share when they were going for $15,000 apiece. He was taking the extra $15,000 a share from me to buy himself more shares on the side without telling me. Trust is vital in any relationship. I trusted Ken and his wife completely, and I got screwed for it. Many of my memories of Ken Lusk are tainted by our partnership in Omnitrition, which ultimately cost me about $200,000. Because he was my partner on it, I never checked up on him, and I didn't realize that he was pocketing half the money.

The only silver lining was that he was investing the half he was taking from me into a bigger share of the company for himself, and he ended up losing all that too. This reminds me of Buddy Rogers's old axiom: "Only friends can screw you, because they are the ones you let get close enough to stab you in the back.

WWF AND THE NEW GENERATION

God bless him, Jim Ross has tried to bring me into places, and I've always been rough to deal with.

When Vince McMahon called me in 1995, I knew, even as I considered going to work for him, that he and I were worlds apart philosophically. I also had a good idea that he was bringing me in, at first anyway, only so he could toy with me. But at the time, my marriage to Sandy had fallen apart, and the old feelings were back. Again I thought that the wrestling business was the one thing I'd always been good at. Nothing else was worth a damn.

Yet I faced the same spiritual struggle over whether I should again get involved. Nowhere in the Bible does it say that life will be a bowl of cherries. In fact, God tells us that it's not going to be easy. It's how we respond to these situations that tells the tale. We have this innate desire to be the captain of our own ship, to be in control. Well, we're not. At different times in life, you might make decisions that aren't good spiritually. You can justify them a million different ways, but those ways are all motivated by the self.

And I justified my return to wrestling through my sense of not having any other real option. So I went to work for Vince McMahon and the World Wrestling Federation.

But I knew, from the moment I arrived in Connecticut, that it wasn't going to last. I also had the sense that Vince really didn't need me. He was just playing a game with me — maybe he could suck some of the juices out of my head, but he probably didn't see me lasting either.

Still, I think going there and working for Vince was a great experience, because I got to see him as a person. He's a controversial figure, but I saw firsthand a lot of good in him as a businessman. He isn't a villain in my book. He's hard-nosed, and he changed wrestling forever, although some-body else would have if he hadn't. And he was first class in the way he handled everything with me.

But Vince put me through my paces, maybe thinking he was going to break me down. The first thing I had to do was go around to all of his executives and listen to them tell me what they thought of me. I answered all of them very tactfully, realizing this was just a game so Vince could see how I would react to these people he was expecting me to work with.

One of them was Bruce Prichard, who was instrumental in convincing Paul Boesch to switch to the WWF in 1987. I really held my tongue in that meeting. He was babbling, and I wanted to say, "Bruce, you're just a pompous ass. You were disloyal to Boesch, and you've got your nose buried so far up Vince's ass it's unreal."

Prichard was completely untrustworthy. I wasn't inclined to believe a word he said. The only reason he was loyal to Vince was that McMahon was where his bread was buttered. Plus the WWF had taken him to the highest level of his career. And I'd had that impression of Bruce from the first time I met him. He used to get all bent out of shape with Boesch for no reason. And in 1992, I had agreed to bring him into WCW. Jim Ross, who was very close to him personally, made the deal, and he stiffed us by not showing up.

Without a doubt, Bruce was a talented, creative kid. But would I trust him? Heck, no. Did I like him? No. But could I work with him? Sure I could, because that was what was expected. Unfortunately, as I would come to learn, Bruce had no real intention of working with me. I think he saw me as a threat to his position and didn't understand that, if I executed my creative role well, all I was doing was strengthening his position.

The whole process of listening to the diatribes from each executive meant nothing. I was obviously there because Vince thought I had something worth bringing to the table, but this was just one of his little games. And I didn't care — he was the boss, the man calling the shots.

And Vince set me up in a nice apartment there and got me a company car, a Lincoln, to drive. I can say this or that, but he treated me great.

The one thing about Vince was that he had to have the last word, the final decision, on everything. He's married to the wrestling business. His wife, Linda, is a very good person, but she's in the business too. You can't be in the business at that level unless you eat, sleep and breathe the business. Vince has been successful not only because he's a brilliant guy and has had a strong vision for where he is going but also because he's a workaholic.

I have a lot of respect, on a worldly level, for what Vince has accomplished, but three months of working for him almost drove me nuts. I think I nearly drove him nuts too.

I would go to his house for a booking meeting, and he might get interrupted by ten phone calls while I just sat there, along with the rest of his "creative team," twiddling my thumbs. He had people to prepare meals for us there, whatever we wanted, and was very hospitable, but the bottom line was everything had to revolve around him.

Vince would assign us to do things and send us to television shoots, but we had no control over the production or the final product. And if the production was screwed up, he'd call all of us together and chew us all out. He was just very passionate about his business.

One time he was reaming everyone out, and I stood up and said, "Wait a minute, Vince. We have no control over the television production. You're the only one who can override anything they do. But you're questioning our loyalty, our desire or our love of the business because you're passionately upset about this show. And you're so upset because of the pressure. Turner Broadcasting has put a show on right against yours, which is what's affecting your ratings right now. And you're reacting to the pressure and taking it out on us. Well, it's not right, and I won't accept it! These other guys might accept it, because they have to work for you, but I don't."

The room became very quiet. I continued.

"All I'm saying is, if you don't let us execute the product, we have no way of measuring what you think our value is. And another thing — don't ever critique me for something your production people did that I have no control over."

He looked at me for a second while everyone else watched on in amazement. Then he said, "You know, you're right."

Another time we all went on a road trip to a TV taping. Well, I didn't know everyone was supposed to caravan. I don't remember who was driving the car I was in — either Pat Patterson or Jerry Brisco — but we got separated from Vince, who took a wrong turn. He got lost and arrived at the taping an hour later than he should have, and he was so mad about being late that at the preproduction meeting he was screaming at everyone in sight.

"Hey, Vince," I called, taking him aside and saying, "We've got a TV show to do. My suggestion to you is, buy a fuckin' map! You grew up in the wrestling business! Buy a map so you can find your way to the arena. Don't play this bullshit game and chew all of our asses when we have a TV program and we're not ready for it."

We had some little skirmishes, but Vince never thought I was flouting his authority. I will say this for him — when we were at a TV taping, he handled all the problems that did come up. Every piece of talent who was important and had a problem had a meeting with him, which, again, screwed up production since everything ground to a halt while Vince was trying to be everything to everyone.

I finally told him, "Vince, when we go to production, I want us to have things running so well that you can turn the production over to me to run, as far as the wrestling, because that's my job. If you want to handle wrestlers' problems, you handle their problems, but while we are doing this production I want you to be a piece of talent there. Your job is the commentary and the color. So be responsible to your job as talent that night instead of trying to solve all these friggin' problems. Let us put you off limits to these crybabies. Let them schedule a time in the office or a time later. The product we're supposed to produce tonight is television."

And Vince agreed to it, and we did it!

A week or so later we were coming back from a TV taping in Chicago, and he told the driver to pull the car over. He said, "Get out of the car and just give me a hug. I have never had a production go like that. That is the best production we've ever had. You have things totally planned out, everybody knows their role, and it flows better than I've ever seen it flow."

Not long after that, though, I had a meeting with Vince in his office. "Bill," he said, "I just can't do it this way. I have to be hands-on in everything."

I said, "Vince, I understand totally. And what I understand is you. You can't delegate authority. Ever since I got here, I've told you — you own the business. Anything I do here couldn't affect that at all. Heck, I wouldn't even want to own a company. But I'm not going to be a broken-down stooge like those others you have positioned who personally report to you — whose every waking moment is about pleasing you and waiting for you, waiting for whatever you need them to do so they can get on with their work. There has to be more to life than just the wrestling business."

"Well," he said, "what are we going to do about it?"

"It's easy," I said. "You're the boss, and I'm going home."

"No hard feelings?"

I smiled. "Vince, we had a three-month deal. You have been good as gold to me, but it's time for me to go home. I don't want to be here, and if I'm going to be here I want to have a position of value. You've played all your games with me and gotten what you wanted from me."

There are a lot of guys who used to be in wrestling, and have come to know the Lord on a personal basis, who are praying for Vince and hoping he will come to have a personal relationship with our Lord. And I am told he has responded, when asked, by saying, "I am not worthy." That too can be a place where many find themselves in their delusion, especially if they have been involved in a performance-based faith as youngsters — and I believe Vince was raised Catholic. His understanding of God's grace may not be fully developed. Grace means without merit. I too am not worthy of God's love. No one is! Yet Christ died for us all. If Vince ever gets that, it will liberate him more than all his wealth, power and fame. I pray for him and his family. So many wonderful believers have prayed for me and are praying for me even now. It's wonderful when someone cares enough to lift us up in prayer to the Lord.

Vince gave me a nice severance package and was going to arrange for me to fly home, but I asked if I could drive the Lincoln home since I'd acquired some things in Connecticut I wanted to keep. He told me, "That's fine, Bill. You do whatever you want."

Vince really treated me like a million bucks. He didn't have to, but he did. He and I disagreed philosophically on a lot of things, but that's OK. You need people who disagree sometimes. You need to sift through different people's ideas and perspectives to get good ideas. When I ran my own companies, I always felt that, if I was surrounded by people who were always going to agree with me, I had nothing. I always wanted guys who were passionate about their own ideas so that we could challenge each other.

As a boss, once I made my final decision, they had to jump on board and work with me to best execute my decision, and that's how it was with Vince and me. We disagreed at times, but whatever he finally decided on something I would do everything I could do to execute it to the best of my ability. The problem was that he was so busy and was under such stress because of WCW nipping at his heels that he couldn't put as much energy into sifting through a bunch of diverging ideas.

One thing Vince did, though, when the WWF went through its lean period, he looked through his company and cut all the fat out of it, which was the complete opposite of what Turner did with WCW. Vince didn't renew contracts for people who weren't key contributors, and he cut positions and trimmed so much of his budget that he turned things around for himself. By contrast, the only time WCW had any fiscal responsibility was the nine months I was there.

Vince and I actually had a laugh about it when I got there. By then, he had already begun the "trim the fat" program in his company. He said, "Bill, I grossed $85 million last year and lost $5 million."

I said, "Boy, you're special — it takes 'special talent' to lose $5 million in wrestling!"

He said, "I know what you mean," and he did too.

I did share a couple of pieces of advice with Vince before I left. Earlier I wrote about the antitrust suits that could have come from the territorial promoters. In 1995, Vince himself could have had a good suit against WCW. Ted Turner's making the call to put the big, new WCW show *Nitro* on Monday nights, directly opposite Vince's *Raw* program, was predatory.

If you're in business, and you want to attract the biggest possible wrestling audience, you certainly wouldn't put your show on directly opposite the show with the biggest wrestling audience. You would choose a different time slot so as not to split the audience. The only reason to do that is to bleed off audience from that competitor to hurt him financially. And TBS had thirty companies it could write off any losses against, so if *Nitro* didn't do well it was nothing to them.

I told Vince this, and he actually started documenting examples of WCW being predatory. He never really needed to use that information, because he ended up following another bit of advice I gave him.

"Vince," I told him, "you've fallen into that old WCW mind-set. They've gotten on a roll and have panicked you so bad that you're reacting to them. You've got to go back to setting the standard. You've got to go back to being the innovator. You know the business; you know the industry. They don't! But you've got a committee in New York watching your shows, and you've toned them down because this committee told you they were too violent. You need to open the gate again and go back to the mud, the blood and the beer."

Finally, Vince did get back to "the mud, the blood and the beer," and *Raw* just kicked *Nitro*'s butt even harder. Now, don't think for one second I'm giving Bill Watts the credit for this, because I'm not. There were a couple of pieces of talent that were instrumental in that turnaround too. One of them was Steve Austin, who'd impressed me so much in wcw. He came to work for the wwF after wcw let him go while he was injured. Vince initially didn't see much personality in him and wanted to put him under a mask.

I said, "Vince, this guy is awesome. Don't hide his identity."

A few months after I left, Austin became very popular after debuting a new catchphrase, "Austin 3:16," which he said meant "I just whipped your ass." Well, John 3:16 is God's demonstration of love, the greatest demonstration of love the world has ever known. It's probably the most important Bible verse of all, because of that demonstration of love. And to use that to put down an opponent and make it a prop in wrestling is not only despicable and immoral but also blasphemous. I hope Steve comes to a point in his life where he realizes what he's doing before it's too late. For him to influence a generation of kids who shoot the finger at authority and have no respect for anything, it just makes me ask, "What is Steve Austin's contribution to our world?" But I don't know that Austin is completely responsible for it.

In any company, the buck stops at the top. In a wrestling company, the moral responsibility comes from the people running it. They also got into shooting the finger, and even double fingers, and when you're in family entertainment (and I don't care what they say — that's what wrestling is) and you start letting people act like that, and even profiting from it by selling foam middle fingers, what are you teaching kids? You're teaching them that, if authority gets in their faces, or tells them something they don't like, they should just shoot it the finger. You're teaching a kid to be rebellious to parents, teachers and everyone who's in authority.

My problem with the wrestling business is that it's gone beyond the pale, and it represents no moral authority. It's teaching our kids the wrong things. It's against not only God but also families and women. It now seems to promote sex of all kinds and drugs through guys who use drug terminology.

So, do I respect Steve Austin as a performer? Yes. Does he have personal responsibility for the double fingers? Yes. But the ultimate responsibility is Vince's.

The feud that really "made" Steve Austin was with Bret Hart, one of the top guys when I was there. My relationship with Bret was a little stiff at first because we didn't know each other. Bret had worked himself into the position of a real star, and he was very protective of that. He liked to walk at his own pace and do things his own way, so he wasn't really cooperative to start with. I just reached out to him conversationally, letting him know I appreciated where he was coming from, as a guy with a family background in wrestling (his father was Canadian star Stu Hart), but also making sure he knew that I needed certain things from him. I wanted to know what he thought about things, and I wanted him to understand that I was relying on him. Bret was working on a TV series called *Lonesome Dove,* and he just had a lot of irons in the fire.

Bret's younger brother, Owen Hart, was also in the company as a heel, and I thought he was great. He was incredibly reliable and incredible in the ring — he was a lot like Ted DiBiase or Ricky Steamboat. Owen could make any match; he could make any opponent look good. He was a catalyst who made a great match happen. It was tragic how Owen Hart died, on a pay-per-view show in 1999, as they were trying to lower him from the ceiling for a gimmicked ring entrance.

Owen was a tag-team champion when I was at WWF, teamed with Yokozuna, a huge man who weighed nearly 600 pounds and had a gimmick of being a sumo wrestler. Yokozuna was another reliable guy and really powerful. He was Rodney Anoia, a Samoan — in fact, he was the son of Sika, who had worked for me as half of The Wild Samoans tag team in Mid-South back in 1982. Like I said, Samoans were warriors, and if they liked and respected you they'd give it their all for you. At his size, the things Yokozuna could do in the ring were amazing.

The guy who was really Bret Hart's top competition for top dog in the company was Shawn Michaels. Michaels was a talented kid. He had no guts, but he had talent and would bust his butt in the ring. He was an unbelievable performer.

Once Bob Backlund (a former collegiate wrestling champion, tremendously conditioned athlete and old enough to have a son Shawn's age) got really mad at Shawn and was ready to take him apart in the locker room. I thought Shawn was going to faint! I don't remember what Backlund was hot about, but I remember how I calmed him down.

"Bob," I said. "You know how Vince is. Why would you wreck your relationship with Vince by kicking the shit out of Shawn Michaels when everyone knows he's scared to death of you anyway? Don't you really think kicking his ass would be a waste of time? I mean, whipping Shawn Michaels is like whipping some little pussy off the street! It wouldn't even be a contest."

Ron and Don Harris, these twins whom I thought were great guys, ended up getting fired after slapping Shawn silly in the locker room, although they both came back later.

I'm told that Shawn also ended up getting whipped so bad at a bar that he ended up in a hospital; Davey Boy Smith and Sean Waltman (The 1-2-3 Kid) were with him and also got roughed up. They must have been blown on drugs. For three wrestlers to get pummeled by six guys is so ludicrous that I can't even fathom it. If it had been Jim Duggan, Scott Steiner and Steve Williams, those guys at the bar could have gotten all the friends they could find, and it still would have been a massacre.

But as far as being a performer goes, Shawn was awesome. He got his start as a job guy for me in Mid-South back in 1984, and he came up to me on one of my first nights in the WWF, and right in front of Vince he said, "You fined me my first two weeks in the business!"

I said, "Did I ever have to fine you again?"

"No."

"Must've worked, then, huh?"

Kevin Nash and Shawn were buddy-buddy, and that was incredibly destructive because they were always stirring things up for their own agendas. I'd met Nash in WCW when he was wrestling as "Vinnie Vegas." At that time, he was so depressed he was thinking about quitting the wrestling business because he wasn't getting anywhere. He was a big guy with an athletic background and was impressive — he just had to learn his trade. But I was the one who talked him into staying in the business.

Nash remembered that when I first got to the WWF, and we got along for a while, but it didn't take me long to realize he wasn't the same kid I'd known. He thought he knew everything there was to know about booking, finishes and the business itself. It was as if he finally became the star he'd always envisioned himself as being, and when he did his melon outgrew the rest of him, as so often hapens. And that's typical because there's an adjustment period for guys who suddenly become stars. The thing with Nash was that he never did adjust. On the one hand, the difference in him was a total shock, but on the other I understood it. Here was this guy making money like he'd never seen before. And the money is what gets guys in this business. We've all got egos, but it's the money that truly changes things.

Nash later tried to book for WCW, which I was told was a colossal failure, but anybody who knew wrestling could have told you that would happen. Still, I have a real soft spot for him as a talent, and he endured the tough times at WCW, stuck it out and became a star. "Personal mentoring" is no longer available in the business, so in some aspects these guys get to be "islands unto themselves" as their egos develop.

Vince also brought in another guy I knew pretty well. Dustin Runnels was the son of Dusty Rhodes, and Dusty had tried to make him into a carbon copy of himself, with the brawling and cowboy boots. But Dustin was limited in his charisma and could never be his dad. Vince went in a totally different direction with him and turned him into "Goldust," who wore gold facepaint and was flamboyant and outrageous. I didn't like it at first, but the more I heard Vince's passion for the idea the more it grew on me, and when I saw Dustin playing the part I thought it was great. It sure was different than anything being done at that time.

Dustin really worked his butt off. Your heart has to go out to a guy like that, who grew up in the business with a superstar for a dad, because such a guy comes into the business with a lot of baggage. Remember, expectations create comparisons, and that really can be a burden, especially if your father has really excelled.

One guy with a bad rap whom I got along with famously was Sid Eudy, who wrestled as "Sid Vicious" and "Sycho Sid." Everyone told me what a problem he was, but I don't know that I ever had anyone try harder for me than he did. He would soak up like a sponge everything I told him, and he tried his heart out. Sid had just never been taught a lot of the basics of pro wrestling. He'd gotten huge pushes because he was such an awesome physical specimen, but no one had taken the time with him. I think Sid's problem with a lot of people was not ego but trust. He'd been burned in the business, I believe, so when he saw that I was shooting straight with him he trusted me. And that doesn't mean Sid and I always agreed on everything.

It took a while before the talent warmed up to me. When you first get somewhere in a creative or executive position like I was in, the boys will test you. They've been through so much and seen so many guys come and go that they want to see if you really have any authority. I think I had their respect, generally speaking, because they knew I'd been successful. As to what they thought of me personally, who knows? So much of that never leaves the car as the guys go from one town to another.

My time in the WWF showed me that, as much as Vince and I often disagreed on things, we also shared a lot of the beliefs about the business and how it should be run. But it also showed me that the business had changed so much that I was truly out of place in the industry.

As a promoter/booker in the 1970s and 1980s, I could take someone only so far with a push. Once he got to a certain point, he had to have that innate quality, that intangible "it" factor. I just had to watch his presence, how he developed and how he reacted to different situations in the ring. Crowd reaction was everything, but we ran the crowds then, as opposed to now, when the crowd runs everything the wrestlers do. The truly great workers controlled the crowd's emotions at all times. Today the guys aren't listening to the crowds because they're out there doing a choreographed set of moves. And no matter what the crowd does, they're going to do the routine.

It was getting that way by 1995. I would tell the wrestlers, "You have given the control of your match over to the crowd. If they're out there chanting, 'Boring, boring,' or 'Bullshit, bullshit,' you guys start to panic and damn near kill yourselves."

In my day, if they'd chanted "Boring, boring," at us, we'd have sat in a hold until we brought them back around to where we wanted them in the first place. Why would I want to go kill myself with a bunch of bumps for an audience that's chanting "Bullshit" at me? The guys today take more spectacular bumps, bigger bumps and more of them, but they take bumps for bumps' sake. And that doesn't necessarily make the match better. We didn't — the bump had to have some meaning in the match's story. It was a matter of timing. We had to sense when it was right to do a particular highspot, and you can't do that if you go out to the ring with a choreographed routine in mind. How do you think Ric Flair can still go out there at age fifty-something? It's because he has timing.

But another part of good timing is knowing when to bow out, and I realized that it was time for me to bow out of the wrestling industry once and for all. I'd never sought to get back into it after selling the UWF in 1987, but I answered the calls that came in. I wouldn't be answering any more of them.

Even when my son Erik worked there briefly in a tag team with his friend Chad Fortune, I didn't see them wrestle on TV. Once I left the WWF, I didn't watch wrestling shows on TV anymore. I realized that that part of my life had to be shut down.

As much as I'd challenged Vince, his wife Linda told me when I was heading out, "I wish you would stay." Linda really impressed me. She was a truly first-class individual, and she understood what I was doing, and what I was trying to do, in terms of taking a little bit of the load off her husband. And one thing I saw was that Vince truly valued his marriage and truly cared for his family. I believe Linda saw what I was doing, and realized it could remove some of the pressure on Vince and help make the company stronger. but it was just not to be — I did write a letter, thanking her. I said, "There just isn't room for more than one 'titan' at Titan Sports."

Vince's competition, Eric Bischoff, ended up running wcw right into the ground, and by the spring of 2001 the wwf was the only major wrestling company in the country. After nearly twenty years, Vince had won the wrestling war he'd started with national expansion.

Eric was the one who replaced me at wcw, and I couldn't believe it when I first heard about his promotion. Bischoff had been a booth announcer, and not a particularly good one. When he got the vice president's job, it was more important to him to hammer the people he hated than to put business first, so he fired Jim Ross.

The funny thing was, the way I remember it, Eric Bischoff should have been gone. I didn't want him, and none of Turner's corporate brass wanted him, because he was a lousy announcer. The only problem was that he'd already signed the contract. He'd worked it out with Kip Frey before I got there and had moved to Atlanta from Minneapolis, so we were stuck with him.

Since we were, I tried to find things for Bischoff to do. He couldn't even do the booth announcing right. What he did was create a game-show concept, which I believe made Bill Shaw and those other executives think he was a smart guy, because they gave credence to someone who could do something outside wrestling, which they looked down on. The next thing we know Bischoff had the position to run wcw.

In 2001, Time-Warner (by then Turner Broadcasting's parent company) and America Online merged, meaning that Ted was now a minority stockholder in the new corporation. He was no longer the absolute boss. I believe that, once he lost control of Turner Broadcasting, he could no longer say, "We're going to keep wrestling," as he had many times before. Then the corporate bean counters looked at the losses and got rid of it.

Eric Bischoff took wcw, which everyone thought at one point he had brilliantly turned around, and broke it, to the point where it could never be fixed. His decisions led to Turner Broadcasting canceling something it had been associated with for more than twenty-five years. That is his legacy.

GETTING IT RIGHT THE
FOURTH TIME

Suzanne —
Everyone knows "I lost my heart in Ada" — I love you so.
You are the most beautiful woman I've ever met — the "keeper of my heart."
As Michael Bolton's song — I want to be your "Soul Provider."
Will you marry me?!
Bill

I met Suzanne in sort of an unusual way. I'd stayed in touch with my old friend Bruce Van Horn and went to visit him and his wife in Ada, Oklahoma, often. It was always good to visit and always good to see their boys play football. I used to tease them and say, "Surely you guys know someone out there who'd be good for me."

One day Bruce called me and said, "I know a good little gal, one who's actually way too good for you, who's been divorced for a while and might be someone you'd be interested in. Heck, if I wasn't married to Sherry, I'd hit on her myself!" Well, that was the best recommendation he could give, since he had extraordinary taste. His marriage to Sherry proved that.

His timing wasn't extraordinary, however, and he waited a couple of months to run it by Suzanne. She was OK with the idea, but according to her she was dating someone else by the time I returned her call. As I recall, I was interested right away.

So it was just not meant to be at that time. When I went to Ada to see

Bruce and Sherry's kids, who were playing football for Ada High School, I'd see Suzanne at the games. She immediately struck me as an impressive person. She seemed to be very well regarded by the people in the community. She had gone to the same church there for years and was quite good looking.

But it was a couple of years before we were formally introduced. I was at a burger cookout to raise money for the team, and as I went through Suzanne's part of the line Sherry said, "This is the guy we've been telling you about!"

Suzanne smiled and said, "I'll shake hands with you," and stuck out a hand.

She was wearing a cellophane glove for food handling, and I tried to come up with something very cool and charming to say. Instead, like a complete idiot, I blurted out, "Oh, no, I don't want to be that safe." Then I asked her, "Why don't you dump that guy you're going out with and go out with me instead? I'm a lot more fun, and I'm better looking too."

She just laughed and said, "I bet you would be fun." But she didn't really say anything else, because she just wasn't a forward person like that.

Later she told the guy she'd been dating who I was and that I'd asked her out. She said he practically turned up his nose and asked, "Why would anybody want to date a wrestler?" Jealousy spoke.

But I guess we just weren't ready yet. Finally, a couple of months after that initial meeting, Bruce called and said she'd broken up with that guy, so I called her. We ended up talking and laughing for a long, long time — and I made a date with her.

I drove to Ada for our date and brought a bottle of champagne. We were going to an Italian restaurant for dinner, and when we got out of the car I took out the champagne bottle because I thought we'd have some with dinner.

She said, "What are you doing? You can't bring that in here — this is a dry county."

I said, "I've never heard of an Italian restaurant you couldn't have wine in."

So I took the bottle in. The hostess seated us, and I told her, "I understand this is a dry county. I'd like you to get the manager or owner because I'm going to hand you this bottle of champagne, and I don't care if you have to serve it to us in coffee cups." I told her I'd also need a pillow.

"Why," she asked, "do you need a pillow, sir?"

"Because I might just propose tonight, and this is a first date, so I might be on my knees for a while, and I'll need it to cushion my knees."

We had everyone tickled, and Suzanne was laughing her head off. The manager came and, sure enough, served us our champagne in coffee cups. And that was our first date.

I was really taken with Suzanne, and she asked really discerning questions. The big one was about my split with Ene. "Why did your marriage of twenty-six years come to an end?"

I said, "It was my fault, because *I was a whore.*"

That blew her away because she'd never heard a man refer to himself as a whore.

She said as much to me, and I asked her, "Do you think being a whore is gender specific? A whore is a whore, and I was a whore. By the time I'd quit being a whore, our marriage was just too damaged."

I really think she appreciated that honesty from me, although as years have passed I've possibly told her a lot more than she ever wanted to know — I've got a big mouth. But the whole night wasn't about regrets and mistakes. We talked and laughed and just really seemed to click. When I got her home at the end of the night, I wanted to kiss her so badly, but I also didn't want to screw up this great first date. So I just said good night and left.

I didn't really like the dating scene; I wanted to be involved in a married relationship, but I also knew that I didn't want to screw up again. I told Suzanne my feelings and said, "So let's take it slowly. You're in control of how fast this relationship goes."

That turned out to be the greatest line I could ever have laid on her, and it was the absolute truth! What woman would ever think that a guy is going to let her have total control and not press the issue sexually? But that was how I felt about her and how much I both respected her and trusted her with my feelings. We laughed a lot, and we still do.

I finally popped the question on December 11, 1997, in a rather unusual way — I took out an ad in the Ada newspaper. I think we both knew that our relationship was heading in that direction. It hadn't been voiced, but we clicked together so well.

A few days earlier we went to a business meeting in Dallas and then to a restaurant owned by my old friend Stanley Abel, Barry Switzer and Dallas Cowboys owner Jerry Jones. We had a ball, and Stan came in, and Switzer came over and hugged her and told her what a great guy I was. Switzer himself is a really great guy — you'd have to be an odd person not to enjoy him. He's just a very personable, outgoing guy. I've never seen him treat anyone any way but great.

Anyway, that night Suzanne and I were dancing, and she told me she loved me. Well, I already knew I loved her.

I wanted to propose to her in a unique way, so I came up with the idea of placing the newspaper ad. With a heart as the outline, it read, "Suzanne — Everyone knows "I lost my heart in Ada" — I love you so. You're the most beautiful woman I've ever met — the "keeper of my heart." As Michael Bolton's song — I want to be your "Soul Provider." Will you marry me?! Bill." We still have a copy of the ad framed and hanging on a wall in our home.

Immediately after, I told her daughter, Jenna, who was still in high school. I didn't want her to be shocked, and I knew she'd see the ad. Jenna is great — she's really special and so close to her mother — just a real blessing. She recently married a man named Wes, who is also a neat person. They are so in love — my heart really goes out to them in this journey of life.

Suzanne's other two children were grown and lived elsewhere. Matt, the middle child, is now an outstanding school teacher in Texas. Craig, her oldest, is a career Army soldier, and I am very impressed with his loyalty to our country and to the service. Whenever he's been deployed in harm's way, Suzanne has really agonized over it, as any mother would when her child is at risk. All the kids are really neat, and so close, which is very important to Suzanne. As I finish this book, Craig has been redeployed back to Iraq, in harm's way.

When Bruce asked Suzanne if she'd like to go out with me, she didn't know who I was. She'd never been a wrestling fan. Her sons were, and they laughed, referring to a wrestling angle I'd done in 1986: "Yes, Mom. You have to go out with 'Cowboy' Bill! He saved us from the Russians!"

I also had a deal with her boss at the salon where Suzanne worked, and when she got to work that day he said, "Suzanne, have you seen the paper?"

She knew I was going to propose, and she had a pretty good idea I'd pull something. She just didn't know what.

We got married in Bruce and Sherry's home, and Suzanne's pastor, Bob Bender, married us.

When we got to New Orleans for our honeymoon, my old friend Emile "Peppi" Bruneau had arranged for a reservation at a nice place, right on Bourbon Street. We had a great time, and things between us have been great since then.

Suzanne is such a blessing in my life and has a real trust in Jesus Christ as Lord. Of course, she gets frustrated with me, because in any relationship there will be disagreements, but she takes her problems to the Lord first.

Another illumination in my life, even at this age (until your life is over, it isn't too late), is the powerful and self-centered behavioral response I installed as a young boy to protect me from pain and from feeling I didn't "measure up" to others' expectations. This was probably because of the unstable emotions of my mother, whom I loved so much. Thus, in order to be "in control," I used my anger and temper to protect me. The result: my delusional attempts at becoming very controlling, resulting in my extreme confrontational behavior, which is damaging to any relationship, as my life's journey has shown. I am so thankful to finally become open to exploring this in myself. I am also going to an excellent Christian family counselor. The emotional liberation has been awesome — and Suzanne has encouraged me in this. I thank God for His loving grace to allow me to see this and to seek help. It's a day-by-day process, but I am making progress. There are moments when that "old self" resurfaces and shows its ugliness, so it's not easy, but it sure is worth it.

Vocationally, by this point in my life, I was fully aware that I'd become a dinosaur in the business where I'd spent most of my adult life. Even if I were comfortable with wrestling on a spiritual level, there just wasn't a place in it anymore for a guy like me. So what else was I qualified to do? As a man, there is an intrinsic desire to be productive.

There wasn't a great demand in the market for a person with my resume, especially if I was thinking about coming even close to replacing the income I was used to from the wrestling business. The only way I saw was to go into business for myself, but there would be an incredible amount of overhead for anything I could do. I had to get out of my "comfort zone" and explore the possibilities available to find another business that was right for me.

I experimented with home-based businesses with extremely mixed results — most of them not good. It's a real "cactus patch" out there, and most companies seem to overpromise and underdeliver. It seems to me that only an extremely gifted few have any real success in this industry. Few companies are really good, long-term deals.

If I was going to have a business, though, it would have to be one that didn't conflict with my faith. And what better way to ensure that than to get into a business where I could truly help others?

The hardest thing for me to get adjusted to, coming from pro wrestling into a full-time, home-based business, was the lack of control. In wrestling, I was in control, told people what to do and ran a tight ship. In network marketing, it's a volunteer army. Every person is his or her own boss; I'm not anybody else's boss. So it's a matter of finding the people who really want to do something with it.

So that's what I'm doing now, and it's something I feel really good about doing. The wrestling world sometimes seems like something from a lifetime ago.

But it also brought me a close friend. I'd played against Jim Meyers when I was on the Indianapolis Warriors team, back when I was breaking into pro wrestling. Jim was playing for the Scranton, Pennsylvania, team. He was a heck of a player — a real animal. A couple of years later he was wrestling as The Animal — George "The Animal" Steele.

This is the story George tells, and since it makes me look so good I'm certainly not of a mind to correct him on it. He says that, when we played against each other in football, he took the wrong key, and I got under his pads and drove him to the sidelines. When we got there, he says I asked him if he was "on roller skates." Now, we both primarily played defense, so I don't know how we'd have ended up facing each other, but, as I said, who am I to correct my friend? What I remember is being impressed with his playing ability. He was a ferocious competitor.

After George got into wrestling, I saw him now and then but didn't really know him. In 1995, I made the speech to induct Ernie Ladd into the wwf Hall of Fame at a ceremony in Philadelphia. George was there, and we talked a bit. A little later, when I went into the wwf, he was working there as a road agent. We were on the same page about a lot of things, but I still didn't know him well.

Later I was working in the company I was with prior to the one I'm currently involved with, the one with the real technological breakthrough in nutritional supplementation. Well, I'd heard George was sick with Crohn's disease. I didn't even know what that was, but I called him to tell him about the breakthrough the company had made and that it might really help him. His first response was to cuss me out for calling and trying to sell him something.

I said, "You grouchy, old bastard! I'm not trying to sell you anything — I'm trying to save your life!"

I really believed in the product, though I told everyone, "We are all different metabolically, so try it and see if it works for you." And we never made any medical claims. This was a food supplement, not a medicine. But good nutrition and our health go hand in hand, and I believe you are what you digest.

He said, "All right, I'll buy a four-month supply, and if it doesn't work I don't ever want to hear from you again."

I didn't know this, but he'd been told he had only four months left to live. He'd been battling this disease for eight years. Doctors had tried numerous procedures and medications, but like much of popular medicine the symptoms, not the causes, of the disease were being attacked.

After he started taking the products, it turned around for him. He called me back and said, "You saved my life!"

George ended up working that business with me, but like me he never made enough money. When we started looking at our current company, he tried it as well — and we are both still involved, along with our wives.

And that was really how our relationship grew. That's one wonderful thing about home-based businesses. It's an industry of relationships. By the time someone you found grows to be a business leader in his or her own right, you've built a relationship with that person.

And over the past couple of years, George's faith in the Lord has grown tremendously, which is the greatest thing of all. George gives me some credit for that too, but God is the one who illuminated his path for him, and that's the most precious gift he could have received. And he always says I saved his life, but I really didn't — I just introduced him to a product. But it really touched my heart recently when he told me, "Reading what you write has really helped me grow in my faith."

George sees Bill Watts with all his warts and blemishes. He's seen me mad. He's heard me cuss. But he also sees the underlying thread of Jesus Christ in my life. Sometimes the pictures of who we are might not be pretty, but once you're Christ's, you're Christ's. Look at the disciple Peter. In the first crisis of his discipleship, he denied Christ three times.

Home-based businesses are really exploding. More people are looking for something that can provide them with an additional income stream and hopefully even replace their primary incomes while at the same time allowing them to have more quality time. But fully investigating one, getting beyond the hype, is so important. We have a twelve-step process to analyze any of these businesses — and that is a real awakening.

LOOKING AHEAD

Between my marriage, my business and my faith, I wouldn't have much time to watch wrestling these days even if I wanted to.

Erik, who's working for a group called NWA TNA, is always trying to get me to watch his show, but I tell him I don't really want to watch the stuff. He wanted to send me a tape, and I finally said, "Okay, I'll watch it, just for you." But I didn't.

Micah sent me a DVD that I did watch — the 1975 movie *Wrestling Queen,* in which I appeared. I saw a lot of old faces that brought back memories. There was Tarzan Tyler, Vivian Vachon and many others, including Danny Hodge. It was also kind of sad watching footage of Andre the Giant, Terry Garvin and so many others who have passed away since then. Even sadder are all the young deaths. Tragically, so many of these guys in their forties are dying because of the damage they've done to themselves with drugs years ago, and some of them kept destroying themselves with that stuff for years.

Many guys who spent years in wrestling have health problems today, whether with their knees, backs or whatever. I have been so blessed, in terms of my health, and I give God all the credit for that. I've had only one major injury, when I tore ligaments in my right knee wrestling in Florida in 1974. But at that point, it didn't matter if your leg was about to fall off — you wrapped it up and went back out the next night. I kept going until I ended up in the hospital with an infection going up my leg. If I'd had the knee surgery to replace the ligaments, it would have been a major operation, and I would have been out of action for a year.

People often ask me why I never watch wrestling these days. Aside from not being comfortable with it spiritually, I also realize that my days in the business are gone. If you know you have to get out of something, why would you go back and watch it only to frustrate yourself?

I was never a *fan* of pro wrestling. I never watched it before I got into it. It's like the private airplane I flew for years. I have about 2,500 hours of time in the air, but since I sold all my airplanes I haven't flown one, and I have no desire to. An airplane to me was just a tool to get me where I needed to go. I never flew my airplane around just for the fun of it. I was flying either to keep my skills sharp or to make a business trip. Yes, I enjoyed flying — it's about ninety-seven percent fun and excitement and about three percent pure terror during those moments when a pilot gets into a situation that overshadows his capabilities. But I just don't have a passion for doing it.

I might catch four or five minutes of a WWE show if I come across it when I'm flipping channels, but I can't remember the last time I sat down and watched an entire show. I don't even go to the events anymore when they're in town.

What little I've seen and what I've heard about current wrestling have given me what might be a very skewed view. There certainly doesn't appear to be any morality in it, and I saw it going in this direction back in 1995. The women end up in *Playboy* and in risqué videos the company puts out in which all they're selling is sex — maybe not directly but at least subliminally. There's no redeeming value. But I know how Vince answers that when he goes on talk shows. I once heard him say, "Well, the woman always wins in the end over the people exploiting her in the story."

Whatever else you or I want to say about him, Vince has won his war. Of course, that might have been the worst thing to happen to the wrestlers themselves. If a guy didn't like me or my rules, there were twenty-six other places to go and work. Today, if someone doesn't like Vince, there's almost nowhere else to go except to companies in Japan or Europe. And I knew it would end up that way as soon as Vince Jr. and the WWF began snatching talent from the regions for more money in 1983.

I used to tell the guys, "Once you guys go to the highest bidder, it'll get to where there's only one company in the United States. And let me tell you something — you'll be able to work as long as that guy has room for you, and then you'll have nowhere to go." And that's exactly what's happened. Of course, the guys who are in there today are making much more money than anyone from past generations, but is it better for the business?

And I think Vince is now reaping what he has sown. After years of battling, he has no more competition. But competition keeps us all sharp, and he has eliminated his, so his business may get soft. It certainly won't be as driven as it was with competition.

In another sense, though, I think the way it turned out is hilarious because, the way I see it, Ted Turner got his butt kicked pretty good! With all the resources Ted had, he allowed WCW to become a corporate mess. How could you lose a wrestling war if you own not only the company but also a number of cable TV networks and eighty percent of the cable outlets in the country? Of course, putting Eric Bischoff in charge seemed to seal WCW's fate.

But while wrestling seems even further away from God than ever, I hear about many wrestlers who have been brought to the Lord. It makes me rejoice. It might be a long time before the sincere converts realize that they can't have it both ways, but eventually they may come to the place where they realize how hard it is to follow Christ and be in the wrestling industry at the same time. But that's between that person and God.

Does that mean I think he or she is less of a Christian? No! I do believe that, as God illuminates Himself to us, through His Holy Spirit, we are held responsible for what we understand. Our redemption, though, is based not on anything we do but on what Christ has done for us at the cross.

Ted DiBiase became a Christian more than a decade ago and does a lot of good work in God's name. Ted and I have remained very close, and he reads things I write on the Internet and in e-mails. I have challenged him on a few spiritual issues, and I've been pleased to sit back and see him eventually come to the same conclusions. His doctrinal beliefs are solid and Scripture based. Ted's at peace with himself and with God's plan for him. He believes that his message of Christ's love is the important thing, and I support his ministry.

When I put something out spiritually, I'm not trying to convince you, and I'm not trying to tell you I know more than you do. I'm not your mentor, your Holy Spirit or your pastor. I'm just trying to stimulate your thought process so that you can search through the Scripture yourself. Does that mean you have to agree with me on everything? No.

So many people in the ministry think it's their job to sell Christianity to someone who's "lost." And they actually think they are the ones doing it! Plus they're making a living from doing that work, so their livelihoods are dependent on the sizes of the crowds they draw. I think that's one of the first seductions, because when you start making a living from it somewhere along the way you'll be tempted to compromise your faith for the sake of making that living.

And, as for wrestling after becoming saved, I'd rather see guys in wrestling who have God in their lives than those who don't. I rejoice to see the changes in their lives as the Lord works through them. "Dr. Death" Steve Williams, who has been going through the toughest health challenges, has been sustained by his faith in the Lord — and that is awesome! There are those who create doubt in my mind, but who am I to say anyone is insincere in his or her faith? Look at my life. There have been times when people would never have believed I'm a Christian based on my actions. But only God can look at a person's heart.

COUNTING MY BLESSINGS

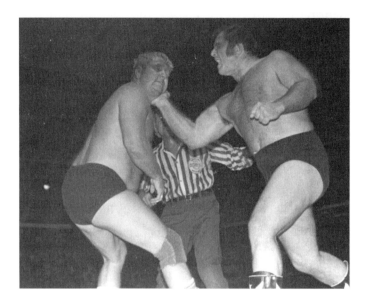

Ene, my daughter, ended up going to the University of Tulsa, and I put her into a house I'd been renting out near the campus. She did well and finished school in Florida, where she double-majored in biology and chemistry. I felt our relationship remained strong until her mother initiated a lawsuit stemming from our divorce, which had been final for over a year. The suit made the children take sides in this legal attack, which polarized us as a family.

I think the kids realize now they should never have become involved in this process, which badly damaged our relationships. I got angry and told them, "If I was such a lousy father, you shouldn't have had anything to do with me. The bottom line is you all 'kept slopping at the trough,' right to the bitter end, and then you turned on me in a court of law." And that is how I felt. I went through a period when I just wouldn't have anything to do with my kids. Pride can be so destructive.

Micah was a loving child and a young man with a lot of heart. My relationship with him started becoming distant when he went to live with his mother. He's had many problems over the years. He's such a chip off the old block — a strong, good-looking kid, but with the same temper I had. He's really had to battle substance abuse too, and I'm proud of him for fighting it.

But Micah was a wonderful kid, and we've recently started talking again. We're on better terms now than we've been in a long time. I'm optimistic because I've come to realize that anyone can change his or her life, starting today. Generally, people think that any change in their lives must be very dramatic, but changes are usually very incremental. A small change can make a huge difference. And I'm sure I have changed too — and hopefully mellowed a lot and become more patient and loving.

With all of the heartbreak of our family falling apart in the 1980s, Erik tried to fix all our problems, to be everything to everybody. And one thing I've found out is that you can't fix people's problems if they don't want them fixed or won't accept your solution. If you feel your solution is correct, whether it actually is or not, you take it personally when it is rejected.

But Erik ended up being the one who reached out to me first after the hurt I'd felt over those affidavits. And we started getting closer again. But it wasn't easy. One day I was talking to my daughter and started thinking about all the things I'd been through with the divorce and having to deal with bankruptcy afterward (which I filed to stop the legal proceedings, not because I couldn't pay my bills), and it just welled up in me. I got so mad I just hung up the phone. See, we never know when Satan will tempt our pride and when we will listen and somehow react, but there are consequences, and in this case it was more estrangement from someone I love. I later told her, "You know, I never asked you to take sides, to say I was right and you or your mother was wrong. All I've ever asked is for you to tell me you were sorry for signing that affidavit."

And I learned one thing about apologies through that. I learned that an apology isn't necessarily someone saying, "You were right, and I was wrong." An apology is, or should be, based on the idea that, if I'm in a relationship with you, and I hurt you, then, if I value that relationship, the apology is to ease the pain of the hurt I caused. So I never asked any of my children to say I was right and they were wrong. All I asked is for them to say, "Dad, I'm sorry I hurt you by getting involved in the legal process of all this mess." It cost me so much financially, and so much anguish personally, and I don't know if they ever understood that.

But both Erik and my daughter Ene later told me they were sorry, and it was actually Suzanne who talked to me about it and got me thinking about those relationships again. I started praying about it, and Suzanne later asked me, "What about if they start calling again? Will you be able to love them again?"

I said, "Well, I promised God I would."

Not long after that, my daughter called me. I told her, "Ene, I love you, and I'm so glad you called."

She said, "I wanted you to know that I've been thinking about it, and I know I did some things wrong, and I'm sorry if I hurt you."

I said, "You know, I'm glad to hear that, but I wasn't even requiring that anymore. Let's just go forward."

And we have ever since. And Erik and I started moving forward too.

I've even started reconnecting with Joel. I recently ran into him in Tulsa, by what seemed to be a complete accident, except I don't believe in random events. Then, in Atlanta in 2004, I saw him when Suzanne and I went to visit my daughter.

The first time I ran into him, I wanted to clear the air. "Let me ask you something," I said. "Was I a bad father?"

"No," he said. "You were the best."

"Did you ever doubt that I loved you?"

"I never doubted that," he said. "I never doubted that you loved me."

What else could I ask for? Joel was always an intelligent kid, and I have wondered if he's started to rethink things since he's recently gone through a divorce of his own.

It's like I told him one time, "You know, with the other children, I had no choice. I'm their father. With you, I had a choice. I chose to adopt you, and you chose to be my son."

Biff, my son from my first marriage, was the only constant in my relationships with my children during this time since, of course, he felt no loyalty toward Ene, the mother of Joel, Erik, Micah and my daughter Ene. Biff was "disenfranchised" due to the divorce of his parents, but because he decided he wanted a relationship with his father he persisted, and we have that precious bond.

I've come to realize how precious our time here is and how important it is to tell the people who are special in our lives how much they mean to us. That was what hit me hardest about JYD's death in 1998. He was driving back from his daughter's high school graduation, the same daughter whose birth he "missed" as a result of The Freebirds "blinding" him in 1980. He fell asleep while driving and crashed into a tree. The car he was driving was the Mercedes I'd sold to him fifteen years earlier. When he died, I realized I'd never told him how much he meant to me personally — how much I loved him as a person. Set aside the situation he had with Vince and his drug problem, because those were things that just got beyond his control and beyond my control — choices and consequences.

Buddy Landel contacted me and asked me to write a eulogy for JYD. When I sat down to write it, I realized, for the first time in a long time and maybe ever, how much I'd truly cared about him and how much he'd impacted my life.

I then got to thinking about some of the other people in my life, and I actually started calling people to let them know how much they had meant to me. I realized that I didn't want anyone else who had impacted my life not to know how much he or she meant to me.

Fortunately, I did have that opportunity with Dick Murdoch. Our last discussion, years earlier, hadn't been a pleasant one. He'd turned so bitter toward the business, and I told him, "Dickie, if you're feeling this way about the business, then you need to get out of it. You've gotten to where you're bad in the dressing room." But I called him in 1996 and got to see him a little later. It was great just to see him again, and we talked and talked. As it turned out, that was only a couple of months before Dickie himself passed away, but at least I'd had the chance to tell him how much he'd meant to me. Dick Murdoch was powerful in my life.

Looking back, even though I see a lot of pro wrestling itself as the promotion of violence and sex, I really was blessed to come across some wonderful human beings. Jerry Oates, whom I met in Georgia; Bob Armstrong, who stayed when everyone else went with Gunkel in 1972; Mr. Wrestling II — what quality guys they are.

And Hawk. I wrote a short eulogy for Mike Hegstrand, "Road Warrior Hawk," in 2003. He died not too long after rededicating his life to God. I heard that "Superstar" Billy Graham asked, "Why would God take him now?" And it is natural, in our grief, to question our Lord. But my reply would be "I look at it like this — God kept him alive long enough to save him." He and Animal could be frustrating, but, gosh, they were good people.

A friend recently sent me a quote, and I wish I knew who originated it, but it certainly applies here: "I would rather live my life as if there is a God, and die to find out there isn't, than live my life as if there isn't, and die to find out there is." And I try to live that way, but I'm not always successful. Like all Christians, I am a work in *process*, and I still rebel against God every day. I try not to, but I do.

A PERSONAL JOURNAL

In wrestling, the fans are the foundation. Without fans, no one could be a star in anything. So often we get disconnected from our fans as we get absorbed in ourselves and become even more self-centered and self-impor-tant. We are so often legends in our own minds way beyond any realistic measure. In my early career, most wrestling areas ran their towns on a weekly basis for live events, so you really got to know the fans — of course, as young men, generally we tried to get to know the young ladies.

But that has changed dramatically. These days money has increased, and pay-per-views have really added another level of insulation from per-sonally interacting with fans. As in all pro sports, insulation becomes a form of isolation, and we get to the point where we really believe it is all about us.

Recently, I attended a big wrestling fans' reunion in Tampa, and it was with mixed feelings that I even went. I got to see some of my peers whom I hadn't seen in years and to re-establish bonds and friendships that in some instances had been damaged. To mention here all the former wrestlers I got to see, many of whom worked with me or for me, would be impossible. But it was priceless to me. Some even took the initiative to come to me, some even with their children along (including some with children in the business), and they told me what working with me or for me had meant to them. How humbling and truly touching. The last time I'd seen some of them we'd had verbal confrontations, sometimes to the point of possibly becoming physical. And for the most part, to see these guys — they would smile, and we would hug — was also priceless. Time has dimmed anger. It was just great to see them alive, for we have lost so many. Each of these people was in my life for a reason, as I was in theirs.

Yes, some are still captive to harbored grievances toward me, and, to tell you the truth, I still harbor resentment toward some of them. What a waste of human emotion! Isn't that aspect of pride so destructive?

But the fans there were awesome! And they paid huge ticket prices to see their heroes, those whose careers they had followed. The Q&A session I was part of — with Jim Cornette, Dennis Condrey, Bobby Eaton and Stan Lane — was truly a walk down memory lane as fans asked their questions to the moderator, Bill Apter. And I was totally impressed by their questions. It was truly an enjoyable experience, and, if these fans got from this event even a small measure of what I carried home in my heart to reflect upon, then they got more than they paid for. I even visited with one of them from the Saint Louis area at the airport while waiting for my flight. He was truly fun to spend time with. He has a very good job and was a bright young man who loved wrestling, which certainly goes against the way some in the media have tried to paint wrestling fans.

In Mid-South Sports, we always tried to give our fans more than they paid for. If attendance was down, we tried to give more, not less. My theory was that, when you get down to the hardcore fans, you'd sure better keep them. If you lost them too, you were in serious trouble. I wanted them going home feeling they truly got more value from our event than they'd expected.

That was also our theory in booking our TV shows, which was why we had so many main-eventers booked against each other on them instead of all the formula matches featuring a superstar against a job guy. We realized that our main area of promotion wasn't a huge population area, so we needed to create more excitement to keep their viewing loyalty and ensure that they wouldn't miss tuning in to events or attending live events in their area.

We also felt a moral responsibility to our fans and their families. That is why we didn't do heat just for heat's sake or make something racial to create emotion at the box office. Our scenarios had to make sense and remain within the bounds of "family entertainment." We didn't allow our wrestlers to use profanity in their interviews or use low blows in their matches. We also didn't allow fans at the TV tapings to show placards with profanity. I'm sure in all those years some slipped by, but if so it was accidental. We took time to demonstrate coaching techniques for amateur wrestling for kids and promoted doing the right thing and that right would win out. We encouraged patriotism for America and its ideals. We promoted going to school, gaining an education and being personally responsible and good citizens. We did all this and still had what I believe were the most exciting TV shows in this business.

Our fans really gave so much to us. And I wish I could relate the many, many incidents of how fans impacted our lives. Our lives' impacts on others are what's important.

One of the fans at the Q&A asked about Hiro Matsuda, my friend from Japan who died of liver cancer. Hiro was a special person. He first came from Japan to Mexico to be a wrestler. What a challenge — to go to a foreign country, learn to speak Spanish and wrestle because there were more opportunities for smaller wrestlers then. Eventually, he immigrated to America and learned yet another language. I met him early in my career in Oklahoma, and we became friends, even more so as time passed. He was a loyal friend. But the thing that is the most important to me is how his life ended. He had cancer of the liver, and I wasn't informed until it was too late because he didn't want those he knew to see the ravages of this fast-moving disease on him physically. He died practically before I knew he was ill. But Brian Blair, an ex-wrestler who had also become a follower of Christ, shared with me that before Hiro died he was there as the Lord allowed him to be called to Christ. And with tears in my eyes, I am rejoicing that the Lord used Brian as a vessel, because now I know that when I go to Heaven, to be with my Savior forever, my friend Hiro Matsuda will be there too.

Here's another example of how some special fans really impacted me and some of my wrestlers. These fans touched our lives in a way that should be shared to illustrate their love, because the most powerful force in this world is love — love is eternal.

As we see the devastation of the tsunami in Asia, of famine, of genocide in Africa, of starving children, we hear people question if there is a God and, if so, "Why does He allow this?" God is sovereign. If He is not in control, then we are all victims of fate. Does God allow these events to happen? Yes. Why? I don't know. Isaiah 55:8 says, "For my thoughts are not your thoughts, neither are your ways My ways. For as the heavens are higher than the earth, so are My ways higher than your ways, and My thoughts than your thoughts." When you admit God's sovereignty, you begin to understand. God "allows" certain events and "causes" certain events, but He loves and cares for every person and desires all to be saved.

Do these disasters mean the victims are worse sinners than we are? When we see events such as the tsunami, we can ask, "Lord, did you allow this — and what is your purpose? What does this mean for me? What are you revealing to me? How am I to respond?"

We are told to live our lives ready to die in Christ, and if we aren't ready to die we aren't ready to live. Our responsibility is not to figure out when He is coming but to be ready for His return. Every tick of the clock moves that time closer.

It's especially difficult when disaster strikes children and babies, because we know our Lord loves children. I believe that children who die before the "age of moral responsibility" are covered by God's love eternally. He is a God of love. Still, even these smallest and most helpless can have tremendous impacts on the lives of others.

Let me share with you a journal. It reads, "For recording your thoughts, feelings, insights — everything and anything that is special to you." I have had this journal since Christmas 1986. Despite all the moves and turmoil of my life, it hasn't been misplaced. It's filled with the loving spirits of the little hearts who wrote to me. I well up in tears just thinking of them.

Life is precious — our Lord paid for us with His life. Children especially can really impact you. There's so much we take for granted — in my case, my health, my strength, being born in America and having parents who loved God and raised me in the church. So when Georgiana Seay showed me a letter written to some of our stars from some little girls with major health challenges (some of them terminal), it really penetrated my calloused heart!

Knowing how busy our wrestlers were, and their brutal travel schedules, I didn't want to leave it to chance that they would answer their letters. I began corresponding with them, knowing we could arrange for them to meet their heroes at the right time. That's just what happened — they got to meet these stars, whose hearts were also touched and who were also so willing to give of themselves for these kids.

The kids also sent me a special journal, which I received right around Christmas of 1986, my last Christmas owning the Universal Wrestling

Federation. We keep this book in our living room area, and Suzanne recently got it out and asked me if I were going to say anything about it in my book. It struck me that this is something I had to share, and I feel Suzanne was led to pick it up and encourage me to do so. God is so faithful — He brings us light in a darkened world. The light from these children still shines in my heart!

I still have the journal's label: "Tammy Cormier & Pam Miller." The last address I had was Groves, Texas. I don't know if the senders are still alive or how to contact their families. Using the Internet, with the limited data I have, I found nothing. As I write this chapter, it is one week before Christmas 2004 — the time we celebrate the birth of our Savior, Jesus Christ. What better time could there be to remember these children?

On the front of the journal, it says, "What is a dream? A magical thing, a rainbow of joy in your heart, your own secret corner where no one can go, where the path to fulfillment can start. A dream lures you on, always one step ahead until you have caught it, and then, there's always another to capture your soul and lead your heart onward again." What a cover to hold the hearts of these children as they pour out their feelings to strangers they have only watched on TV, wrestling stars who were so strong, so healthy, so exciting — living a life they could only dream of. And, I'm sure, in those kids' dreams, these lives were wonderful and golden.

Each of their letters to me in this journal was written by hand, either by themselves or, if they were too young to write, by someone they dictated to. A few of them talked about their favorite wrestlers, but many of them made a request. What touched me was that, even as they were dying, their thoughts were not to make a request for themselves but often for another child. So, although a little of the "personal touch" may be lost in this reproduction, I hope you can still feel their hearts. Remember too that their heroes were the wrestlers featured on our TV show at that time. It's a snapshot of the impact we could have on young lives. Unfortunately, I can't include all of them, but I still believe you'll be able to see their hearts.

Page 1

Everyone has a Special Dream that keeps you going. That's what "our" Book is all about. It contains some of our most Special Thoughts and also some pictures. We all hope you Enjoy it as much as we enjoyed writing it.

There may be some stories written by another person, because some are too young to write. So Merry Christmas to All!

Page 2

My name is Kyle. I love everything. My favorite Wrestlers are Hacksaw, Taylor, Magnum and Rock-N-Roll Express.

If I had 1 wish it would be to become strong and happy and to climb a mountain top.

Merry Christmas!

Kyle Jason Weaver

Note: Kyle is 11 years old and he has a heart condition that is inoperable. Last August, he was granted his wish. He was able to go to the Smoky Mountains and camp out.

Page 3

My name is Carrie and I'm 12. My mom is writing this because I had an accident and broke my arm.

To me a dream come true is something you know will never happen and when it does, then life stops.

My dream is to see Disneyland, but in a way I hope I never do — Because wishes only come true when you don't have time left.

Love, Carrie

Note: Carrie has Leukemia and Thank God has been in remission for 1 and ½ years.

Page 7

These are the pictures of my daughter Stephanie. She is 4 years old. Her father and I go to most of the matches in Lake Charles. Stephanie loves wrestling. She gets all excited at the sight or mention of Terry Taylor. Even at 4, She knows good taste! Ha!

When asked what she wants she'll look up and say she wants Terry Taylor to wait until she grows up and she'll marry him. Stephanie has Leukemia and is now taking Chemo at MD Anderson [a hospital in Houston].

She also wants to draw a picture for Terry Taylor.

Her photo was enclosed when she was 2 years old. On the next page when she was 4 years old, on the next 2 pages her crayola drawings.

Page 13–15

Dear Mr. Watts,

My name is Suzanne Jacobs. I'm 15 years old and I have Cancer. I'm not able to attend many of the matches but I do watch on TV. I'm just glad to see ya'll back on Channel 4. We really missed ya'll. I just hope someday soon ya'll be coming here to Beaumont.

Here is what I want for my dream. First I'd love to be well but I'm not so I can live with it. But my wish is for someone else. I think you know her. Her name is Tammy Cormier. She just got back from the hospital yesterday. According to Mrs. Miller she's not doing very good. It seems she got a cold and when she went to the hospital it was real bad. There's a spot on her right lung. They say her cancer is back. Tammy doesn't know yet

Tammy is a good person. She has done so much to build up our morale when things were down. When Magnum T.A. got hurt she wrote him a special letter. She sent him some Rosary beads that was given to her by someone. She called them her good luck charm because the Pope himself blessed them. She wanted him to have them. One time in church she asked for a special prayer service just for Magnum.

No matter how sick she would get she always looked on the positive side. And that's hard for anyone to do while in Chemo.

I know you know she is a big fan of wrestling, especially the Rock-N-Roll Express but she's also a big fan of Terry Taylor.

One time she and I went to a match in Houston. She wanted to meet Terry Taylor but every time he came out he was just swarmed. Since she and I both have amputated legs it was hard to push through.

Anyway last summer me and about 6 others raised money by washing cars and a few other things. The money was put up in order to Grant a Wish for Someone Special. That someone special is Tammy.

We've talked it over with Mrs. Miller and she said she would help in any way. What we want is to arrange a meeting so Tammy could meet Terry Taylor. We have raised $500 and we would pay him for his room expenses and travel and his time. We know these things take time so we aren't in any hurry.

Tammy would have a nurse with her and a clearance from the doctor. Mrs. Miller said she or one of the other ladies would be willing to meet with Terry to arrange things anytime that is convenient.

We know how busy he is and we wouldn't ask him to go out of his way. They could meet him in some town where he will be wrestling. It's just it'll have to be on a weekend because of school.

It would be nice if it could be somewhere where it snows because she has this thing for a snowman.

I hope you can help us out — I know it's a lot to ask but only if it was for 15 minutes it would be great! I know $500 isn't much but we could probably raise more.

Thank you and Merry Christmas to all!

Note: Suzanne is a very special person. Like Tammy she thinks about the other person. Everything she said in her letter is true. We found out the other day that Tammy has a spot on her right lung. Everyone here's main goal is to grant a wish for a dying child. We've all gotten together and we want to grant Tammy's wish.

As I'm sure you know, Tammy is a big fan of wrestling. Her favorites have always been the Rock-N-Roll Express and Terry Taylor. I know it is impossible for her to meet the R-N-R Express but it would mean of lot if we could arrange for her to meet Terry. I know how busy these men are and I'm not asking for them to go out of their way.

All I'm asking is for a few minutes. We have a fund that would pay his expenses.

Either myself or one of the other two ladies would be glad to meet with Terry to explain everything. My husband and I attend most of the matches in Houston and Lake Charles, and we usually stay the night in Houston.

At this time Tammy knows nothing about the spot on her lung. She believes it is the flu.

I want to Thank You for the time you've given me and I really hope that you and Terry can help us make a wish come true.

Merry Christmas!

Pam Miller

[Note: We made this happen. We also had several other wrestlers meet with these children. And they too were glad to do it — their hearts were moved.]

Page 19

Merry Christmas!

My name is David. I love wrestling and I wish ya'll would come to Beaumont.

I'm 15 and have Muscular Dystrophy. To me I most admire the strength the wrestlers have. You know, when they get thrown over the ropes and they still get back up to fight. I know how they must feel.

There's a lot of times when it's hard for me to get up out of bed, but no matter how bad it hurts, I keep going because if I give in I'll never get back up.

So keep up the good work. You make my day.

Page 20

To all UWF Wrestlers,

I wish you all a Merry Christmas. Like everyone else, I'm a fan of wrestling. My name is Monica and I'm 18. I'm a freshman at Lamar. I'm sort of new at this so forgive me for being clumsy.

I'm one of the lucky ones. I have Leukemia but in remission for almost 2 years. Even though I'm free of the disease I'm still cursed. I found out 4 years ago I was sick. Since that time I've never had a date. It seems the hardest thing for people to understand is I can't give you my cancer just by being near me.

For me my dream would be for people not to treat me different. After all I'm a person first and I have the same feelings as everyone else. The only difference is I don't take living for granted. Each day is better than yesterday.

So guys, have a Great New Year.

Monica Broune

Page 21

Dear UWF Wrestling

We all wish you a Merry Christmas. Every one of us love wrestling and attend whenever possible.

I for one think UWF is the #1 wrestling on TV.

The only thing ya'll lack is Rick Morton and Robert Gibson. But we can't have everything.

I really hope you can help in granting Tammy's dream.

Although I'm older than she is, she has really taught me a lot. She has taught me how to make the most out of living. Without her I don't think I would ever have made it.

She has more courage then anyone I have ever met — no matter how bad she may feel she never lets it get in the way of what she wants to do.

I for one can't imagine what life would be without her. I'm just so glad that I have known her.

Keep up the good work and keep bringing us #1 wrestling!

Love,
Kassy Williams

Page 24

Dear Mr. Watts

Merry Christmas!

My name is Sam (Samantha) and I'm 17.

Like everyone else I really love wrestling. Whenever I can I go to Lake Charles matches and sometimes Houston. Ya'll truly number one.

I'm really sorry you won't get it before Christmas but we tried.

The other night we had a Christmas Party. We all talked about what we hoped for in 1987. Wouldn't it be great if a cure for cancer be found. Or some way to ease the pain.

We also talked about some of our memories of Christmas last year. And the memory of some of our friends who no longer is with us, it really made me sad.

There's a very special person that we want so much to grant a wish come true. I know a few other has written about it so I want to tell my reason.

Page 25

The wish is for Tammy Cormier. I know you know her. There's no bigger wrestling fan around.

She likes the Rock-N-Roll Express and Terry Taylor the best.

Tammy is very special to everyone she meets. She has such a bright outlook on life. Through everything she has been through she still has hopes. In the past 3 years she has lost a twin sister to cancer. Countless chemotherapy, radiation. Lost her leg to cancer, then recently bone marrow transplant. And now we found out she has a spot on her lung that she doesn't know about.

Through all this she still has hope. It all seems so cruel. There's so much to do, yet she'll never know.

Our wish for Tammy is to meet her favorite wrestler. Since Terry is closer could it be him? We have a fund that would pay for his time and expense. Mrs. Miller or one of the other sponsors would meet and explain everything. Could you help make our present come true?

Merry Christmas!

Love
Sam

Page 26

To Mid South Sports,

Hi! And Merry Christmas. My name is Wayne Ross. And yes, I'm a big fan of wrestling. I never miss a match in Lake Charles.

My favorites are Hacksaw, Williams, and Taylor. I can't wait to see Duggan and Taylor become tag team champs.

I'm sort of new to the group. I'm 17 and I have stomach cancer. I'm a patient in Galveston. I find it real hard talking about my illness. I must still be in the shock stage. I figure if I don't talk about it, it will go away. Stupid. Everyone here seems so positive I feel angry. Before getting sick I played football and baseball. Now I feel like a freak with a bald head.

I hope ya'll can help Mrs. Miller with Tammy's dream. She's a great kid. When asked what my dream was for 1987, it would be to stop being angry and learn to cope.

Wayne

Then, handwritten on yellow legal paper, was this letter from Tammy:

Dear Mr. Watts,

I hope you had a nice Christmas. Sorry I'm so late. I was so glad to hear from you. You always come through whenever I get down. I'm glad you are my friend.

I'm surprised Ricky and Robert still remember us, they have so many fans. They are also special and we miss them.

Your trip to Colorado sounds exciting, I really think you should try ice skating. I love winter and snow. It never snows in Beaumont. When I see pictures of the snow and snowmen I really miss the snow.

I heard about Magnum T.A.'s accident. It was terrible. I hate to hear something like that happening but it must be extra hard for such an active person. Each night I say a prayer for him and his family. I'm glad he has some movement. It will just take time. One day after we heard about his accident some of my friends were talking saying how they all hope he's able to wrestle again. I told them I too would like to see him back wrestling but more important I was glad he is alive and improving.

Then one day while watching wrestling Dusty Rhodes was saying how hard it was for T.A. It really brought back memories of when I lost my leg. I was so down I didn't want to go on. But I made it and it was hard. I still get uneasy in crowds because without meaning to people stare at the radiation markings and the chemo-burns, and now my leg. You always say how much courage I have. I don't really, I just learned to take it a day at a time. But if I could I'd give it all to Magnum because he needs all our support now.

I've been back in the hospital. They say it was the flu. I'm not totally convinced. I haven't felt this bad in a long time. I've got to go back to the doctor in 2 weeks.

My dad took me to Houston Dec. 26th to see the wrestling matches. I was watching the fans take pictures, they really get wild. We had to leave after Terry and Hacksaw's match. It was exciting. Terry seems like a nice guy. He seems sincere. Maybe someday I can meet him.

Another year is here. I have really had a great year. The best one so far, because I'm still alive and able to get around. Who knows? I may go down in medical history as the girl who wouldn't give up.

I hope everyone's year is as Great as mine!

Your friend,
Tammy Cormier

AFTERWORD

As we have traveled together in this journey, with you reading what I've written about my life, it is my sincere hope to leave you with some "nuggets of gold" to value and to stimulate your heart and mind — to plant a seed of discovery beyond the outward surface, the realm of the physical and material.

As you have read about the choices I've made and their consequences, you've also read my comments concerning my spirituality (which is way more important and meaningful than my physical and material life, which is mortal and thus temporary), my understanding of God and what I feel He has illuminated of Himself to me in this process of relationship with Him — starting with the depth of His passion demonstrated at the cross.

The key point I'm sharing is that, because of the cross of Christ, I have a deep, personal, *eternal* relationship with Him (God the Father) through His precious Son, Jesus Christ, and His Holy Spirit, which dwells in me.

This is the Holy Trinity — one God in three persons. It all starts at the cross and what Jesus did there for you and me.

One must answer these questions. *Is Jesus Christ whom He says He was and is, or is He a liar? Is God whom He says He is and has revealed Himself as, or is He a liar? Is the Bible God's revelation of Himself to us, or is it a book of fables and legends?* The Bible is the only true source we really have to learn about Jesus. Human opinions are not the truth; they are skewed or biased by our interpretations and agendas.

One thing that really struck me about the Bible is that it was written over a period of some 2,000 years by about forty different authors whom God inspired to write specific books under His revelation to them. These authors were men from all walks of life, from highly educated to simple fishermen, from kings to paupers, and there isn't a single contradiction in the Bible — it is totally harmonious. To me, that is impossible without divine inspiration.

Yes, we can read the Bible and misinterpret it or take verses out of context to prove our own agendas and opinions, but it is the only source of absolute truth on this planet. And we have attempted for centuries to disprove and discredit it but can't, because it is God's Word, and He is divine.

So friend and fellow traveler, as you approach the end of this life (for any moment can be our last here), consider this question: *Where are you going to spend eternity?* It is time to think about it. In Christ, I love and respect you, so I am sharing with you this truth as I understand it, and it is up to you to decide whether or not to believe it.

Whether or not you believe what I am saying to you, there is an eternal life: one with God or one without God. One in Heaven or one in Hell. And the difference is huge, except that we can't fully grasp how wonderful Heaven will be and how horrible Hell will be. Where do you want to spend eternity?

What you believe about what Christ did at the cross has eternal consequences. I want to emphasize here that this isn't about religion or ritual; rather, it's about a relationship. God desires an intimate, personal and *eternal* relationship with each of us and has provided the "bridge" to accomplish that in His son, Jesus Christ, who undertook the most dramatic and powerful act of love ever: his "substitutional" death on a Roman cross. Christ took *our* place and paid in full God the Father's just demand for all of our sins, past, present and future; he did this in order to redeem us, to reconcile us forever to Himself! God *the just* became God *the justifier.*

In the Bible, He has made the understanding of this so simple that a child can grasp it and choose to accept the gift of merciful grace (meaning "without any merit on our behalf"), His eternal salvation. At the same time, the Bible can challenge the most gifted scholar for a lifetime because it truly is the living Word of God revealed.

In this relationship, He wants to be our friend. In the New Testament, in John 15: 12–15, it says, "This is My Commandment, that you love one another, just as I have loved you. Greater love has no one than this, that one lay down his life for his friends. You are My friends if you do what I command you. No longer do I call you slaves, for the slave does not know what his master is doing; but I have called you friends, for all things that I have heard from My Father I have made known to you" (NASB).

Salvation is based not merely on the confession and repentance of sin but also on the fact that Jesus Christ Himself laid down His life and paid our debt in full. When He went to the cross, He died a sacrificial death on our behalf so that we can be absolutely sure that our sins are forgiven *forever*. Salvation has nothing to do with our behavior or performance, but it has everything to do with the loving and merciful grace of God and the shed blood of Christ. It is about His performance on the cross for us, which ensured our full reconciliation to God the Father. So Christ on the cross is the most important event ever witnessed in this world!

God the Father's complete satisfaction in and approval of Christ's sacrifice at the cross is fully demonstrated in His resurrecting Him from the dead. Christ lives! And, through Him, I too can live eternally with Him, and so can you if you so choose.

Too often the church takes this simple and pure concept and, although well meaning, creates a certain legalism of religion and ritual that can smother and confuse people by creating such a list of dos and don'ts by which they must live their lives to maintain their position in the family of God. People can be made to feel that they don't measure up to the expectations required, and this feeling can drive them away from a relationship with God.

So can teachings such as the loss of salvation. To me, that is horrendous and isn't supported by Scripture as I read and understand it. I believe that *once saved, always saved.* To me, anything added to or subtracted from the total sufficiency of Christ's death and resurrection is misleading and false. (This does not mean that divine election dulls human responsibility.)

God is intimate in His relationship with us, and He speaks in ways that are particular to our own hearts — not just through the Bible but also through the whole of creation. Life is not to be solved but to be lived by faith in Him, and this requires us to get to know Him (through the Bible) and to follow Him obediently.

In any family, or in any relationship, there can be challenges and trying times. This also happens in our relationship with the Lord because of our natural pride and sinful nature. But God is faithful and loves us unconditionally, so once members of His family we are never in any danger of being rejected or kicked out. We may, of course, be disciplined, and that is further proof of His love.

The hardest part of this relationship with God is surrendering our lives to Him. The concept (or process) of surrender in our culture is so negative, because submission goes totally against our concepts of control and success. We may even view it as *weakness,* yet in relation to God obedience epitomizes strength. God is a warrior, a conqueror, our hero, and His heart is fierce for us, as shown by what He did for us at the cross. Yet God is love — perfect love — as fully revealed in Christ.

Obedience to the Lord is empowering. The challenges and circumstances that we will experience will strengthen our faith as our trust in Him grows. This process of relationship will continue from the miraculous moment of being reborn when we accept Jesus as Lord and Savior to the day He calls us home, because our old sinful nature will struggle with our new being in Him and against His leadership. Thus, surrendering ourselves to Him is also an ongoing and daily process; I may have to surrender something in me to Him fifty times today — and again tomorrow. There will be times of both victory and failure in that, but He is faithful.

As Charles Stanley has said in *Full Surrender,*

> What is involved in making a full surrender? It is the definite, deliberate, voluntary transfer of undivided possession, control, and use of our entire being to the rightful owner: Jesus Christ. It is like saying, "God, here is my life. Until now, I have had it my way, but from this point on, it's Your call. Whatever You want, that's what I will do. I will trust You and obey, regardless of my own preferences." That means no reservations, no bargaining.
>
> Is that difficult? Yes, it is. But is it worth it? Absolutely! Because God assumes total responsibility for the life fully surrendered to him. So stop clutching onto pennies; open your hands in surrender so that you can receive the vast treasure of blessings God wants to pour into your life.

In the book *Wild at Heart* by John Eldredge (in which he captures the warrior hero persona of God and fully reveals "the enemy" too), he says, "The most important aspects of any man's world — his relationship with his God and with the people in his life, his calling, the spiritual battles he'll face — every one of them is fraught with mystery." He also quotes Oswald Chambers in *My Utmost for His Highest:*

> Naturally we are inclined to be so mathematical and calculating that we look upon uncertainty as a bad thing. . . . Certainty is the mark of the common-sense life; gracious uncertainty is the mark of the spiritual life. To be certain of God means that we are uncertain in all our ways, we do not know what a day may bring forth. This is generally said with a sigh of sadness, it should rather be an expression of breathless expectation.

Eldredge goes on to say that God is a person — not a doctrine. He operates not like a system, not even a theological system, but with all the originality of a truly free and alive person, though, I believe, never against His revealed traits and never against what's in the Bible. Eldredge also says,

> The Modern Era hated mystery, we desperately wanted a means of controlling our own lives and we seemed to find the ultimate Tower of Babel in the scientific method. Don't get me wrong — science has given us many wonderful advances in sanitation, medicine, transportation. But we've tried to use those methods to tame the wildness of the spiritual frontier. We take the latest marketing methods, the newest business management fad, and we apply it to ministry. The problem with modern Christianity's obsession with principles is that it removes any real conversation with God. Find the principle, apply the principle — what do you need God for? So Oswald Chambers warns us, "Never make a principle out of your experience, let God be as original with other people as He is with you."
>
> What God did offer Adam was friendship. He wasn't alone to face life, he walked with God in the cool of the day and there they talked about love and marriage and creativity, what lessons he was learning and what adventures were to come. That is what God is offering to us as well.
>
> The only way to live this adventure — with all its danger and unpredictability and immensely high stakes — is in an ongoing, intimate relationship with God. The control we so desperately crave is an illusion. Far better to give it up in exchange for God's offer of com-

panionship, set aside stale formulas so that we might enter into an informal relationship.

He goes on to say that, "As Dallas Willard writes, 'The ideal for divine guidance is . . . a conversational relationship with God: the sort of relationship suited to friends who are mature personalities in a shared enterprise.'"

So this golden nugget is that Jesus Christ desires a deep, personal, intimate and eternal relationship with you and me — and He paid the ultimate price for that for us at the cross of Calvary! If for some reason you have some grievance — real or perceived — against the church, religion or ritual, then my question is "What did Jesus Christ ever do to hurt you? What do you have against Him?" He loves you unconditionally and will respond to your plea to come into your heart as Savior and Lord.

Although much is revealed in the Bible, certainly more than enough for us to accept or reject God's Son, we can only glimpse what Heaven will be. Our vision of Christ is likewise filtered through our limited understanding and skewed by our very nature. After this life, though, which is but an instant compared to eternity, in our "glorified bodies" we will see Him as He really is and remain in His perfect love, and His perfect light, which is so illuminating that there will be no shadows. And I believe that time will be so wondrous and He will be so awesome — it will take eternity for Him to fully reveal Himself to us. What an exciting time and life to look forward to in Him! What a wonderful prize for our finishing the course of life here. I hope to see you there too, along with everyone I know and love — but that choice is between you and the Lord. If you already have that relationship, or if you make the choice to give your life to Him, then you'll have riches well beyond anything this world can offer, and they'll be eternal.

May the good Lord bless and keep you, and make His light to shine upon you, until He comes again or calls you home.

Bill Watts

PS: There are a couple of appendices below of areas that have been illuminated for me over time; they may further stimulate your heart and mind. Also, if you'd like, visit us at www.cowboybillwatts.com.

APPENDIX 1

CHRIST ON THE CROSS —

HOW WRONG I WAS ABOUT IT!

This is a personal understanding by me, Bill Watts, neither a theologian nor a Bible scholar but a grateful sinner whom Christ has saved, also in times past referred to as "Cowboy" Bill Watts of professional wrestling fame, or is it "infamy"?

First, to paraphrase a thought by Keats in one of his poems, at this time in the world, when the best lack conviction and the worst are filled with passionate intensity, it is important that we all declare ourselves openly and hopefully with passionate conviction. Here is also the perfect place to add the most defining and convicting thought, as in Acts 16:30, when the jailer in charge of the place where Paul and Silas had been imprisoned, after the events of that situation, cried, "What must I do to be saved?" That is the place where we must all start to experience the salvation of Christ.

As William MacDonald wrote in *Believer's Bible Commentary*, "This question must precede every genuine case of conversion. A man must know he is lost before he can be saved. It is premature to tell a man how to be saved until first he can say from his heart, 'I truly deserve to go to hell.'" If a person isn't aware of being lost, of sinning against the only righteous and holy God and facing an eternity in Hell, then nothing that I write here will have any impact, nor will that person grasp the enormity of his or her personal situation in relation to God and eternity. First and foremost, we must acknowledge our "position" in relation to our God and Creator.

I Corinthians 1:18 says, "For the preaching of the cross is to them that perish foolishness; but unto us which are being saved it is the power of God." And I Corinthians 2:14 notes, "But the natural man receiveth not the things of the Spirit of God: for they are foolishness unto him; neither can he know them, because they are spiritually discerned." As a sinner, I am without merit or favor, in a corrupt body of flesh, but saved by grace through faith in the redeeming work of Jesus Christ at Calvary, where He died for my sins (and yours). I deserve an eternity in Hell, but His death and resurrection, and my faith in His work, have reconciled me fully to God the Father.

Let me share with you what Christ has done for me — and can do for you. This is not about religion but about a deep personal relationship with Christ, who accepted me with all my transgressions and flaws and loved me enough to die that horrible death for me. He took my place and yours, and He paid the price for our sins. He loved me enough to seek me out and reveal that to me, and He loves you that much too.

Let me share with you my understanding of this. I use the Bible as the basis for many of the things I write since it is the infallible Word of God. As II Timothy 3:16–17 says, "All scripture is given by inspiration of God and is profitable for doctrine, for reproof, for correction, for instruction in righteousness, that the man of God may be perfect [meaning to have all that is necessary for his understanding], furnished unto all good works." If you don't accept the Bible as the inspired Word of God, then none of this has any meaning for you. The Holy Bible is the only written source wherein God reveals Himself to us and gives us the basis for His relationship to us through his Son, Jesus Christ.

My life, as those who know me can certainly attest, has been a mercurial testimony of what I am now relating. But God is faithful, and even in my periods of darkness His light shines. Once you are His, He never lets go; no one, nothing, can ever take you away from Him — not even you can. God never quits striving for your heart to conform to His will for you. Praise Him! Thank Him for His undying, unconditional love!

There have been periods in my life when He has illuminated so much of Himself to me, as He does to all of His own. Those moments have been breathtaking and humbling as His spirit has illuminated to me, again, the lack of understanding I have had at times, how woefully wrong and short-sighted I was and still am. Thus, this isn't written as "holier than thou" or from any point of criticism except of myself, but hopefully it stimulates your thoughts and better focuses or clarifies your relationship with Jesus, because there is no middle ground (in John 14:6, Jesus says, "I am the way, the truth, and the life; no man cometh unto the Father, but by Me," so there is only one way to God — through Christ, as I Timothy 2:5 also confirms).

To see our position in relation to Christ, we must first realize that we are lost, that "all have sinned and fallen short of the glory of God" (Romans 3:23). We must realize that we are sinners against God and that the "wages of sin are death" (Romans 6:23). And when you read this Scripture reference, note that it is sin –– singular, not plural — so the consequence of even one sin is condemnation in relation to God's holy and just standard of righteousness.

We must also realize that there is nothing we can do on our own (Ephesians 2: 5, 8: "Even when we were dead in sins, he hath quickened us together with Christ; by grace ye are saved"; "For by grace are ye saved through faith; and that not of yourselves: it is the gift of God, not of works, lest any man should boast"). We have no merit of ourselves and cannot earn His favor or aspire to His righteousness. If even one person on Earth had been able to measure up to God's standard of holiness, then Christ need never have died for us at Calvary.

We must realize too that God's law (the Ten Commandments) isn't just some random rules; rather, it reveals His intrinsic traits — His righteous character. But once revealed as the standard, the law of God also becomes the curse, because it holds us accountable and reveals our shortcomings and fallen state. Does that make the law bad? Never, for it is just, but it reveals us and our predicament in relation to righteousness. Being a good person in the eyes of the world isn't the way to salvation. It is how we measure up to God's standard — as Galatians 2:16 reveals.

We must understand this awesome and only God, the Creator, sovereign Lord of the universe, who "spoke" everything into existence through His Son — who was always with Him and is Him, for they are inseparable. We must come to the point where we see just how much He (who was without sin) suffered on our behalf. He paid our dues as He substituted Himself and received our judgment and punishment, so that we might be freed from slavery to sin and be reconciled to God through Him.

We are saved by grace. It can't be earned or bought. Grace is "unmerited favor," God's gift to us through His Son. This is the highest form of love ever demonstrated on Earth. To receive it, all we must do is come to Him and believe in Him, not from the head but from the heart, to know He is God and to receive Him into our hearts as our Lord. He is sovereign!

This is not religion, which humans in our arrogant pride and rebellious disobedience have tried to make it and led so many astray (as Proverbs 14:12 states, "There is a way which seemeth right unto a man, but the end thereof are the ways of death"). But it is about our personal relationship with Jesus Christ!

I feel so inadequate to the task of describing what the Holy Spirit has illuminated to me. I feel that I somehow demean by not fully grasping all that Christ accomplished at the cross and how much more he endured than I can perceive or understand. Yes, I accepted His loving sacrifice for my salvation, but in my heart of hearts, in my "pride of life," I didn't give Him nearly enough recognition for the unprecedented agony of what He endured for me as He took my place on that cross so that I won't ever have to experience such torture.

Some time ago I wrote a note in my Bible: "Had I been the only person in the world, Christ would still have died on the cross for me. Had I been the only person in the world, I would have been the one to nail Him to the cross!" That is the darkness of sin in the human heart (Romans 3:10–18). How we can delude ourselves to think there is anything of merit in our hearts is frightening, but in our pride we do. The only "right" I've earned based on my efforts and merits is to spend an eternity in Hell. But Christ sought me out and called me, and the Holy Spirit convicted me of my lost and sinful state. He redeemed me and gave me His salvation.

Christ did it all. It is all done. No one can add to it or take away from it. That He loves me, such an immoral sinner, and has chosen me to be His is beyond any comprehension I have. But I am so thankful! Now I share with you what I feel the Lord has let me see. I only hope it stimulates you to consider this for yourself, so that you don't ever have to face God on your own merits in judgment for your sins. Because we shall all face Him. The separating factor is whether we face Him on our own and answer Him based on our own merits or whether we accept His Son as our advocate and Savior and rely on his merits.

Hebrews 12:1–2 states, "Therefore, since we have so great a cloud of witnesses surrounding us, let us also lay aside every encumbrance, and the sin which so easily entangles us, and let us run with endurance the race that is set before us, fixing our eyes on Jesus, the author and perfector of faith, who for the joy set before Him endured the cross, despising the shame, and has sat down at the right hand of the throne of God." Reflecting on that verse drew me to the words "who for the joy set before Him endured the cross, despising the shame," and I wondered, "How could He have considered it a joy?"

Then I think of Christ and the entire crucifixion event, reflecting on His suffering for us. May He forgive me for my thoughts, how I could have demeaned the purest and greatest act of love and obedience ever and, in so doing, demeaned Him. How treacherous foolish pride, how deceitful my heart of flesh!

I had, in some periods of my life, considered that Christ, in His death on the cross, was a young man, in the prime of His life, a very strong man, a carpenter by trade. His labor was very physical, and He was forceful and intimidating when angry — as when He drove the money changers out of the temple. Yet He died sooner than either of the two thieves crucified on either side of Him. Why? I thought that He was God, so it really didn't hurt Him as bad, and seemingly, when He had accomplished the task, He just gave up His life, and the suffering ended.

Consider this: God almighty comes to Earth to redeem His fallen creation. He is the God of the universe, has been in Heaven for eternity, praised and glorified by angelic choirs, sung to by His entire creation, and He must come to Earth to redeem his own fallen creation. He divested Himself of all that! Think about that for a moment. Read Philippians 2:5–8 and put it into perspective. Now think of all the forms He could have taken — an angel, a king, a conqueror or any number of supernatural forms. But he comes in all the physical frailty of humanity and as a baby, without pomp or ceremony, born in total poverty. He never accumulated any earthly trappings or honors for Himself — total humility, a servant. He was hounded by kings and authorities, misunderstood, accused, hated — a man of sorrow, without an estate, a huge following or wealth. He was tested by Satan, accused by the religious leaders, rejected by His chosen people; He who sinned not came here not to conquer but to serve and to die for our sins.

And if dying was all Christ had to do, there were many ways that would have been much less painful and shameful. But He endured the worst death devised by humanity to that date. He was beaten, tortured, made a spectacle. Without being found guilty of anything more than being who He said He was, He was condemned to that horrible death in order that we might live. His death took hours! Dying between two criminals — the God of the universe.

Christ was scourged by the Romans, who weren't bound like the Jews to forty lashes lest they kill the person. These were battle-hardened Roman legionnaires, conquerors of the world, known for their vicious effectiveness, certainly never cited for mercy, and lives other than their own weren't highly valued. Jerusalem wasn't a "cushy" post that got the sophisticated, highly intelligent or especially kind Roman functionary. It was rather like the Russian front was for German soldiers — the feared banishment for the disfavored or incompetent of the army. Therefore, it certainly was very brutal. Their whips had sharpened bits of metal in the braids to tear the flesh, and they were masters at making a person suffer — whipping him to the point of death, his very organs exposed through his shredded back!

Christ was also struck and spit on. A crown of huge thorns — I'm sure their natural toxin would increase the pain — was likely jammed on His head as a mock crown, causing Him to bleed. He'd been forced to carry the horizontal cross member — no small physical feat, especially under such duress. Surely food and drink were withheld. And His divinity knew how it was to end — think how we dread something bad, or something that could hurt, and how that stress drains our strength before we even experience it.

And then there was the extreme brutality of the actual crucifixion — being nailed to the cross. These weren't slender, stainless steel surgical nails (as if that would make it less painful) but likely rough, wide nails (by some accounts seven inches long) driven through the hands or wrists into the rough cross. Can you even imagine? Then that cross member was roughly hoisted into position on the vertical part, and more nails were driven through the feet or ankles!

The terrible ripping pain to the nail-pierced limbs, to an already pain-wracked body, in front of jeering masses, His very creation that He'd come to save! The shame heaped upon an innocent man, our Lord. The emotion and pain washing over Him and engulfing Him like a tidal wave. Christ refused the drink they gave in those days to deaden the pain and awareness so that He would have the fullness of His faculties to endure His mission, our salvation.

I am the sinner that, but for Him, should have to endure that judgment. Yet I had diluted that too in my mind to the point where it just wasn't that bad. I thought others (but certainly not me) had endured worse physical torture than that in history — oh, our sinful pride, the ever-present desire to elevate ourselves to equality with God or to mentally or subliminally reduce God to our own understanding!

I have experienced the emotion of hatred. As a young man, I wrestled in Madison Square Garden before over 18,000 screaming fans, the largest crowd ever in the "old" MSG for any event in its history. These fans were screaming for my blood. Their hatred of me, the "villain" wrestling their "hero," was washing over me in waves, like a physical force. This was an era when fans still took their wrestling seriously. This crowd was insane with rage. It hit with such a force that it seemed physical. It completely changed my demeanor! It was worse than being slapped, as far as the affront to my senses, and more powerful than the strongest blow.

I knew I had to combat it, or it would dominate me. I attacked all that emotion with my own anger. I became enraged and hated all those faceless people. I loathed them, and that permeated my very being. I projected it back at them like a weapon, and I was able without any remorse or conscience to react toward those people, transformed by the force of all that emotion focused at me into a blood-lusting beast. Emotion, whether love and adulation, or anger and hatred, is such a powerful force, as history has recorded with lynch mobs, racial riots and war, where atrocities have been perpetrated against innocent people.

After that match, I was in similar situations in my career in that godless venue, but I knew what to expect. I still felt it, but I understood it, even though the violence of my reaction was barely under control when, at certain times, things nearly got out of control. Just like when we think we have our sinful flesh under control — we don't.

Christ on the cross never summoned any "weapons," whether anger or hatred, in self-defense; He never struck back at that blood-lusting crowd. He loved us so much that He endured the shame. But can you imagine from my example how the power of mass emotion directed at you can feel and how this innocent Lamb of God must have felt? No, because we are not God and can only feel it from our limited perception as humans. This gentle man of sorrows was the focal point of the fury of this mob, who sought his innocent blood. This true and perfect man was thrust, with the helplessness of a lamb led to slaughter, into this maelstrom of hate.

I also thought I understood Matthew 27:46, where He cried out from the cross, *"Eli, Eli, lama sabachthani?"* That is, "My God, my God, why hast thou forsaken me?" Taken from the 22nd Psalm, with His last breath, knowing this event would be preserved and scrutinized, He validated the scriptures already written. During His time on Earth, He was in perfect communion with the Father in Heaven. But He who knew no sin became our sin on the cross, and that communion, that eternal bond, had to be severed. Christ had to suffer and die (Hebrews 9:22); as the sacrifice for us, He had to be separated from God the Father. I even thought that for an instant Satan had some "access" to His mind and that facing that evil without God the Father was so horrible that He cried out. The really abominable thought seemed to creep into my mind on occasion that, after all, He is God. As God, even in the flesh, He was supernatural, so all this didn't hurt Him as much as it would me! And He seemingly died when His "job" was done — He gave up His own spirit, so He was in control to some extent of the suffering.

I've read about crucifixion, how the joints just slowly pull apart as the muscles can no longer resist. The pain from the nails hurts so bad that each breath is harder to take, and finally the victim dies of suffocation. As the joints come apart and the muscles relax and tear, you can no longer breathe (traditionally, they would break the condemned person's legs to deny that support to breathe and ensure death, but they didn't do that to Christ, as was prophesied in the Old Testament).

I'm familiar with how prolonged pain defeats our will to resist. In athletics, training plus emotion and reaction distract us from the effects of pain, unless we are defeated by it and react to inflict pain back. Conversely, I hate to get a shot or have my blood taken in a doctor's office, because I have to be passive, to just endure it without retaliating. The most significant pain I know, even though I know it only as a spectator, is illustrated by prolonged labor in childbirth. I don't know how a woman endures it!

So I'm not trying to diminish what Christ endured — *I* sure couldn't have endured it without crying out. I probably would have begged for mercy even prior to enduring it. I'm an avid reader and have read many accounts of prisoners of war and the inhumane treatment and torture many of them endured, for years in many instances, and they survived. So, you see, I was diluting what He endured on the cross.

Athletes often withstand great pain, and I've read accounts of the Christian martyrs being fed to the wild beasts, burned alive and suffering all the other fiendish savagery humans can inflict. So, yes, the pain and suffering Christ endured based on that perspective were horrible but not worse than others have endured. But keep in mind that everything described thus far was what He suffered at the hands of humans in broad daylight and what was predominantly physical.

What I hadn't yet really grasped, much less considered and understood, was the real issue, the real trial, the unbearable aspect that no one has ever experienced except Jesus Christ — having to face the wrath of God in paying the penalty for sin! I hadn't yet grasped that.

Then my brother, Bobby, was sharing with me in Isaiah 52 and 53 concerning the prophetic descriptions of Christ on the cross. We came to Isaiah 52:14, the second half of which says, in the NAS translation, "So His appearance was marred more than any man, and His form more than the sons of men." The KJV says, "As many were astonished at Thee; His visage was so marred more than any man, and His form more than the sons of men." Even Scofield's notes on it say, "So marred from the form of man was His aspect that His appearance was not that of a son of man," that is, not human.

With all my "worldly wisdom" and pride of the flesh (the Bible calls it foolish pride, ignorance and darkness of understanding), I said, "How was

His visage marred more than any man? I just don't see it. Yes, He suffered, but not *that* much!"

Bobby took me to Isaiah 53:4–6: "Surely our griefs He Himself bore, and our sorrows He carried; yet we ourselves esteemed him stricken, smitten of God, and afflicted. But He was pierced through for our transgressions, He was crushed for our iniquities; the chastening for our well-being fell on Him, and by His scourging we are healed. All of us like sheep have gone astray, each of us has turned to his own way; but the Lord has caused the iniquity of us all to fall on Him." Isaiah 53:10 states, "But the Lord was pleased to crush Him, putting Him to grief; if He would render Himself as a guilt offering." Wait a minute! What is *this?* Strong words: "smitten," "stricken," "afflicted," "crushed" — and by God, a supernatural, omnipotent power, not by humans! Am I missing something? Is there something I'm not seeing (foolish, ignorant man that I am)?

Consider this: three of the Gospels in their recounting of the crucifixion — Matthew 27:45–46; Mark 15:33–34; and Luke 23:44–45 — state that, from about noon to 3 p.m., total darkness fell at Calvary. What is the significance of that? We know that in everything God has a purpose, and in His word there is completeness, so for three hours Christ was crushed for our sin! Not just an instant but three long, excruciating, horrible, indescribable hours of anguish unbearable even to our Lord. He suffered this for me — and for you! What marred His visage more than any man was what He endured facing God's wrath in receiving the judgment for sin — the spiritual and mental anguish, not just the physical torture.

God's Son, Jesus Christ, became sin! He was sacrificed. The penalty for sin is death. That payment for sin is before a wrathful God in judgment, a God who has declared, "I hate sin!" No one has yet faced our wrathful God in relation to judgment for sin. No one, that is, except Christ. But there will be a final judgment for all.

Hebrews 10:31 tells us, "It is a terrifying thing to fall into the hands of the living God." In even more of an insight, Moses describes the "sight" of His holiness in Hebrews 12:21: "And so terrible was the sight that Moses said, 'I am full of fear and trembling.'" Moses also referred to Him as a "consuming fire."

Facing God in wrath is what marred Christ's visage more than that of any man (not the physical torture). It was so horrible that even the physical shrank in comparison. I believe that God the Father "covered" His Son by darkness on the face of the Earth while He underwent judgment for sin. He didn't allow His creation to view the effects of His wrath as He dealt with our sin and crushed His own Son for us. Some scholars speak of the "blood and water" referred to in John 19:34, which came out when the soldier thrust the spear into His dead body, as the sign of one dying of a "broken heart." If so, I can now understand!

My God, my God, forgive me for my ignorance, my futility, my darkness, my lack of understanding. Most of my life I've considered self only. All my thoughts and efforts were focused on self and its desires rather than on Christ, or I'm sure the Holy Spirit would have revealed all this to me much sooner! I am thankful that God is a faithful and loving God. His loving kindness, mercy, forgiveness and grace are unfathomable and never-ending — until the Day of Judgment, predicated by Christ's return, or our earthly death in denial of the truth revealed to us by the Holy Spirit. One thing is certain — we are all going to meet Him. Will it be as our conqueror and judge or as our loving Lord? He will not come again as a lamb or suffering servant but as a king!

Thank You, Heavenly Father, praise You for Your Holy Spirit, who reveals Jesus Christ to us, who opens our eyes that we may see, our ears that we may hear. Thank You that Your Spirit illuminated, through my loving and faithful younger (but greater in stature) brother, the wonderful sacrifice Christ made for me at Calvary that I've finally been able to see. Thank You, Lord! Thank You also for the saints who have prayed for me.

Without Christ, each person will face the same wrathful God our Savior faced on the cross in judgment for sin. Just try to imagine the forces that will come to bear in extracting that penalty — Christ Himself, in His role as substitute for our sin, wasn't spared, and God won't spare anyone from facing His wrath in judgment. That realization should cause each person to examine his or her personal relationship (or lack thereof) with Christ. If you are reading this, then it's not too late for you to come to Him.

Now, back to the verse we started with, the part that says, "who for the joy set before Him, endured the cross." Here there are two wonderful kinds of joy. First, Christ was totally obedient to the Father, glorifying Him as He satisfied Him completely in relation to sin and fulfilling God the Father's righteousness and justice without compromising any of His attributes. Second, Christ had such great love for us that He could sacrifice Himself for us. And God the Father was forever glorified and satisfied, and He then glorified the Son — He is risen and sits at the right hand of God in Heaven. Praise Him! As horrible a sinner as I am, living in this garbage dump of flesh, I won't have to face a wrathful God in judgment for my sins.

As long as I'm in this "body of flesh," I will sin and live with the consequences of that sin while here on Earth, but I am still saved from its eternal penalty. The Holy Spirit will contend with the war waged in my flesh that is contrary to His will for me. I am freed from the bondage of my sin and have within me, through Him, the strength to resist, even though my flesh, in its self-centered rebellion, will always compete with that will.

Thank You, Jesus, for setting me free from my sins and washing me white as snow in your precious blood!

I hope that you know Christ as your Savior. Otherwise, you'll meet God as your judge. If you already know Christ as your Savior, I hope this brings you even closer to His intense love for us. The following poem was found in a man's Bible after he died.

> Low at Thy feet, Lord Jesus,
> This is the place for me;
> Here I have learned deep lessons,
> Truth that has set me free.
> Free from myself Lord Jesus,
> Free from the ways of men;
> Chains of thought that have bound me,
> Never bind again.
> None but Thyself, Lord Jesus,
> Conquered this wayward will,
> But for Thy love constraining,
> I had been wayward still.

This is my prayer of thanksgiving and praise for all He has already done for me. I can rest because I am in Him, and He is in me. I accept that my salvation is only by and in the Lord Jesus Christ. I cling to His love and His righteousness, not mine, which is so corrupt, fallible, self-serving and conditional.

Here are some excerpts of poetry by George West Frazer, who went to the Lord on January 24, 1896.

> 1) God's house is filling fast —
> "Yet there is room!"
> Some soul will be the last —
> "Yet there is room!"

Yes, soon Salvation's day
From you will pass away,
Then grace will no more say —
"Yet there is room!"

2) Down to the depths of Woe
Christ came to set me free:
He bared His breast,
Received the blow,
Which justice aimed at me!

3) On that same night, Lord Jesus,
When all around Thee joined
To cast its darkest shadow
Across Thy holy mind,
We hear Thy voice, blest Savior,
"This do, remember Me!"
With joyful hearts responding,
We do remember Thee.

I am in the autumn of my life, but I know I am saved by God's grace. I know that, once saved, always saved. As I John 5:10–13 reveals,

He that believeth on the Son of God has the witness in himself: he that believeth not God hath made Him a liar; because he believeth not the record that God gave of His Son.

And this is the record, that God hath given to us eternal life, and this life is in His Son.

He that hath the Son hath life; and he that hath not the Son of God hath not life.

These things have I written unto you that believe on the name of the Son of God; that ye may know that ye have eternal life, and that ye may believe on the name of the Son of God.

I am not afraid to die because I know without any doubt that I'll be with my Savior, Jesus Christ, but, as I look back on my life and how I've wasted it in relation to Him, I am ashamed to die! Isn't it wonderful, though, that it's His infallible and unconditional love and righteousness to which we cling and not our own?

Do you know Him? Is He your Lord and Savior? That is the real issue — the only issue with eternal consequences. There is no in-between.

APPENDIX 2
THE LANDMINE
OF INSECURITY

How we feel about ourselves is so important. From a young and impressionable age, we install emotional mechanisms because of what we experience, and here I'd like to share with you my understanding of this.

God addresses this over and over in the Bible. Romans 8:33–39 offers powerful truths worth meditating upon. These truths should become the foundation of your self-esteem as you see the value our Heavenly Father places on each of us.

I also listened to a well-respected biblical teacher named Charles Stanley on the topic of "the landmine of insecurity." His message really spoke to me about this topic. Looking back, it might explain many of my experiences and my reactions to life. We don't need to live in insecurity, but it's a powerful land mine we can step on that can have dramatic effects on our lives. Here are the ideas that Stanley brought forth, in my own words.

What Causes a Person to Feel Insecure?

In my case, it began with an unpredictable childhood environment. My mother, whom I loved the most, became bipolar, which made my environment very unpredictable on a daily basis in regard to her expectations of me. Those expectations could fluctuate dramatically, along with emotional rewards or punishments. Also, her wide mood swings gave me no solid, consistent role model for conducting my own life realistically. Her dominance in our household made this even more dramatic since my father never stood up to her for me.

Insecurity can also be the result of a tragedy such as death, divorce or some financial failure. Other major factors can be underdeveloped skills and talents, with no encouragement from parents and coaches, whose methods can be very beneficial or detrimental. Living under unrealistic rules and regulations set by parents or coaches, who themselves cannot live by them, can be devastating because of the tremendous authority given to them. We can never please them, nor can we really know what the standard of approval is today, or this week, since they too don't demonstrate consistent behavior or leadership.

Another tremendous factor is poor body image (being considered too fat, too slow, too skinny, not "buff" enough, not good looking or beautiful enough, etc.), and its effects can last a lifetime. This continues even when those body image statements are no longer true, because you might have made tremendous changes — if not consciously, then just by maturing.

A further factor is growing up without positive feedback or being compared to others (in the family to a brother or sister) instead of being encouraged individually. The standards set for you should be based not on someone else but on your unique abilities. This generally starts in the home but can also be carried forward to school, the athletic field, the workplace and even the church, where it should never occur.

What Does an Insecure Person Feel?

Why is this so important? Because the way you imagine yourself to be is the way you will become!

"I can never accomplish this task. I just can't do it." Remember, the Lord does not call us to do anything that He doesn't fully equip us to do. "I'm a failure." We may not succeed every time and in everything, but that does not make us failures! "I'm ugly. I'm a loser. People are only being nice to me because they want something from me." If you believe these things, they are emotionally devastating and can make you a "slave" to this type of self-degradation and poor image.

When we think negatively about ourselves, we are only pouring gasoline on the fire of our insecurity! We need to focus on the promises of God and on how He views us. His love is unconditional — we can't earn it. He freely loves us and will never forsake us! By accepting Christ as my Savior and Lord, I am a child of God forever. There are so many positive promises God reveals to us in His Word.

What are the effects of insecurity? They can include difficulty establishing good and lasting relationships, which we need. We can be perceived as snobbish or prideful, one of the cover-ups of insecurity. We can suffer from indecisiveness, fear of failure (which severely limits what you can do in life and limits God's use of your life — it's OK to fail, for God won't forsake you) or anger (which creates a critical attitude).

We can be passed over for promotions and honors because of messages we send about being inadequate, indecisive or afraid of failure. There are problems with others (this has permeated my life). We can even come to believe that success in life is based on the approval of others (look whom we lift up as heroes in this nation — athletes and movie stars, but eventually both ability and beauty fade). Even though you are doing your best to hide it, it often shows through.

How Do You Overcome the Feelings of Insecurity?

There is no quick solution, but you can do it! The first and most important factor is to acknowledge your feelings and identify the causes. Then, if you have a personal relationship with the Lord, make a decision in Christ to overcome insecurity. If you haven't made a decision to trust Christ as your Savior, then it will be very hard for you, because you have no assurance of your future after death. Realize that it is more than self-esteem ("Am I the way I see myself or not? How does God see me?"). The most important factor is that He values you so much He sent His Son to die for you on a cross so that He could have an eternal relationship with you.

Don't focus on negative feelings — focus on the Holy Spirit within you. Focus on the positive qualities in your life. You might not see them, but I'll bet others see many good qualities in you. You'd probably be happily surprised. Take a sheet of paper and ask the Lord to help you write out the positive qualities in your life. This will help you to visualize what is still lacking. Each day, if we visualize that we are saints for the Lord, we will walk closer to Him, so fill your mind with the principles of God's Word, which has the "right stuff."

And stop comparing yourself with others. Avoid the trap of blaming others! Reward yourself when you do the right thing. Do something that makes you feel good about what you have accomplished. Overcome any doubts about the Word of God. Trust Him! Set your mind on what He wants you to be, on His promises and precepts.

Is it easy? No, but He is with you forever. His Word is the most life-changing gift ever provided to the world. To see myself as He sees me is the most liberating and loving reality. My Creator loves me; He understands me and accepts me "just as I am."

This truly is the pathway to being an emotionally healthier person, one who can interact so much better in relationships with those around me. It is my hope that others do not wait until they are sixty-six, as I am, to explore themselves more fully and be set free from harbored behavioral mechanisms that can be self-destructive, as most of my life illustrates. Life is all about our choices and their consequences — good and bad.

ABOUT THE PHOTOS

Forewords: Kicking "The Spoiler," Don Jardine (1976).

Preface: One of my earliest publicity shots, Indianapolis (1962).

Chapter 1: At Super's Gym in NJ with 500 lbs on the bench press.

Chapter 2: Senior Year at Putnam City High School in 1956–57. Duayne Miller, who later became an NCAA Champion wrestling for OU, Coach TJ Snyder, and me (at about 235 lbs).

Chapter 3: My "O-Club" 1960 Membership Card, given to those who letter in varsity sports at OU.

Chapter 4: Cranking up a chinlock on World Champion Jack Brisco, with Stu Schwartz refereeing (Florida, 1974).

Chapter 5: Clubbing Bruno Sammartino during my first big heel run in 1965. This picture was taken at MSG. (It was the only ring with 4 ring ropes.)

Chapter 6: Being hip-tossed by Verne Gagne, circa 1969, in Minneapolis.

Chapter 7: Three titans: Ed "Strangler" Lewis (who also went blind in later life), Leroy McGuirk (with his seeing-eye dog), and Lou Thesz.

Chapter 8: President Jimmy Carter with Wrestling II. (President Carter's mother was a big fan of wrestling in Georgia.)

Chapter 9: These billboards, a wrestling first, and something I created, were strategically placed all over Tampa to promote our show and top story-line.

Chapter 10: Me with tag partner Ray Candy. Candy surprised me, pleasantly, by drawing a big house at the Superdome for a match with Ernie Ladd.

Chapter 11: Calling the Mid-South action with Boyd Pierce at a Shreveport TV taping (1984).

Chapter 12: Me and Steve "Dr. Death" Williams — a four-time NCAA All-American and two-time Big 8 football player under Barry Switzer. We're standing behind OU's football stadium before a game with Missouri. I presented Steve with an award at halftime.

Chapter 13: Putting the boots to Dennis Condrey during "The Last Stampede" (New Orleans, April 7, 1984).

Chapter 14: Junkyard Dog, my biggest box office star!

Chapter 15: Punching Buddy Colt.

Chapter 16: A TV match with Sting (1986).

Chapter 17: Kerry Von Erich with a headlock on Terry Gordy. Michael Hays is ringside and Buddy Roberts stands on the apron.

Chapter 18: Being interviewed for radio by assistant Houston promoter Paul Boesch in 1963. Boesch would take over as lead promoter after Morris Sigel's death in 1967.

Chapter 19: My Cheyenne III. Turbine engines, fast, long-range — a great airplane.

Chapter 20: In Japan for WCW, with Dusty Rhodes and Hiro Matsuda.

Chapter 21: Vince McMahon.

Chapter 22: My marriage proposal to Suzanne. See, I'm still a romantic . . .

Chapter 23: Being measured for my first custom-made suit. (I do not remember the tailor, but I sure was a handsome young man, wasn't I?)

Chapter 24: "Drop-kicking" (our personal joke) Dick Murdock. Also pictured is Jerry Usher, a loyal, dependable, and very good referee.

Chapter 25: My daughter, my heart. Ene hugs me on the balcony overlooking the Gulf of Mexico in Destin, Florida. Sons are awesome—but daughters steal a father's heart.

Afterword: Now — just plain Bill, Senior Citizen. Sharing his choices and their consequences with you.